P9-DMO-824

Resegregation

School Resegregation

Must the South Turn Back?

Edited by John Charles Boger
and Gary Orfield

The University of North Carolina Press
Chapel Hill and London

Designed by April Leidig-Higgins
Set in Minion by Copperline Book Services, Inc.
Manufactured in the United States of America

This book was published with the assistance of the H. Eugene and Lillian Youngs Lehman Fund of the University of North Carolina Press. A complete list of books published in the Lehman Series appears at the end of the book.

The paper in this book meets the guidelines for permanence and durability of the Committee on Production Guidelines for Book Longevity of the Council on Library Resources.

Chapters 1–4 have been reprinted by permission of the publisher in revised form from articles in *North Carolina Law Review* 81 (May 2003); chapter 10 has been reprinted by permission of the publisher in revised form from *Redesigning Accountability Systems for Education*, ed. Susan Fuhrman and Richard Elmore (New York: Teachers College Press, 2004), 220–44; © 2004 by Teachers College, Columbia University; all rights reserved.

Library of Congress Cataloging-in-Publication Data
School resegregation: must the South turn back? /
edited by John Charles Boger and Gary Orfield.
p. cm.
Includes bibliographical references and index.
ISBN 0-8078-2953-6 (cloth: alk. paper)
ISBN 0-8078-5613-4 (pbk.: alk. paper)
1. Segregation in education—Southern States—Congresses. 2. School integration—Southern States—Congresses. 3. Public schools—Southern States—Congresses. I. Boger, John Charles. II. Orfield, Gary.
LC212.622.S35 2005 379.2'63'0975—dc22 2005001619

cloth 09 08 07 06 05 5 4 3 2 1
paper 09 08 07 06 05 5 4 3 2 1

Contents

Tables & Figures

Tables

Figures

Acknowledgments

This book had its inception at a conference, "The Resegregation of Southern Schools?: A Crucial Moment in the History (and the Future) of Public Schooling in America," which was conceived simultaneously in the winter of 2001 by the University of North Carolina School of Law's then-fledgling Center for Civil Rights and by The Civil Rights Project at Harvard University. Happily, the Center and the Project joined forces to cosponsor a combined conference, held in Chapel Hill, North Carolina, on 30 August 2002. Many people had important roles in framing that conference. Gary Orfield, Chris Edley, Elizabeth DeBray, Jacinta Ma, and Erica Frankenberg in Cambridge; Jack Boger in Chapel Hill; and John Brittain at the Thurgood Marshall School of Law at Texas Southern University commissioned the original research for the conference from which this book has resulted. *North Carolina Law Review* student editors John Fleming, Jodi Luster, and Kara Millonzi recruited speakers, organized production of materials, and performed many other tasks as cohosts. The UNC Center's program assistant, Allison Stelljes, provided wonderful overall logistical direction for the conference and for the preparation of conference materials. At that time, Marilyn Byrne of The Civil Rights Project also began her involvement, which has ranged from conference support to coordination of final manuscript preparation.

Public and scholarly response to the conference was so strong—more than five hundred attendees crowded into the William and Ida Friday Center for Continuing Education on a Labor Day weekend, southern news media offered extensive coverage of the discussions, and hundreds of scholars and activists requested copies of the conference papers—that the UNC Center and The Civil Rights Project agreed to extend their collaboration. The John S. and James L. Knight Foundation and the Ford Foundation provided generous financial support for the UNC Center and The Civil Rights Project to address southern school resegregation in academic and community settings. In addition, the Charles Stewart Mott Foundation and the John D. and Catherine T. MacArthur Foundation provided core funding to The Civil Rights Project during the period in which this volume's research was initially commissioned. The *North Carolina Law Review* planned a special symposium issue (vol. 81 [May 2003]), coedited by John Fleming and Jodi Luster, that offers nine articles by scholars expanding on their earlier summary conference papers.

In the winter of 2003, Chuck Grench, a wise and supportive editor who serves as assistant director and senior editor at the University of North Carolina Press, encouraged the UNC Center and The Civil Rights Project to consider editing a volume built on the conference papers. This volume reflects our response to his kind invitation. That winter, Rebecca High, a recent UNC Law graduate with prior editorial experience, joined the UNC Center as a fellow. Rebecca soon began collaboration with Erica Frankenberg, a commissioned researcher with The Civil Rights Project, to turn this idea into a published volume. Working diligently and patiently with all of the volume's authors and coeditors, Rebecca and Erica coaxed drafts and revisions out of overbusy scholars; offered thousands of gentle, useful suggestions; and spent many early mornings and late evenings performing necessary editorial and revision tasks.

The authors were helpful both in preparing their own manuscripts and in offering suggestions to each other and the coeditors. The volume received much-appreciated technical support from UNC Center program assistants Allison Stelljes, Austin Johnson, and Anne Peele. Law student Catalina Azuero was a great help in various research tasks for coeditor Boger, and Jennifer Blatz provided valuable assistance in the preparation of Orfield's contribution. UNC law students Atinuke Akintola, Larissa Bixler, Kerry Burleigh, Andrew Owens, Andrea Schrag, Allison Smith, Danielle Ward, Sara Warf, and Junghoon Yum cheerfully carried out numerous copyediting tasks. Lori Kelley and Abby Bielagus of The Civil Rights Project provided helpful assistance in proofreading and the formatting of chapters in their final stages, and Allan Klinge tracked down missing or incomplete references to finish the bibliography.

UNC Law School Dean Gene R. Nichol has offered steadfast intellectual and institutional support to the UNC Center in general and to this project in particular. The Center's director, Julius Chambers, whose brave and resourceful civil rights practice led the way toward southern school desegregation for nearly forty years—first with the Chambers, Stein, Ferguson law practice in Charlotte, North Carolina, and then as director-counsel of the NAACP Legal Defense and Educational Fund in New York—remains a special source of inspiration and support for this book.

School Resegregation

INTRODUCTION

GARY ORFIELD

The Southern Dilemma

Losing *Brown*, Fearing *Plessy*

The Supreme Court's 1954 decision declaring segregated schools unconstitutional directly threatened the South's social traditions. After Reconstruction was dismantled in the 1870s and 1880s, the South gained the right to manage race relations as it wished. It built a comprehensive system of racial separation, a system legitimized by the Supreme Court in the 1896 *Plessy v. Ferguson* "separate but equal" decision. But then, in *Brown v. Board of Education*, the Court said that this system of mandatory racial segregation was illegitimate. To its advocates, *Brown* promised a new day in which the color lines at the heart of all major southern institutions would finally come down and opportunity and access would no longer depend on race. To its opponents, *Brown* directly threatened the racial system on which the region was founded.

The year that *Brown* was decided, the University of North Carolina Press published a remarkable book, Harry Ashmore's *The Negro and the Schools*, that summarized the work of forty scholars studying the South's segregated schools. The volume portrayed a region with deeply unequal schools and last-minute efforts at equalization under the threat of imposed desegregation but with pervasive separation and inequality remaining after nearly sixty years of "separate but equal" education. This book, published just after the fiftieth anniversary of *Brown*, tells of a South where schools have been transformed beyond recognition, where apartheid gave way as southern schools became the nation's most integrated, but where there is now a strong trend backward toward greater racial separation in an ever more diverse and urbanized region.

Brown is almost universally celebrated as the greatest twentieth-century Supreme Court decision; in its wake, the South changed deeply. Yet *Brown*'s legacy for southern schools is still uncertain. In fact, in the early twenty-first century, segregation is again growing after decades of progress toward integration. If the present period turns out to be another turning point for southern society, it deserves the most careful analysis. Although most Americans prefer to think of their history as a story of continuous progress, the South has a sense of tragedy, a sense of its original sin of slavery, and the knowledge that progress is deeply mixed with reverses. A third of a century after the South's schools became the least segregated in America, the region is leading a backward slide toward renewed segregation under way more slowly in other parts of the country. This book is about resegregation and the choices and consequences the region faces as separation grows.

John Hope Franklin, the great African American historian, often talked about the era when Reconstruction ended, the Northern troops left the South, the new civil rights laws were not enforced, and the Supreme Court began interpreting away into nothingness the post–Civil War amendments to the Constitution.[1] American intellectuals were largely silent or approving, often dismissing civil rights enforcement as futile or disruptive. Reformers were dismissed as "radicals," and those who reimposed systems of intense racial subordination were hailed in their states as "redeemers." As the twentieth century began, most whites quietly accepted the return to racial subordination and blatant inequality.

The twenty-first century has begun with seeming parallels. The most conservative Court in several generations is interpreting away protections won by nonwhite students a half century earlier. All three branches of the federal government support limiting civil rights enforcement. The country is slipping back into deeper separation. The impact of the Supreme Court's decisions on the South has been particularly dramatic for three reasons: the South was the most desegregated region; the South had the most districts whose demographic composition was compatible with extensive long-term desegregation (e.g., countywide metropolitan districts containing substantial percentages of both white and minority students); and major parts of the South were under the most conservative federal appellate court, the Fourth Circuit Court of Appeals, which aggressively terminated desegregation plans and limited even voluntary action promoting integration.[2] This court basically repudiated the idea that integrated education was a compelling interest justifying race-conscious policies, a position undermined by the Supreme Court's 2003 decision in *Grutter v. Bollinger*, which found that college integration was a compelling interest and that some affirmative policies to create it could continue.

Although many educators have silently accepted the claim that segregation now can actually be equal, many others oppose the historic reversal, which has quietly abandoned the dream of *Brown* to return to the failed promise of *Plessy*. Southern districts resegregating their schools often have superintendents and other leaders who tell the public that things will be all right, that they know what to do to equalize education, but these districts also frequently have skeptics who remember the conditions that existed in the black schools before desegregation or have seen profoundly unequal ghetto schools in other districts. Often newly resegregated schools appear on the official list of failing schools sanctioned under the No Child Left Behind Act of 2001.

This book originated in research commissioned for a conference on resegregation of the South at one of the South's greatest research universities, the University of North Carolina at Chapel Hill. The conference, held on Labor Day weekend in 2002, drew more than five hundred participants, more than even the largest venue in the university's conference center could hold. They came to hear and discuss nineteen studies of the changes in the region's schools and their consequences. Many participants had deep roots in the struggles for integrated education in southern cities and counties; some were prominent educators or civil rights leaders; others were young people, products of interracial schools produced by the desegregation struggle, who wanted to be involved in the debate over the future. That weekend of intense discussion enriched the region's debate and began a long effort to bring the new research into sharper focus. That work has led to the publication of this book, which offers important conclusions and ideas about the fateful changes now under way.

A half century ago, the Supreme Court's decision in *Brown v. Board of Education* set in motion what became a fundamental challenge to the racial system of the southern and border states, with their apartheid laws and institutions. A generation later, in the late 1960s and early 1970s, decisions in the urban desegregation cases helped open up a much shorter and more limited attack on the racial institutions and practices of segregation and inequality in the North and West as well as the South's cities. In 1974, however, the Supreme Court began to set limits, making it very difficult—and usually impossible—to address the remaining problems of segregation and inequality in the nation's great metropolitan areas, problems based on segregation among separate school districts. Yet not until the 1990s did that period of limits change into a period of retreat and reversal, triggered by three Supreme Court decisions supporting resegregation. By 2005, the South had been resegregating for more than a decade.

Why Focus on the South?

School segregation and inequality are national problems, and the most intense segregation in the country today is in older northern metropolitan areas, so why focus this book on the South? Historically, slavery and the Civil War had their roots in the South. The South also had the greatest number of blacks and the deepest inequalities, although the nation's racial division spread to other regions on a large scale with the Great Migration from the rural South that began during World War I. The South, however, remained the home of the most extreme and comprehensive systems of racial subordination and the deepest resistance to racial change. The region has been central to the black experience in America. The eleven states of the Confederacy have always been home to a majority of U.S. blacks. Since the 1970s, this concentration has been intensifying, with a substantial, decade-by-decade net in-migration of African Americans back to the South.[3]

When *Brown* was decided, the South was totally segregated. Beginning with the creation of schools for blacks after the end of slavery, the region's educational institutions had always been organized along racial lines. Those schools were profoundly unequal. Even after the legal threat of desegregation motivated southern leaders to work seriously to close the gaps in the early 1950s, the differences remained huge. In 1940, southern white schools were receiving 133 percent more per child in funds than black schools received; the gap remained at 43 percent when the South argued in the Supreme Court for continuing "separate but equal."[4] The one black educator warmly embraced by the white South after Reconstruction, Booker T. Washington of Tuskegee, Alabama, advocated separate and different education for blacks, a kind of practical education for the limited range of jobs available to young blacks.[5] White educators in the South had provided no significant leadership in desegregating their schools and had demonstrated little enthusiasm for equalization before the Court forced the issue.

Brown's promise combined very broad goals with very narrow means. The 1954 decision sought to end imposed segregation, thereby halting what the Court found to be irreversible harm inflicted on students in segregated schools. The means of the 1955 *Brown* remedial decision, conversely, were far more limited: the Court instructed local federal district courts to begin some kind of change in ways the courts decided would be feasible in view of local conditions. Considering the two decisions together, one could say that the promise of *Brown* was contradictory —to change fundamentally the basic structure of southern society and race relations yet to do so in a way that would not seriously disturb white racists. This compromise, which united the diverse elements on the Supreme Court, was based on the vain hope that a strategy of gradualism would ease the transition while displaying caution about the limits of judicial power.

But in fact, intense white political resistance rather than moderate compliance crystallized across the region. The black community read *Brown*'s first part—its promise—and wondered why it was not being fulfilled, while white leaders read *Brown*'s invitation to gradual, locally designed change and became confident that the color line could be maintained with only very minor modifications. Without any concrete requirements or guidance from the higher courts, and facing intense state and local resistance from virtually all white leaders, most southern federal district judges, themselves products and residents of a segregated society, decided that extremely limited change was all that would be necessary—policies permitting a handful of black students to transfer to white schools.

After 1954, the South's federal judges kept the pace of desegregation very slow. Virtually the entire elected leadership of the region mobilized under the banner of "massive resistance," enacting scores of laws to try to block any significant desegregation, attacking the Supreme Court, opposing even the most modest voluntary desegregation, closing public schools, and stirring up deep racial polarization.[6] White resistance was much more intense during the period in which leaders were exploiting fear of racial change that had not yet begun than when large-scale desegregation actually came. At the outset of the 1960s, it seemed as if the intensity of white southern resistance had grown so great that desegregation would remain a minor exception in an overwhelmingly segregated region, an area whose political unity made the *Brown* decision seem of little more than symbolic importance—and mostly an empty symbol at that. Only 1 percent of black students in the South were in majority white schools in the summer of 1963, when President John F. Kennedy asked Congress to pass a sweeping new civil rights law following national outrage against the violent attack on Martin Luther King Jr.'s civil rights march in Birmingham, Alabama.

Brown was a smashing disappointment in producing desegregated schools during its first decade, but it was nonetheless a huge force in terms of delegitimizing all aspects of the southern system of apartheid and spurring a social movement to produce changes that the courts were unwilling to order on their own. Southern blacks, drawing inspiration from *Brown*, began to confront entrenched racial practices not only in the courts but in the streets as well. *Brown* helped spur the civil rights movement and prod the Democratic Party into making a deep commitment to serious racial change. *Brown* produced a model for creation of new legal rights that would motivate other movements for legal changes that forbade discrimination based on language, gender, handicap, and other irrelevant personal circumstances. The model of the legal campaign for *Brown* also strongly influenced other educational campaigns, such as the battles for equalizing school funding and guaranteeing all students a minimally adequate education, that remain active in the courts a half century later. The decision's ultimate influence was vast. But its impact on its first target, segregated schools, remained small until the social and political forces outside the courts produced larger changes.

Widespread desegregation came to the South suddenly, beginning in the mid-1960s. Congress passed the 1964 Civil Rights Act, the first major civil rights law in nearly a century, and President Lyndon Johnson, the first president elected from the South since the Civil War, set out to enforce seriously the law. It brought the power of the federal government squarely to bear on southern schools. The law authorized the Department of Justice to go to court to enforce civil rights laws and required the schools to desegregate or face cutoff of rapidly increasing school aid funds being allocated under the 1965 Elementary and Secondary Education Act, which was the largest such act in U.S. history and which provided substantial boosts in the budgets of the region's high-poverty schools.[7] Acceptance of change came after southern leaders suffered decisive defeats in the battle over the 1964 act, the rise of a powerful black movement, and President Johnson's sweeping 1964 reelection, a campaign in which the GOP candidate, Barry Goldwater, who opposed the civil rights law, carried only five of the fifty states.

It looked as if the South had lost and would have to change. In communities wishing to fight desegregation, leaders learned that they would be in court not only against a civil rights lawyer but also against the vastly more powerful U.S. Department of Justice, which virtually never lost a civil rights case in that era. Desegregation soon began in earnest, and the dual system of black and white segregated schools was radically restructured into systems of comprehensively desegregated schools. By the end of the 1960s, the South experienced a level of interracial schooling that had probably never been seen anywhere in American history on a large scale.[8]

As the 1970s began, the federal courts had fashioned a set of policies designed to produce rapid and full desegregation in the southern districts where desegregation was feasible. In a 1968 decision, *Green v. New Kent County*, the Supreme Court said that the time for "deliberate speed" was over and that no more delays were permissible. *Green* also announced that *Brown* sought not merely to give students from minority groups a choice about transferring from a segregated school to a white school but to end segregation itself. To accomplish that goal, separate racially defined school systems would be converted to unitary systems in which the schools were not racially identifiable and the faculties were desegregated, with resources and curriculum equalized. It was a sweeping mandate.

Three years later, in 1971, a generation after *Brown*, the *Swann v. Charlotte-Mecklenburg* decision tackled the South's urban segregation and upheld the use of districtwide busing when necessary to overcome unconstitutional segregation. Except in a small share of rigidly racist counties in the Black Belt, where whites were a minority and largely abandoned public schools for "segregation academies," and in the large central cities, where the schools already had few remaining whites, very substantial and rapid desegregation occurred under these policies. Since many large cities in the South, unlike the North, were part of countywide school districts that included both city and suburbs, some full metropolitan regions rapidly reached high levels of school integration.

When Richard M. Nixon's administration tried to delay enforcement of these new requirements, the Supreme Court unanimously rejected that delay,[9] and the lower federal courts, in very unusual decisions, first found that the government was intentionally failing to enforce the requirements of the 1964 Civil Rights Act and then ordered the Office for Civil Rights to quickly update many older and less adequate desegregation plans to meet the new Supreme Court standards.[10]

In spite of a hostile White House and an unenthusiastic Congress, the South continued to become more and more integrated into the late 1980s. Rural and small-town America, where resistance had seemed most intractable, became the most integrated segment of the population. White students in the South began to attend schools with far higher proportions of black classmates than did whites in any other region.[11] Recognizing that desegregation had become inevitable, Congress and President Nixon agreed in 1972 on the creation of a large federal program to assist in the desegregation process, the Emergency School Aid Act. This act gave no money for busing costs but funded programs to help the positive operation of desegregated schools by retraining teachers, providing appropriate curriculum and strategies, and working on interpersonal relations among students.[12] The programs were intended to assist desegregated schools in becoming genuinely integrated, with good race relations and rising achievement. School districts competed eagerly for these funds, and research showed that those programs enjoyed considerable success.[13] (Unfortunately this program was shut down in 1981 as part of President Ronald Reagan's first budget.)

Impact

At the time of *Brown*, very little was known about interracial schools, about how to create them or how to make them more effective. By the 1970s it had become clear that desegregation offered significant gains for minority students and that the most important of these gains were not measured by test score increases but by changes in students' life chances. It was also clear that the precise design of a desegregation decree mattered and that some approaches could increase student gains in all dimensions.

The black-white achievement gap closed substantially during the desegregation era (1964 through the late 1980s), particularly in the South, although the gaps have grown wider during the recent resegregation period. Some estimates suggest that the black-white achievement gap fell by half during the earlier period. Further, during the desegregation era, large increases occurred in both high school graduation levels and college-going rates among black students, although those gains have eroded seriously in the recent past. Only about one-quarter of blacks were graduating in the early 1950s, but the rate soared toward its high point—more than three-quarters, according to some federal statistics—in the

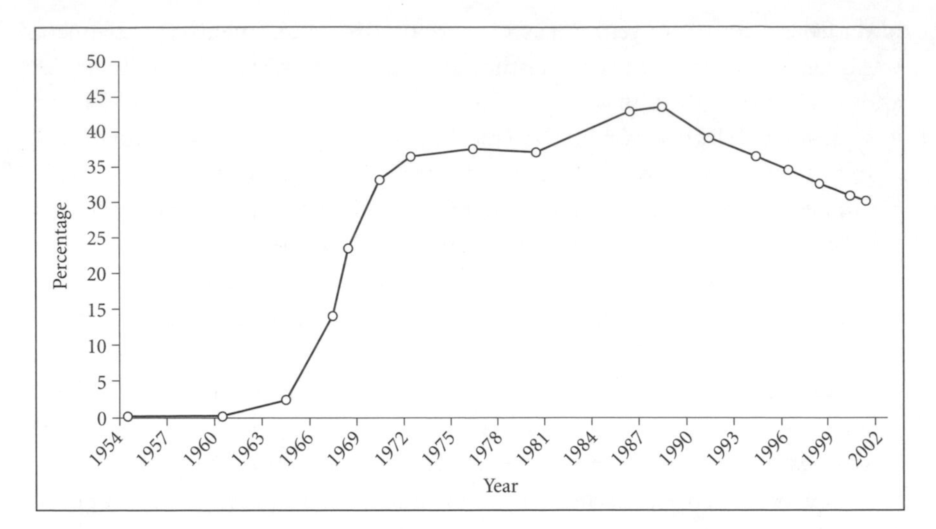

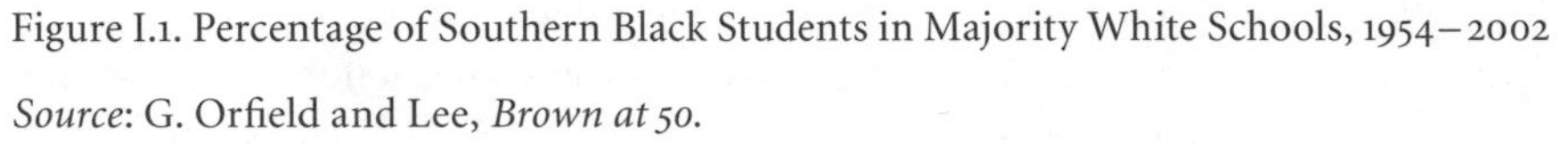
Figure I.1. Percentage of Southern Black Students in Majority White Schools, 1954–2002

Source: G. Orfield and Lee, *Brown at 50*.

period before resegregation and other policy changes such as high-stakes testing took hold.[14] Other changes obviously took place at the same time, making it impossible to know the precise impact of desegregation. The least we can say is that (1) desegregation occurred at the same time as substantial educational progress for blacks and improved racial attitudes among whites, and (2) the conservative agenda of the late 1980s and the 1990s was implemented at the same time that reversals of some of these gains took place. Direct research on desegregation impacts suggest that it had substantial influence and that resegregation has created new obstacles to equal educational opportunity and attainment.

Attitudes toward housing integration improved during the desegregation era. Since the issue has not been systematically researched, one can only speculate about the relationships between school desegregation and the rise of successful cross-racial political coalitions in many communities and states. (Contemporary surveys show that students in desegregated schools feel that they understand people from other backgrounds better and are more confident of their ability to discuss issues across racial and ethnic lines. These skills and attitudes seem strongly related to leadership and coalition building.) The school desegregation movement can claim rare and extremely important accomplishments for African American students: breaking a deeply rooted social and political pattern of stratification, maintaining such change for decades, and producing real academic gains. Desegregation largely disappeared from southern politics after the 1970s: very few people listed it as a serious problem after that time, and desegregation levels remained very high for decades without additional judicial intervention despite the attacks of the Nixon and Reagan administrations. It looked in many ways like a successful social revolution, though many secondary problems of inequality within desegregated schools remained to be addressed, and equitable policies for metropolitan communities without metropolitan school districts were not found.

How did these incredible accomplishments begin to come apart? Why has the South returned to segregation since the 1980s? Whenever these questions are discussed in public, people tend to answer that desegregation failed or the public turned against it. Yet while the percentage of students in private schools in the South increased, it remained well below the national average. In fact, although local problems arose, overall levels of desegregation remained highly stable, and schools were integrated at very high levels in most of the rural and small-town South as well as in metropolitan areas with countywide districts. This does not mean that problems and failures did not occur or that desegregation represented an educational panacea but rather that the general pattern was surprisingly positive in the light of southern history. Further, public opinion about the acceptance and value of desegregation became more positive over time.[15]

Others answer that the growing segregation of the 1990s is just a result of demography or housing patterns. School districts wishing to end their desegregation plans often present this basic explanation to the courts. Such districts point to white flight (a decline in white students caused by desegregation) and contend that housing segregation has expanded but argue that these demographic trends are not the schools' problem and that the schools should not be required to redress these issues, which are merely the product of private decisions.

Some facts are clear. The percentage of black and Latino students in the South has grown since the 1960s, while the percentage of white students in the region has gradually declined, a process often described as "white flight." It is also true that by 2000 only a small white majority remained in the South's public schools. Yet the South had a much higher percentage of all its students in substantially desegregated schools and a much smaller percentage of white students in private schools. Although the South's enrollment changes did relate to the proportion of minority students in white schools, some of the most rapid losses of whites occurred in cities such as Atlanta[16] where busing had never been pursued. Racial transition continued in some places where desegregation orders had been abandoned and segregated neighborhood schools created. It is also true that levels of school desegregation for black and white students increased—in spite of the shrinking white majority—until the 1990s, when such levels went into a period of continual decline, a sudden change that corresponded to no sudden demographic change. The basic housing changes at work in the 1990s were actually more posi-

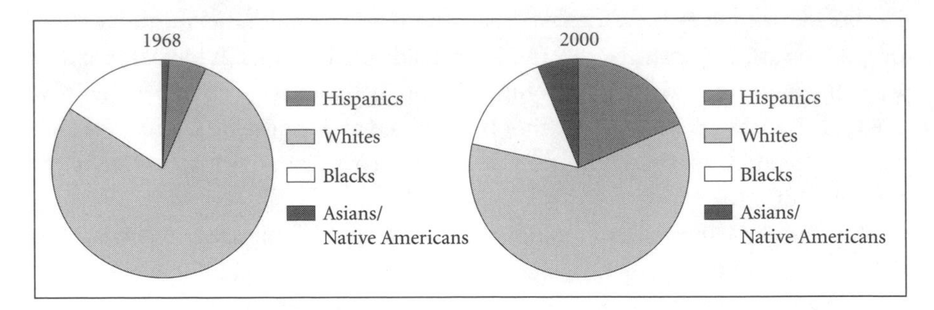

Figure I.2. Percentage of Public School Enrollment by Race/Ethnicity, 1968 and 2000

Sources: G. Orfield, George, and A. Orfield, "Racial Change"; 2000–2001 NCES Common Core of Data.

tive from a desegregation standpoint than those during the era of increasing school desegregation. In fact, as this book will show, residential desegregation has been increasing even as school desegregation has been declining. No simple white flight explanation accounts for increasing school segregation.

The basic causes of the declining percentage of white students in the South are the age structure and birth rates of the white population, the impact of internal migration within the United States, and, most important, the effects of international migration. The percentage of nonwhite students in U.S. schools more than tripled from the time of *Brown* through the beginning of the twenty-first century. Whites are the oldest group in terms of median age and, on average, have families that are much smaller than Latino families and somewhat smaller than black families. Therefore, whites are producing relatively fewer students. A substantial return migration of blacks to the South has also occurred since the 1970s, probably reflecting the area's economic growth and its improved racial climate. In addition, a very large internal and international migration of Latinos into the South and its schools has taken place. The largest southern state, Texas, has the lowest share of white students of any state in the region because of the immense expansion of its historic Latino population. That change is certainly not caused by desegregation orders, since few court orders are presently in place in the state, since Latinos were never significantly desegregated, and since the state's largest city, Houston, has never been desegregated by court order.

Though school desegregation plans and neighborhood residential transition undoubtedly produce white flight at times, this is a secondary issue in explaining the South's growing school segregation, especially because the region has had very few new desegregation orders for decades and is now more than a decade into the process of terminating those that do still exist. As research by Sean F. Reardon and John T. Yun shows, residential segregation declined in the region as school segregation rose, indicating that a key problem was the declining role of school-assignment plans, which had made schools substantially less segregated than neighborhoods.

The resegregation of the South has clearly been related to court decisions. Desegregation of southern blacks increased from the early 1960s until the end of the 1980s, even during periods when national political administrations were hostile to desegregative policies. For decades, even though the South had the highest share of African American students to desegregate and a bitter history of resistance, it has been the most integrated region of the country. After President Nixon withdrew the federal executive branch from the enforcement process in 1969 and after Congress took away the enforcement authority of the U.S. Department of Education's Office for Civil Rights during the Carter administration, the federal courts became the central policy makers. Then began a long period in which the law was relatively clear and constant and little active conflict erupted about desegregation at the community level. School desegregation plans became a normal part of life.

The reversal in the South was clearly related to a 1991 Supreme Court decision, *Board of Education of Oklahoma City v. Dowell*, that authorized federal courts to end desegregation plans. In a stunning reversal of earlier expectations, the Court adopted the basic ideas first put forward by President Reagan's Justice Department —that desegregation was a temporary rather than a permanent goal for schools and that courts could dissolve existing orders and permit the restoration of segregated neighborhood schools as long as the school districts said that they made these changes for educational rather than racial reasons. This change came from a Court on which seven of the nine members had been appointed by Republican presidents with conservative views on civil rights; it was headed by a chief justice who had opposed *Brown* while serving as Supreme Court clerk.

In striking contrast to the extreme gradualism that characterized the implementation of desegregation in the decade after *Brown* and the era's consistently passive judicial posture and very limited remedies, a number of federal district judges in the 1990s took an activist role in enforcing and even expanding on the Supreme Court's resegregation decisions.[17] These courts, particularly the Fourth Circuit, clearly believed that the Rehnquist Court was headed toward an outright prohibition of any kind of race-conscious action to maintain even voluntary desegregation after a district had been released from its historic constitutional obligation to convert to a "unitary" system. When the district court said that this obligation had ended, many judges thought that taking race into account to maintain integration was constitutionally impermissible. Based on this line of reasoning, federal courts in the late 1990s forbade a number of communities from using race-conscious student-assignment policies to keep magnet schools integrated, including major districts in the Virginia and Maryland suburbs of Washington, D.C., and in Charlotte, North Carolina.[18] Although the Supreme Court refused to review those decisions, the basic assumption on which they rested —that race-conscious policies to maintain desegregation were illegal without a court order—has since been undermined by the Supreme Court's 2003 decision upholding race-conscious college admissions policies.[19]

New Dimensions of Segregation

While the South is abandoning or being forced to abandon efforts to integrate black and white students, another major segregation issue has often been ignored. In the 1991 *Dowell* decision, in which the Supreme Court first approved ending desegregation plans and permitting the Oklahoma City Board of Education to return to segregated neighborhood schools, the Court concluded that enough had been done to desegregate blacks but made no mention of the rapid growth of a segregated Latino population in the same school district. This and many other decisions that followed declared school districts unitary and ended their desegregation obligations even though no remedy had ever addressed the special isolation of Latino students, for whom neighborhood school policies meant more severe segregation. A much more complex system of racial and ethnic stratification has developed in southern schools than *Brown* ever contemplated, and this system is usually ignored. Since the 1960s, the proportion of Latino students in American schools has quadrupled, while the share of whites has fallen significantly. Much of the national population growth, including a majority of the growth in the first years of the twenty-first century, is driven by the Latino migration. The Latino population soared 10 percent in just the first two years of the new century. National and regional statistics show the increasingly multiracial character of our society and the very high and increasing segregation of Latino students.[20] The data also show the great academic success (on average) and high level of integration of Asian students. The country is seeing a rapid increase in the number of schools with three or more significant racial and ethnic groups.[21] Issues of multiracialism are here, but they have not been addressed.

As desegregation is abandoned, a variety of policies have emerged that purport to resolve issues of educational inequity for minority students. Such policies often make sweeping claims about what can be accomplished but often ignore inequalities rooted in race and, in the worst cases, actually compound them. The No Child Left Behind Act, which dominates educational policy in the early twenty-first century, is a classic example of a policy that sounds a ringing affirmation of minority rights but ends up undermining desegregation and punishing the schools and children that are the worst victims of segregation by race and

Table 1.1. U.S. Public School Enrollment by Race/Ethnicity, 1968–2000 (in Millions)

Race/Ethnicity	1968	1980	1994	1996	1998	2000	Change, 1968–2000
Latinos	2.0	3.2	5.6	6.4	6.9	7.7	+5.7 (283%)
Whites	34.7	29.2	28.5	29.1	28.9	28.8	–5.9 (–17%)
Blacks	6.3	6.4	7.1	7.7	7.9	8.1	+1.8 (29%)

Sources: DBS Corp., 1982, 1987; G. Orfield, George, and A. Orfield, "Racial Change"; 1996–97, 1998–99, 2000–2001 NCES Common Core of Data.

poverty. The act is based on the Children's Defense Fund's slogan, "leave no child behind" and embodies President George W. Bush's desire to end what he called "the soft bigotry of low expectations."[22] It sounds like a minority equity policy. The act, however, incorporates requirements for annual test score gains that pose huge challenges for minority, high-poverty schools where children often lack qualified teachers and educational materials and face additional burdens of language, health, and high mobility. The law imposes sanctions that take students and funding away from schools after just two years if they do not produce gains far in excess of what has ever been achieved across a major school district. Because the act sets a single achievement goal and requires that all schools progress at the same rate, the formula has the perverse impact of imposing far tougher achievement requirements on schools that start far behind. Because it judges each school on the yearly progress of each group of students, segregated white schools have far fewer standards to meet to avoid sanctions than do integrated schools. Amy Stuart Wells and Jennifer Jellison Holme point out in their chapter in this volume how the branding of interracial schools as academically inadequate deepens the problem by driving middle-class whites from integrated schools to overwhelmingly white schools and neighborhoods. Trying to impose accountability while ignoring the inequalities built into segregation can result in punishing those who are working in the most difficult situations, encouraging them to leave for schools with less demanding requirements, and thus only exacerbating the inequalities. The policy sounds good but ends up punishing the victims of segregation yet another time.

A striking thing about the recent discussion of educational reforms, moreover, is the reductionist nature of their definition of education. They tend to equate education with test scores and weigh desegregation only along that metric. Desegregation's educational impact, however, is clearest in the way it produces access to schools, teachers, and curriculum of differing quality and in its impact on students' life chances (such as college enrollment and success), preparation to live and work and participate effectively in a multiracial society, and deeper understanding of other parts of our society. The Supreme Court emphasized precisely these goals in *Grutter*, its 2003 decision upholding affirmative action.

Public beliefs about integration are full of complexities and contradictions—strong and growing support for racially integrated schools but much less support for any means to achieve them. Generalized support of integrated education has reached a very high level: it has increased rather than declined as resegregation has taken place. Yet courts and local leaders seldom offer any serious discussion of the nature and consequences of intense segregation by residence and schools. At the same time, however, those officials adopt policy changes that rapidly create highly segregated minority schools that become centers of urban pathology and often move to the list of officially designated "failing" schools.

The press usually does not mention the racial composition of student bodies enrolled in the failing schools. Public leaders rarely challenge the public to consider the incompatibility of its social and educational goals and to choose integrated education. The public opinion data seem clearly to indicate that the turn back to resegregation did not result from any negative turn in public opinion or any public perception that desegregation was one of the major problems in the nation's schools. It has not appeared for many years as a serious worry on the annual Gallup Poll surveys of such problems.[23] Just as the courts opened the issue in the 1950s, leading public opinion, they were trying to close the topic a half century later, leading public opinion backward.

The Contributions of the New Research

The South's leaders, judges, scholars and journalists, educators, and parents all need answers to a few basic questions in thinking about and deciding the future of race relations in the region's schools. In what way is the South resegregating? Where does resegregation appear, and whom does it affect? Why is this happening? What are the region's choices, how feasible are they, and what are their probable consequences? Thinking seriously about the future of southern education requires coming to terms with these issues, all of which this volume addresses.

One might think that it would be relatively easy to clarify the trends and relationships—how much and what kind of resegregation is occurring. Surely that is just a statistical fact. Well, of course, there are different ways to set up categories, different ways to measure segregation, and different ways to determine whether changes are large or small. Several authors in this book describe the trends, measuring it in different ways. All show that segregation in the South is growing. It is not an extremely rapid growth, like the growth of desegregation in the mid-1960s and early 1970s. Rather, it is a gradual but now very clearly established long-term trend toward racial isolation of black students after previous decades of movement in the opposite direction. In some individual districts where desegregation plans were dismantled, segregation grew rapidly.

Although contemporary issues of resegregation and desegregation are often discussed using simple slogans, these matters are really complex and multidimensional, and this book seeks to move the discussion forward. Scholars from many institutions and disciplines have written essays that greatly enrich our understanding of what is happening, the consequences, and possible alternatives.

This book adds a vital focus on Latinos—largely ignored in the South during the civil rights era—to the conventional discussion of the dynamics of racial change in the region. *Brown* was a decision about the exclusion of black students from white schools, but the South has become more diverse as a massive wave of Latino immigration has swept the country. Latinos have clearly faced a history of illegal segregation and discrimination, particularly in Texas. A number of early civil rights battles against segregation were organized by Latino groups, including the American G.I. Forum and League of United Latin American Citizens, which fought these practices for decades. The Supreme Court's 1973 *Keyes* decision belatedly recognized that discrimination against Latino students resembled that against blacks in the South and that Latino students had a right to seek judicial orders against school districts to repair the damage caused by segregation and discrimination.

The South includes two of the eight states with the highest populations of Latino students, Texas and Florida, and other states, including North Carolina and Georgia, are now experiencing an extremely rapid growth in this segment of the population. Texas had about one-fifth of all the Latino students in the United States in 2000. The state experienced a vast immigration from Mexico, and population projections show that in the future it will become a majority Latino state. Luis M. Laosa's chapter, "School Segregation in Texas at the Beginning of the Twenty-first Century," examines the segregation of Texas public school students by race/ethnicity, poverty status, and English-language proficiency and asks whether the composition of schools stratified along these three measures is related to the academic performance of the students in these schools. He finds a strong positive correlation between the percentage of minority students and the percentage of economically disadvantaged students. Laosa also reports that Spanish-speaking students tend to be isolated from white students and students of higher socioeconomic status. These relationships suggest that racial (and socioeconomic) desegregation could help to improve performance for all students in desegregated schools. Since Latinos across the South have very low rates of high school completion and college attendance, the long trend toward resegregation may be deeply threatening. Linguistic segregation plus high-stakes testing in English can be a toxic combination for Latino students.

Why Are the Region's Schools Resegregating?

Resegregation is widely explained as a result of a combination of factors—the inherent limits of the courts and enforcement policies, the relentless spread of housing segregation reflecting private choices, and the rising number of minorities and declining white population in the nation and its schools.

Since the time of *Brown*, critics have argued that the federal courts had simply bitten off more than they could chew, that they had begun something they lacked the capacity to finish. If this were true, it would mean that the courts' efforts to overreach would inevitably fail and, worse, would lose legitimacy and discredit the policy they were attempting to pursue. Several authors in this book address the role of the courts, including John Charles Boger and Jacinta S. Ma and Michal Kurlaender. Erwin Chemerinsky argues that the courts failed to do all that was in their power, not that they tried to do more than they were able. The major reason for this failure of will, Chemerinsky contends, was the politics of Supreme Court appointments that produced an anti-civil-rights majority by the late 1980s, not the inherent limitations of courts as institutions. The Supreme Court failed to adopt workable urban desegregation and financial equalization policies after President Nixon broke the Warren Court's unity: Nixon appointed four of the five justices who voted against equalizing school funding in *San Antonio v. Rodriguez* (1973). The Nixon Court also voted against requiring the integration of metropolitan areas that had fragmented into many small racially segregated school districts, a decision that guaranteed growing metropolitan segregation as residential segregation expanded within individual school districts.[24] Chemerinsky further argues that resegregation of desegregated districts was not the inevitable consequence of judicial failure (since southern desegregation continued to increase in the 1980s) but was the foreseeable consequence of the High Court's decisions in the 1990s that initiated the resegregation now occurring in the South. His argument suggests a possible positive future role for the courts in reversing the current resegregation if the Court were altered by new appointments.

Ma and Kurlaender agree and believe that the Supreme Court's 2003 *Grutter* decision on affirmative action for college admissions shows how the legal doctrines could be shaped. *Grutter* clearly recognizes both that integration is a compelling educational need for American students and colleges and that state universities properly should take race into account to achieve integration—that there is really no other effective way to accomplish it. This decision, considered by many to be the most important civil rights decision in a quarter century, naturally undermines some key legal assumptions of the southern courts that have pressed to end school desegregation and then to block voluntary integration efforts. If the colleges and universities have a compelling interest in diversity, how much greater, many people ask, is the interest of the nation's public schools? Ma and Kurlaender argue that recent developments both in the courts and in the research community could give new life to the struggle to keep integrated schools in the South. If the courts are a central factor driving resegregation, a different directive obviously could increase desegregation. If the rulings turn on proof of important benefits from desegregation, the experiences of students recently studied in seven school districts across the United States—showing benefits for high school students that parallel those the Court found compelling for college students—are of the greatest importance.

Is It Just Demography?

Another central theme in the resegregation discussions is the belief that the courts are trying to impose artificially integrated schools in a society where the continuous spread of residential segregation will inevitably undo this process. Proponents of ending desegregation orders use this argument in a fundamental way. Judges have to make findings about whether school districts have taken all practical steps before ending court orders, and some districts argue that nothing more can be done because they cannot deal with the spreading housing segregation. Sean F. Reardon and John T. Yun's chapter, "Integrating Neighborhoods, Segregating Schools: The Retreat from School Desegregation in the South, 1990–2000," analyzes the relationship between school and residential segregation in the South. The statistics show that because of desegregation plans, southern children had been substantially more integrated in schools than in neighborhoods. During the 1990s, however, residential segregation declined but school segregation increased. This suggests that the increase in school segregation results not from private residential choices but from changes in school policy. In short, less segregated neighborhoods had more segregated schools. These trends may foreshadow even more rapid resegregation in the South as courts release increasing numbers of school districts from desegregation plans. This finding does not, however, mean that demography does not constitute part of the problem. Everything else being equal, less black contact with white students will obviously occur as the percentage of whites in the total population falls. However, the desegregation level rose for decades even as this process of white student decline proceeded, suggesting the joint impact of slowly declining residential segregation and school desegregation plans. Then the trend turned, consistently going in the other direction. The underlying demographic trend did not change—the courts and school policies did.

In decisions about whether to end court orders, school districts often argue that any desegregation plan is futile because of white flight and spreading housing segregation. Desegregation in metropolitan school districts in the South, however, was far more extensive and stable than what happened in the city districts. In this book, Erica Frankenberg argues that a comprehensive school desegregation plan can indeed produce a positive impact on housing integration and thus reduce segregation in both schools and housing. By comparing two school districts with different levels of metropolitan desegregation, she finds that the most extensive school desegregation is related to lessened housing segregation. In other words, the higher the cost of opting out of desegregation plans via residential moves, and the more uniform the school desegregation provided throughout a metropolitan area, the greater the probability of integrated neighborhoods.

Another new vision of the relationships between school and housing issues comes in a pioneering qualitative study. A great deal of discussion has taken place about the relationship between testing and opportunity for minority students, but very little evidence has been produced on the impact of extensive publicity about test results on the residential preferences of families—that is, the effect on the stability of integrated communities. Since the average American family moves every six years, integrated neighborhoods rapidly resegregate unless they have a continuing inflow of both white and nonwhite residents.[25] Wells and Holme's chapter, "No Accountability for Diversity: Standardized Tests and the Demise of Racially Mixed Schools," suggests that the practice of marketing residential neighborhoods by exclusive reliance on standardized test scores to describe local schools seriously threatens interracial communities and their schools because racially diverse schools usually have at least modestly lower scores than outlying all-white suburban communities. Wells and Holme argue that the increased emphasis on statewide standardized testing has led to a narrowing definition of what a good school is and consequently has contributed to white flight from previously racially mixed schools. Parents mistake the average score for what their own children will achieve, not knowing that powerful evidence demonstrates that families are much more important than schools are for determining the test scores of middle-class children and that no evidence indicates that attending desegregated schools harms white achievement. (In fact, white students report substantial gains on other dimensions.)

Standardized testing and widespread publicity are central elements embodied in the No Child Left Behind Act of 2001. However, this kind of testing appears to be unfair to poor and minority students, to give huge advantages to schools serving children from affluent and well-educated homes, and also tends to raise already high dropout rates. Because publication of test scores makes the most affluent schools look best, and since the tests do not measure many of the most important advantages of integrated schools, continued community integration may be threatened. If Wells and Holme are correct, this environment of increased high-stakes testing (and publicity) can tend to resegregate communities that are residentially desegregated: white parents who believe politicians' claims that test scores represent the full measure of effective schools (rather than simply reflect the relative affluence of their communities) will tend to follow high scores when making housing choices. Differing ways of reporting both test scores and other school offerings and achievements might be far more positive for lasting residential integration.

Effects of Segregation and Resegregation

The central part of this book answers the query about why segregation is an important issue and resegregation an educational threat. Before considering the extent of current resegregation, the book examines the limits to the desegregation that occurred in the region. From the early days of the desegregation battles, advocates talked about the need to move beyond getting students of more than one racial/ethnic group in the same building (desegregation) to full-blown mixing of students and staff in classes and activities under conditions of respect and equal status (integration). Classroom-level segregation greatly erodes the benefits of school-level desegregation. Charles T. Clotfelter, Helen F. Ladd, and Jacob L. Vigdor examine this issue in their chapter, "Classroom-Level Segregation and Resegregation in North Carolina." They show that during the 1994–2001 period, when resegregation of the state's schools was under way, modest increases also occurred in classroom segregation across all grade levels and areas. The authors argue that much of this negative trend resulted from decisions by the Fourth Circuit Court of Appeals, which has pushed to end desegregation orders in the four states under its jurisdiction. The rising segregation also may result from rapid immigration of Hispanics to North Carolina, since they are often segregated in special English-language development classes, at least for a time. Thus, segregation was rising within as well as among schools.

Roslyn Arlin Mickelson's "The Incomplete Desegregation of the Charlotte-Mecklenburg Schools and Its Consequences, 1971–2004" examines a nationally prominent desegregated school system in which students' track placement correlated with race, often irrespective of students' academic potential. She finds that desegregated classrooms had positive effects on students' academic achievement. These data suggest that the rapid racial and economic resegregation in Charlotte after the Fourth Circuit lifted the desegregation order[26] hurt student achievement and that efforts to increase classroom desegregation in the city would have increased scores.

School administrators, public officials, and the press in communities undergoing resegregation almost always publicize assurances that all neighborhood schools will be equal and that education might even be better because kids will be closer to home and transportation money can be used for other things. Although *Brown* declared that separate schools were inherently unequal based on generations of bitter experience under *Plessy*, current rhetoric strongly suggests that school officials have somehow learned how to make separate schools equal. In fact, however, the combined adverse impact of segregation by race, poverty, and inequality on major educational outcomes normally takes hold rapidly in most resegregating schools. Nine-tenths of highly segregated black and Latino neighborhood schools must deal with concentrated poverty and its educational impacts, a situation rarely found in highly segregated white schools, which still account for almost half of the nation's educational institutions.[27]

With resegregation comes increasing concentration of poor children in segregated minority schools. Russell W. Rumberger and Gregory J. Palardy's chapter, "Does Resegregation Matter?: The Impact of Social Composition on Academic Achievement in Southern High Schools," shows that a school's social class composition, which is very strongly related to its racial composition, is also strongly related to student achievement, particularly in southern schools. The authors conclude that if students are to have a fair chance, either they should attend less impoverished schools or the nature of the high-poverty schools that kids attend must be dramatically altered. Family characteristics are very powerful predictors of student success in the South, and large educational differences exist even among kindergarten children. This is an invaluable reminder of the fact that the great leaders of the civil rights movement had no delusions that desegregating the schools alone would be sufficient. The movement sought full access to voting, jobs, housing, and equality in every sphere of life. The great march where Martin Luther King Jr. made his "I Have a Dream" speech was called the March on Washington for Jobs and Freedom. Increasing concentrations of children in isolated poor neighborhoods will produce growing gaps in achievement. Dealing with the poverty of black families would surely help school success.

If schools filled with poor children from families with low educational levels and few resources are systematically unequal, and if funds alone make relatively small differences, securing good teachers becomes a central need that becomes more urgent as the isolation and poverty intensify. Increasingly powerful evidence confirms the importance to students' educational success of highly qualified teachers with significant experience. This evidence is clearly reflected in the No Child Left Behind Act's requirement that all Title I classrooms have "highly qualified" teachers. A classic complaint about segregated minority schools has been that they cannot attract and retain excellent teachers. Research on schools that are unusually successful with disadvantaged students tends to identify a strongly committed and highly qualified faculty as a key element. In fact, good evidence shows that serious reforms take years of concerted effort by a faculty that buys into the reforms.[28] As southern schools resegregate, one crucial question is what happens to the teachers. Catherine E. Freeman, Benjamin Scafidi, and David L. Sjoquist take on this question in their chapter, "Racial Segregation in Georgia Public Schools, 1994–2001: Trends, Causes, and Impact on Teacher Quality." They show that the more heavily minority a school is, the more likely it is that white teachers have fewer advanced degrees and years of experience and the more likely that they will leave more rapidly. The supply of nonwhite teachers lags far behind the share of minority children in the schools, so white teachers' decisions are very important and have serious implications for student achievement. A 2001 study of Texas teachers reported similar findings.[29]

One thing that is very clear about resegregated schools in the South is that school-level test scores strongly relate to the level of segregation. This is a particular problem in the South, which not only has by far the highest percentage of African American students (and in the states of Texas and Florida is home to leading centers of Latino settlement) but also is the region most committed to graduation and promotion testing. The South began this movement earlier and has embraced it more thoroughly than any other area. In 2003, ten of the eleven southern states had mandatory high school graduation tests, and many other tests controlled students' ability to move from grade to grade and to attend college. Jay P. Heubert's chapter, "High-Stakes Testing, Nationally and in the South: Disparate Impact, Opportunity to Learn, and Current Legal Protections," discusses the growth of high-stakes testing and details its particularly harsh impact on minority children. He cites disturbing evidence of failure to provide real opportunity for students to learn tested materials. Standardized tests, especially when coupled with high stakes, cause disproportionate harm to minority students because differences in family education, in peer groups, and in school quality are linked to test scores and disproportionately affect the South—especially the region's segregated schools. Heubert, who coauthored a National Academy of Sciences report on this issue, sees the trend toward resegregation and extreme emphasis on testing as a toxic combination for the future of the region and its students. If minority students are sent back to inferior schools and then denied high school graduation on the basis of material that they were never effectively taught, it is a new cost of segregation. Other recent studies show that the national dropout rates are higher than previously reported and that the problem is most severe in segregated high-poverty high schools.

What Should Be Done?

If southern schools are resegregating, if the cause to a considerable extent lies in changes in the policy of the courts, if the consequences lead inexorably toward many forms of educational inequality, and if no evidence demonstrates that separate schools are or can plausibly become equal, what can be done? This policy issue is addressed implicitly or explicitly in a number of the chapters in this volume. Both Chemerinsky and Ma and Kurlaender strongly suggest that the courts could do more, that the Supreme Court's 2003 decision in *Grutter* may open the way, and that serious leadership is needed from educators if we are to avoid losing diverse schools and to take full educational advantage of diversity where it does exist.

Other critics argue that school districts should pursue a nonracial alternative. Some have touted the value of social-class desegregation as a viable alternative to race-conscious desegregation. This call has stirred public discussion, but only a handful of districts have undertaken serious initiatives, and these districts have had positive previous desegregation experiences—San Francisco; Cambridge, Massachusetts; and Wake County, North Carolina (metropolitan Raleigh, the only major southern example). Of these districts, Raleigh is the largest and includes both city and suburbs, and it has for years been a national leader in desegregation. Facing a real risk of being forced to rapidly resegregate, like Charlotte, the Wake County district decided to try to preserve diversity by assigning students in ways that balance students in schools by their test scores and poverty levels. Susan Leigh Flinspach and Karen E. Banks's chapter, "Moving beyond Race: Socioeconomic Diversity as a Race-Neutral Approach to Desegregation in the Wake County Schools," explores the early years of this experience. Their study shows that the district, in contrast to San Francisco, had considerable success with this process, perhaps in part because students in the area were already attending racially desegregated schools and had done so for many years. This study discusses some of the difficulties as well as advantages Wake County has experienced in operationalizing this approach. It has generated a substantial backlash, proving that busing poor kids is really not much better accepted than racial desegregation. A parallel study of San Francisco found that there was substantial resegregation when an assignment plan using socioeconomic status was adopted.[30] In San Francisco, in the aftermath of the Supreme Court's affirmative action decision, members of the school board are considering returning to court to ask for the resumption of the use of race-conscious policies. The Wake County plan is reportedly stirring increasing resistance over time. Nonetheless, it is a very important example of a policy that might be considered by many districts not desiring severe resegregation and its consequences. Powerful evidence certainly shows that high-poverty schools have negative educational impacts, and Wake County's educational gains show real progress.

john a. powell is well known not only as an attorney and writer but as a philosopher of the movement for an integrated society. In his chapter on strategies, "A New Theory of Integrated Education: *True* Integration," he takes the debate beyond the political and empirical realities to think again about the true goals of the desegregation movement and what must be done to pursue them. His discussion of true integration is provocative, and his thoughts about how the South could move in that direction are very useful. Like Dr. King, powell sees desegregation as a limited measure, only the first essential step toward integration. Contemporary political beliefs, he explains, undermine the pursuit of true integration. At a time when almost every part of the South is moving toward greater segregation, powell offers a vision of much deeper integration. Many people considered the vision that led to the ending of southern apartheid in the 1960s and 1970s to be audacious. So is powell's. If there is to be a turn back toward a civil rights agenda, a broad vision will be invaluable.

Must the South Retreat toward *Plessy*?

School desegregation is celebrated as a historic accomplishment even as it is abandoned in practice as much of urban America turns back to segregated neighborhood schools, driven, in part, by Supreme Court decisions ending desegregation orders. Some observers say that this phenomenon demonstrates that desegregation failed and that we are worse off than before the famous court decision whose fiftieth anniversary we are celebrating. Others assume, perhaps because the issue is generally neglected in policy debate, that we have done all that can be done.

It is a good time to think about these issues, since an overwhelming majority of Americans favor desegregated schools and almost all parents want their children to be prepared to get along with children of all backgrounds in a society that will become half nonwhite within their lifetimes.[31]

Much can be learned from the experience of school desegregation. In some parts of the country, levels of desegregation that would have seemed inconceivable were achieved and maintained for a long time. The basic factors determining the most successful experiences are known to researchers and many educators but are not being applied. Federal courts sometimes force districts supporting desegregation to resegregate. Desegregation, a difficult but successful option, is being abandoned in favor of another option—separate but equal—that never worked on any significant scale and does nothing to address issues of successfully preparing students for a diverse society. At a time when we still have generations of southerners who benefited from the most desegregated schools in the history of the South or any other region, it is especially important to reflect on what has been learned and not to let the gains quietly be lost.

The truth about the desegregation story is that we did accomplish a great deal when we were serious about it—when all branches of government worked together briefly in the 1960s—and in just a few years the South went from almost complete racial separation to having the nation's most integrated schools. Most parents whose children went to integrated schools and most students who now attend them see doing so as a very positive experience that has lasting impacts on their lives. We have not put any real effort into desegregation in several decades. Our political and educational leaders are generally silent, the federal government has done nothing for a long time, and the courts have been leading the backward trend toward segregation. It is crucial to think about the possibilities for avoiding the profound inequalities of opportunity normally associated with segregated high-poverty minority schools.

The August 2002 gathering of more than five hundred people in Chapel Hill to discuss an issue many observers thought to be dead was an important sign that the South will not forget the civil rights revolution. So were the many 2004 celebrations of *Brown*'s fiftieth anniversary in universities and communities across the region. Millions of Americans have been shaped by *Brown*'s successes, and the thought of going back in the direction from which the region has been emerging is deeply troubling. Our political leaders and our courts have failed to preserve the gains and are spreading the false impression that *Plessy* can now work in a region where it failed comprehensively for more than sixty years. This is a period in which serious analysis of the kind presented in this book is essential. If no leadership on this question comes from our courts or from our elected officials, it may have to come again from the people, from a movement of those who know and value integration and wish to preserve a hard-won legacy. Southern educators and citizens need to give careful attention to the lessons of this new generation of research and analysis. The region's future will depend, to a considerable extent, on whether these decisions are made correctly.

Notes

1. These amendments (Thirteenth, Fourteenth, and Fifteenth) prohibited involuntary servitude, required equal protection of the laws, and supported voting rights.

2. Sontag, "Power of the Fourth."

3. U.S. Bureau of the Census, *Migration.*

4. Ashmore, *Negro and the Schools*, 153.

5. Washington, *Up from Slavery.*

6. Peltason, *Fifty-eight Lonely Men*; Wilhoit, *Politics of Massive Resistance*; Shoemaker, *With All Deliberate Speed*; Lewis, *Portrait of a Decade.*

7. G. Orfield, *Reconstruction.*

8. Ibid.

9. *Alexander v. Holmes.*

10. Panetta and Gall, *Bring Us Together*; *Adams v. Richardson.*

11. Office for Civil Rights, U.S. Department of Education, data reported in G. Orfield and Yun, *Resegregation.*

12. G. Orfield, *Congressional Power*, chap. 9.

13. System Development Corporation, *Third Year.*

14. Grissmer, Flanagan, and Williamson, "Why Did Black Test Scores Rise?" High school completion statistics from the Census Bureau's Current Population Survey show this pattern. For a discussion of dropout data, see G. Orfield, *Dropouts in America.*

15. For example, southern attitudes became overwhelmingly positive: in 1959, 83 percent of white southerners objected to having white children attend schools that were 50 percent African American, but only 38 percent objected by 1975. *Gallup Opinion Index*, 9.

16. G. Orfield and Ashkinaze, *Closing Door*, chap. 5.

17. G. Orfield, "Conservative Activists."

18. *Tuttle v. Arlington County School Board*; *Eisenberg v. Montgomery County Public Schools.*

19. *Grutter v. Bollinger.*

20. Frankenberg, Lee, and Orfield, *Multiracial Society.*

21. Ibid.

22. See "Remarks by the President on Education Implementation," 4 September 2002, ‹http://www.ed.gov/news/pressreleases/2002/09/09042002presdoc.doc›, 31 August 2004.

23. Frankenberg, Lee, and Orfield, *Multiracial Society.*

24. *Milliken v. Bradley.*

25. U.S. Bureau of the Census, *Migration.*

26. *Belk v. Charlotte-Mecklenburg Board of Education.*

27. Frankenberg, Lee, and Orfield, *Multiracial Society.*

28. Elmore and McLaughlin, *Steady Work.*

29. Hanushek, Kain, and Rivkin, *Why Public Schools Lose Teachers.*

30. Flinspach, Banks, and Khanna, "Socioeconomic Integration Policy."

31. *Gallup Opinion Index*, 9.

PART ONE

The History of the Federal Judicial Role

From *Brown* to *Green* to Color-Blind

CHAPTER ONE

ERWIN CHEMERINSKY

The Segregation and Resegregation of American Public Education

The Courts' Role

A half century of efforts to end school segregation have largely failed. Gary Orfield's powerful recent study, *Schools More Separate: Consequences of a Decade of Resegregation*, carefully documents that during the 1990s, America's public schools have become substantially more segregated. In the South, for example, he shows that from "1988 to 1998, most of the progress of the previous two decades in increasing integration in the region was lost. The South is still more integrated than it was before the civil rights revolution, but it is moving backward at an accelerating rate."[1]

The statistics presented in his study are stark. For example, the percentage of African American students attending majority white schools has steadily decreased since 1986. In 1954, at the time of *Brown v. Board of Education*, only 0.001 percent of African American students in the South attended majority white schools.[2] In 1964, a decade after *Brown*, this number had increased to just 2.3 percent. From 1964 to 1988, however, significant progress occurred: the figure grew to 13.9 percent in 1967, 23.4 percent in 1968, 37.6 percent in 1976, 42.9 percent in 1986, and 43.5 percent in 1988. But since 1988, the percentage of African American students attending majority white schools has declined. By 1991, the percentage of African American students attending majority white schools in the South had decreased to 39.2 percent, and over the course of the 1990s this number dropped even more, reaching 36.6 percent in 1994, 34.7 percent in 1996, and 32.7 percent in 1998.[3]

Orfield's study shows that the nationwide percentage of African American students attending majority African American schools and schools where more than 90 percent of the students are African American also has increased in the past fifteen years. In 1986, 62.9 percent of African American students attended schools that were 50–100 percent nonwhite; by 1998–99, this number had increased to 70.2 percent.[4]

Quite significantly, Orfield's study shows that the same pattern of resegregation is true for Latino students.[5] Desegregation efforts have historically focused on integrating African American and white students, but the burgeoning Latino population requires attention, too.[6] The percentage of Latino students attending schools where the majority of students are of minority races or where students are almost exclusively of minority races increased steadily during the 1990s. Orfield notes that Latinos "have been more segregated than blacks now for a number of years, not only by race and ethnicity but also by poverty."[7]

The simple and tragic reality is that American schools are separate and unequal. As Orfield documents, to a very large degree, education in the United States is racially segregated.[8] By any measure, predominantly minority schools are not equal in their resources or their quality. Wealthy suburban school districts are almost exclusively white; poor inner-city schools are often attended exclusively by African American and Hispanic students. The year 2004 was the fiftieth anniversary of *Brown v. Board of Education*, and American schools marked that occasion with increasing racial segregation and gross inequality.

There are many causes for the failure of school desegregation. None of the recent presidents—Reagan, George H. W. Bush, and even Clinton—have done anything to advance desegregation. None have used the powerful resources of the federal government, including the dependence of every school district on federal funds, to further desegregation. "Benign neglect" would be a charitable way of describing recent presidents' attitudes toward the problem of segregated and unequal education: the issue has been neglected, but nothing about this neglect has been benign. A serious social problem that affects millions of children has simply been ignored.

The federal government—and, for that matter, state and local governments—also have failed to act to solve the problem of housing segregation. In a country deeply committed to the ideal of the neighborhood school, residential segregation often produces school segregation. But decades have passed since the enactment of the most recent law to deal with housing discrimination,[9] and efforts to enhance residential integration seem to have vanished.

There is no simple explanation for the alarming trend toward resegregation. In this chapter, I argue that the courts must share the blame: courts could have done much more to bring about desegregation, but the judiciary has instead created substantial obstacles to remedying the legacy of racial segregation in schools. I do not want to minimize the failure of political will, but every branch and level of government is responsible for the failure to desegregate American public education. I contend that Supreme Court decisions over the past thirty years have substantially contributed to the resegregation that Orfield and others document.

Desegregation will not occur without judicial action: desegregation lacks sufficient national and local political support for elected officials alone to remedy the problem. Specifically, African Americans and Latinos lack adequate political power to achieve desegregation through the political process. This relative political powerlessness was true when *Brown* was decided and remains true today. The courts are indispensable to effective desegregation, and over the past thirty years the courts, especially the Supreme Court, have failed. To be sure, as I discuss later in this chapter, individual court orders have brought about desegregation in many areas of the country. Courts could have done more, but even merely continuing rather than ending existing desegregation orders (as the Supreme Court has mandated) would have limited resegregation of southern schools.

This chapter focuses on two major sets of Supreme Court decisions that have contributed to resegregation. I will first examine the Supreme Court's decisions of the 1970s, especially those decisions rejecting interdistrict solutions to segregation and funding inequities.[10] Second, I will turn to the Supreme Court's decisions of the 1990s ordering an end to desegregation efforts.[11] These cases and subsequent lower court decisions have substantially contributed to resegregation of public schools. The third part of the chapter looks at why this judicial failure has occurred.

Some commentators, including Gerald Rosenberg, have argued that the failure to achieve desegregation reflects inherent limits on judicial power.[12] I strongly disagree: the judiciary's failure instead lies in its actions. Had the Supreme Court decided key cases differently, the nature of public education today would be very different. Although segregated schools have many causes, the overarching explanation for the Court's rulings is simple: justices appointed by Republican presidents have undermined desegregation. Four justices appointed by President Richard Nixon are largely to blame for the decisions of the 1970s: the crucial cases were 5–4 decisions, with those four justices helping to make up the majority.[13] Five justices appointed by Presidents Ronald Reagan and George H. W. Bush are responsible for the decisions of the 1990s that have contributed substantially to resegregation of schools.[14] The resegregation of schools has resulted largely from the Court's decisions, not from the inherent limits of the judicial process.

Today, there are voices—often strong voices—in minority communities that have turned against desegregation as the solution. The rejection of desegregation as a policy objective very much results from the lack of success—and possible success—given the current realities of desegregation described in this chapter. In cities with minority populations of 80–90 percent, meaningful desegregation just is not possible under current law. Understandably, many in these minority communities say that efforts at strengthening education should no longer focus on desegregation but should instead concentrate on improving schools for minority students. But history offers little reason for hope that dual school systems ever will be equal. As Thurgood Marshall expressed thirty years ago in a prophetic dissent in *Milliken v. Bradley* (1974), "we deal here with the right of all children, whatever their race, to an equal start in life and to an equal opportunity to reach their full potential as citizens. Those children who have been denied that right in the past deserve better than to see fences thrown up to deny them that right in the future. Our nation, I fear, will be ill served by the Court's refusal to remedy separate and unequal education, for unless our children begin to learn together, there is little hope that our people will ever learn to live together."[15]

The Decisions of the 1970s: The Supreme Court Contributes to the Resegregation of American Public Education

The 1970s were a particularly critical time in the battle to desegregate American schools. From *Plessy v. Ferguson* in 1896 until *Brown* in 1954, government-mandated segregation existed in every southern state and in many northern states. As mentioned earlier, in 1954, when *Brown* was decided, only 0.001 percent of the South's African American students attended majority white schools. After *Brown*, southern states used every imaginable technique to obstruct desegregation. Some school systems attempted to close public schools rather than desegregate.[16] Some school boards adopted "freedom of choice" plans, which allowed students to choose the school where they would enroll and resulted in continued segregation.[17] In some places, school systems outright disobeyed desegregation orders.[18] The phrase "massive resistance" appropriately describes what occurred during the decade after *Brown*. By 1964, in *Griffin v. County School Board*, the Supreme Court had grown tired of the delay, lamenting that there had been far too little speed, and ordered that all vestiges of prior segregation be eliminated "quick[ly] and effective[ly]."[19]

The result of this massive resistance was that a decade after *Brown*, little desegregation had occurred. In the South, just 1.2 percent of African American schoolchildren were attending schools with whites.[20] In South Carolina, Alabama, and Mississippi, not one African American child attended a public school with a white child in the 1962–63 school year. In North Carolina, only 0.2 percent of the African American students attended desegregated schools in 1961, and the figure did not rise above 1 percent until 1965. Similarly, in Virginia in 1964, only 1.63 percent of African Americans attended desegregated schools.[21]

But the persistent efforts at desegregation had an impact. One by one, the obstructionist techniques were defeated. Finally, by the mid-1960s, desegregation began to proceed. By 1968, the integration rate rose to 32 percent, and by 1972–73, 91.3 percent of southern schools were desegregated.[22]

Many factors explain the delay between *Brown* and any meaningful desegregation. Efforts to thwart *Brown* had to be defeated. Title VI of the Civil Rights Act of 1964, which tied local receipt of federal funds to agreement to eliminate segregation, played a crucial role.[23] But so did renewed Supreme Court attention to segregated schools. For a decade after *Brown*, the Court largely stayed out of the desegregation effort.[24] Not until 1964 did the Court lament, "There has been entirely too much deliberation and not enough speed" in achieving desegregation.[25]

By the 1970s, as described earlier, the nation finally saw substantial progress toward desegregation. But three crucial problems emerged: white flight to suburbs threatened school integration efforts; northern school systems, which had not enacted Jim Crow laws, required desegregation; and pervasive inequalities existed in funding, especially between city and suburban schools. The Court's handling of these issues was critical in achieving desegregation. In each instance, the Court, with four Nixon appointees in the majority, ruled against the civil rights plaintiffs and dramatically limited the effectiveness of efforts to achieve desegregation and equal educational opportunity.

White Flight

By the 1970s, a crucial problem had emerged: white flight to suburban areas. White flight came about in part to avoid school desegregation and in part as a result of the larger demographic phenomenon of suburban development.[26] In virtually every urban area, the inner city was increasingly composed of racial minorities. By contrast, the surrounding suburbs were almost exclusively white, and what little minority population resided in suburbs was concentrated in towns that were almost exclusively African American.[27] School district lines often parallel town borders, meaning that racial separation of cities and suburbs results in segregated school systems. For example, by 1980, whites constituted less than one-third of the students enrolled in the public schools in Baltimore, Dallas, Detroit, Houston, Los Angeles, Miami, Memphis, New York, and Philadelphia.[28]

Thus, effective school desegregation required interdistrict remedies. The lack of white students in most major cities prevented desegregation, and intradistrict remedies could not desegregate suburban school districts because of the scarcity of minority students in the suburbs.[29]

In *Swann v. Charlotte-Mecklenburg Board of Education* (1971), the Supreme Court held that district courts have broad authority in formulating remedies in desegregation cases.[30] The Court upheld the power of the district courts to take "affirmative action in the form of remedial altering of attendance zones to achieve truly nondiscriminatory assignments."[31] The Court also stated that courts could use busing as a remedy where needed and that bus transportation is an important "tool of school desegregation."[32] The Court found that busing students is a constitutionally acceptable remedy unless "the time or distance of travel is so great as to either risk the health of the children or significantly impinge on the educational process."[33] But *Swann* focused exclusively on remedies *within* a school district. The holding did not address interdistrict remedies. When a school system comprises predominantly minority students, there is a limit to how much desegregation can be achieved without an interdistrict remedy.

In 1974, the Supreme Court took a different turn in its jurisprudence on the powers of federal courts in desegregation cases. In *Milliken v. Bradley*, the Court imposed a substantial limit on the courts' remedial powers.[34] *Milliken* involved the Detroit-area schools. Like cities in so many areas of the country, Detroit was a mostly African American school district surrounded by predominantly white suburbs and school districts. A federal district court imposed a multidistrict remedy to end de jure segregation. The Supreme Court ruled that this desegregation technique is impermissible, concluding that "without an interdistrict violation and interdistrict effect, there is no constitutional wrong calling for an interdistrict remedy."[35]

Milliken has had a devastating effect on efforts to achieve desegregation in many areas. In a number of major cities, inner-city school systems are substantially African American and are surrounded by almost all-white suburbs. Desegregation would require transferring students between city and suburban schools because there are simply too few white students in the city and African American students in the suburbs to achieve desegregation without an interdistrict remedy. Yet *Milliken* precludes such a remedy unless plaintiffs offer proof of an interdistrict violation.[36] In other words, a multidistrict remedy can be formulated only for those districts whose policies fostered discrimination or if a state law caused the interdistrict segregation. Otherwise, the remedy can include only those districts found to violate the Constitution. While such proof is often unavailable, plaintiffs in relatively rare cases have met *Milliken*'s requirements.[37]

I grew up in Chicago, an urban area in which the city is predominantly minority but surrounding suburbs are virtually all-white. For example, on the west side of the city, the Austin neighborhood is composed almost entirely of African Americans and Latinos. But just across the city line, suburban Oak Park and especially River Forest are overwhelmingly white. An interdistrict remedy could help to desegregate both the Chicago public schools and the nearby suburban schools. Little would be required except redrawing attendance zones. But *Milliken* has ensured that this kind of remedy will not be used.

This segregated pattern in major metropolitan areas did not occur by accident but rather was the product of myriad government policies.[38] Moreover, *Milliken* has had the effect of encouraging white flight. Whites who wish to avoid desegregation can do so by moving to the suburbs. If *Milliken* had been decided differently, one of the incentives for such moves would be eliminated. In reality, in many areas the *Milliken* holding makes desegregation impossible.

In an important paper presented at the conference on the resegregation of southern schools, Charles T. Clotfelter quantified the causes for segregation of public schools.[39] Clotfelter's study dramatically proves *Milliken*'s impact in perpetuating segregation and preventing effective remedies. According to Clotfelter, private schools lead to only about 17 percent of the nation's segregation.[40] By far the most important factor accounting for segregation is racial disparities among public school districts.[41] In most instances, *Milliken* precludes courts from remedying this problem and thus is significantly responsible for the segregation of U.S. schools today.

Proving Discrimination in Northern School Systems

Plaintiffs had no difficulty in proving discrimination in states that by law had required separation of the races in education. But in northern school systems, where segregated schools were not the product of express state laws, an issue arose about what would suffice to prove an equal protection violation and to justify a federal court remedy. Northern school systems were generally segregated; the issue was what plaintiffs had to prove for courts to provide a remedy.

The Supreme Court addressed this issue in *Keyes v. School District no. 1, Denver, Colorado* (1973). Substantial segregation existed in Denver's public schools even though Colorado law had never mandated the separation of the races.[42] *Keyes* held that absent laws requiring school segregation, plaintiffs must prove intentional segregative acts on the part of a school board or other local officials and affecting a substantial part of the school system.

The Court therefore drew a distinction between the de jure segregation that existed throughout the South and the de facto segregation that existed in the North. The latter is deemed to be a constitutional violation only if there is proof that the racially separate student populations were the product of some official discriminatory purpose. This approach is consistent with the Supreme Court cases holding that when laws are facially neutral, proof of a discriminatory impact is not sufficient to show an equal protection violation; proof of a discriminatory purpose must also exist.[43] But requiring proof that local school officials acted with discriminatory purpose created a substantial obstacle to desegregation in northern school systems, where residential segregation—a product of myriad discriminatory policies—caused school segregation. *Keyes* in reality created an almost insurmountable obstacle to judicial remedies for desegregation in northern cities. The government was responsible for segregation in northern schools, but plaintiffs often found it impossible to prove that responsibility.

Inequality in School Funding

By the 1970s, substantial disparities existed in school funding. In 1972, education expert Christopher Jencks estimated that, on average, the government spent 15–20 percent more on each white student's education than on each African American child's schooling.[44] This disparity existed throughout the country. For example, the Chicago public schools spent $5,265 for each student's education, but the Niles school system, just north of the city, spent $9,371.[45] The disparity also corresponded to race: in Chicago, 45.4 percent of the students were white and 39.1 percent were African American; in Niles Township, the schools were 91.6 percent white and 0.4 percent African American.[46] In New Jersey, largely black Camden spent $3,538 on each pupil, while highly white Princeton spent $7,725.[47]

A simple explanation exists for the disparities in school funding. In most states, education is substantially funded by local property taxes. Wealthier suburbs have significantly larger tax bases than poor inner cities and can tax at lower rates and still have more to spend on education.[48] The Court had the opportunity to remedy this inequality in education in *San Antonio Independent School District v. Rodriguez* (1973) but failed profoundly, concluding that the inequalities in funding did not deny equal protection.[49]

Rodriguez involved a challenge to the Texas system of funding public schools largely through local property taxes.[50] Texas's financing system meant that poor areas had to tax at a high rate but had little to spend on education; wealthier areas had low rates and more funds. One poorer district, for example, could afford only $356 per pupil, while a wealthier district spent $594 per student.[51]

The plaintiffs challenged this system on two grounds: it violated equal protection as impermissible wealth discrimination, and it denied children in the poorer districts the fundamental right to education.[52] The Court rejected the former argument by holding that poverty is not a "suspect classification"; consequently, discrimination against the poor need meet only rational basis review.[53] Under equal protection analysis, discrimination against racial minorities is treated as highly suspect and must meet "strict scrutiny"—that is, must be found necessary to achieve a compelling government interest. The government usually loses when strict scrutiny is used. At the opposite end of the continuum, laws that do not discriminate with regard to "suspect classifications" have to meet only rational basis review. That is, they only have to be "reasonably related to a legitimate government interest." The government usually wins under rational basis review. Thus, the Court's choice of rational basis review ensured the government's triumph. The Court explained that where wealth is involved, the Equal Protection Clause does not require absolute equality or precisely equal advantages. In thoroughly reviewing the Texas system of funding schools, the Court determined that the state had plausible concerns about maintaining "local control" of educational funding that were constitutionally adequate if not very compelling.[54]

Moreover, the Court rejected the claim that education is a fundamental right. Justice Lewis Powell, writing for the majority, concluded that "education, of course, is not among the rights afforded explicit protection under our Federal Constitution. Nor do we find any basis for saying it is implicitly so protected."[55] The Court came to this conclusion in spite of the fact that education obviously is inextricably linked to the exercise of constitutional rights such as freedom of speech and voting.

The Court also noted that the Texas government did not completely deny an education to students; the challenge was to inequities in funding. In concluding, the Court found that strict scrutiny was inappropriate because neither discrimination based on a suspect classification nor infringement of a fundamental right occurred.[56] The Court found that the Texas system for funding schools met the rational basis test.

In *Kadrmas v. Dickinson Public Schools* (1988), the Court reaffirmed that education is not a fundamental right under the Equal Protection Clause.[57] *Kadrmas* involved a challenge brought by a poor family against a North Dakota statute authorizing local school systems to charge a fee for the use of school buses. The Court reiterated that poverty is not a suspect classification and that discrimination against the poor must meet only rational basis review.[58] The Court found that the law did not deny any child an education because the fee did not preclude the student from attending school. Hence, the Court said that rational basis review was appropriate and concluded that the plaintiffs "failed to carry the 'heavy burden' of demonstrating the challenged statute is both arbitrary and irrational."[59]

These decisions are wrong—tragically wrong—in holding that no fundamental right to education exists. The Court should have recognized a fundamental right to education under the Constitution, as it has recognized other rights that are not enumerated, including the right to travel,[60] the right to marry,[61] the right to procreate,[62] the right to custody of one's children,[63] the right to control the upbringing of one's children,[64] and many others.[65] Education is essential for the exercise of constitutional rights, for economic opportunity, and ultimately for achieving equality. Chief Justice Earl Warren eloquently expressed this view in *Brown*:

> Today, education is perhaps the most important function of state and local governments. Compulsory school attendance laws and the great expenditures

> for education both demonstrate our recognition of the importance of education to our democratic society. It is required in the performance of our most basic public responsibilities, even service in the armed forces. It is the very foundation of good citizenship. Today it is a principal instrument in awakening the child to cultural values, in preparing him for later professional training, and in helping him to adjust normally to his environment. In these days, it is doubtful that any child may reasonably be expected to succeed in life if he is denied the opportunity of an education.[66]

The combined effect of *Milliken* and *Rodriguez* cannot be overstated. *Milliken* helped to ensure racially separate schools, and *Rodriguez* ensured that the schools would be unequal.[67] American public education is characterized by wealthy white suburban schools that spend a great deal on education surrounding much poorer African American city schools that spend much less.[68]

The Decisions of the 1990s: The Supreme Court Ends Desegregation Orders

Orfield briefly but accurately notes a cause for the resegregation of the 1990s: Supreme Court decisions ending successful desegregation orders.[69] In several cases, the Court concluded that school systems had achieved "unitary" status and consequently decreed that federal court desegregation efforts were to end.[70] These decisions resulted in the cessation of remedies that had been effective and, ultimately, in resegregation. Many lower courts followed the lead of the Supreme Court and have likewise ended desegregation orders, causing resegregation.

In several cases during the 1990s, the Supreme Court considered when a federal court desegregation order should end. In *Board of Education of Oklahoma City Public Schools v. Dowell* (1991), the Court determined whether a desegregation order should continue even when its termination would mean a resegregation of the public schools.[71] Oklahoma schools had been segregated under a state law mandating separation of the races. Not until 1972—seventeen years after *Brown*—did courts finally order desegregation. The federal court order subsequently succeeded in desegregating the Oklahoma City public schools. Evidence indicated that ending the desegregation order would likely result in dramatic resegregation.[72] Nonetheless, the Supreme Court held that after Oklahoma City's racially dual school system had become "unitary," a federal court's desegregation order should end, even if the action could lead to resegregation of the schools.[73]

The Court did not define "unitary system" with any specificity; it simply declared that the desegregation decree should end if the school board has "complied in good faith" and "the vestiges of past discrimination have been eliminated to the extent practicable."[74] In evaluating these two factors, the Court instructed the district court to look "not only at student assignments, but 'to every facet of school operations—faculty, staff, transportation, extracurricular activities and facilities.'"[75]

In *Freeman v. Pitts* (1992), the Supreme Court held that a federal court desegregation order should end after a school district complies with the order, even if other desegregation orders for the same school system remain in place.[76] A federal district court ordered desegregation of various aspects of a school system in Georgia that previously had been segregated by law. Part of the desegregation plan had been met: the school system had achieved desegregation in pupil assignment and in facilities. Another aspect of the desegregation order, concerning assignment of teachers, had not yet been fulfilled, however.[77] The school system planned to construct a facility that likely would benefit whites more than African Americans.[78] Nonetheless, the Supreme Court held that the federal court could not review the discriminatory effects of the new construction because the part of the desegregation order concerning facilities had already been met. The Court stated that when a portion of a desegregation order is met, the federal court should cease its efforts to enforce that part and remain involved only with those aspects of the plan that had not been achieved.[79]

Finally, in *Missouri v. Jenkins* (1995), the Court mandated an end to a school desegregation order for the Kansas City schools.[80] Missouri law had previously required the racial segregation of all public schools, and not until 1977 did a federal district court order the desegregation of the Kansas City schools. The federal court's desegregation effort made a difference. In 1983, twenty-five schools in the district had an African American enrollment of greater than 90 percent. By 1993, no elementary-level student attended a school with an enrollment that was 90 percent or more African American. At the middle school and high school levels, the percentage of students attending schools with an African American enrollment of 90 percent or more declined from about 45 percent to 22 percent.[81]

This progress was halted, however, in an opinion authored by Chief Justice William Rehnquist that ruled in favor of the state on every issue. The Court's holding consisted of three parts. First, the Court ruled that the district court's effort to attract nonminority students from outside the school district was impermissible because the plaintiffs had not proved an interdistrict violation. Chief Justice Rehnquist applied *Milliken v. Bradley* to conclude that the interdistrict remedy—incentives to attract students from outside the district into the Kansas City schools—was impermissible because there was proof only of an intradistrict violation.[82]

Second, the Court ruled that the district court lacked authority to order an increase in teacher salaries. Although the district court had found that an across-the-board salary increase to attract teachers was essential for desegregation, the Supreme Court concluded that the increase was not necessary as a remedy.[83]

Finally, the Court ruled that a continued racial disparity in student test scores did not justify continuance of the federal court's desegregation order. The Court concluded that the Constitution requires equal opportunity, not equal result; consequently, disparities between African American and white students on standardized tests were not a sufficient basis for concluding that desegregation had not been achieved. Disparity in test scores is not a basis for continued federal court involvement.[84] The Supreme Court held that when a district has complied with a desegregation order, the federal court effort should end.[85]

Together, *Dowell*, *Freeman*, and *Jenkins* have given a clear signal to lower courts: the time has come to end desegregation orders, even when the effect could be resegregation. And the lower courts have followed this lead. Indeed, it is striking how many lower courts have ended desegregation orders in the past decade, even when provided with clear evidence that the result will be to increase segregation of the public schools. For example, in *People Who Care v. Rockford Board of Education* (2001), the U.S. Court of Appeals for the Seventh Circuit reversed a federal district court decision that refused to end desegregation efforts for the Rockford, Illinois, public schools.[86] The court began its analysis by observing that the Supreme Court has called for "bend[ing] every effort to winding up school litigation and returning the operation of the schools to the local school authorities."[87] The Seventh Circuit noted the substantial disparity in achievement between white and minority students but stated that although the board "may have a moral duty [to help its failing minority students], it has no federal constitutional duty."[88] This analysis is the same reasoning followed by other courts throughout the country in ending desegregation orders.

Similarly, the U.S. Court of Appeals for the Fourth Circuit recently ended federal judicial oversight of the Charlotte-Mecklenburg school system.[89] Although the school system had historically been segregated and although desegregation had succeeded, the court nonetheless ordered an end to desegregation efforts. In Charlotte, local control was taken away by the court's order not to use race in student assignment, even though the school district fought to maintain the desegregation policy.

The U.S. Court of Appeals for the Eleventh Circuit ended the desegregation order for the Duval County schools in Jacksonville, Florida, concluding that district had achieved unitary status.[90] At the time of the Eleventh Circuit's conclusion, Latino students outnumbered whites and African Americans combined at thirteen Duval County schools.[91] The Eleventh Circuit stated that the segregation resulted from white flight and voluntary residential segregation and thus did not provide a basis for continued desegregation efforts.[92]

In addition to these decisions by federal courts of appeals, many district courts have ordered an end to desegregation efforts, including several in 2002.[93] In none of these cases did the courts give weight to the consequences of ending the desegregation orders in causing resegregation of the public schools.

The nationwide trend of federal courts ending desegregation efforts means that resegregation will increase, potentially dramatically, in the next decade. Orfield documents the resegregation that occurred during the 1990s. Recent decisions indicate that the first decade of the twenty-first century may see a much worse return to resegregation.

Why Have Courts Failed?

Scholars such as Gerald Rosenberg see the failure to achieve desegregation as reflecting inherent limitations of courts. I strongly disagree. Desegregation likely would have been more successful and resegregation less likely to occur if the Supreme Court had made different choices.

If from 1954 to 1971 the Court had acted more aggressively in imposing timetables and outlining remedies, desegregation might have occurred more rapidly. If the Court had decided *Milliken* differently—not a fanciful possibility considering that the case was a 5–4 decision—interdistrict remedies could have produced much more desegregation of American public education. If the Court had decided *Keyes* differently, courts could have fashioned desegregation remedies if the plaintiffs could offer proof of a discriminatory impact. Requiring nonwhite plaintiffs to show that a school system has acted with discriminatory intent dramatically limited the ability of the federal courts to order desegregation of de facto segregated northern city school systems. If the Court had decided *Rodriguez* differently, there would have been more equality in school funding and educational opportunity.[94] If the decisions of the 1990s had differed, successful desegregation orders in many cities would have remained in place. Therefore, the dismal statistics about current segregation are less an indication of the inherent limits of the judiciary and more a reflection of the Supreme Court's choices.

What, then, explains the Court's choices? The answer is obvious: its decisions result from the conservative ideology of the majority of the justices who sat on the Court in the 1970s, when these cases were decided. *Milliken* and *Rodriguez* were both 5–4 decisions, and the majority included the four Nixon appointees who joined the Court in the few years before those rulings. If the Warren Court had decided the cases in 1968, six years before *Milliken* and five years before *Rodriguez*, the cases would almost certainly have been resolved in favor of interdistrict remedies. If Hubert Humphrey had won the 1968 presidential election and appointed the successors to Justices Warren, Abe Fortas, Hugo Black, and John Marshall Harlan, these cases would likely have had different results.

Similarly, the decisions of the 1990s were the product of conservative, Republican justices. In each of the cases, five Reagan and George H. W. Bush appointees—Chief Justice Rehnquist (whom President Reagan nominated as chief justice) and Justices Sandra Day O'Connor, Antonin Scalia, Anthony Kennedy, and Clarence Thomas—constituted the majority in ordering an end to desegregation orders.

The cause for the judicial failure could not be clearer: conservative justices have effectively sabotaged desegregation. In June 2002, Justice Thomas wrote a concurring opinion in *Zelman v. Simmons-Harris*, in which the Court upheld the constitutionality of the use of vouchers in parochial schools.[95] Justice Thomas lamented the poor quality of education for African Americans in inner cities and urged voucher systems as a solution.[96] The irony—and indeed, hypocrisy—of Justice Thomas's opinion is enormous. The rulings of his conservative brethren have contributed significantly to the educational problems of racial minorities. Justice Thomas has never suggested that the Court reconsider any of the decisions discussed in this chapter. But he is very willing to allow vouchers, which would take money from the public schools and transfer it to private, especially parochial, institutions.

Conclusion

During the Vietnam War, Senator George Aiken said that the United States should declare victory and withdraw from Vietnam.[97] The Supreme Court seems intent on declaring victory over the problem of school segregation and withdrawing the judiciary from solving it. But as Orfield demonstrates, the problem has gotten worse, not better.[98] The years ahead look even bleaker as courts end successful desegregation orders.[99]

People can devise rationalizations to make this desegregation failure seem acceptable: that courts could not really succeed; that desegregation does not matter; that parents of minority students do not really care about desegregation. But none of these rationalizations are true. *Brown v. Board of Education* stated the truth: separate schools can never be equal. Tragically today, America has schools that are increasingly separate and unequal.

Notes

1. G. Orfield, *Schools More Separate*, 2.
2. Ibid., 29.
3. Ibid.
4. Ibid., 31.
5. Ibid.
6. Desegregation in the South has traditionally focused on whites and African Americans because they were the concern of the litigation of the civil rights movement. At the time, the states did not have a significant Latino population. Now, however, the growth in the Latino population requires that this group also be considered in evaluating desegregation efforts. See Gricco and Cassidy, "Overview" (on file with the *North Carolina Law Review*) (illustrating that Latinos are the largest minority group in the United States); see also G. Orfield, *Schools More Separate*, 17, table 1 (indicating that from 1968 to 1998, the Latino population enrolled in public schools has grown from 2 million to 6.9 million, a 245 percent growth in thirty years).
7. G. Orfield, *Schools More Separate*, 2.
8. Ibid., 48. Orfield explains that segregation by race relates to segregation by poverty and to many forms of educational inequality for African American and Latino students.
9. The last national housing law addressing discrimination, the Fair Housing Act, was enacted in 1968.
10. *San Antonio Independent School District v. Rodriguez* held that inequities in school funding do not deny equal protection; *Milliken v. Bradley* limits the power of the courts to impose interdistrict remedies for school segregation.
11. *Board of Education v. Dowell* held that after a public school system has achieved unitary status, desegregation orders should end, even if a resegregation of the public schools would result; *Freeman v. Pitts* clarified that partial compliance with a desegregation order should end that part of the order, even if other parts of the order remain to be met; *Missouri v. Jenkins* (1995) held that disparities in white and African American students' test scores alone does not prove the lack of a unitary system or justify continuing desegregation orders.
12. Rosenberg, *Hollow Hope*.
13. The four Nixon appointees—Warren Burger, Harry Blackmun, Lewis Powell, and William Rehnquist—were joined by Justice Potter Stewart to comprise the majority opinion. *Milliken*, 720; *Rodriguez*, 2–3.
14. Recent desegregation cases, such as *Missouri v. Jenkins*, have been 5–4 decisions, with the majority comprised of Chief Justice Rehnquist and Justices Sandra Day O'Connor, Antonin Scalia, Anthony Kennedy, and Clarence Thomas. *Missouri v. Jenkins* (1995), 72.
15. *Milliken*, 783 (Marshall, J., dissenting).
16. See, e.g., *Griffin v. County School Board*, holding that the closing of public schools, combined with tuition grants and tax breaks to private segregated schools, violates the Constitution.
17. See, e.g., *Green v. County School Board*, overturning New Kent County's "freedom of choice" plan as unconstitutional, finding that it burdened students and parents with a responsibility that properly remained on the school board.
18. See, e.g., *Cooper v. Aaron*, demanding that states follow Supreme Court orders.

19. *Griffin*, 232.
20. Klarman, "*Brown*," 9.
21. Ibid.
22. Ibid., 10.
23. See Devins, *Judicial Matters*, 1034.
24. *Cooper* is a notable exception: the Court insisted on state compliance with a federal court desegregation order.
25. *Griffin*, 229.
26. See Asher, "Note," 1173–74, which discusses white flight in many major cities and argues that federal and state constitutional grounds justify interdistrict relief in a wide range of situations.
27. See *Milliken*, 785 (Marshall, J., dissenting): "Negro children had been intentionally confined to an expanding core of virtually all negro schools immediately surrounded by a receding herd of all white schools."
28. See Smedley, *Developments*, 412.
29. Ibid.
30. See *Swann v. Charlotte-Mecklenburg Board of Education*, 30.
31. Ibid.
32. Ibid.
33. Ibid., 30–31.
34. *Milliken*, 752–53.
35. Ibid., 745.
36. Ibid., 744–45. But see *Evans v. Buchanan*, implementing a metropolitan plan, and *United States v. Missouri*, finding a school district to be a remaining vestige of segregation.
37. See, e.g., *United States v. Board of School Commissioners*, 191–92, finding that housing discrimination warranted interdistrict desegregation; *Metropolitan School District v. Buckley*; and *Evans*, 352–53, approving interdistrict remedies when disparity in enrollment patterns are caused by government activity. See also *Hills v. Gautreaux*, allowing an interdistrict remedy for housing discrimination.
38. See Massey and Denton, *American Apartheid*; and powell, Kearney, and Kay, *In Pursuit*.
39. See Clotfelter, "Private Schools," 3–4.
40. Ibid., 13, 32, table 5.
41. Ibid., 8–14.
42. *Keyes v. School District no. 1, Denver, Colorado*, 201.
43. See, e.g., *McCleskey v. Kemp*, holding that proof of disparate impact is insufficient to establish a constitutional violation in administration of the death penalty; *Washington v. Davis*, 239–45, holding that proof of discriminatory impact alone is not enough to prove a racial classification; there also must be proof of discriminatory purpose.
44. Jencks, *Inequality*.
45. Kozol, *Savage Inequalities*, 236, table 1.
46. Steele, "Note," 620 n. 173.
47. Kozol, *Savage Inequalities*, 236, table 2.
48. Coons, Clune, and Sugarman, *Private Wealth and Public Education*, 45–51; Shalala and Williams, *Political Perspectives*, 368.

49. *San Antonio Independent School District*, 55.

50. Ibid., 10–11.

51. Ibid., 12–13.

52. Ibid., 17.

53. Ibid., 28–29. The Court determined that the system of alleged discrimination and the class it defines did not have the "traditional indicia of suspectness" (28). In the Court's view, the class was not saddled with such disabilities, subjected to such a history of purposeful unequal treatment, or relegated to such a position of political powerlessness as to command extraordinary protection from the majoritarian political process.

54. Ibid., 47–53. After analyzing the various aspects of the Texas plan, the Court determined that it was "not the result of hurried, ill-conceived legislation [or] the product of purposeful discrimination against any group or class" (55). To the extent that the plan of school financing resulted in unequal expenditures between children who resided in different districts, the Court found that such disparities were not the product of a system that is so irrational as to be invidiously discriminatory.

55. Ibid., 35.

56. Ibid., 28, 37–39.

57. See *Kadrmas v. Dickinson Public Schools*, 457–59.

58. Ibid., 458.

59. Ibid., 463 (quoting *Hodel v. Indiana*, 332).

60. See *Shapiro v. Thompson*, 629–31.

61. See *Boddie v. Connecticut*, 382–83.

62. See *Skinner v. Oklahoma*, 541–43.

63. See *Stanley v. Illinois*, 650–51.

64. See *Troxel v. Granville*, 63–66.

65. See, e.g., *Cruzan v. Director, Missouri Department of Health*, 278–80, finding a fundamental right under the Due Process Clause to refuse unwanted medical treatment; *Roe v. Wade*, 153: "Th[e] right of privacy . . . is broad enough to encompass a woman's decision . . . to terminate her pregnancy"; *Griswold v. Connecticut*, 485, finding that the right to use contraceptives falls within a constitutionally protected zone of privacy.

66. *Brown v. Board of Education (I)*, 493.

67. This is not to minimize the adverse effects of the other decisions, but *Milliken* and *Rodriguez* are crucial because the former ensured the separateness of American public education and the latter ensured their inequality. In theory, effective desegregation could still have occurred through actions of the federal or state legislatures, but such actions did not occur, and *Milliken* and *Rodriguez* ensured that courts, the most likely agents for change, could not achieve desegregation.

68. See generally Patterson, *Brown*, discussing the combined impact of *Milliken* and *Rodriguez*.

69. G. Orfield, *Schools More Separate*, 16.

70. See, e.g., *Missouri v. Jenkins* (1995).

71. *Board of Education v. Dowell*, 249–50.

72. Ibid., 242. After the school board was released from the continuing constitutional supervision of the federal court, it adopted the Student Reassignment Plan (SRP). Under the plan, which relied on neighborhood assignments for students in grades K–4, a student

could transfer from a school where he or she was in the majority to a school where he or she would be in the minority. In 1985, it appeared that the SRP had caused a return to segregation. If the SRP were to continue, eleven of sixty-four schools would be greater than 90 percent African American, twenty-two would be greater than 90 percent white plus other minorities, and thirty-one would be racially mixed. In light of this evidence, the district court refused to reopen the case.

73. Ibid., 247–49.

74. Ibid., 249–50.

75. Ibid., 250 (quoting *Green*, 435).

76. *Freeman*, 490–91.

77. Ibid., 481, finding that a racial imbalance existed in the assignment of minority teachers and administrators.

78. Ibid., 483.

79. Ibid., 490–91.

80. *Missouri v. Jenkins* (1995), 103. Earlier in *Jenkins*, the Supreme Court ruled that a federal district court could order a local taxing body to increase taxes to pay for compliance with a desegregation order, although the federal court should not itself order an increase in the taxes.

81. Ibid., 75.

82. Ibid., 90, 92–94, 97.

83. Ibid., 100.

84. Ibid., 102.

85. Ibid.

86. *People Who Care v. Rockford Board of Education* (2001), 1078.

87. Ibid., 1074, quoting *People Who Care v. Rockford Board of Education* (1998), 835.

88. Ibid., 1076.

89. *Belk v. Charlotte-Mecklenburg Board of Education*, 335.

90. *NAACP v. Duval County Schools*, 976.

91. M. Brown, “Beyond Black and White,” A1.

92. *NAACP v. Duval County Schools*, 971–72.

93. See, e.g., *Berry v. School District*, ending desegregation efforts for the Benton Harbor, Michigan, public schools; *Lee v. Butler County Board of Education*, ending desegregation order for the Butler County, Alabama, public schools; *Lee v. Opelika City Board of Education*, ending desegregation order for Opelika, Alabama, schools; *Davis v. School District*, ending desegregation order for the Pontiac, Michigan, public schools.

94. Indeed, a number of state supreme courts have found that inequalities in funding violate provisions of their state constitutions. See, e.g., *Serrano v. Priest*, holding that the California school financing system violated equal protection provisions of the state constitution; *Rose v. Council for Better Education*, finding Kentucky’s common school financing system unconstitutional; *McDuffy v. Secretary of Education*, holding that the Massachusetts school financing system violated the state’s constitution; *Abbott v. Burke*, finding New Jersey’s Public School Education Act unconstitutional; *Tennessee Small School System v. McWherter*, declaring educational funding statutes unconstitutional; *Edgewood Independent School District v. Kirby*, finding the Texas school financing system in violation of the state constitution.

95. In *Zelman v. Simmons-Harris*, the Supreme Court upheld the constitutionality of an Ohio law that allowed parents to use vouchers in the Cleveland city schools. Approximately 96 percent of parents used their vouchers in parochial schools (2466). In a 5–4 decision, the Court upheld this use as constitutional (2480). The Court's division was identical to that in the 1990s decisions ordering an end to desegregation orders: the majority comprised Rehnquist, O'Connor, Scalia, Kennedy, and Thomas (2462).

96. Ibid., 2480 (Thomas, J., concurring). Indeed, Justice Thomas lamented the current condition of inner-city schools in very powerful language: "Frederick Douglass once said that '[e]ducation . . . means emancipation. It means light and liberty. It means the uplifting of the soul of man into the glorious light of truth, the light by which men can only be made free.' Today many of our inner-city public schools deny emancipation to urban minority students. Despite this Court's observation nearly 50 years ago in *Brown v. Board of Education*, that 'it is doubtful that any child may reasonably be expected to succeed in life if he is denied the opportunity of an education,' urban children have been forced into a system that continually fails them."

97. Krebs, "George Aiken," B10.

98. See G. Orfield, *Schools More Separate*, 2. Orfield's report, including statistics from the 2000 Census, illustrates that from 1988 to 1998 southern school segregation intensified (see esp. tables 1, 3, 6). This trend occurred during a period in which three Supreme Court decisions authorized a return to segregated neighborhood schools and limited the reach and duration of desegregation orders. Orfield concludes that from 1988 to 1998, "most of the progress of the previous two decades in increasing integration in the [South] was lost" and provides numerous recommendations for a stable interracial education system.

99. The issue of what could be done differently is beyond the scope of this essay, except as it is implicit in the criticism of what the Supreme Court has done. A major national initiative for school desegregation is needed. This initiative could come through Congress, which could document extensive segregation and inequalities in the public schools and adopt a comprehensive statute mandating interdistrict remedies and equity in school funding. There would be constitutional challenges based on recent federalism decisions, yet remedying such inequalities lies at the core of Congress's powers under the Thirteenth and Fourteenth Amendments. Alternatively, the Supreme Court could reverse course and reconsider the decisions discussed in this chapter, which have contributed so much to the resegregation and inequalities in American public education. There is no indication whatsoever that these—or any—actions from Congress or the Supreme Court are likely in the foreseeable future.

PART TWO

The Color of Southern Schooling

Contemporary Trends

CHAPTER TWO

SEAN F. REARDON | JOHN T. YUN

Integrating Neighborhoods, Segregating Schools

The Retreat from School Desegregation in the South, 1990–2000

After decades as the most successfully integrated schools in the United States, the schools of the South appear to be moving slowly toward resegregation. During the 1990s, public schools throughout the South became increasingly segregated. Black-white public school segregation, in particular, increased in almost every state in the South from 1990 to 2000. Indeed, black-white school segregation increased in more than three-quarters of the one hundred counties in the South with the largest black student enrollments.

In this chapter, we describe these trends in public school segregation in the South. We then examine the relationship between residential and school segregation to determine the extent to which changes in school segregation are attributable to changes in patterns of residential segregation. The relationship between residential and public school segregation is particularly important because of the Supreme Court's insistence that states and their public school systems cannot be held legally responsible for school segregation patterns that result from segregated residential patterns that may be the result of private choices of individuals.[1] One plausible explanation for this trend of increasing school segregation is that public schools are becoming more segregated as a result of increasingly segregated residential patterns—particularly because of increasing residential segregation *between* school districts. Segregation between school districts is even more difficult to counter than segregation within school districts because courts can transfer students across school district lines only when it can be shown that the state has actively contributed to segregation through its delineation of district boundaries.[2] To the extent that white and black families reside in separate school districts, available within-district integration policies will be relatively ineffective in producing racially integrated schools no matter how strongly such policies are enforced.

A second possibility is that public schools are becoming more segregated not as a result of changing residential patterns but rather as a result of a retreat from active school board efforts to integrate public schools. A set of recent Supreme Court rulings has made it easier for many school systems to weaken or voluntarily abandon their desegregation plans,[3] which is likely to result in a wholesale trend toward resegregation in many school districts. In school districts in Charlotte and Greensboro, North Carolina, and Tampa–St. Petersburg, Florida, for example, public school segregation was low in 1990 as a result of effective desegregation plans but rose sharply in the 1990s as a result of a policy retreat from desegregation goals.[4] If changes in segregation result from a retreat from active desegregation efforts in the wake of the *Dowell*, *Freeman*, and *Jenkins* decisions, we can expect more rapid increases in public school segregation in the future as federal courts declare more formerly segregated school districts "unitary" and release them from further judicial oversight.

If increasing school segregation results from increasing residential segregation, plaintiffs may have little legal recourse for opposing the resegregation of schools. If, however, increasing segregation in public schools is a result not of increasing residential segregation but of school action (or inaction) in student-assignment policies, the courts may offer more leverage for addressing this issue, or a willing school board could simply alter its policies to increase integration. Thus, from a legal and policy perspective, it is important to distinguish between these two possible proximal causes of the trend toward increasing school segregation, because each has distinct legal and policy implications.

This chapter is organized into two parts. First, we describe patterns and trends of public school segregation in the South from 1990 to 2000. We describe both white-black and white-Hispanic segregation, although in our discussion of white-Hispanic segregation we focus on Texas and Florida, the two states that enroll the vast majority of the South's Hispanic students. Second, we describe the relationship between residential and public school segregation in the South from 1990 to 2000. Here we focus on white-black segregation patterns, since white-black segregation is much more ubiquitous in the region.

Measuring Segregation

To measure how evenly students are distributed among schools by race, we use a measure of segregation called the information theory index (referred to as *H*).

This measure does not depend on the race/ethnic composition of the population but only on how evenly population groups are distributed among schools or tracts.[5] It ranges from 0 to 1, with a value of 0 indicating perfect integration (the racial/ethnic proportions are identical in all schools or tracts) and a value of 1 indicating complete segregation (meaning that each school or tract is monoracial).[6] In general, values of *H* above 0.40 indicate extreme segregation, while values of 0.25–0.40 indicate moderate segregation.[7] By convention, a change in *H* of .05 or more in a decade represents a significant change in segregation levels.[8]

We use several primary sources of data for this chapter. For patterns of residential segregation, we use tract-level race/ethnic counts from the 1990 and 2000 Censuses. In 1990, we use counts of the non-Hispanic white population (referred to as "white" in this chapter), the non-Hispanic black population ("black"), the Hispanic population ("Hispanic"), and all others combined ("other"). In 2000, we use the same categories with the exception that we classify all those falling into the "two or more races" category as "other."[9]

For patterns of public school enrollment and segregation, we use data from the 1989–90 and 1999–2000 Common Core of Data Public Elementary/Secondary School Universe Survey Data Files.[10]

The region included in the data reported here is that included in the Census definition of the South.[11] We use definitions of metropolitan areas based on the metropolitan statistical area definitions from 1993, the year that the definitions were updated based on 1990 Census data.

How Did Public School Segregation Change in the South during the 1990s?

Nationally, public school segregation increased slightly from 1990 to 2000.[12] Table 2.1 shows that in the South, segregation between white and black students increased modestly (using the segregation index *H*), while segregation between white and Hispanic students decreased substantially.

White-black public school segregation in the South—as in the rest of the country—is largely attributable to segregation between public school districts; in 1990 and 2000, between-district differences in public school racial compositions accounted for nearly three-quarters (71–72 percent) of the overall public school segregation in the South. Between 1990 and 2000, both the between- and within-district components of white-black segregation increased slightly.

Figure 2.1 shows that within many individual states, black-white public school segregation levels are moderately high. Segregation is greatest in the District of

Table 2.1. Changes in Public School Segregation in the South, 1990–2000

	Public School Segregation between Whites and					
	Blacks		Hispanics		Nonwhites	
	1990	2000	1990	2000	1990	2000
Total school segregation (*H*)	.379	.400	.581	.520	.348	.354
Between-district						
Portion	.272	.284	.522	.453	.260	.264
Proportion	71.8%	71.0%	89.8%	87.1%	74.7%	74.6%
Within-district						
Portion	.107	.116	.059	.067	.088	.090
Proportion	28.2%	29.0%	10.2%	12.9%	25.3%	25.4%
Average within-district segregation (*H*)						
All districts	.049	.053	.058	.047	.040	.037
Districts in large Metropolitan Statistical Areas	.066	.057	.063	.050	.050	.042
Districts in small Metropolitan Statistical Areas	.068	.070	.071	.050	.056	.048
Rural districts	.040	.047	.053	.045	.035	.033

Source: Authors' tabulations of Common Core of Data, 1989–90 to 1999–2000.

Note: *H* = information theory index.

Columbia, Tennessee, Maryland, Arkansas, and Alabama and least in Delaware, South Carolina, and North Carolina. As in the South as a whole, public school segregation rose modestly in most states during the 1990s, with the largest increases occurring in Alabama, Arkansas, Louisiana, and Mississippi.

Unlike white-black segregation, which rose slightly in the 1990s, overall, white-Hispanic public school segregation declined substantially in the 1990s. Nonetheless, white-Hispanic segregation remained quite high in 2000—much higher, in fact, than white-black school segregation. This high segregation level results largely from the fact that Hispanic students are concentrated in only two states, Texas and Florida, which together enrolled more than 95 percent of all Hispanic public school students in the South in 1990 and 87 percent in 2000. While Hispanic enrollment in the rest of the South is increasing, southern Hispanic segregation patterns remain dominated by these two states.

The trends in white-Hispanic segregation in Texas and Florida differ substantially from the white-black segregation trends in the South. Figure 2.2 shows that

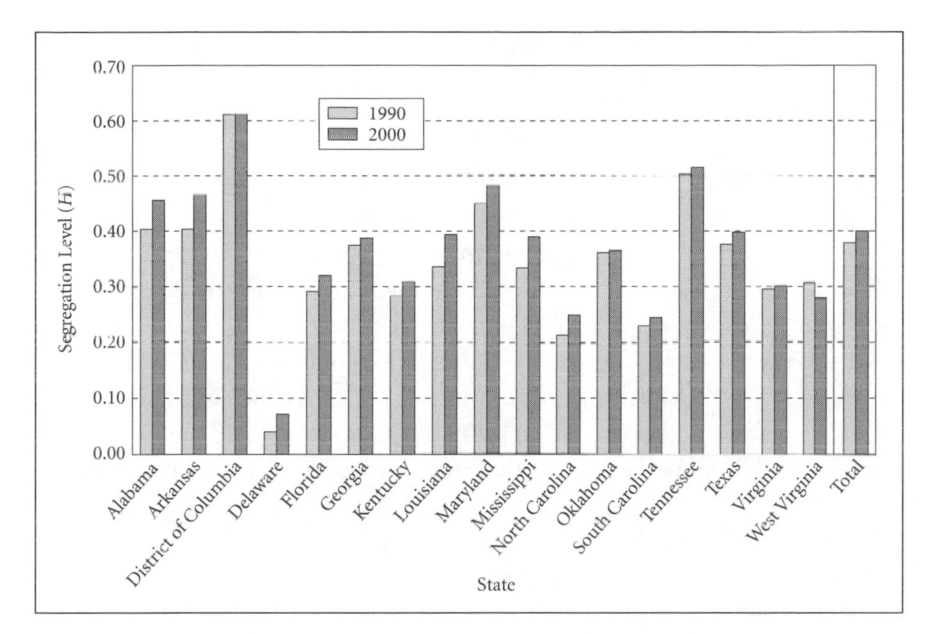

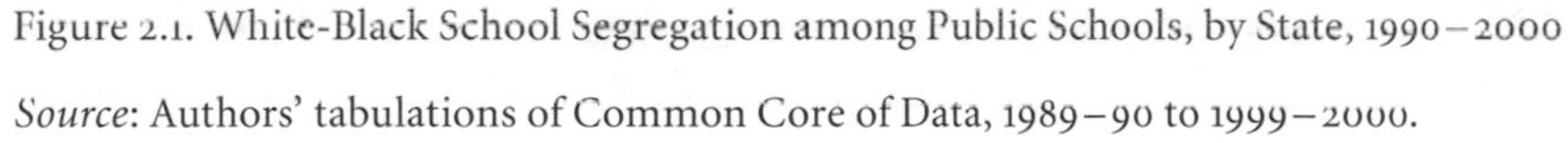
Figure 2.1. White-Black School Segregation among Public Schools, by State, 1990–2000

Source: Authors' tabulations of Common Core of Data, 1989–90 to 1999–2000.

the total segregation between Hispanic and white students decreased from 1990 to 2000 in both states. However, when we separate this trend into its between- and within-district components, we see that this decrease results entirely from a reduction in between-district segregation—in fact, the within-district portion of white-Hispanic segregation changed very little in both states.[13] This means that within-district white-Hispanic segregation levels remained roughly constant, on average, in Texas and Florida from 1990 to 2000, even as Hispanic student populations became more evenly dispersed among school districts throughout the two states. Any explanation of white-Hispanic segregation trends in the South must account for these patterns.

Given the trends reported here, we can make several general points. First, public school segregation in the South clearly is slowly increasing for black students and is decreasing rather rapidly for Hispanic students. The increase in white-black segregation results from increases in both within- and between-district segregation, while the decline in white-Hispanic segregation arises entirely because of a decline in between-district segregation. Second, the levels of public school white-black and white-Hispanic segregation in the South remain very high, regardless of the changes in segregation during the 1990s.

Did the Increase in Public School Segregation Result from Increases in Residential Segregation?

From a legal and policy perspective, it is important to know the extent to which the trend of increasing school segregation in the South results from increases in residential segregation and/or changes in school-assignment policies. If increasing residential segregation drives increasing school segregation, we would expect local changes in school segregation to correlate positively with local changes in residential segregation. If, however, changes in school-assignment policies (including a retreat from active desegregation efforts) drive increasing school segregation, we would expect local changes in school segregation to be uncorrelated with changes in residential segregation. Instead, we might expect the increases in school segregation to be greatest in areas that have high residential segregation but relatively low school segregation—places where prior school desegregation efforts had been most active and effective and where a return to neighborhood schools would lead to a rapid resegregation of schools. To investigate these alternatives, we first describe the general trends in residential segregation in the South. We then examine the relationship between residential and school segregation.

Changes in Residential Segregation in the South, 1990–2000

Residential white-black segregation declined in the South from 1990 to 2000, just as it did elsewhere in the United States.[14] In addition, white-Hispanic residential segregation declined overall in the South over the period. Table 2.2 illustrates the changing patterns of residential segregation in the South as a whole from 1990 to 2000.

The overall levels of black-white residential segregation in the South declined only modestly from 1990 to 2000, though this modest decline masks two conflicting trends: white-black segregation *between counties* actually increased during the 1990s, while segregation *within counties* declined. This means that black and white families were more likely to live in separate counties in 2000 than they were in 1990. For the most part, this increase in between-county segregation resulted from increases in segregation among counties in metropolitan areas (likely a result of growing white suburbanization) rather than from changes in the segregation between rural and metropolitan counties or from changes in segregation patterns among rural counties. In other words, the counties surrounding major southern cities such as Atlanta, Birmingham, Charlotte, and Jacksonville

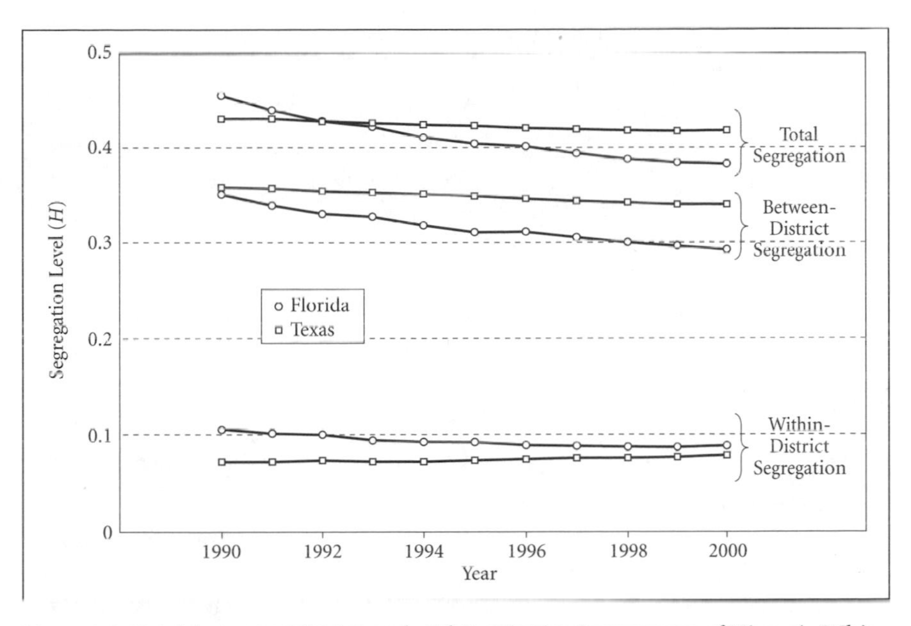

Figure 2.2. Total, between-District, and within-District Components of Hispanic-White Segregation in Texas and Florida, 1990–2000

Source: Authors' tabulations of Common Core of Data, 1989–90 to 1999–2000.

tended to become more racially identifiable—more disproportionately black or white—during the 1990s, though the racial balance between metropolitan and rural areas did not change substantially during that time. In contrast, average segregation within counties fell during the 1990s, though within-county segregation still accounted for the majority of white-black segregation in 2000.

The overall levels of white-Hispanic residential segregation also fell in the 1990s in the South and did so even more sharply than white-black segregation levels. This decline was wholly attributable to declines in the between-county segregation of whites and Hispanics—Hispanic populations grew dramatically in every state in the South, even those with relatively few Hispanics in 1990. Nonetheless, in 2000 as in 1990, the bulk of Hispanics in the South lived in Texas (6.7 million Hispanics, 57 percent of the region's Hispanics in 2000) and Florida (2.7 million, 24 percent); thus, white-Hispanic segregation levels reflect primarily between-state differences in Hispanic proportions rather than more localized segregation patterns.

Within individual states, black-white residential segregation levels generally declined as well. Figure 2.3 shows that segregation between blacks and whites in all southern states was high or extremely high in 1990, and though it declined

Table 2.2. Changes in Residential Segregation in the South, 1990–2000

	Residential Segregation between Whites and					
	Blacks		Hispanics		Nonwhites	
	1990	2000	1990	2000	1990	2000
Total residential segregation (*H*)	.412	.391	.475	.422	.343	.308
Between-county component						
Portion	.157	.167	.375	.314	.155	.154
Proportion	38.1%	42.7%	78.9%	74.4%	45.2%	50.0%
Within-county component						
Portion	.255	.224	.100	.108	.188	.154
Proportion	61.9%	57.3%	21.1%	25.6%	54.8%	50.0%
Average within-county segregation (*H*)						
All counties	.132	.114	.074	.047	.096	.077
Counties in large Metropolitan Statistical Areas	.204	.178	.079	.080	.150	.124
Counties in small Metropolitan Statistical Areas	.227	.188	.093	.070	.169	.133
Rural counties	.099	.087	.070	.036	.071	.057

Source: Authors' tabulations of U.S. Census, 1990 and 2000.

Note: *H* = information theory index.

slightly in all states except Arkansas and the District of Columbia in the 1990s, black-white residential segregation remained nonetheless in the high or extremely high range for almost all southern states in 2000. As figure 2.4 illustrates, Hispanic-white segregation levels, in contrast, generally remained in the low to moderate range for all states except Texas and Florida. White-Hispanic segregation increased substantially in Arkansas, the District of Columbia, Georgia, and Maryland, all places where the Hispanic population grew sharply.

Relationship between Patterns of Residential and Public School Segregation

The preceding results show that residential segregation between whites and nonwhites has generally declined in the 1990s, while school segregation—at least white-black segregation—has increased moderately. In this section we examine the relationship between these two trends at a more local level. Specifically, we

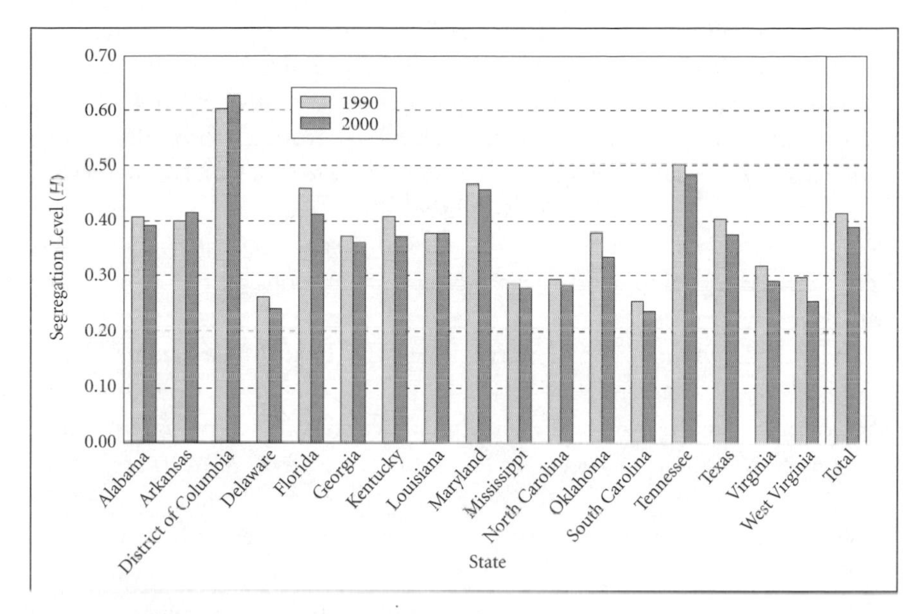

Figure 2.3. White-Black Residential Segregation among Census Tracts, by State, 1990–2000

Source: Authors' tabulations of U.S. Census, 1990 and 2000.

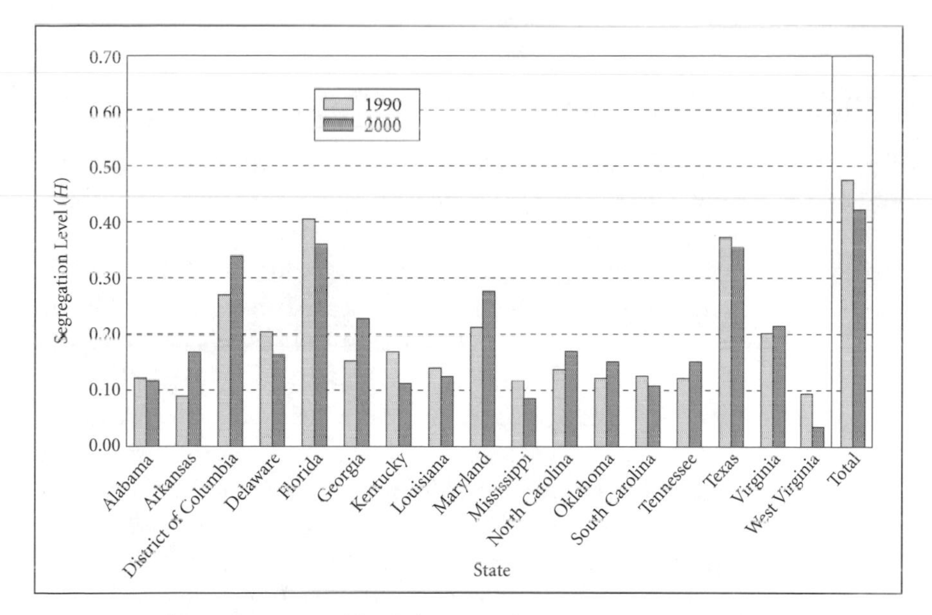

Figure 2.4. White-Hispanic Residential Segregation among Census Tracts, by State, 1990–2000

Source: Authors' tabulations of U.S. Census, 1990 and 2000.

examine whether and how local changes in school segregation relate to local changes in residential segregation. If school segregation tended to increase, on average, primarily in local areas with increasing residential segregation, then we can explain the trend toward increasing school segregation as a result of rising local housing segregation, which may occur even as aggregate levels of residential segregation are declining. If, however, local school segregation *increases* even where local residential segregation *decreases*, this suggests that policy retreats from school integration efforts bear at least some responsibility for increasing school segregation.

Under the Supreme Court's 1974 ruling in *Milliken v. Bradley*, federal courts are not allowed to order interdistrict (and thus, intercounty) desegregation remedies except when the state can be shown to have contributed to segregation by its delineation of school district boundaries. In essence, federal courts are limited in their ability to ameliorate patterns of between-district residential segregation. As a result, desegregation policies can have their strongest effects within school districts. However, because we do not have residential segregation data tabulated by district, we cannot examine the relationship at this level. In most southern states, school districts are coterminous with counties (Texas and Oklahoma are notable exceptions), so county-level analyses provide a good proxy for district-level analyses in all states except Texas and Oklahoma.

County-Level Residential and School Segregation

Figure 2.5 presents a plot of 1990 white-black school segregation levels (on the vertical axis) against white-black residential segregation levels (on the horizontal axis) for metropolitan area counties in the South, with larger circles indicating counties with larger black populations. Because values of H above .40 are considered extremely segregated, the figure shows first that almost all of the southern metropolitan area counties with the largest black public school student populations in 1990 had extremely high levels of both residential and public school segregation. Second, in 1990, many southern metropolitan area counties had far lower levels of public school segregation than of residential segregation (those counties well below the diagonal on the figure), meaning that their school systems had largely succeeded in integrating the schools despite sometimes very high levels of residential segregation. A number of these counties are noted in figure 2.5: Jefferson County, Kentucky (Louisville); Pinellas County, Florida (St. Petersburg); Mecklenburg County, North Carolina (Charlotte); Chatham County, Georgia (Savannah); Davidson County, Tennessee (Nashville); and East Baton Rouge Parish, Louisiana (Baton Rouge). In these counties, public school segrega-

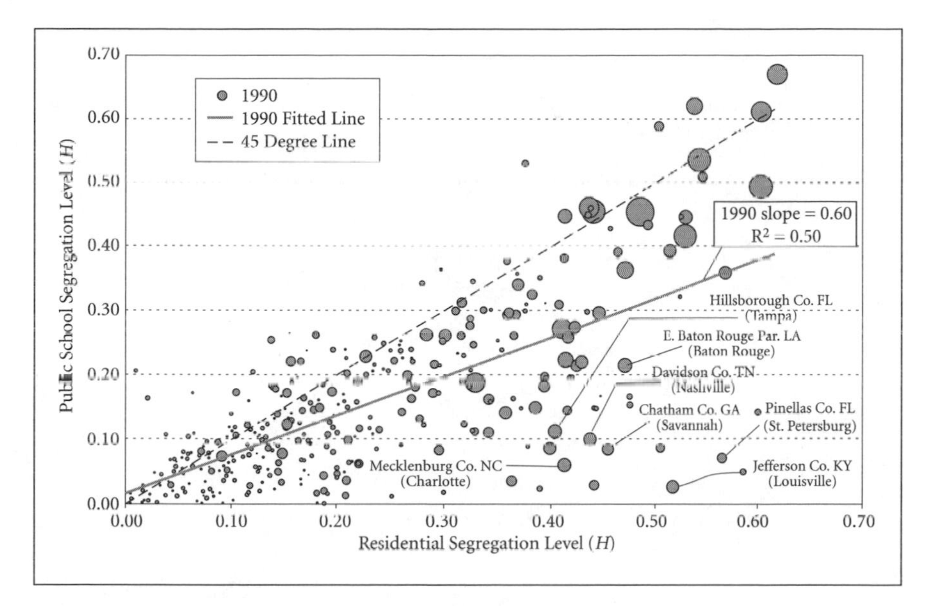

Figure 2.5. Relationship between Residential and Public School White-Black Segregation, All Counties in Southern Metropolitan Areas, by Size of County Black Population, 1990

Sources: Authors' tabulations of Common Core of Data, 1989–90, and U.S. Census, 1990.

tion efforts had largely succeeded by 1990 in overcoming high levels of within-county residential segregation to produce relatively integrated public schools.

In some other counties, however, the public schools were even more segregated than housing patterns would predict. Fulton County, Georgia (Atlanta), is an example of this pattern. In such places, the public schools may be more segregated than residential patterns not only because the public school systems have failed to integrate the schools but also as a result of white flight to the private school sector in districts with large black populations.

Considerable variation exists among southern counties in levels of both residential and public school segregation as well as in the correspondence of the two. A summary measure of the relationship between residential and school segregation is given by the statistics on the fitted line in figure 2.5, which represents the average pattern of association between the two types of segregation. If school enrollment patterns simply replicated residential patterns, the level of school segregation in each county would be roughly the same as the level of residential segregation, the fitted line in figure 2.5 would follow the forty-five-degree line, and the R^2 (the proportion of variance in school segregation explained by residential segregation) would be close to 1. Conversely, if there were complete

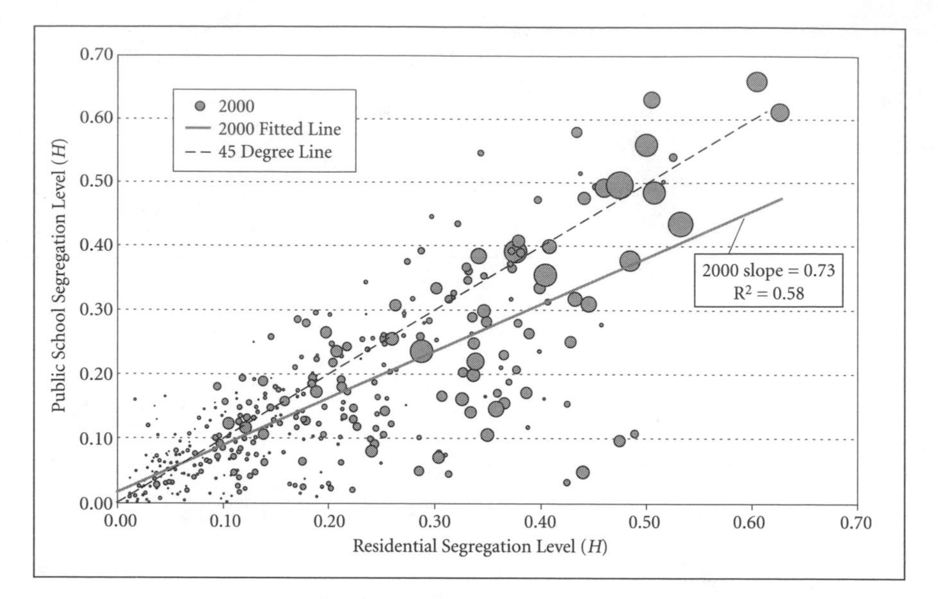

Figure 2.6. Relationship between Residential and Public School White-Black Segregation, All Counties in Southern Metropolitan Areas, by Size of County Black Population, 2000

Sources: Authors' tabulations of Common Core of Data, 1999–2000, and U.S. Census, 2000.

school integration in each county, the slope of this line would be flat, and the R^2 would be 0. Given the size of some counties, this level of school integration may be an unrealistic expectation, since achieving full integration in large counties might require transportation of residentially segregated students over very large distances. Nonetheless, a flatter slope indicates a weaker pattern of association between residential and school segregation and would suggest that schools are effectively ameliorating the effects of residential segregation by creating racially integrated school systems. The slope (.60) of the fitted line in figure 2.5 indicates that, on average, public school segregation in 1990 was 40 percent lower than residential segregation among the metropolitan counties of the South.

Figure 2.6 presents the same data as figure 2.5 but for 2000. Several trends are evident from a comparison of the two figures. First, the counties are much more closely clustered around the forty-five-degree line. This indicates that many of the counties with high levels of 1990 school integration had changed considerably by 2000, moving up and to the left in figure 2.6: they had become less residentially segregated but more educationally segregated. The slope of the fitted line is now steeper (.73), meaning that, on average, in 2000, public school segregation within a county was only 27 percent lower than residential segregation within the

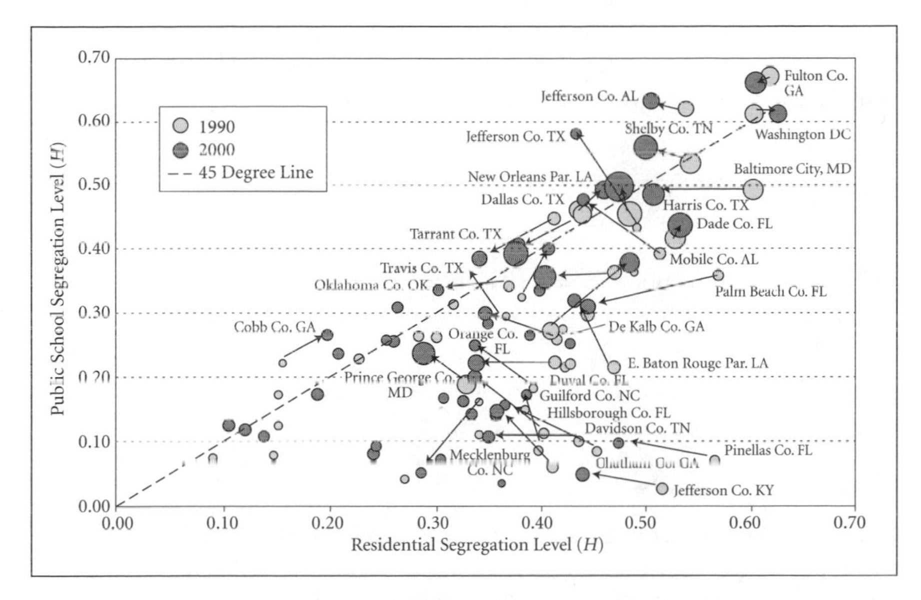

Figure 2.7. Relationship between Residential and Public School White-Black Segregation, Fifty Largest Counties in Southern Metropolitan Areas, by Size of County Black Population, 1990–2000

Sources: Authors' tabulations of Common Core of Data, 1989–90 to 1999–2000, and U.S. Census, 1990 and 2000.

same county. By this measure, the effectiveness of public school desegregation efforts had been reduced by a third (from a 40 percent to a 27 percent reduction in segregation) in the 1990s.

Figure 2.6 also shows that a number of counties in 2000 were above the diagonal—public school segregation was greater than residential segregation in these counties. Again, in such places, the public schools may be more segregated than residential patterns not only because the public school systems have failed to integrate the schools but also as a result of white flight to the private school sector in districts with large black populations.

Figure 2.7 overlays the 1990 and 2000 data (for the fifty southern counties with the largest black populations) to facilitate comparison between the years. The changes in segregation levels in many of these counties are quite dramatic considering that a change of .05 or more is considered substantial. Segregation changes were less dramatic for counties at the upper right of the figure—those where levels of both school and residential segregation were already high—but the general trend across the fifty counties with largest black populations was toward decreasing residential segregation (the average change in *H* was −0.042) and increasing public school segregation (the average change in *H* was +0.020). With the exception of a very few counties, the aggregate pattern of declining residential segregation coupled with increasing public school segregation is remarkably consistent across most metropolitan area counties in the South.

Consequences of the Retreat from Desegregation Efforts

In the preceding section, we saw that local increases in school segregation in southern metropolitan area counties cannot, in general, be attributed to increases in residential segregation. In this section, we approach the issue from another perspective by examining trends in public school segregation in a handful of districts that were declared unitary during the 1980s and 1990s.

Austin Independent School District

A federal district court declared the Austin (Texas) Independent School District (AISD) unitary in 1983 after eleven years under a desegregation order. In 1987, the school district adopted a new race-blind student-assignment plan that placed elementary students in neighborhood schools. In the academic year prior to the plan, only six schools in AISD enrolled more than 80 percent minority students; the following year (1987), AISD had nineteen such racially isolated minority schools.[15] The plaintiffs in the original case (the American Civil Liberties Union and a group of parents) sued the district over the new plan, but federal courts upheld the neighborhood school-assignment plan, and AISD remained unitary.[16] Following the initial sharp increase in school segregation between 1986 and 1987, both white-black and white-Hispanic segregation have continued to grow in AISD. From 1987 to 2000, the level of white-black segregation measured by *H* increased by 50 percent, from .26 to .39, and white-Hispanic segregation increased from .17 to .28. During the same period, white-black residential segregation declined in Austin (from .36 to .33), and white-Hispanic residential segregation increased slightly (from .20 to .24). So, some thirteen years after the return to neighborhood schooling in AISD, white-black and white-Hispanic public school segregation levels were higher than the corresponding residential segregation of the surrounding area. While we cannot say with certainty that these changes can be attributed to the granting of unitary status, given the timing of the trends and the lack of any corresponding trend in residential segregation, the retreat from active school integration efforts is the most plausible explanation for the patterns.

Charlotte-Mecklenburg School System

The Charlotte-Mecklenburg School System (CMS) was declared unitary in 2001 after a long and successful history of school desegregation efforts. This history is reflected in the large difference between black-white school and residential segregation levels prior to the granting of unitary status. In 2000, the CMS school and residential segregation levels were .15 and .36, respectively, indicating that district efforts to desegregate the schools were holding the level of school segregation well below what would be expected from strictly neighborhood based school-assignment policies.

Because unitary status was granted after our data were collected, it is unclear how the change to unitary status has affected segregation in the district, though Roslyn Arlin Mickelson (this volume) reports dramatic increases in school segregation under the current assignment plan. It is interesting to note as well that despite the CMS's successful school desegregation efforts, the district had experienced a trend toward resegregation even in the years prior to the granting of unitary status. During the late 1980s and early 1990s, the CMS moved away from its desegregation policy of student busing and multiracial attendance zones toward a system of controlled choice that featured magnet schools and racially targeted enrollments.[17] During this period, white-black school segregation increased from .06 in 1990 to .15 in 2000, while residential segregation decreased from .41 to .36. These are very substantial changes—in opposing directions—over a ten-year period. Moreover, while the overall level of school segregation in the district remained relatively low (.15) even in 2000, the increase of 150 percent in white-black segregation during the CMS era of controlled choice suggests that the controlled-choice plan may not have been as effective as the previous desegregation efforts in keeping the district desegregated. It will be very important to attend to future changes in segregation levels, particularly in the years immediately following the unitary-status decree, to see if the changes to neighborhood-based school choice will continue this trend toward resegregation in Charlotte-Mecklenburg.

De Kalb County Schools

The De Kalb County Schools in the Atlanta metropolitan area were declared unitary for student assignment in 1988 and declared fully unitary in 1996.[18] Following the unitary-status decree in 1996, De Kalb County schools no longer used race in school-assignment policies.[19] From 1993 (the first year for which data are available) to 1996, white-black school segregation in De Kalb increased from .27 to .29; following the unitary decree, segregation increased much more rapidly, from .29 in 1996 to .38 in 2000. This is an extremely large change that occurred contemporaneously with the unitary-status decree. While residential segregation in De Kalb increased during the 1990s as well—from .41 in 1990 to .48 in 2000—the timing of the school segregation increase suggests that the increase in residential segregation alone does not bear responsibility for the change in school segregation. The sharp increase in school segregation indicates a need for greater scrutiny of the causes of these changes, particularly if school choice or charter or magnet schools constitute a secondary cause of the increase in school segregation in the district. Because the granting of unitary status does not prohibit a district from using race as a factor in school assignment but rather simply frees the system of the requirement to do so, student-assignment policies could be modified to restore some racial balance.

Broward County Schools

Finally, we examine the changes occurring in Broward County, Florida. The Broward County schools were declared unitary in 1994 through an unpublished judgment.[20] Nonetheless, although the district is no longer required to consider race in school assignment, district policy explicitly states that each school should have a diverse student body, with diversity defined by race, special education status, English-language status, and socioeconomic status.[21] In addition, the district revises the school boundaries each year based on demographic changes and community input from public hearings. Finally, many of the choice and charter school programs also have a diversity component explicitly listed in their admissions policies.

During the 1990s, Broward County schools experienced rapid demographic changes—the share of white enrollment in the district fell by 18 percentage points, and the Hispanic share more than doubled, from 8 to 17 percent. However, despite this change, the white-Hispanic segregation level—already quite low in 1990—fell from .10 to .08 by 2000, while white-black segregation remained stable but high at .36. During this time, residential segregation for Hispanic students increased from .06 to .10, and residential segregation for black students fell from .47 to .40.

These trends suggest that unitary status need not necessarily lead to rapid increases in school segregation. When residential segregation levels are low (as is the case with white-Hispanic residential segregation in Broward County), neighborhood schools will not be highly segregated, particularly when school districts actively seek to create diverse school environments. Likewise, when both residential and school segregation levels are high (as is the case with white-black segregation in Broward County), the granting of unitary status and the return to neighborhood schools is unlikely to result in rapidly increasing school segregation, since in such a case, school segregation is already high, suggesting that the prior desegregation efforts had not been particularly successful.

Conclusion

Public school segregation between white and black students in southern states increased in the 1990s, reversing several decades of stable integration patterns in much of the region. This trend—although at present only moderate in magnitude—is notable not only because it reverses a long decline in school segregation in the South but also because the increase in school segregation came during a decade during which residential segregation in the South declined rather substantially. Seen in the context of these decreases in residential segregation, the increase in school segregation represents a substantial change in the effectiveness of public school desegregation efforts. In 1990, the public schools in metropolitan area counties were, on average, 40 percent less segregated than the housing patterns in their corresponding county—school systems countered two-fifths of the segregative effects of housing patterns. By 2000, however, public schools were only 27 percent less segregated than their local housing markets, a one-third reduction in the effectiveness of desegregation efforts.

Given these patterns, residential segregation changes clearly are not responsible for the increases in school segregation in the South. In fact, it is likely that school segregation levels would have increased more were it not for the substantial declines in residential segregation occurring in the 1990s. Nonetheless, while the recent increases in school segregation in the South are not attributable to changes in residential segregation, residential desegregation is increasingly important in shaping school segregation patterns. In the absence of active school desegregation efforts, residential segregation will increasingly determine patterns of school segregation, as neighborhood public schools mirror neighborhood racial composition patterns.

These trends may represent the leading edge of a rapid process of resegregation of public schools in the South. The Supreme Court has made it easier for school districts currently operated under federally supervised desegregation orders to be declared unitary and released from judicial supervision, but the effects of the Court's rulings are only recently being felt as districts are released from desegregation orders. A number of important districts have recently been declared unitary, but these declarations have occurred so recently that their effects are not yet evident in our data. If this trend continues, however, it is likely that the resegregation of the South will accelerate rapidly, both in places that have traditionally had large minority populations and in places where minority populations are only recently present in significant numbers.

Notes

1. See *Freeman v. Pitts*, 494–96, 506–7.

2. See *Milliken v. Bradley*; *Milliken v. Bradley II.*

3. In *Board of Education of Oklahoma City Public Schools v. Dowell*, the court emphasized that desegregation orders were intended to be temporary and that a return to local control was preferable when a district had "complied in good faith with the desegregation decree since it was entered, and the vestiges of past discrimination had been eliminated to the extent practicable" (249–50). In *Freeman*, the Court ruled that districts could be released from desegregation orders piecemeal; district courts might end their judicial oversight in areas where sufficient progress had been shown—for example, in student or faculty assignments—while retaining oversight in other areas where progress was still needed (489–90). Moreover, the Court has placed particular emphasis on a district's "good faith commitment" to ending segregation (491) rather than the stronger requirement that desegregation efforts "work, and work *now*," which the Court had previously emphasized (*Green v. County School Board of New Kent County*, 439). Finally, in *Missouri v. Jenkins* (1995), the Court appeared to shift the burden of proof from school districts (which, since *Green*, had been required to explain racial disparities) to plaintiffs, who, it said, must identify "the incremental effect" that prior *de jure* segregation had on any continuing racial disparities if they are to be considered by federal courts (101).

4. Logan, Stowell, and Oakley, *Choosing Segregation.*

5. Massey and Denton, "Dimensions of Residential Segregation"; Reardon and Firebaugh, "Measures of Multigroup Segregation."

6. The information theory index is computed as one minus the ratio of the average diversity of individual schools or tracts to the diversity of the total population in all schools or tracts combined. If all schools or tracts have the same race/ethnic composition as the population, the diversity will be the same in all schools, and H will be 0. If many schools or tracts have substantial overrepresentations of a race/ethnic group, then the average diversity within schools or tracts will be low, compared to that of the population, and H will be large. For more detail on the properties of the information theory index, see Reardon, Yun, and Eitle, "Changing Structure"; Reardon and Firebaugh, "Measures of Multigroup Segregation."

7. Reardon and Yun, "Integrating Neighborhoods."

8. Lewis Mumford Center, *Ethnic Diversity Grows*; Reardon and Yun, "Suburban Racial Change."

9. This is not an ideal treatment of the "two or more race" respondents but probably influences the results only slightly, since there are relatively few such respondents (1.3 percent of those in the South).

10. National Center, "Common Core of Data." The common core of data (CCD) contains race/ethnic enrollment counts for virtually all schools in the country. Because Georgia and Virginia did not report race/ethnic enrollment data in 1989–90, for these states we use data from the 1993–94 school year, which in both cases is the earliest year for which data are available. Tennessee data for 1999–2000 were obtained from the state of Tennessee's Web site, since Tennessee data were not included in the 1999–2000 CCD. For both 1989–90 and 1999–2000, the CCD uses race/ethnic classifications comparable to the 1990 Census.

11. Alabama, Arkansas, District of Columbia, Delaware, Florida, Georgia, Kentucky, Louisiana, Maryland, Mississippi, North Carolina, Oklahoma, South Carolina, Tennessee, Texas, Virginia, and West Virginia.

12. Logan, Stowell, and Oakley, *Choosing Segregation*; G. Orfield, *Schools More Separate*.

13. In decomposing *H* into between- and within-district components, the within-district component is a weighted average of the within-district segregation levels, where each district's segregation level is weighted by the size and ethnic diversity of the district. In general, this within-district component may change as a result of changes in within-district segregation levels, from a shift in the population from low- to high-segregation districts, and/or from disproportionately large increases in the diversity of districts with high levels of segregation. See Reardon, Yun, and Eitle, "Changing Structure." The stability of the within-district segregation component here largely results from the overall stability of within district segregation levels.

14. Lewis Mumford Center, *Ethnic Diversity Grows*; Reardon and Yun, "Suburban Racial Change."

15. *Price v. Austin Independent School District* (1990); *Price v. Austin Independent School District* (1991); Karatinos, "*Price v. Austin Independent School District.*"

16. *Price* (1990); *Price* (1991).

17. Mickelson, this volume.

18. Frankenberg, Lee, and Orfield, *Multiracial Society*.

19. Interview with De Kalb County staff at the School Assignment office, 3 October 2003.

20. Frankenberg, Lee, and Orfield, *Multiracial Society*.

21. See the approved Broward Public Schools memo located at ‹http://www.browardschools.com/districtreports/pdf/boundaries.pdf›.

CHAPTER THREE

CHARLES T. CLOTFELTER | HELEN F. LADD | JACOB L. VIGDOR

Classroom-Level Segregation and Resegregation in North Carolina

In the two decades following the momentous *Brown v. Board of Education* decision, the South's public schools underwent an astounding transformation. Whereas all of its public schools had been strictly segregated by race in 1954, they had become by 1974 the nation's most racially integrated schools.[1] In North Carolina, official resistance to desegregation initially forestalled all but token integration as late as 1960, but subsequent federal court orders and increased local compliance transformed it by 1980 into the most integrated state in the South and one of the most integrated states in the nation.[2]

In this chapter we document two forces working to reduce this high level of interracial contact. The first of these is resegregation—an increase in racial disparities between schools. Reflecting this trend, the share of white students in the average black student's public school in the state decreased from 54 percent in 1980 to 47 percent in 1996 and then, accelerating the decline, to 43 percent in 2000.[3] The second blemish on the state's record of school desegregation is racial segregation within schools. Even schools that appear, on the surface, to be integrated can contain wide racial disparities among their classrooms. This form of segregation is often associated with the academic tracking of students, commonly practiced in North Carolina and elsewhere. If disparities exist in the racial or socioeconomic composition of students assigned to various academic tracks, tracking will obviously produce some degree of segregation within schools, with the extent of the segregation depending on those disparities. As the ongoing debate over the merits of tracking makes clear, this tendency to segregate students by race is a major reason for opposition to tracking.[4]

Using data on the racial composition of classrooms in North Carolina, we document the course of segregation between the 1994–95 and 2000–2001 school years. Over this period, segregation in the public schools increased. While its absolute magnitude remained modest, the increase is noteworthy for its ubiquity. In both urban and rural districts, from the majority-black coastal plain to the predominantly white mountainous regions, and from the elementary to high school levels, white and nonwhite students increasingly gravitated toward separate classrooms in the late 1990s.

Our discussion begins by providing a broad overview of North Carolina's public schools and their students. After introducing and explaining the methods we use to quantify segregation, we present evidence on recent trends in the tendencies for white and nonwhite students to attend different schools and to sit in different classrooms within the same school. We then briefly discuss the factors that impel these trends. Signs of fading federal commitment to enforce integration, made evident by court rulings in North Carolina and elsewhere, undoubtedly bear substantial responsibility for the recent rise in segregation. We also highlight the state's changing racial composition and note the limited extent to which recent declines in residential segregation have yielded reductions in school segregation.

An Overview of Public Education in North Carolina

North Carolina's public school system has several distinctive institutional characteristics. As in most southern states, the state government plays a large role, relative to local districts, in financing and giving direction to public schools. In 1997–98, the state paid for two-thirds of the cost of the state's elementary and secondary schools, compared to an average of only 48 percent in the United States as a whole.[5] In 1990 the state adopted an accountability program with a state report card comparing performance by districts, and in 1997 it instituted a formal school-based accountability system featuring widespread student testing, monetary rewards to teachers in successful schools, and greater scrutiny of unsuccessful schools.[6] Like those adopted elsewhere, this program attempted to improve the quality of public schools by providing additional incentives to administrators and teachers in the form of financial bonuses for gains in measured performance.[7] The advent of charter schools represented another important policy innovation in this period. In 1996 the state legislature provided for up to one hundred such schools, all to be chartered at the state level.[8]

North Carolina's public school districts, like others in the South, are noteworthy for their large average size. Whereas the typical American school district serves 19,200 residents, the average North Carolina district is countywide and serves 65,400.[9] In practice, this broader geographic coverage offers fewer options for households that might want to avoid racially mixed public schools by moving to nearby, more segregated districts. The state's 117 public school districts are dis-

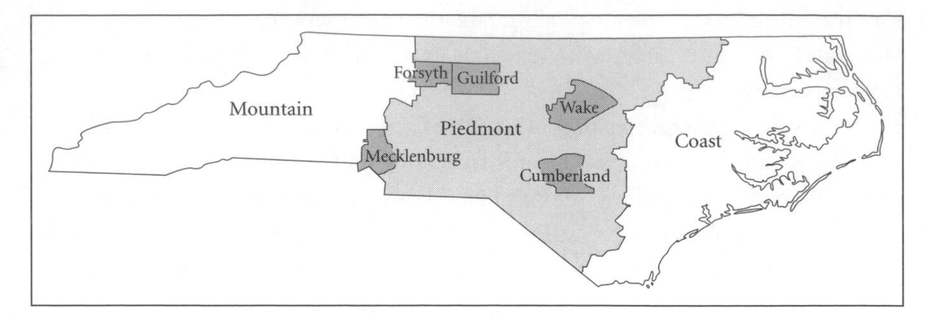

Figure 3.1. North Carolina School Districts, 2000–2001

Table 3.1. Enrollment and Racial Composition in North Carolina Public Schools, State and District Groups, 2000–2001

District	Total Enrollment	Percentage of Students: Black	Hispanic	Other Non-white	All Non-white	Annual Growth Rate 1994–95–2000–2001
State of North Carolina	1,281,201	31.1	4.4	3.3	38.9	1.9
Five largest districts						
Charlotte-Mecklenburg	104,260	43.1	5.5	4.9	53.4	3.4
Wake	98,975	27.7	4.6	4.2	36.4	4.2
Guilford	63,585	41.9	3.3	4.4	49.6	2.3
Cumberland	50,927	48.4	5.3	3.3	57.1	0.4
Winston-Salem/Forsyth	45,914	39.0	6.5	1.3	46.8	2.6
Other urban						
Coastal	133,246	42.4	3.3	1.3	47.0	0.5
Piedmont	128,288	37.6	6.1	2.5	46.2	2.2
Mountain	96,980	17.5	3.2	2.9	23.7	1.1
Rural						
Coastal	79,269	37.5	3.6	0.6	41.6	0.5
Piedmont	299,922	30.3	4.6	5.4	40.2	1.9
Mountain	179,835	8.5	3.6	2.2	14.3	1.7

Sources: North Carolina Department of Public Instruction, North Carolina Education Research Data Center; Membership Data, 1994–95 and 2000–2001 and North Carolina Public Schools Statistical Profile, 2001; authors' calculations.

tributed across a wide array of urban, suburban, and rural locations. To reflect broad patterns in the state without undue complexity, we split the state's districts into eleven groups—the five largest districts, plus three urban and three rural groups divided geographically into the state's principal regions, the coastal plain in the east, the mountains in the west, and the Piedmont in the middle.[10] Figure 3.1 shows these divisions.

All five of the largest districts are countywide, as are a majority of all districts in the state. Charlotte-Mecklenburg (which includes the city of Charlotte) was in 2000 the largest district in the state, followed by Wake County (which includes the state capital of Raleigh), Guilford County (which includes Greensboro and High Point), Cumberland County (which includes Fayetteville), and Winston-Salem/Forsyth. Together, these five urban districts accounted for a third of the state's public school students in 2000–2001, roughly the same number as were contained in the state's remaining thirty-two urban districts.

Ranking eleventh among states in population, North Carolina enrolled some 1.3 million students, including those in charter schools, in grades K–12 in 2000–2001.[11] As the summary statistics in table 3.1 show, the state's minority population is sizable, accounting for 39 percent of public school enrollment. African Americans constitute the largest minority group by far, but the 1990s witnessed rapid growth in the Hispanic population.[12]

The coastal and Piedmont regions have roughly twice the proportion of nonwhite students found in the mountain region. Reflecting the state's moderately rapid overall growth rate, enrollments increased at an annual rate of 1.9 percent between 1994–95 and 2000–2001, paced by annual growth rates of more than 3 percent in the state's two largest districts, Wake County and Charlotte-Mecklenburg.

Measuring Segregation between and within Schools

We use the term "segregation" to mean unevenness in patterns of enrollment or the extent to which these patterns are racially unbalanced. To measure the degree of segregation, we employ a numeric index based on the gap between the overall percentage of nonwhite students in a district and the percentage of nonwhite students in the school attended by the typical white student in that district. We present evidence both on the degree of segregation between schools (that is, the extent to which white and nonwhite students attend different schools within a district) and on the degree of segregation within schools (the extent to which white and nonwhite students sit in different classrooms within the same school).

This evidence is based on a unique and comprehensive data set provided to us by the North Carolina Department of Public Instruction, which provides information on the racial composition of every class offered in every public school in the state.

These data allow us to calculate segregation across schools and within classrooms. Most statistical studies of school segregation employ the first of these approaches; they typically ask to what extent the schools in a district differ by racial composition. At one extreme is complete segregation, where students are strictly separated on the basis of race. At the other extreme is no segregation, where schools are racially balanced—that is, where every school has exactly the same percentage of nonwhite students. Like most segregation indexes, the index we use yields a value of 1 for complete segregation and 0 for the case of no segregation, with patterns in between taking on values between 0 and 1. For example, if 40 percent of a district's students were nonwhite but the school attended by the average white student was only 30 percent nonwhite, our across-school segregation index would be 0.25 ([40 − 30]/40), indicating that the gap between the actual and the maximum possible nonwhite percentage was 25 percent of the total nonwhite percentage.[13] If all schools were racially balanced, no gap would exist and the index would be 0. In contrast, if schools were entirely segregated, the index would be 1, since the average white student would attend a school that was 0 percent nonwhite, leaving a 40 percent gap between actual and maximum nonwhite percentage.

By virtue of the detailed data made available to us, we applied this approach at the classroom level. Instead of measuring interracial contact by the nonwhite percentage in the typical white student's school, we base our second measure on the composition of the typical white student's classroom. To the extent that classrooms within schools differ in racial composition, this classroom-based measure of average interracial contact will be both more accurate and smaller than that based on the schoolwide average. By the same token, the resulting gap between the average and the maximum nonwhite percentage will be larger than that based on comparisons across schools, leading to higher measured segregation.

We calculate our indexes separately by grade level. To measure classroom-level segregation at the elementary level, in most cases we examine the racial composition of "self-contained" classrooms, where students spend most of their time. At the middle and high school levels, where students attend several different classes during the course of each day, measuring classroom-level segregation is inherently more complicated. Our measures for these grades are based on the racial composition of English classes.[14]

Statewide Segregation Indexes

Table 3.2 displays our basic findings, listing statewide average school- and classroom-level segregation indexes. We report indexes for two school years and three grade levels. The indexes shown in the table demonstrate three essential points:

1. *Classroom segregation is fairly modest in North Carolina.* In the 2000–2001 school year, classroom-level segregation index values averaged between 0.20 and 0.23, indicating that the average district in North Carolina is closer to being completely racially balanced than to being completely segregated. A classroom-level segregation index value of 0.20 suggests that the typical white student is in a class with a nonwhite share that is 20 percent lower than that of the district as a whole. Thus, in a district that was 40 percent nonwhite, the average white student would be in a classroom that was 32 percent nonwhite.[15] In a class of twenty-two pupils, the typical white would have seven nonwhite classmates rather than nine, as would be the case if the classrooms were racially balanced. Nonwhite students, correspondingly, tend to be in classrooms with a higher percentage of nonwhite students than perfect evenness would dictate.[16]

2. *Although the changes are modest, segregation levels have been increasing.* Between 1994–95 and 2000–2001, both between-school and within-school segregation levels increased at all three grade levels in North Carolina. In some cases, these increases were quite large in percentage terms. First-grade students, for example, witnessed an increase in classroom segregation of 33 percent. These large relative increases, however, generated only modest numerical changes in the racial composition of classrooms. In the hypothetical 40 percent nonwhite district discussed in the previous paragraph, the average white first-grader sat in a class with 34 percent nonwhite students in 1994–95 but only 32 percent nonwhite students in 2000–2001. This change in composition would be roughly equivalent to starting with a classroom of eight nonwhites among twenty-four students and adding one additional white student.

An interesting footnote to this rising segregation is the role played by charter schools. Only authorized in North Carolina in 1996, and comprising only 1.2 percent of the state's overall enrollment in 2000–2001, charter schools could nevertheless be blamed for a part of the rise in segregation over the period. If charter schools had been omitted from the calculations of segregation in 2000–2001, the overall segregation index for the state would have increased slightly less than it did.[17] Charter schools have this effect because they include a large number of predominantly black schools. Their effect in increasing overall racial segregation is ironic, since the state legislature had inserted language into the authorizing legislation to prevent charters from becoming havens for whites.[18]

Table 3.2. School- and Classroom-Level Segregation in North Carolina, 1994–1995 and 2000–2001

	School-Level Segregation		Classroom-Level Segregation	
Grade Level	1994–95	2000–2001	1994–95	2000–2001
Elementary (first)	0.13	0.17	0.15	0.20
Middle (seventh)	0.09	0.11	0.18	0.23
High (tenth)	0.08	0.09	0.20	0.23

Source: North Carolina Department of Public Instruction, North Carolina Education Research Data Center; authors' calculations.

Note: Table entries are weighted averages of segregation levels in each of the state's 117 school districts. The weights are equal to the district's share of statewide enrollment in the specific grade.

3. *Older students attend more integrated schools than younger students but sit in more segregated classrooms.* In the first grade, classroom-level segregation is only slightly higher than school-level segregation, suggesting that the degree of within-school segregation in elementary schools is quite small. In fact, the degree of segregation within elementary schools is within the range that would be expected if students were randomly assigned to classrooms. After the transition to middle and high school, students attend larger campuses that draw students from a wider area, which generally leads to a lower degree of school-level segregation. Yet once inside their relatively integrated schools, students of different races tend to be sorted into different classrooms, with the net result of greater segregation measured at the classroom level.

Segregation in Large Districts and across Geographic Regions

Our examination of broad trends in segregation levels for the state as a whole masks interesting variation in the experiences among districts. Table 3.3 uncovers some of this variation by examining school- and classroom-level segregation trends for the state's five largest school districts, which serve the cities and immediate suburbs of Charlotte, Raleigh, Greensboro, Fayetteville, and Winston-Salem. Generally speaking, the patterns in each district match those of the state. With only one exception, schools and classrooms at every grade level in each district became more segregated between 1994 and 2000. Moreover, the only

Table 3.3. School- and Classroom-Level Segregation in Large Districts, 1994–1995 and 2000–2001

	School-Level Segregation		Classroom-Level Segregation	
Grade Level/District	1994–95	2000–2001	1994–95	2000–2001
Elementary (first)				
Charlotte-Mecklenburg	0.17	0.25	0.19	0.28
Wake (Raleigh)	0.08	0.11	0.09	0.14
Guilford (Greensboro)	0.25	0.34	0.27	0.37
Cumberland (Fayetteville)	0.13	0.14	0.15	0.18
Winston-Salem/Forsyth	0.11	0.34	0.12	0.36
Middle (seventh)				
Charlotte-Mecklenburg	0.12	0.19	0.28	0.34
Wake (Raleigh)	0.06	0.07	0.20	0.27
Guilford (Greensboro)	0.23	0.26	0.37	0.38
Cumberland (Fayetteville)	0.11	0.13	0.18	0.20
Winston-Salem/Forsyth	0.02	0.24	0.16	0.38
High (tenth)				
Charlotte-Mecklenburg	0.10	0.13	0.26	0.31
Wake (Raleigh)	0.05	0.07	0.21	0.24
Guilford (Greensboro)	0.28	0.26	0.39	0.37
Cumberland (Fayetteville)	0.08	0.10	0.14	0.17
Winston-Salem/Forsyth	0.04	0.11	0.19	0.26

Source: North Carolina Department of Public Instruction, North Carolina Education Research Data Center; authors' calculations.

case of declining segregation, among and within Guilford County high schools, occurred in the district with the highest overall segregation levels. In each district, elementary schools exhibited the lowest classroom-level segregation, even though their school-level segregation was the highest.

These five districts have had remarkably different degrees of success in integrating their schools and classrooms. Wake County, for example, came very close to racial balance at the school level, as indicated by its low index values of school-level segregation. At the classroom level, Wake's average white first-grade student in 2000–2001 was assigned to a classroom where more than 30 percent of students were nonwhite, reasonably close to the district average of 36 percent. The district's track record was somewhat less impressive at the middle and high school levels. Although older students attend schools that are among the most racially balanced in the state, the tendency to sort by race within Wake County schools made classrooms resemble those in the other districts. The evidence shows that Cumberland County has had more success in restricting the within-school sorting of students at higher grade levels.

At the other end of the spectrum, Guilford County consistently displayed school- and classroom-level segregation indexes well above the state average. In a district where approximately half of all students were nonwhite, the average white student at all grade levels sat in a classroom where fewer than a third of the pupils were nonwhite. In other words, the typical white student in Guilford attended classes with nearly the same racial composition as the typical white student in Wake despite the fact that the overall percentage of nonwhite students in Guilford was 13 points higher. The school systems serving Charlotte and Winston-Salem showed the greatest evidence of change over this time period, moving closer to the levels witnessed in Guilford County.[19]

Similar trends were evident in the state's 112 smaller school districts. Classroom-level segregation increased in every region of the state, in both urban and rural schools, at the elementary, middle, and high school levels. As in the larger districts, these increases were quite modest. Segregation levels in smaller districts generally are in the same range as in larger districts, and within each region segregation levels in the urban districts typically exceed those in rural districts. The lowest segregation levels among urban districts tend to occur in the mountain region, which features the most racially homogeneous underlying population. Segregation levels in the coastal region, home to rural counties with the state's highest nonwhite population density, also are generally low.

Possible Explanations for the Rising Levels of Segregation

In other work we formulate and test hypotheses explaining the patterns and trends in segregation observed in North Carolina.[20] We base our hypotheses on the premise that school administrators must attempt to balance social and political pressures for and against segregation. The adoption of policies that result in a high degree of school segregation might expose administrators to unfavorable scrutiny from parents or federal courts and could generate negative publicity on a local or national scale. Moving toward complete integration of public schools could also generate ill will, most likely from white parents who seek to limit their children's degree of exposure across racial or socioeconomic lines.[21] Totally ignoring white parents' desires to limit exposure might result in "white flight" to other districts or private schools, with consequent reductions in white student enrollment, reduced political support for public schools and their leadership, and lower property values in some neighborhoods.

Moreover, treating classroom segregation levels as purely the result of administrative decisions is clearly an oversimplification. Parents and students play a critical role in determining the distribution of students across classrooms, especially in later grades, when students choose electives. Nonetheless, our model provides a framework for considering three possible explanations for the recent rise in classroom-level segregation in North Carolina: changes in racial attitudes, the waning judicial enthusiasm for racial balance in schools, and the unprecedented influx of Hispanic immigrants to many parts of the state.

Changing Racial Attitudes

It is tempting to attribute the rise in segregation within North Carolina's schools to a decline in the tolerance of one racial group for another. Yet the facts do not support this explanation. Evidence from the General Social Survey shows that white residents of the South Atlantic region, like those in other regions, have moderated their racial views significantly over the past thirty years. Whereas prior to 1980 more than one-third of whites in the South Atlantic region strongly agreed with the statement "whites have a right to a segregated neighborhood, and blacks should respect that right," fewer than 10 percent strongly agreed after 1990.[22]

While many social scientists are rightly skeptical of the candor of some survey responses, housing market trends also point toward increased racial tolerance. North Carolina's metropolitan areas are noteworthy both for their comparatively low levels of residential segregation and for the recent rate of decline in these levels. While the state's neighborhoods are far from integrated, a comparison with cities of the Northeast and Midwest, where high degrees of segregation are the norm, and with the West, where blacks are often the third-largest minority group, offers a remarkable contrast. Thus, a puzzle arises. Why has classroom-level segregation increased in North Carolina at the same time that racial attitudes appear to have softened?

One explanation for this puzzle may be the changing political pressures that result when a formerly dissident group (here, racial segregationists) decides to rejoin the educational mainstream. Intolerance may have coexisted with integrated schools because the most intolerant segment of the white population opted out of public schools, freeing administrators to tailor school integration patterns to the preferences of the remaining, more tolerant group. Following the same line of reasoning, increased tolerance could accompany higher levels of school segregation if the most intolerant parents became slightly more tolerant and thus willing to take an active role in the public schools but did so only in exchange for implicit or explicit concessions, such as school-choice programs or the greater use of tracking.

Even though North Carolina's neighborhoods are integrating and its classrooms are segregating, the state's children continue to experience more racial interaction at school than at home. We compared the average classroom-level school segregation in each of the state's one hundred counties with a measure of neighborhood-level segregation. For all but one county, the index of school segregation was smaller than that for residential segregation, implying that classrooms in virtually every part of North Carolina offer children a more integrated experience than do their neighborhoods.

Relaxed Judicial Oversight

Another possible explanation for the increase in school segregation lies in changes in judicial mandates. In a series of decisions in the early 1990s, the Supreme Court invited a speedy end to judicial oversight for school districts after they had freed themselves of the vestiges of past racial discrimination. School districts that had labored under court-ordered plans requiring racially balanced enrollments were released from these obligations.[23] Most of the districts in our data set were not directly affected by court rulings during the time period studied, but these rulings probably indirectly affected district decision making. The lower probability of judicial intervention reduced pressure on administrators to pursue integration in schools and classrooms. Perhaps as a result of these judicial developments, several North Carolina districts changed their school-assignment policies in the late 1990s. Winston-Salem/Forsyth is a case in point. After operating for twenty-three years under a judicial order calling for strict racial balance, it implemented in the 1995–96 school year a controlled-choice plan permitting parents to choose among schools within a geographic zone. The plan produced racial disparities among schools, which sparked complaints. After investigating these complaints, the Office for Civil Rights, in light of the Fourth Circuit decisions disallowing the use of race in assignment, officially gave its blessing to the plan in 2000.[24] The result of instituting the choice plan in Winston-Salem/Forsyth was a rise in measured segregation, as shown in table 3.3. A contrasting case is Guilford County, where schools had a comparatively high rate of segregation throughout the period. In that county, three previously independent and diverse districts merged their operations without making major changes in school-assignment patterns.

Hispanic Immigration

A third explanation for North Carolina's increase in segregation points toward marked increases in immigration to the state. While North Carolina's African American and Native American populations remained relatively steady in the 1990s, its Hispanic population grew at a rate four times higher than the national average. Changes in a community's racial composition could alter the balance between classroom integration and segregation in several distinct ways. Increases in the overall nonwhite percentage of a community give administrators a choice between imposing greater degrees of interracial exposure or increasing the level of segregation. White opposition to classroom integration may well increase as communities become more nonwhite.

At the same time, increases in the nonwhite population might decrease the white community's political influence on administrative decisions. The net impact of changes in community composition on pressure to segregate or integrate is not clear a priori. Figure 3.2 presents some evidence that illuminates this point by plotting the degree of segregation in each school district against the percent nonwhite in each district. The data display an inverse U-shaped pattern, indicating that the districts with the greatest racial diversity, as indicated by a nonwhite share close to 50 percent, tend to have the highest levels of segregation. In other words, higher nonwhite shares predict greater degrees of segregation up to a point, beyond which the opposite pattern holds. It is plausible, then, that growth of the Hispanic population could push districts toward higher degrees of segregation, particularly in areas that began with relatively small nonwhite populations. Broad patterns across North Carolina school districts are consistent with this view. Districts with large increases in percentages of nonwhite students, particularly the urban districts of the Piedmont and mountain regions, tended to exhibit large increases in segregation. Exceptions to this pattern, such as Cumberland County, often began the period with nonwhite majorities.

The nonwhite share of school enrollment increased in 105 of the state's 117 districts between 1994–95 and 2000–2001, with the average increase on the order of 4 percentage points. Since three-quarters of the state's districts and most of the state's urban districts had white majorities at the beginning of the period, the net impact of this demographic change was to increase diversity. We examined the statistical association between changes in segregation and the growth in three major racial groups of students. For first grade, we found no statistically significant relationship. In seventh grade, we found that segregation decreased in districts where black and white enrollments increased. For tenth grade, we found that segregation increased in districts with higher Hispanic growth.[25]

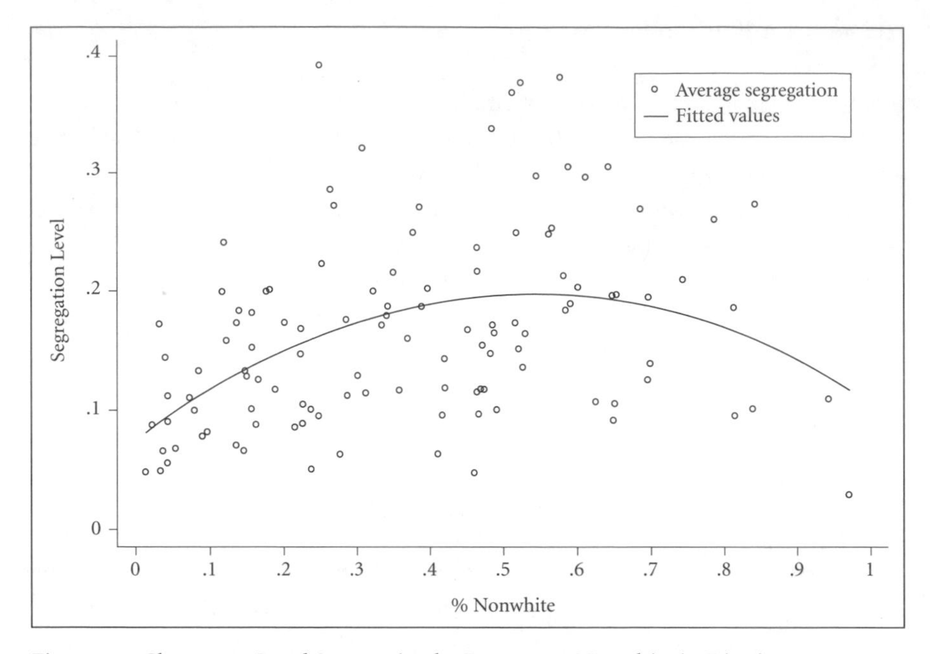

Figure 3.2. Classroom-Level Segregation by Percentage Nonwhite in District, 2000–2001

Another possible link between the growing Hispanic population and school segregation involves the tendency for those students who speak a language other than English to be educated in separate classrooms, especially when such students form a critical mass within the school. Although these classroom-assignment decisions may be made entirely for instructional reasons, higher white-nonwhite segregation is a quite likely side effect. Table 3.4 investigates this hypothesis by presenting elementary (first-grade) classroom-level segregation indexes for two different racial pairings: whites and Hispanics and whites and blacks. The table shows a pronounced increase in segregation between whites and Hispanics, evident both statewide and in each of the five large districts and six categories of smaller districts. In some large school systems, the degree of white-Hispanic segregation is quite high: in Charlotte-Mecklenburg, for example, the average white first-grade student has only half the number of Hispanic classmates as would be expected if all classrooms were racially balanced.[26]

At the same time, the placement of Hispanic students in settings designed for students of limited English proficiency clearly cannot explain the entire increase in segregation observed between 1994–95 and 2000–2001, because the separation of black and white students also increased during this time period across the state.

Table 3.4. First-Grade Classroom-Level Segregation Indexes Using Alternate Racial Groupings, 1994–1995 and 2000–2001

	Hispanic vs. White		Black vs. White	
District	1994–95	2000–2001	1994–95	2000–2001
State of North Carolina	0.11	0.20	0.16	0.23
Five largest districts				
Charlotte-Mecklenburg	0.18	0.46	0.20	0.28
Wake	0.10	0.16	0.10	0.18
Guilford	0.16	0.38	0.27	0.41
Cumberland	0.11	0.14	0.16	0.22
Winston-Salem/Forsyth	0.18	0.38	0.12	0.42
Other urban				
Coastal	0.09	0.18	0.18	0.26
Piedmont	0.13	0.18	0.18	0.21
Mountain	0.08	0.14	0.13	0.19
Rural				
Coastal	0.11	0.17	0.11	0.16
Piedmont	0.11	0.21	0.16	0.21
Mountain	0.07	0.11	0.12	0.17

Source: North Carolina Department of Public Instruction, North Carolina Education Research Data Center; authors' calculations.

Conclusion

Thanks to a number of factors, including relatively low levels of residential segregation and relatively large school districts (most of which are coterminous with counties), North Carolina's public schools and classrooms retain a noteworthy degree of racial integration. The evidence presented in this chapter, however, suggests that progress toward racial balance has stalled and reversed over the past several years. Although increases in segregation were relatively modest in degree over the six-year period we examined, they were striking in their pervasiveness across grade levels and in urban and rural districts in all parts of the state. Our data also predate Charlotte-Mecklenburg's adoption of a school-choice plan, which occasioned a significant jump in racial separation in that district beginning in the fall of 2002.

Decreased white tolerance of nonwhites is clearly not the explanation for the rise in segregation. Indeed, racial tolerance among whites appears to have increased during the period.[27] A more compelling explanation for the rise in school segregation is the gradual waning of judicial oversight, combined with admonitions that school officials not use race in making school assignments.[28] Whether this prohibition will be reversed in light of the Supreme Court's 2003 ruling in *Grutter v. Bollinger* remains very much an unanswered question at this writing. One additional factor appears to be the rapid immigration of Hispanics to the state. While many unforeseen circumstances will undoubtedly influence the future path of segregation in North Carolina's classrooms, the persistence of these trends in the first decade of the twenty-first century portends further lost ground in years to come.

Notes

The authors are grateful to Roger Aliaga and Thomas Ahn for research assistance, to the North Carolina Education Research Data Center for providing data, and to the Spencer Foundation for financial support. The views expressed herein are those of the authors and do not necessarily reflect those of any organization.

1. G. Orfield, *Public School Desegregation*, table 2. Regions were ranked by the percentage of black students attending schools that were 90 percent or more minority or 50 percent or more minority.

2. Frankenberg, Lee, and Orfield, *Multiracial Society*, table 40. Ranked by percent white in the average black student's school, North Carolina was fifth out of twenty-eight listed states in 1980 and third in 2000, and highest among southern states in both years.

3. Ibid.

4. See, e.g., Oakes and Guiton, "Matchmaking"; Loveless, *Tracking Wars*.

5. Snyder and Hoffman, *Digest of Education Statistics, 2000*, table 159.

6. Ladd, "School-Based Accountability Systems"; North Carolina Department, "History of Public Education."

7. For description and analysis of such programs, see Ladd, *Holding Schools Accountable*.

8. The act setting up charter schools is in General Statutes of North Carolina, chap. 115C-238.29.

9. U.S. Bureau of the Census, *Statistical Abstract*. Data on districts are for 1997, population 1999, tables 491, 20. Alaska and Hawaii are omitted from calculations.

10. All districts in counties that were 45 percent or more urban in 1990 were classified as urban, as were all city districts in any county with enrollments of at least 2,000 in 2001–2, not counting charter school enrollments. The boundaries between coastal, piedmont, and mountain counties were taken from North Carolina Division of Travel and Tourism, *Yours to Discover: North Carolina State Parks and Recreation Areas* (Raleigh: North Carolina Division of Travel and Tourism, 1998).

11. Charter schools were included with the districts in which each was located, although they were administratively independent of those districts.

12. Between 1992 and 2000 the state's Hispanic population grew from 84,000 to 379,000, for an annual rate of 18.8 percent, compared to 4.7 percent a year for the nation (24.3 to 35.3 million).

13. The nonwhite percentage in the typical white's school, referred to as the exposure rate *E*, is a weighted average of school racial compositions, where white enrollment is the weight. The segregation index *S* is equal to $(n - E)/n$, where *n* is the racial composition of the district.

14. For details on the exceptions to this general strategy, see Clotfelter, Ladd, and Vigdor, "Symposium."

15. 40 percent − .20 × 40 percent = 32 percent.

16. Focusing on the experience of the "average" member of the group obscures the fact that some individuals witness dramatic segregation in schools and classrooms. As stated in the introduction to this chapter, one in every fifteen nonwhite students attended a school that was at least 90 percent nonwhite in 2000–2001. This probability varied widely across districts. In the Winston-Salem/Forsyth school district, for example, one in every five nonwhite students attended a school with at least 90 percent nonwhite students. There had been no such schools in that district in the 1994–95 school year.

17. To be valid, such a conclusion assumes that, in the absence of charter schools, the students who would have attended them would have been distributed among public schools by racial composition in the same proportions as were actual public school students in 2000–2001.

18. The act stated that each charter school's racial composition should reflect that of the local school district or the special population in the school district it was designed to serve. General Statutes of North Carolina, chap. 115C-238.29F.

19. Mickelson, this volume, also finds disparities in racial composition within high schools in Charlotte-Mecklenburg. Instead of a segregation index, she shows disparities between schools by noting schools whose racial compositions depart by more than 15 percent from the district average. She shows disparities within schools by showing differences in racial composition among classes in different tracks for the same subject.

20. Clotfelter, Ladd, and Vigdor, "Racial Segregation."

21. That white parents might prefer to limit interracial contact in schools is suggested by evidence from the housing market, variations in rates of private school enrollment, and patterns of white parents' choices of schools. For an extended discussion of the basis for apparent white aversion to racially mixed schools, see Clotfelter, *After Brown*, chap. 3.

22. National Opinion Research Center, "General Social Survey."

23. The first of these decisions was *Board of Education of Oklahoma City Public Schools v. Dowell*. For a discussion of the effect of this and other cases, see G. Orfield and Eaton, *Dismantling Desegregation*.

24. Ziegenbalg, "Civil-Rights Inquiry"; telephone conversation with Doug Punger, attorney for the Winston-Salem/Forsyth School Board, 15 May 2003. For a discussion of related rulings in the Fourth Circuit, see Boger, "Willful Colorblindness."

25. The dependent variable in the regressions was change in segregation, and independent variables included the percent growth in black, white, and Hispanic enrollments plus dummy variables for urban districts and districts in the mountain and coastal regions. In the equation for seventh grade, the coefficients for percent growth in black and white

enrollment were negative and significant at the 95 percent level. In the tenth-grade equation, the coefficient for Hispanic enrollment growth was positive and significant at the 90 percent level.

26. Reardon and Yun, this volume, find that white-Hispanic segregation more than doubled between 1987 and 2000 in Charlotte-Mecklenburg and Guilford County and increased slightly in Wake County.

27. See National Opinion Research Center, "General Social Survey."

28. For a discussion of the *Eisenberg* and *Tuttle* decisions, in which the Fourth Circuit Court stated these admonitions against race-conscious assignments, see Boger, "Willful Colorblindness."

CHAPTER FOUR

ROSLYN ARLIN MICKELSON

The Incomplete Desegregation of the Charlotte-Mecklenburg Schools and Its Consequences, 1971–2004

Advocates look to desegregation as the touchstone to equality of educational opportunity. Critics call it a failed social experiment.[1] As judicial mandates to desegregate end across the country, the history and consequences of desegregation in the Charlotte-Mecklenburg Schools (CMS) offer us the opportunity to assess the contributions of desegregation and segregation to racial differences in student achievement. From 1971 to 2002, the Charlotte-Mecklenburg community grappled with the mandate of *Swann v. Charlotte-Mecklenburg* (1971) to provide equality of educational opportunities to all children. CMS employed mandatory busing (from roughly 1969 through 2002) or controlled choice among magnet schools (from 1992 to 2002) to achieve a racial balance among students in every school—approximately 40 percent black and 60 percent white (and other students).[2] Under this system, almost all students were bused to schools outside their neighborhoods for at least some part of their educational careers. As a result, the majority of students in CMS from 1969 through 2002 attended a racially desegregated school at some stage in their education.[3]

The legal foundation for desegregation in CMS collapsed in the spring of 2002, when the U.S. Supreme Court declined to review a decision of the U.S. Court of Appeals for the Fourth Circuit that CMS had fully met its obligations imposed under *Swann*, had overcome its racially dual past and become a single "unitary" school system, and could therefore be released from further judicial supervision. Even before the U.S. Supreme Court denied the plaintiffs' petition for review,[4] CMS designed a new pupil-assignment plan, built around neighborhood schools, for the 2002–3 school year.[5] Two years into the new plan's operation, CMS is resegregating at a quickening pace.

These are difficult times for those in Charlotte and across the nation who believe that compelling reasons still exist to require public schools to pursue racial and ethnic integration. Not only are the federal courts declaring other segregated school districts to be unitary,[6] but the interracial coalitions of progressive citizens and their allies among corporate and civic elites that once supported desegregation also appear to be disintegrating.[7] In the face of claims that desegregation does little to improve minority students' educational outcomes yet inflicts heavy burdens on the children and communities it is intended to serve,[8] growing numbers of African Americans now embrace neighborhood schools or vouchers as attractive alternatives that may provide greater educational opportunity to black students than desegregated schools offer.[9]

Most overt educational discrimination—de jure separate schools for blacks and whites, racist curricula and teachers—has been eliminated.[10] Nevertheless, discrimination in education survives, and the most harmful manifestation of it today is arguably de facto segregation.[11] When it occurs at the school level, it is considered first-generation segregation. Classroom-level segregation, known as second-generation segregation, takes the form of ability grouping or tracking. Most American schools organize secondary school instruction by tracks.[12] Blacks, Latinos, and Native Americans disproportionately are found in lower tracks, where curricula and instructional practices are weaker.[13] Not only are blacks and other ethnic minorities (other than Asians) more likely than whites to be assigned to lower tracks, but research indicates that blacks and whites with similar ability often learn in different tracks, especially in racially desegregated school systems[14] or systems where blacks are a numerical minority.[15] The relative absence of black students in higher-level courses and their disproportionate enrollment in lower-level ones is an underemphasized component of the race gap in achievement.[16]

In this chapter, I report findings from a fifteen-year-long investigation of desegregation, segregation, and academic achievement in CMS. I provide empirical data that show that students—both blacks and whites—gain academically from learning in desegregated schools and classrooms. The inverse is also true—all students suffer academically in segregated learning environments. I demonstrate that although CMS achieved renown for its efforts to implement court-ordered desegregation from roughly 1971 to 2002, many of the district's practices and policies actually worked to subvert the *Swann* decision's mandate to provide all students with equitable opportunities to learn. Most notable among these practices were student-assignment policies that allowed growing resegregation beginning in the mid-1980s and the practice of tracking academic courses in secondary schools. Even in the desegregated schools, students' core academic courses in math, science, social studies, and English were commonly organized in ways that tended to enroll blacks into the lower-level courses and whites into the higher, college-preparatory ones. In this way, resegregation by tracking within schools undermined the potential benefits of school-level desegregation. I show how Charlotte's new, post-unitary-status Family Choice pupil-assignment plan, based on neighborhood schools, has accelerated this trend toward school-level resegregation. Finally, I offer preliminary achievement outcomes showing how black and white low-income students in schools with concentrated poverty score lower on standardized tests than do low-income students in middle-class schools. I conclude by considering the implications of the CMS case for the prospects for equality of educational opportunity in the present era.

How the CMS Research Study Was Conducted

The CMS system offers a unique opportunity to explore the relationships among desegregation, segregation at the school and classroom levels, and academic achievement. CMS operated under the *Swann* mandate to desegregate until 2002, by which time the majority of its students had attended desegregated schools for most of their educational careers. Due to the creeping resegregation of the district since the mid-1980s, increasing numbers of students also have experience with racially imbalanced black and white schools. Secondary schools—even those that are racially balanced—are highly tracked. Because tracking is racially correlated, widespread tracking translates into systematic resegregation by classroom within schools.

Sample

In the spring of 1997, my team of researchers collected survey data from every middle school and high school in CMS.[17] Working with a complete list of eighth-grade language arts and twelfth-grade English classes offered by CMS during the spring 1997 semester, we randomly selected a 50 percent sample of classes from every school. We used a table of random numbers to select at least one language arts and English class from every track level at each school. For example, if a particular high school's twelfth-grade English offerings included two advanced placement (AP), two academically gifted (AG), two advanced, and four regular classes, our randomly selected sample of classes from that school included one AP, one AG, one advanced, and two regular English classes. On average, 90 percent of the students enrolled in the selected classes completed the survey.

Of the 1,833 CMS high school students who completed surveys, 611 (33.3 percent) were black, 1,119 (61.1 percent) were white, and 103 (5.6 percent) were Asian, Hispanic, or Native American. A total of 2,730 middle school students completed the survey: 1,014 (37.1 percent) were black; 1,538 (56.3 percent) were white; and

178 (6.5 percent) were Asian, Hispanic, or Native American. Because of the small number of Hispanic, Asian, and Native American respondents, I analyzed only data from black and white students.[18] Since 1997, I have continued to collect CMS documents and aggregate school system data available from the district's Web site or from the North Carolina Department of Public Instruction.

I supplement the survey and aggregate school system data with in-depth interviews with educators, parents, and civic leaders. I also use CMS documents and reports and expert witness reports from the 1999 desegregation trial.[19] Finally, I use a set of phone interviews with CMS secondary principals, senior administrators, and several current and former school board members conducted from December 1998 through May 1999. These interviews were designed to elicit information about the formal and informal policies and practices associated with race, desegregation, and the allocation of students to specific courses in CMS schools.[20]

Survey Data

The middle school and high school surveys were almost identical. The primary difference is that the high school version included questions about respondents' school-to-work educational experiences. The survey instruments ascertained students' demographic characteristics (age, race, gender), their family background (mother's and father's educational and occupational attainment), attitudes toward education and the future, educational and occupational aspirations, work and leisure activities, and self-reported effort. CMS also provided multiple measures of achievement and the history of prior schools attended by each student. CMS records provided indicators of school-level variables such as the proportion of teachers with full licensure and with advanced degrees.

Analyses

The analyses of the survey data proceeded in several steps. First, because students attended different schools, I explored the possible relationship between students' outcomes and the characteristics of schools that they attended. I used multilevel modeling to estimate individual students' achievement as a function both of school-level factors and of characteristics of the students themselves.[21] I separately analyzed the middle school and high school samples. Second, I examined the racial compositions of English, social studies, math, and science classes by track in CMS middle and high schools. This procedure permitted me to assess whether resegregation by track within schools was taking place.

Third, I used CMS data on enrollment by student race and free/reduced-price lunch status for each school to examine and compare schools' demographics before and after the implementation of the neighborhood-schools-based Family Choice Plan. I examined fall 2001 (prior to unitary status) student demographics by school and compared them to those of the 2002 (after unitary status) and 2003 school years. The comparison enabled me to determine whether, after the first two years of post-unitary-status operation, the racial balance of CMS schools had changed, and if so, in what directions. Together, the survey data and the longitudinal enrollment data by race enable me to examine the academic consequences for CMS students of the court's withdrawal from *Swann*.

Findings

Effects of School Racial Composition on Achievement

Effects of Segregation

The results of the data analyses indicate that students who learned in segregated schools had lower scores on North Carolina standardized tests than their predicted scores if they had attended integrated schools.[22] While the findings confirm that many factors most people expect to affect achievement in fact do so—positive effects come from higher socioeconomic status; access to private art, music, or dance lessons (experiences that some social scientists refer to as cultural capital); academically oriented peer groups; positive attitudes toward education; and greater effort—the results also show that attending segregated schools negatively affects students' achievement.

Table 4.1 presents the results of the statistical analyses for 1997 CMS students' North Carolina middle school end-of-grade (EOG) and North Carolina high school end-of-course (EOC) standardized test scores. Reading top left to right, the first column identifies the student, family, and school racial composition factors I investigated. The middle column gives results for middle school students, and the column on the right gives results for high school students.[23] The middle school results show that effort, prior achievement, positive educational attitudes, being female, and being white are associated with higher test scores. Receiving private art, music, or dance lessons and higher family socioeconomic status also positively affect test scores. Higher tracks (which are disproportionately white) have a positive effect on EOG reading scores, while attending segregated minority middle and elementary schools negatively affects test scores.

The high school results indicate that effort, family socioeconomic status, and private art lessons do not significantly affect EOC test scores, but prior achieve-

Table 4.1. Influence of Various Factors on Charlotte-Mecklenburg Middle and High School Students' Standardized Test Scores, 1996–1997

Factor	Middle School ß	High School ß
Student Factors		
Race (African American)	−2.347***	−5.331**
Gender (female)	.778**	−9.780***
More effort	.716***	2.053
Higher prior achievement	.104***	.428**
Positive concrete attitudes	.937***	3.253*
Abstract attitudes	.105	−2.258
Academic-oriented peer group	—	31.881**
Family Factors		
Family background (higher SES)	.722***	.760
Private art lessons (yes)	.553*	2.342
School Factors		
Greater % segregated elementary education	−.018**	−.167**
Higher % middle school black students	−.054**	—
College track (yes)	2.638***	11.682**
More gifted students in school	—	−.282
School is a magnet (yes)	.632	2.576
N of students	1,748	1,313
N of schools	24	11

Note: "—" indicates that variable is not in model.

* $p < .05$, indicating a 1 in 5 chance of a false positive finding of statistical significance.
** $p < .01$, indicating a 1 in 100 chance of a false positive finding of statistical significance.
*** $p < .001$, indicating a 1 in 1,000 chance of a false positive finding of statistical significance.

ment, positive educational attitudes, being in a college-bound track, and having academically oriented peers all positively influence scores. Holding other factors constant, male and white students achieve higher test scores than female or black students.[24] However, there are no significant influences on test scores from magnet school attendance, the percentage of gifted students in the respondent's school, or abstract educational attitudes.

After holding constant (controlling for) the numerous individual and family background factors discussed previously, the statistical analyses indicate that the more time that students—both black and white—spend in segregated black elementary schools, the lower are their grade 8 EOG reading scores and grade 12 EOC scores.[25] Holding constant (controlling for) the same individual and family background factors, the larger the percentage of black students in a middle school, the lower are all its students' EOG reading scores.

Effects of Desegregation

The results of the regression analysis also indicate that the more time both black and white students spend in desegregated elementary schools, the higher their standardized test scores in middle and high school and the higher their track placements in secondary school.[26] Because track placement contributes substantially to achievement—over and above students' family background, effort, and other individual characteristics—the fact that students who had more of their elementary education in desegregated schools tend to have higher track placements is an important academic outcome of desegregation.

Effects of Racial Composition of Classrooms on Achievement

Because ability grouping and identification for gifted or special education begin early in students' educational careers,[27] grouping and labeling practices contribute to secondary school track placement. Since I concentrate on secondary students in this chapter, I will discuss only briefly the roots of tracking in elementary school ability grouping practices. During early elementary school, disproportionate numbers of black students, especially males relative to their numbers in the overall student population, are placed in special education, and disproportionate numbers of whites are identified for gifted education. To illustrate this pattern in the early sorting of students, I refer to findings from two studies.

Mindy Kornhaber's research on the identification process for gifted and talented education in CMS reveals how certification as AG is an early source of racially correlated tracking in the district.[28] Kornhaber reported that throughout the early 1990s, African Americans in CMS were markedly underreferred for AG assessments; consequently, programs for the gifted became and remain largely the domain of white students. According to one CMS central office educator Kornhaber interviewed, gifted education has been used widely as a white track, and the CMS gifted program has been an "elitist, isolated, white-only program" that has only recently begun to change.[29] Kornhaber described how formal AG identification is a high-stakes process that some parents pursue and cultivate. She quoted one high-level staff member who observed, "Parents want elementary school identification as gifted because it allows entrance into middle school gifted classes."[30] Savvy parents know that AG identification in elementary school launches the children onto a trajectory of high-track secondary school courses.

The second illustration comes from Tamela Eitle's examination of the relationship between special education placement rates among black students and the desegregation status of different school districts.[31] Using a nationally representative data set, she found that in districts under court-ordered desegregation rulings, the proportions of blacks in special education are significantly higher than in otherwise comparable districts. Eitle suggests that higher rates of second-generation segregation through special education placements of black students during elementary school may constitute a response to desegregation orders.

The patterns of racially correlated sorting of elementary students into special education and gifted programs as described by Eitle and by Kornhaber suggest some of the covert processes countering desegregation efforts in districts under court mandates to end segregation, such as CMS. In virtually all CMS secondary schools, core academic classes are tracked. All secondary school tracks are far more racially homogeneous at the low and high ends of the continuum than are the schools themselves. This conclusion arises from my analysis of a CMS document that identifies the course name, track level, and student count by race, period, and teacher's name for every course offered in the system's eleven high schools and twenty-four middle schools.[32]

This pattern of resegregation by track within secondary schools is illustrated in table 4.2 with 1997 data from schools emblematic of racially isolated black, racially balanced, and racially isolated white schools during a time when CMS was lauded as a successfully desegregated school system. The table shows the percentage black in a given school and in classes by subject and track level. Cochrane Middle School, for example, is 78 percent black—a racially isolated black school—but its AG math classes enroll no black students. Its special education children's math class is 86.3 percent black. The track is, nonetheless, racially balanced because 86.3 percent is just barely within the ±15 percent range (an increase in 1 percent of black students in special education would tip the track into the racially imbalanced category). South Charlotte Middle School, with 11 percent black students, is a segregated white school. Although its regular and exceptional children's mathematics classes average more black students than the school as a whole and the gifted classes have fewer, all math classes are racially balanced because they fall within the ±15 percent range around the school's population of 11 percent black students. Carmel, a desegregated middle school, displays a pattern that is common throughout CMS secondary schools. The top track has almost no black students, while blacks are strikingly overrepresented in the lowest track (special education). Only the regular math class is desegregated

Table 4.2. Typical Racial Composition of Charlotte-Mecklenburg Middle School Mathematics and High School Biology Classes by Track and School, 1996–1997

	Percentage of Blacks in			
School	School	College Prep Class[a]	Regular Class	Special Education Class
Middle School Mathematics				
South Charlotte	11.0	3.0	20.6	13.2
Carmel	35.3	1.5	23.5	69.0
Cochrane	78.0	0.0	78.1	86.3
High School Biology				
North Mecklenburg	21.6	0.0	36.2	37.4
Myers Park	35.1	1.9	76.0	100.0
Garinger	63.2	0.0	74.8	80.0

[a] Eighth-grade academically gifted mathematics and high school biology advanced placement.

Source: Mickelson, expert report, Exhibits 1A–H; CMS, *Class Counts*, 1996–97.

and then just barely: if the percentage of blacks enrolled in regular math fell by 3 points, that track, too, would be racially imbalanced.

Table 4.2 shows a similar pattern among high school biology classes. Schools' top-track classes are almost always disproportionately white, irrespective of the schools' racial composition; special education courses are almost always disproportionately black; and only regular classes are racially balanced. Because track placement powerfully influences academic outcomes, the existence of racially correlated tracks in a desegregating school system seriously reduces the potential that school-level desegregation policies can improve black students' achievement.

One might argue that track placements merely reflect objective decisions to enroll students in classes in keeping with their merit and that any correlations with race are coincidental or result from racial differences in social class or in ability. To test this argument, I analyzed track assignments by student race in middle and high schools, holding constant students' prior achievement during their elementary school years. I divided students into deciles based on eighth-grade students' scores on their second-grade California Achievement Test (CAT) and twelfth-grade students' scores on their eighth-grade CAT. I then compared track placements for blacks and whites within each decile range. If race were not

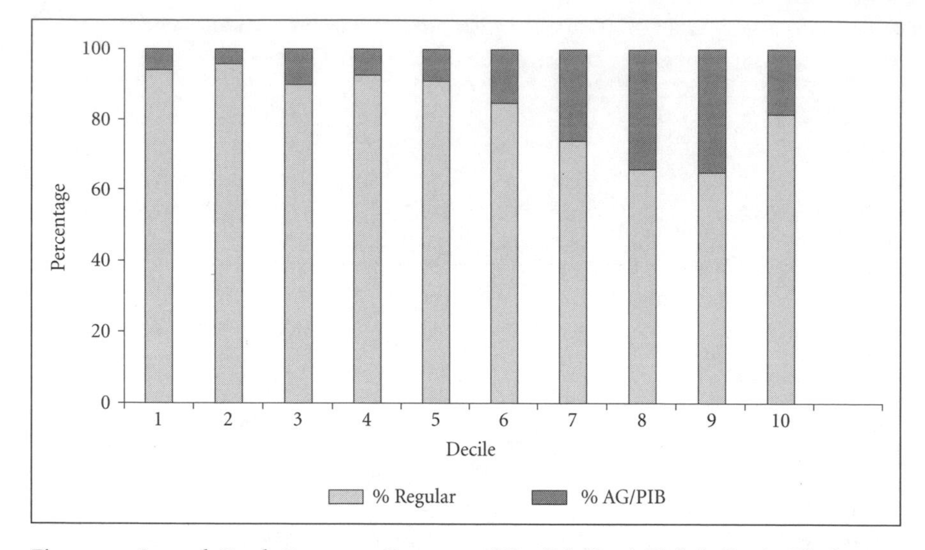

Figure 4.1. Second-Grade Language Battery and English Track Eighth Grade: Black Students

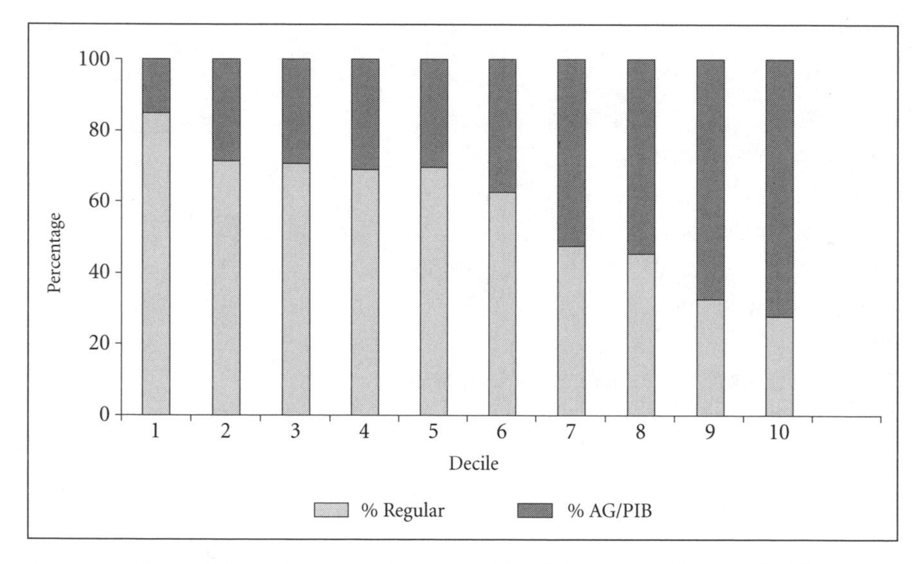

Figure 4.2. Second-Grade Language Battery and English Track Eighth Grade: White Students

a factor in track placements, within each decile range the proportions of blacks and whites in each track would be similar.

The analyses show that students' track assignments were related to their race. The pattern among the most academically able students (those with scores in the highest decile) reflects the overall tendencies found throughout the other decile ranges: irrespective of their prior achievement, blacks are more likely than their comparably able white peers to be in lower tracks. Figure 4.1 presents the percent of black grade 8 students in different language arts tracks controlling for their achievement when they were in second grade. Figure 4.2 presents the same for white grade 8 students. The dark area indicates the top track. Moving left to right, when we compare the increase in percent of students by decile in the top track in figures 4.1 and 4.2, we find distinctly different placement patterns for blacks and whites, with whites more likely than blacks with similar CAT scores to be in the top tracks. For example, among grade 8 students in the top decile (ninetieth to ninety-ninth percentile), only 27.6 percent of whites but 81.3 percent of blacks were enrolled in regular English classes, while 72.3 percent of whites but only 18.7 percent of blacks were assigned to the top English track (AG or pre–International Baccalaureate).

Figure 4.3 presents the percentages of black grade 12 students in various English tracks, controlling for their prior achievement. Figure 4.4 presents the same for white grade 12 students. In these figures, the gray area represents the top track. Moving left to right across the deciles as we compare the top tracks in figures 4.3 and 4.4, we again find distinctly different placement patterns for blacks and whites: whites are more likely than blacks to be in the top tracks, although the differences are not as stark among seniors as they are for grade 8 students. For example, among twelfth-grade students whose grade 6 CAT scores were in the top decile (ninetieth to ninety-ninth percentile), 20 percent of blacks but 53 percent of whites were enrolled in the AP/International Baccalaureate English track. These comparisons are among comparably able students.

These findings using 1997 data indicate that prior achievement alone does not explain the pattern of racially correlated access to top (or bottom) tracks. Four years later, racially correlated patterns of track assignment continued. In the fall of 2001, several thousand CMS middle school students, a majority of whom were black, were placed into lower-level mathematics classes even though all had passed or excelled on their previous year's EOG math tests. The superintendent ordered the misplaced students to be moved into higher-level, reconstituted math classes.

How did this happen? Although parents and students participate in course placement decisions, in fact, families typically rely on the advice of educators, who

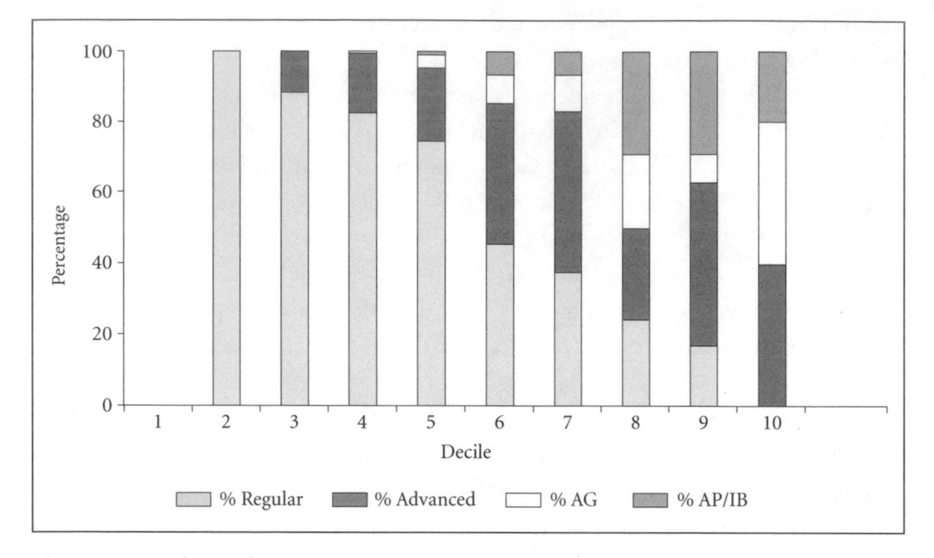

Figure 4.3. Sixth-Grade Language Battery and English Track Twelfth Grade: Black Students

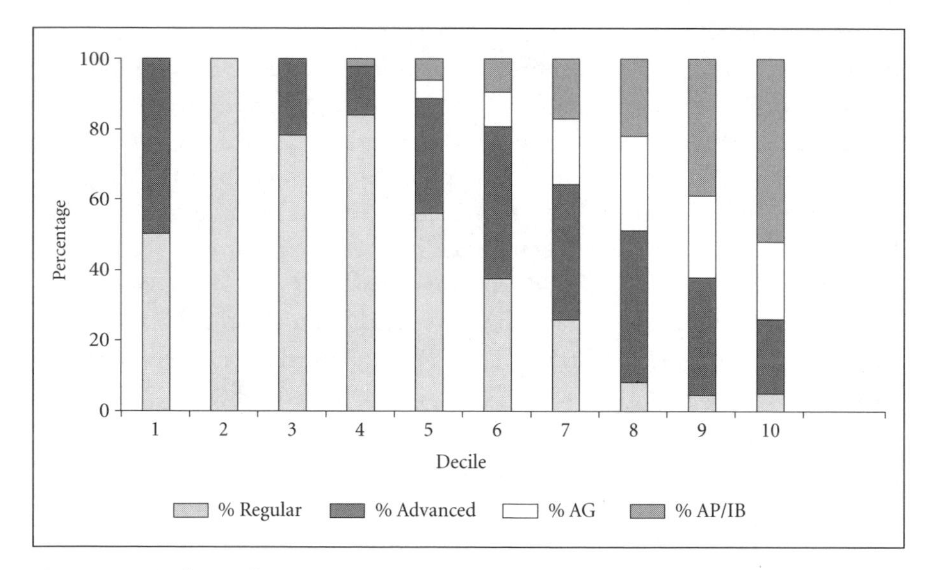

Figure 4.4. Sixth-Grade Language Battery and English Track Twelfth Grade: White Students

often powerfully shape students' educational career trajectories. The superintendent explained that a number of decisions led to the misplacement of so many blacks into lower-level math courses, including racial stereotyping: "I think people need to face that there are issues of bias and prejudice that play into this."[33]

Family Choice, Neighborhood Schools, and Resegregation in Postunitary CMS

School-level segregation in CMS was never eliminated entirely, but during the early 1980s the district came very close to fulfilling the court's order to eliminate the dual system.[34] At that time, only a handful of schools were racially identifiable as minority or white. By the late 1980s, despite a mere 1 percent increase in the proportion of CMS students who were black (from 38 to 39 percent), the percentage of racially identifiable schools began to grow. In the 1998–99 school year, despite an increase of only 2 percent during the previous ten years in the proportion of CMS students who were black (from 39 to 41 percent), nearly one-fourth of all CMS schools had become racially identifiable black or white at the building level.[35] By 1999, even though Charlotte-Mecklenburg remained a majority white community and Mecklenburg County as a whole was more residentially integrated than it had been thirty years earlier,[36] CMS was resegregating at the school level.[37]

The trend toward resegregation began to accelerate with the implementation of CMS's Family Choice Plan in the fall of 2002.[38] As designed, the plan's key features include (1) maximum stability of school assignments over a student's educational career; (2) a guaranteed school assignment near the family's home if parents so choose; (3) guaranteed options to choose enrollment in high-performing schools for poorly performing or low-income students in schools with concentrations of other poorly-performing or low-income students (as long as seats are available in the high-performing schools);[39] (4) magnet school choices offering a variety of themes; and (5) maximum utilization of all school seat capacities. In another resolution, adopted in July 2001, the board pledged to ensure equity across all schools.[40]

Using CMS enrollment data, I examined the shifting racial composition of CMS schools between the 2001–2 (before unitary status) and 2003–4 (two years after unitary status) school years. Table 4.3 presents the changing demographics of the Charlotte-Mecklenburg school district in the first and second years of post-unitary status. In the 2003–4 school year, 22.6 percent fewer elementary schools, 7.4 percent fewer middle schools, and 20.6 percent fewer high schools were racially balanced than in 2001–2. In fact, 9 percent more elementary schools, 3 percent more middle schools, and 16.6 percent more high schools became racially

Table 4.3. Changes in Charlotte-Mecklenburg Schools' Racial Demographics by School Level, 2001–2002 (prior to Unitary Status) through 2003–2004 (Two Years Postunitary Status)

	Percentage Change from 2001–2 through 2003–4		
Racial Demographics	Elementary	Middle[a]	High
Racially balanced	−22.6	−7.4	−20.6
Racially identifiable black	+9.0	+3.0	+16.6
Racially identifiable white	+11.6	+4.5	+4.0

[a] Based on ±15% CMS black population for each year.

Sources: CMS, *Class Counts*, May 2002; CMS, Monthly Membership at End of Month One, 17 September 2002, 18 September 2003.

identifiable as black, while 11.6 percent more elementary schools, 4.5 percent more middle schools, and 4 percent more high schools became racially identifiable as white.[41]

The new CMS pupil-assignment plan generates and sanctions the concentration of low-income students in predominantly minority schools. Figure 4.5 shows the intersection of race and social class in the eighty CMS elementary schools. The figure is based on the results of parents' school selections for the 2003–4 academic year, the second year of the choice plan. Reading left to right, the figure shows that schools with the highest percentage of white students were also those with the lowest percentage of students on free or subsidized lunches. Although the association between concentrations of minority students and concentrations of low-income students is well known,[42] figure 4.5 portrays this association in CMS. When the resegregation data in table 4.3 are juxtaposed with the race/poverty concentration data in figure 4.5, we can see how current CMS pupil-assignment policies structure potential inequities in opportunities to learn.

The initial implementation of the new Family Choice Plan led to significant imbalances in the utilization of schools' seating capacities.[43] Under- and overutilization patterns were related to the schools' racial composition. In the 2002–3 academic year, thirty-eight of the thirty-nine underutilized schools were racially imbalanced minority schools. (Because of the growing number of Hispanic students in CMS, I calculated imbalance summing black and Hispanic students into one "minority" category.) Of the thirty-three overutilized schools, thirteen were racially balanced, fourteen were racially identifiable white, and only six (three elementary and three high schools) were racially identifiable minority.

With two exceptions, underutilized schools also underperformed on North Carolina's statewide standardized tests. CMS designates a school as an Equity Plus

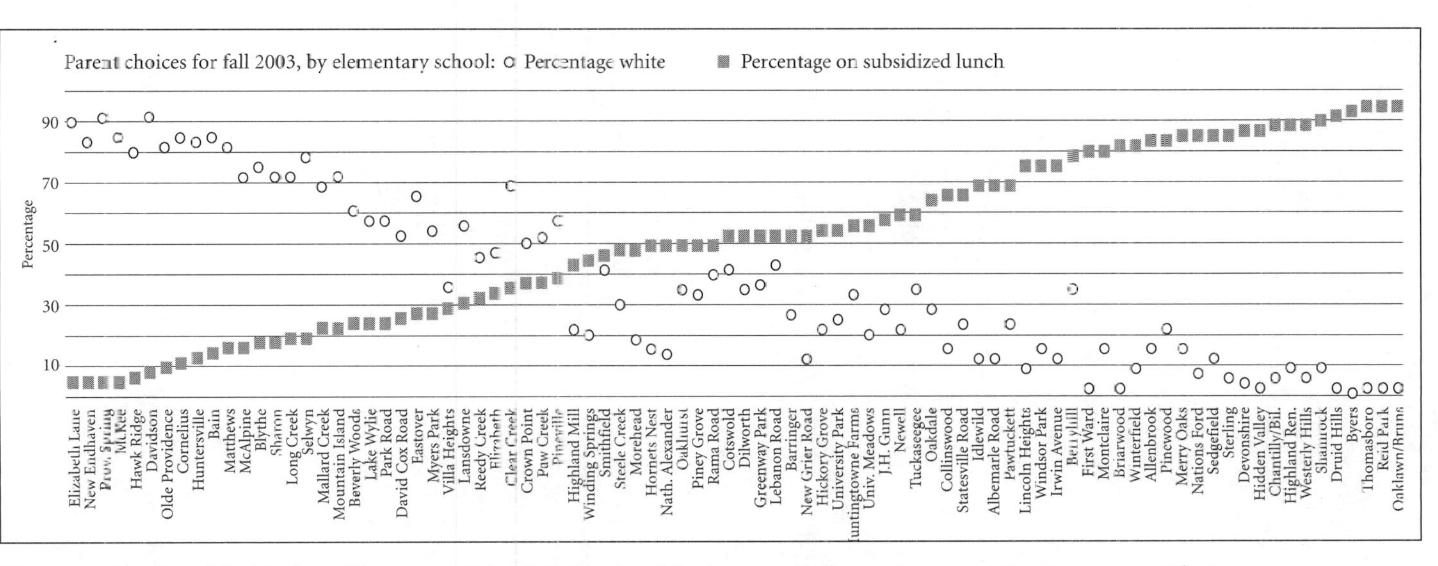

Figure 4.5. Charlotte-Mecklenburg Elementary Schools by Race and Socioeconomic Status Concentration, 2003–2004 Choices

II school if it has high concentrations of low-performing and poor students and proportionately fewer qualified teachers (based on their licensure and experience). Equity Plus II status means that the school receives additional resources, including smaller classes and teacher bonuses.[44] At every level, underutilized schools that were also Equity Plus II schools were racially isolated minority schools. Conversely, none of the overutilized schools, irrespective of their racial composition, had Equity Plus II status.

Several likely reasons exist for the relationship between underutilized schools and Equity Plus II status. One is that class size is smaller by design in Equity Plus II schools. Another reason is that parents tended not to choose low-performing neighborhood schools.[45] The apparent relationships among underutilization of seat capacity, Equity Plus II status (a measure of low school quality), and high concentrations of low-income and minority students in the schools will require further study before tentative conclusions about the association of these forces can be reasonably drawn. Nevertheless, the concentration of low-income students in underutilized, low-performing schools does not bode well for those students' chances of receiving a high-quality education.

Individual-level longitudinal data are necessary for assessing the academic consequences of resegregation by race and social class. Such data are not yet available as of this writing. However, school-level data, disaggregated by student race and free/reduced-lunch status, are available for the 2002–3 school year, the first year of implementation of the neighborhood school-based choice plan. Table 4.4 presents the percentage of students in each school who passed their standardized tests, displayed by students' race and poverty status, according to degree of concentrated poverty in the particular school students attend.[46] For example, only 64 percent of elementary school students in high-poverty schools (a school with 80 percent or more students qualifying for free or reduced-price lunch) passed their North Carolina year-end standardized tests, compared to 95 percent of students in low-poverty schools (20 percent or fewer free/reduced-lunch students). In low-poverty elementary schools, 77 percent of black students passed, compared to 62 percent in high-poverty schools. At the high school level, 34 percent of all students attending high-poverty schools passed their North Carolina standardized tests, compared to 75 percent in low-poverty schools. In low-poverty high schools, 44 percent of black students passed, compared to 31 percent in high-poverty schools. Although far from definitive, these initial findings from CMS's return to neighborhood schools—especially the growing nexus of race, poverty, and low performance—suggest some of the ways that segregation contributes to the persistence of the race gap in academic outcomes.

Table 4.4. Percentage Passing North Carolina Statewide Tests by School Poverty Level, Student Poverty, and Student Race, 2002–2003 (Year 1 Unitary Status)

	% Passing by School Poverty Level		
Student Group	High	Moderate	Low
Elementary Schools			
All students	62	77	91
Low income	60	65	69
Not low income	77	89	94
Black	60	70	74
White	76	90	94
Middle Schools			
All students	54	70	88
Low income	50	55	64
Not low income	69	84	93
Black	60	70	74
White	71	88	93
High Schools			
All students	23	46	71
Low income	21	27	34
Not low income	27	56	76
Black	22	36	39
White	62	70	82

Note: Elementary and middle school poverty formula: 75% High; 74–26% Moderate; 25% Low; high school poverty formula: 55% High; 54–26% Moderate; 25% Low.

Sources: NC DPI End-of-Grade Test Results 2002–3, 2003–4; NC DPI End-of-Course Test Results 2002–3, 2003–4.

Conclusion

Desegregated schooling benefits the academic outcomes of students who experience it, and segregated schools and classrooms harm those who learn in them. Using 1997 survey data and aggregate school system data from CMS, I examined the academic consequences of attending segregated and desegregated schools. My findings indicate that

- Racially segregated schools and racially segregated tracks still exist in CMS a generation after the Supreme Court's order to desegregate the school system, and both forms of segregation harm students' academic achievement.[47]

- The greater the number of elementary school years that a student spends in a desegregated elementary school, the higher a student's scores on standardized tests and the higher the track placement in secondary school.
- The greater the number of elementary school years that a student spends in a racially isolated black elementary school, the lower the student's later scores on standardized tests are and the lower the track placement in secondary school will be.
- Track placement is influenced not only by prior experience with segregated elementary education but also by a student's race: black CMS students are more likely to be found in lower tracks than white students with comparable prior achievement, family backgrounds, and other individual characteristics.
- Irrespective of race and socioeconomic background, CMS students who attend schools with lower concentrations of poor students perform better on average on North Carolina standardized tests than do students in schools with higher concentrations of poor students.
- Since CMS was declared unitary and implemented a neighborhood school-based choice pupil-assignment plan in 2002, resegregation by race and social class has intensified. Thus, CMS in the 2003–4 school year had a higher percentage of schools marked by concentrations of poor, low-performing, and minority students than it had prior to being declared unitary.

Despite significant narrowing over the past quarter century, the black-white gap in achievement that existed in 1954 continues today. The findings from the Charlotte case study suggest some of the important reasons for the race gap's persistence. For example, in Charlotte, covert resegregation processes worked to re-create white privilege in the school system even as it desegregated. Elsewhere, Stephen S. Smith and I contend that, insofar as racially identifiable grouping and tracking can be considered second-generation segregation, one can plausibly argue that the establishment and maintenance of second-generation segregation in CMS was a political precondition of using busing to dismantle school-level first-generation segregation.[48]

Future analyses will need to examine the extent and effects of tracking under the new neighborhood-based assignment plan. If extensive tracking is a response to school-level desegregation efforts, ironically, we may find that while the new neighborhood-based assignment plan leads to greater resegregation among schools, the political and social forces that stimulate racially correlated tracking will be weaker. Under such circumstances, we may find that in-school resegregation by track is reduced, an academic sliver of sunlight on resegregation's otherwise cloudy horizon.

In many ways, CMS's history offers us a strategic case study on the relationship of desegregation and segregation to racial equality in educational processes and outcomes. My findings suggest why so many desegregation programs seem to offer minority students such limited redress for historical inequalities in educational opportunities. Following the withdrawal of *Swann*'s legal imprimatur for desegregation, Charlotte, once an icon of successful desegregation, may soon become a district emblematic of postunitary resegregation. The larger lesson from CMS's rapid resegregation and the growing concentration of low-performing and poor children in racially isolated minority schools reminds us of a bitter historical truth: Jim Crow education is America's most spectacularly failed social experiment. Segregated schooling will not—cannot—offer equality of educational opportunities to our children.

Notes

1. Lino Graglia, for example, referred to desegregation in this manner in his debate with fellow law professor john a. powell on National Public Radio's *Justice Talking.*

2. Gaillard, *Dream Long Deferred*; S. Smith, *Boom for Whom?*

3. Mickelson, "Subverting *Swann*," 217.

4. See *Belk v. Charlotte-Mecklenburg Board of Education*, 152.

5. Charlotte-Mecklenburg Schools, "Board Resolution 2001"; Charlotte-Mecklenburg Schools, "Board Resolution 2002–2003."

6. See *Board of Education of Oklahoma City Public Schools v. Dowell*; *Freeman v. Pitts*; Chambers, "Judge in KY." There is considerable variation in both the social science and legal literature in the usage of terms used to describe the racial composition of districts and schools. See G. Orfield and Eaton, *Dismantling Desegregation.*

7. Mickelson and Ray, "Fear of Falling"; Welner, *Legal Rights.*

8. Armor, *Forced Justice*; Armor, Rossell, and Walberg, "Outlook for School Desegregation"; Cook, *School Desegregation and Black Achievement*; Morris and Morris, *Price They Paid*; Shujaa, *Beyond Desegregation.*

9. Breed, "One-Race Schools"; Chambers, "Judge in KY"; Flake, "Drowning"; Fuller, "Continuing Struggle."

10. Gamoran, "American Schooling"; Armor, Rossell, and Walberg, "Outlook for School Desegregation."

11. In 1966, the Coleman Report (Coleman et al., *Equality of Educational Opportunity*) demonstrated that blacks attending desegregated schools achieved more than their counterparts in segregated schools. Recent empirical research offers further evidence of the harm segregation causes, not only to minorities but to whites as well. See Bankston and Caldas, "Majority African American Schools"; S. Brown, "High School Racial Composition"; Kelly, "Black-White Gap"; Grissmer et al., *Student Achievement*; Mickelson, "Subverting *Swann*"; Mickelson, "How Middle School Segregation Contributes." In their independent reviews of the empirical literature on diversity effects on learning, Hawley, "Diversity and Educational

Quality," and Hallinan, "Diversity Effects," conclude that students who learn in schools that have students from different races and ethnicities are likely to gain an education superior to that of students who lack this opportunity.

12. Research on the effects of tracking is extensive and, with few exceptions (see Kulik and Kulik, "Effects of Ability Grouping on Secondary School Students"; Kulik and Kulik, "Effects of Ability Grouping on Student Achievement"), suggests the harmful effects of the practice. See Kornhaber, "Seeking Strengths"; Lucas, *Tracking Inequality*; Lucas and Berends, "Sociodemographic Diversity"; Oakes, *Keeping Track*; Oakes, Muir, and Joseph, "Course Taking"; Wheelock, *Crossing the Tracks.*

13. Hallinan, "Diversity Effects"; Kelly, "Black-White Gap"; Lucas, *Tracking Inequality*; Lucas and Berends, "Sociodemographic Diversity"; Mickelson, "Subverting *Swann*"; Oakes, *Keeping Track*; Oakes, Muir, and Joseph, "Course Taking"; Welner, *Legal Rights.*

14. Eitle, "Special Education or Racial Segregation."

15. Kelly, "Black-White Gap."

16. Even some of the harshest critics of race-sensitive remedies to educational inequality acknowledge the existence of racially correlated tracking and its contribution to the race gap in educational outcomes. See Armor, Rossell, and Walberg, "Outlook for School Desegregation."

17. The design of this research is unique and is an improvement over most previous studies of desegregation. Unlike most prior desegregation research, I look at the effects of individual and school characteristics on students' achievement using a technique called multilevel regression analysis. In addition, my study employs a longitudinal measure of each student's exposure to elementary school segregation and measures of academic track placement in middle and high school. Most prior desegregation research fails to use multilevel regression analysis or to examine simultaneously school- and classroom-level segregation. Finally, no previous study has had a longitudinal measure of the effects of elementary school segregation on secondary school achievement.

The research design also offers a clear advantage over studies employing national samples. Nationally representative data sets often have only a handful of students from a single school in selected districts. By focusing on a single district, this study considers CMS middle and high schools (their processes and practices) and their students (the distribution of demographic characteristics and achievement outcomes across the schools) in their interdependent social, educational, and political contexts. This kind of holistic contextual analysis is impossible with nationally representative samples. In this way I detect districtwide trends and patterns that are missed in the large national samples typically used in desegregation research. Greater details of the methods, data, and analyses are available by request.

18. I did not collect survey data from students in special educational English classes. The disproportionate number of black students in special education classes and special programs causes the proportion of black students in the non-special-education classes to be less than the district's 1997 overall percentage black. The samples therefore are biased toward *underestimating* the effects of segregated schooling on black children's achievement.

19. *Capacchione et al. v. Charlotte-Mecklenburg Schools.*

20. Mickelson, expert report.

21. Kreft and de Leeuw, *Introducing Multilevel Modeling*; Rabe-Hesketh and Everitt, *Handbook*.

22. For purposes of this study, to ascertain if a school is racially segregated, I follow the standards used by the CMS Board of Education while it operated under the *Swann* orders. I use a ± 15 percent bandwidth around the district's percentage of black students. Any school with a student population less than 15 percent black I consider to be racially isolated. For my analyses of within-school segregation of secondary school academic courses, I again draw on the ± 15 percent bandwidth standard and consider a classroom to be racially isolated black if the black proportion of students in it exceeds the school's proportion of black students by 15 percentage points; I consider a classroom to be racially isolated white if the black proportion of the population is more than 15 percentage points below the school's overall percentage of black students, and I consider all other classrooms to be racially balanced. At the time that I conducted this research, very few secondary students were neither black nor white.

23. The numbers with asterisks indicate the factors my research found significantly affected test scores; numbers with multiple asterisks are more highly significant.

24. Female high school students tend to earn higher grades and attain more education than males, but male students tend to earn higher scores on standardized tests like the EOC and SAT (see Mickelson, "Why Does Jane Read?").

25. One of the unique aspects of this study derives from the fact that because CMS was a majority white school system until roughly 2002, black *and* white students in my sample experienced both desegregated and segregated schooling. When the students in the sample attended CMS elementary schools in the early 1980s, the district was about two-thirds white. Thus, even the racially isolated minority elementary schools often had many white students (up to 45 percent white).

26. This chapter's report of the positive effects of desegregation on academic achievement is certainly not the first time researchers have found this association. Beginning with James Coleman et al.'s pathbreaking *Equality of Educational Opportunity* and continuing through a host of more recent studies, the positive relationship between desegregation and achievement has been well established. Readers interested in this topic may wish to consult S. Brown's examination of the relationship using a national data set ("High School Racial Composition"), and Borman, "Half Century," which reports research using data from the state of Florida. See also Hallinan, "Diversity Effects"; Hawley, "Diversity"; Braddock and Eitle, "Effects of School Desegregation," for synthetic reviews of empirical research. For a different perspective, see Armor, Rossell, and Walberg, "Outlook for School Desegregation."

27. Entwistle, Alexander, and Olsen, *Children, Schools, and Inequality*; Kornhaber, "Seeking Strengths."

28. Kornhaber, "Seeking Strengths."

29. Ibid., 105.

30. Ibid., 119.

31. Eitle, "Special Education or Racial Segregation."

32. See Charlotte-Mecklenburg Schools, *Class Counts*. For my analyses of within-school segregation of secondary school academic courses, I draw on a ± 15 percent bandwidth

standard and consider a classroom to be racially isolated black if the black proportion of students in it exceeds the school's proportion of black students by 15 percentage points; to be racially isolated white if the black proportion of students in it is 15 percentage points or more below the school's overall proportion of black students. I consider all other classrooms racially balanced. Clotfelter, Ladd, and Vigdor, this volume, use a different measure of within-school segregation, but their results are consistent with mine. It is significant that Clotfelter, Ladd, and Vigdor's results are consistent with mine because their data are four years more recent than the CMS data I used. Together, our findings suggest a persistent pattern of second-generation segregation.

33. Cenzipur, "New Standards Hit Minorities Hard."

34. Charlotte-Mecklenburg Schools, *Monthly Reports*.

35. Armor, expert report; Mickelson, expert report; S. Smith, expert report.

36. Lord, expert report.

37. In the early 1980s, fewer than 5 percent of black CMS students attended schools whose black enrollment exceeded court-mandated ceilings; by the mid-1990s, the corresponding figure was approximately 27 percent (see S. Smith, expert report). Among grade 12 CMS students who participated in the 1997 study, 37 percent of blacks and 15 percent of whites had some experience with segregated black elementary education during their careers; among grade 8 students in the 1997 study, 56.4 percent of blacks and 21.2 percent of whites experienced some of their elementary education in segregated black schools.

38. On 3 April 2001 the CMS school board adopted the Family Choice Student Assignment Plan for the 2002–3 school year (see Charlotte-Mecklenburg Schools, "Board Resolution 2001"). To participate in the Family Choice Plan, parents were required to fill out a choice application and to select three schools within one of four geographic areas into which the county is divided. They were guaranteed their "home" school if that was their choice and, based on a number of criteria (such as their child's academic profile, the family's socioeconomic background, the home school's academic and socioeconomic status profile, what schools siblings attend), families could choose another school within their zone and receive free public transportation to it. If they were admitted to a magnet school outside their zone, students did not receive free public transportation. Students in countywide magnets receive free transportation.

Starting in the 2003–4 school year, students assigned to home schools that fall at least 30 percentage points above the district's average concentration of low-income students were to be able to move to the top of the list for admission to schools with below-average poverty if there were seats available (see Helms, "Parents' Choice"). This provision became problematic because of overcrowding at the most desirable schools. In the spring of 2004, CMS eliminated the term "choice" from its new pupil-assignment plan's name. School officials explained that they made this name change to reduce the chances that parents would be misled into thinking that, other than entering a lottery for magnet schools, they had any choice of schools other than their neighborhood school.

39. Lack of seating capacity may not be a legitimate reason to deny students from low-performing schools a seat in an overcrowded high-performing one. According to Taylor ("Title I," 1757), the new federal No Child Left Behind Act of 2001 (P.L. 107-110) gives parents an unrestricted right to transfer their children to better schools irrespective of seat

capacity if their assigned school fails to make adequate yearly progress for two consecutive years.

40. Charlotte-Mecklenburg Schools, "Board Resolution 2002–2003."

41. Following CMS's long-standing practice, I consider an elementary school whose black student population is greater than 15 percentage points above the school district's average to be racially isolated black; a school with a black proportion of the population more than 15 percentage points below the school district's average to be racially isolated white; and all other elementary schools to be racially balanced or desegregated. I use similar standards for secondary schools, a standard more conservative than CMS's practice of considering schools greater than 50 percent black to be racially isolated black and less than 35 percent black to be racially isolated white.

42. The effects of school-level poverty on student achievement, net of individual family background, were established definitively in Coleman et al.'s *Equality of Educational Opportunity.* More recent studies have demonstrated that low-income students perform better in schools without concentrations of other poor students. Readers interested in this topic may wish to consult Natriello, McDill, and Pallas, *Schooling Disadvantaged Children*; Kahlenberg, "Unambiguous Legacy"; and V. Lee and Burkam, *Inequality.* An even more salient piece of research by Hudgins, "Comparison," compared three North Carolina counties (Wake, Forsyth, and Mecklenburg). Hudgins found that students in Wake County outperformed students in North Carolina as a whole as well as Mecklenburg and Forsyth Counties and that Wake is closing the race gap faster than the other sites. Wake County's guidelines are that no school should have more than 40 percent of its students on free or reduced-price lunch and that no more than 25 percent of any school's students should have failed the previous year's EOG tests (Mickelson, "Achieving Equality").

43. Schools with underutilized seating capacity have fewer students than their physical plants were designed to serve. Overutilized schools have more students than their physical plants were designed to serve, necessitating the use of mobile units and nonclassroom space, such as art or music rooms, as classrooms.

44. Charlotte-Mecklenburg Schools, "Board Resolution 2002–2003."

45. Helms, "High-Poverty Schools."

46. Qualifying for free or reduced-price lunch status is CMS's measure of poverty.

47. This pattern of resegregation by track within CMS is not recent. In 1973, two years after the *Swann* decision, the administration reported to the CMS school board on the status of desegregation efforts. The report noted, among other problems arising from efforts to implement the court's order, that "'ability-grouping' too frequently is de-facto resegregation" (see Charlotte-Mecklenburg Schools, *Pupil Assignment Plan Study,* 14). William Poe, the chair of the school board in 1975, explained to me in a 1998 interview why the district began "ability grouping" when it began to desegregate. He drew an example from the desegregation of West Charlotte, at that time the flagship high school of the black community. Poe stated that when students from the politically powerful "old money" white Myers Park neighborhood desegregated West Charlotte, an optional Open Program (a rigorous college prep track) was instituted to encourage whites to participate in desegregation. As Poe recalled, the Open Program "was created as an impetus for whites to enroll their kids in the school. The school board viewed it as a sop to white people." He explained that the creation

of this track necessitated the hiring of new chemistry, calculus, and foreign-language teachers at West Charlotte. According to Poe, "Whites needed to be assured that their children would get the same quality of education they had received at Myers Park High, not just the culinary and cosmetology classes offered to blacks at West Charlotte."

48. Mickelson and Smith, "Race, Tracking, and Achievement."

CHAPTER FIVE

LUIS M. LAOSA

School Segregation in Texas at the Beginning of the Twenty-first Century

The increasing size and diversity of the population of the state of Texas—particularly when considered in regard to the distribution of children among schools by ethnorace, home language, and socioeconomic status—pose serious questions and challenges for educational policy and practice in the state and generally for the nation. These issues include those concerning school segregation. During the past three decades, changes have occurred in the levels of ethnoracial segregation of students in Texas. Gary Orfield reported the following trends. From 1970 to 1980, the level of isolation of Hispanic/Latino students from white non-Hispanic students in Texas decreased slightly; however, since 1980 it has been rising, reaching in 1998 a level higher than that in 1970. Similarly, the level of isolation of African American from white non-Hispanic students decreased slightly between 1970 and 1980; since then, it has increased to approximately the same level as that in 1970. By 1998, Texas was among the four states with the highest levels of isolation of Hispanic/Latino students from white non-Hispanic students and was among the nine states with the highest levels of isolation of African American from white non-Hispanic students.[1]

I recently conducted a study of the public schools in Texas to illuminate these issues.[2] The study had four principal aims. First, I examined how the student population is distributed among the state's public schools by students' ethnorace, family socioeconomic status, and English-language proficiency status. An aim of these analyses was to ascertain the level of isolation of students by ethnorace, socioeconomic background, and English-language proficiency level. Second, I examined the interrelationships among these student body characteristics to shed light on the linkages among them, including particularly the linkages of ethnoracial and linguistic isolation to economic poverty. Third, I examined the relationships of these student body characteristics to academic performance to determine how the school's level of academic performance for pupils from particular ethnoracial, linguistic, and socioeconomic backgrounds is (or is not) related to the school's student body's ethnoracial, linguistic, and socioeconomic composition. Finally, I sought to determine whether, for a bilingual population (i.e., Hispanics/Latinos), the relationships of these student body characteristics to the school's academic performance level depend on the language (i.e., English versus Spanish) through which this performance is tested. (As used in this chapter in reference to the study's findings, the term "school segregation" or "isolation" does not necessarily imply that the school boards or other public school officials caused the ethnoracial, socioeconomic, or linguistic segregation of students observed.)

Before turning to the study itself, I will review certain characteristics unique to the geography, history, and peoples of Texas to provide a context for the study's findings.

Geographical, Historical, and Sociodemographic Context

Geography

Two geographic characteristics are particularly relevant. First, Texas is physically very close to and easily accessible from a number of Spanish-speaking countries. Texas shares a common international border with Mexico, a very long boundary formed by the Rio Grande, an often shallow, narrow river that sometimes can be crossed on foot. From the Rio Grande Delta to the Texas-Louisiana border, the Texas border is the shore of the Gulf of Mexico, linking Texas with the ports of four other southern states, Mexico, Caribbean island nations, and Central and South America. Second, Texas is very large. Covering an area of 266,807 square miles,[3] it is the largest state with the exception of Alaska. For these reasons, Texas has a high percentage of transnational immigrants, and their absolute numbers are also high.

Sociohistorical Context

Texas was initially colonized by Spain. Texas was a part of Spanish Mexico, situated on the border of Spain's North American empire, which for three centuries (1519–1821) sought to incorporate the indigenous peoples of Texas into the Spanish colonial empire, including its religion, its language, and facets of its culture.[4] When Mexico gained independence from Spain in 1821, Texas entered the Mexican nation as one of its states. Anglo Americans soon began settling in Texas; many came from the South, bringing African American slaves with them.[5] Texas became an independent republic in 1836 and was admitted to the United States as the twenty-eighth state in 1845. Anglos became the overwhelming majority, and Mexican Americans became a politically and economically powerless minority.[6]

Historically, a triethnoracial school system developed in Texas, with segregated facilities for Mexican American, African American, and white non-Hispanic students. Separate "Mexican schools" were maintained on the grounds that the separation benefited Mexican American children. These ostensible altruistic reasons stand in apparent contradiction to several observed practices: (1) the placement of all Spanish-surnamed students in segregated schools, even though some were fluent in English; (2) the tendency of these "Mexican schools" to have vastly inferior physical facilities; (3) the lax enforcement of attendance laws in those schools; and (4) the tendency to discourage many Spanish-surnamed children from pursuing advanced schooling.[7] Policies regarding children's use of their native language in school and language policies in general were additional factors that contributed to the social exclusion and isolation of Hispanics/Latinos in the United States.[8]

Immigration—mostly from Mexico but increasingly from other Spanish-speaking countries as well—and fertility differentials have steadily increased the size of Texas's Hispanic/Latino population. Cultural and linguistic ties between Texas and Mexico remain strong to the present because of continued migration, geographical proximity, and communications technology.

Population Characteristics at Present

At present, Hispanics/Latinos are the second largest ethnoracial population group in Texas. Population projections predict that they will soon be the largest. The U.S. Census showed that in 2000, Hispanics/Latinos in Texas numbered 6.67 million, or 32 percent of the state's total population.[9] Hispanics/Latinos may be of any race, although nearly all the Hispanics/Latinos in Texas identified themselves as either white alone (71 percent) or "some other race" alone (25 percent), a category that excludes African American/black, American Indian, and Asian/Pacific Islander.[10] The vast majority (76 percent) of the Hispanic/Latino population is of Mexican descent, although both the number and percentage of persons of Puerto Rican, Cuban, and Central and South American origin are increasing.[11]

White non-Hispanics constituted about 53 percent (i.e., 10.9 million or 11.1 million, depending on whether the count includes only persons who indicated only one race [e.g., white alone] or also individuals who indicated more than one race [e.g., white-black biracial]) of the state's total population. African Americans (non-Hispanic) constituted about 12 percent (2.36 or 2.43 million). The remaining 3–4 percent were non-Hispanics from other racial groups, including Asian/Pacific Islander American and American Indian.[12]

In the *school-age* population, however, Hispanics/Latinos are already nearly as numerous as white non-Hispanics. In the 2000–2001 academic year, Texas had 4,059,619 public school students (early childhood education through grade 12). Of these students, 40.6 percent were Hispanic/Latino; 42.0 percent were white non-Hispanic; 14.4 percent were African American; 2.7 percent were Asian/Pacific Islander American; and less than .5 percent were American Indian.[13]

Among the fifty states, only California surpasses Texas in number of Hispanics/Latinos. According to the U.S. Census, in 2000, there were 10.97 million Hispanics/Latinos in California and 6.67 million in Texas. Third is New York with 2.87 million, followed by Florida with 2.68 million, Illinois with 1.53 million, Arizona with 1.30 million, and New Jersey with 1.12 million; each of the other fifty states had fewer than 1 million Hispanics/Latinos.[14] Of the fifty states, only two surpass Texas in the percentage of Hispanics/Latinos: California and New Mexico, wherein 32.4 percent and 42.1 percent of the population are Hispanic/Latino, respectively.[15]

Among the southern states, Texas has the highest percentage of Hispanics/Latinos and the lowest percentages of African Americans and whites who are not Hispanic/Latino.[16] Given the large size of the state's total population, however, Texas has a larger number of African Americans than does any other southern state—indeed, every ethnoracial group is numerically larger in Texas than in any other southern state.[17]

Languages Spoken in the Home

Since the sixteenth century, Spanish-speaking people have lived in what is now the state of Texas. In 2000, according to the U.S. Census, 31 percent of the total population of Texas age five years and older, or 6.01 million persons, spoke a language other than English in the home. For 86 percent of them, or 5.2 million individuals, that language was Spanish.[18] In the Census Bureau definition, the population that speaks a language other than English includes only persons who sometimes or always speak that other language in the home; it excludes those who know languages other than English but do not use them at home and those who are limited to a few expressions or slang.[19] Thus, in 2000, more than one-fourth of the total population five years and older in Texas spoke Spanish in the home, either in addition to English or instead of English.

Population Projections

Population projections suggest that Texas will likely remain among the nation's fastest-growing states. The changes in the ethnoracial composition of the state's population will also be substantial. By 2040, the Hispanic/Latino population will reach an estimated 52–59 percent of the state's total population, while the Anglo population will likely total 24–32 percent, the African American population 8–9 percent, and the "other" population around 6–9 percent.[20]

The Study

The principal questions the study's data analyses were designed to answer regarding the public schools in Texas are as follows:

- What is the ethnoracial mix of the schools' student bodies?
- What is the socioeconomic mix of the schools' student bodies?
- What is the linguistic composition of the schools' student bodies?
- What, if any, are the relationships among these student body characteristics?
- What, if any, are the relationships of these student body characteristics to the school's level of performance on academic achievement tests? Are these relationships the same for the different ethnoracial groups? For Hispanics/Latinos, are these relationships the same for the English- and Spanish-language versions of the tests?[21]

To answer these research questions, I used publicly available data collected by the Texas Education Agency through its Public Education Information Management System on each of the state's public schools. For the statistical data analyses, I treated the school (campus) as the unit of analysis.

Results

Ethnoracial Composition

The Texas public schools have, on average, a student body that is 44.9 percent white non-Hispanic, 38.8 percent Hispanic/Latino, 14.3 percent African American, 1.8 percent Asian/Pacific Islander American, and 0.4 percent American Indian. Schools differ widely from each other around each of these averages: that is, many schools have very high concentrations of a single ethnoracial group, while many other schools have a more balanced student body. For example, Hispanics/Latinos constitute 70 percent or more of the student body in approximately one-fifth of the schools, while in another fifth of the schools, Hispanics/Latinos constitute between 0.1 percent and 9.9 percent of the student body. Similarly, white non-Hispanics constitute 70 percent or more of the student body in about one-third of the schools, while in one-fifth of the schools they constitute between 0.1 percent and 9.9 percent of the students. African Americans are the majority of the student body in nearly one-tenth of the schools, while they are 0.1–9.9 percent of the student body in about half of the schools.

Considerable ethnoracial isolation of students occurs in Texas. Many schools have very dense concentrations of Hispanic/Latino students. Hispanics/Latinos are the majority of the student body in 2,452 schools, or 32.6 percent. This ethnoracial group constitutes 90–100 percent of the student body in 937 schools, or 12.5 percent.

White non-Hispanic students are the majority in 3,525 schools, or 46.9 percent; this ethnoracial group accounts for 90–100 percent of the student body in 572 schools, or 7.6 percent.

The corresponding figures for African Americans are much smaller. African American students are the majority in 552 schools, or 7.4 percent (or 8.5 percent of the schools with pupils from this ethnoracial group). (There are no African American pupils in 14 percent of the schools, while there are no Hispanic/Latino or white non-Hispanic pupils in fewer than 3 percent of the schools.) African Americans account for 90–100 percent of the student body in 113 schools, or 1.5 percent (or 1.8 percent of the schools with pupils from this ethnoracial group). When summed into a single group, however, Hispanics/Latinos and African Americans constitute 90–100 percent of the student body in 1,617 schools, or 21.5 percent.

There are no schools in which Asian/Pacific Islander American students are the majority. American Indians are the majority in 2 schools.

Intense ethnoracial isolation, therefore, if measured in this way (i.e., the percentage of public schools in which a particular ethnorace constitutes 90–100 percent of the student body), is by far highest for the Hispanic/Latino population. Next in descending order is the white non-Hispanic population, whose isolation is about half as intense as that of Hispanics/Latinos. Third is the African American population, whose isolation is considerably less intense than that of either of the previous two populations. The level of isolation of the combined population of African Americans and Hispanics/Latinos (i.e., the sum of the school's African American and Hispanic/Latino students) is, however, considerably higher than the sum of the levels of isolation of the two individual populations. No ethnoracial isolation of the American Indian population exists except in one school, and no ethnoracial isolation of the Asian/Pacific Islander American population exists.

Many students in Texas attend schools in which their ethnoracial group constitutes the vast majority of the student body. In such schools, therefore, students have only limited opportunity to interact with those from different ethnoracial backgrounds.[22] Although the number of highly segregated schools is thus indeed large, also large is the number of schools with an ethnoracially balanced student body. At the same time that many schools experience increasing levels of segregation, many schools in which a single ethnoracial population predominated in the past have at present a more highly diverse student body, thus increasing the opportunity for interethnoracial contact. To all indications, both trends will likely continue to increase.

Socioeconomic Composition

Considerable isolation of students by socioeconomic background also occurs. For example, in 910 schools, or 12.1 percent, 90 percent or more of the student body is economically disadvantaged.[23]

Particularly disturbing is the strong correlation between ethnoracial segregation and socioeconomic isolation. Schools with dense concentrations of Hispanic/Latino or African American pupils tend to have dense concentrations of economically disadvantaged pupils. The opposite is true for other ethnoracial groups. That is, schools with relatively dense concentrations of white non-Hispanic, Asian/Pacific Islander, or American Indian pupils tend to have relatively few economically disadvantaged students. Hispanic/Latino and African American pupils are much more likely than those from other ethnoracial groups to attend schools with relatively dense concentrations of economically disadvantaged students.

For example, in schools in which 90–100 percent of the student body is economically disadvantaged, the student bodies are, on average, 72.84 percent Hispanic/Latino and 7.30 percent white non-Hispanic. In contrast, in schools in which less than 10 percent of the student body is economically disadvantaged, the student bodies are, on average, 16.10 percent Hispanic/Latino and 70.80 percent white non-Hispanic.

Also disturbing is the relationship found between socioeconomic isolation and English-language proficiency status, as described subsequently.

Linguistic Composition

The schools have, on average, a student body of which 12.09 percent of the students are formally classified by the school system as "limited English proficient" (LEP). (Also called "English-language learners" [ELLs], this classification can be applied only to pupils who are not native speakers of English.) Considerable variability occurs around this average. For example, in 131 schools, or 1.8 percent,

LEP/ELL students constitute 70 percent or more of the student body, while in 3,797 schools, or 50.5 percent, such students constitute less than 10 percent but more than 0 percent of the student body. Only 16.0 percent of the schools do not have LEP/ELL students.

There is a definite tendency for LEP/ELL students to attend schools with dense concentrations of economically disadvantaged students. For example, in schools in which economically disadvantaged pupils constitute 90–100 percent of the student body, LEP/ELL pupils constitute, on average, 32.52 percent of the student body. In contrast, in schools with less than 10 percent of pupils who are economically disadvantaged, LEP/ELL pupils constitute, on average, only 2.36 percent of the student body. Thus, LEP/ELL students tend to be isolated from students who are not economically disadvantaged.

LEP/ELL students tend to be isolated also from white non-Hispanic students. For instance, white non-Hispanics make up, on average, 1.87 percent and 57.76 percent of the student body in schools in which LEP/ELL students constitute 90–100 percent and 0–9.9 percent of the student body, respectively.

Relationships to Academic Performance

Relationships of the Student Body's Ethnoracial Composition to the School's Performance Level on the English-Language Version of the Academic Achievement Tests

The study also discovered alarmingly high correlations between ethnoracial segregation and academic performance. The denser a school's concentration of Hispanic/Latino or African American students, the worse the school's performance as measured by the student body's passing rates on the English-language version of the reading, writing, and mathematics achievement tests. In contrast, the denser a school's concentration of white non-Hispanic or Asian/Pacific Islander American students, the better the school's performance on these tests. These correlations occur for the school's performance for its student body as a whole; they also occur for its performance for particular ethnoracial groups. That is, the school's passing rates for Hispanics/Latinos, African Americans, and white non-Hispanics are better in schools with denser (than in those with lighter) concentrations of white non-Hispanics or Asian/Pacific Islander Americans but are worse in schools with denser (rather than lighter) concentrations of Hispanics/Latinos or African Americans.

For example, in schools in which Hispanics/Latinos constitute 90–100 percent, 40–49.9 percent, and 0–9.9 percent of the student body, the average passing rates for Hispanic/Latino sixth-graders on the English reading test are 77.39 percent, 81.56 percent, and 88.78 percent, respectively. In contrast, in schools in which white non-Hispanics constitute 90–100 percent, 40–49.9 percent, and 0–9.9 percent of the student body, the average passing rates for the Hispanic/Latino sixth-graders on this test are 90.13 percent, 82.92 percent, and 75.95 percent, respectively.

No correlation occurs between the school's passing rates for Asian/Pacific Islander Americans (on the English-language version of the tests) and the school's concentration of students from this ethnoracial group (i.e., Asian/Pacific Islander American). Like the school's passing rates for the other ethnoracial groups on the English version of the tests, however, the school's passing rates for Asian/Pacific Islander Americans on these tests are better in schools with denser (rather than lighter) concentrations of white non-Hispanics but are worse in schools with denser (rather than lighter) concentrations of Hispanics/Latinos or African Americans. Separate analyses of the school's passing rates for American Indians are not reported because of this ethnoracial population's relatively small size and extremely thin distribution among schools.

Relationships of the Student Body's Ethnoracial Composition to the School's Performance Level on the Spanish-Language Version of the Tests

Each Hispanic/Latino student took either the English- or the Spanish-language version of the academic achievement tests. The correlations for the Spanish-language version of the tests are in a direction opposite to those for the English-language version. The school's passing rates for Hispanics/Latinos on the Spanish version of the tests correlate positively with the student body's percentage of Hispanics/Latinos but negatively with the student body's percentage of students from the other ethnoracial groups. Thus, the denser a student body's concentration of white non-Hispanics, the better the school's academic performance for Hispanics/Latinos as measured by the English version of the tests but the worse this performance if measured by the Spanish version of the same tests. In contrast, the denser a student body's concentration of Hispanics/Latinos, the worse the school's academic performance for Hispanics/Latinos as measured by the English version of the tests but the better this performance if measured by the Spanish version.

Relationships of the Student Body's Socioeconomic Composition to Academic Performance

The study also found a pervasive relationship between concentrated poverty and the school's academic performance. Specifically, the denser a school's concentration of economically disadvantaged students, the lower the school's performance as measured by the English-language version of the reading, writing, and mathematics achievement tests. This linkage is evident in the school's performance for each ethnoracial group, including Hispanics/Latinos. In contrast, the school's percentage of economically disadvantaged students either is not associated or is positively associated with the school's passing rates for Hispanics/Latinos on the Spanish version of the tests.

Relationships of the Student Body's Linguistic Composition to Academic Performance

The analyses also found relationships between the school's relative concentration of LEP/ELL students and the school's level of academic performance. The larger a student body's percentage of LEP/ELL students, the lower the school's academic performance as measured by the English-language version of the reading, math, and writing tests; this is true of the school's performance for each of the four ethnoracial groups, including Hispanics/Latinos. This relationship is in a direction opposite to that of the relationship for the Spanish version of these tests. That is, the larger a student body's percentage of LEP/ELL students, the higher the school's academic performance for Hispanics/Latinos as measured by the Spanish-language version of these tests. Thus, the relationship of the student body's percentage of LEP/ELL students to the school's academic performance level for its Hispanic/Latino students is negative if that performance is measured using the English version of the tests but is positive if measured using the Spanish version of the same tests.

Conclusion

The issues concerning school segregation and integration are now even more complex than they were in the past. This study's findings bring to light various facets of the current complexity. The public debate concerning school segregation and integration has typically been cast in terms of black-white isolation. This study demonstrates how school segregation is not only a black-white issue. School segregation extends to other ethnoracial populations, including particularly the Hispanic/Latino population. The study also shows that, in addition to ethnoracial segregation, school segregation by socioeconomic status and by English-language proficiency status also exist, that these three forms of segregation are interrelated, and that each is related to academic performance.

School segregation by socioeconomic status is linked both to school segregation by ethnorace and to school segregation by English-proficiency status. School isolation is very closely linked to concentrated poverty.

Moreover, each of the three forms of school segregation (i.e., by ethnorace, by socioeconomic status, and by English-proficiency status) is linked to the academic performance of schools. These linkages of school segregation to how well (or how badly) schools perform for their students are particularly disturbing.

The existence of school isolation of children who are native speakers of Spanish and not yet fully proficient in English raises questions about possible consequences of this isolation for language development—for example, How much is the children's English-language development affected by a lack of models of proficient English, a scarcity of opportunities to interact in English, and an absence of a need to communicate in this language with peers?

Adding to this complexity, the relationship of school segregation to academic performance is not the same for all ethnoracial groups. For the Hispanic/Latino population—a bilingual population—the correlation between school segregation and academic achievement can be either positive or negative, depending on whether the level of achievement is measured using English- or Spanish-language versions of the achievement tests.

All these facets and complex realities of school segregation are evident in Texas but likely are not unique to this state. In many parts of Texas—and in a growing number of schools in other states[24]—the demographic trends that are rapidly transforming the composition of the population pose or soon will pose difficult challenges for educators, students, and policy makers. These challenges bear also on the future of the larger society. If the issues concerning school segregation continue to be conceived as they traditionally have, significant forms of isolation will be overlooked. One should not neglect the increasing school segregation of Hispanic/Latino children, the segregation of students who are learning English as a second language, or the segregation of students by family socioeconomic level. Approaches to solutions of problems of segregation that were effective in the past may not be effective for the present.

This study's findings bring forward an urgent need for new conceptualizations—a need to frame the issues of school segregation and integration in the light of the new and emerging knowledge about educational isolation, including a need for new definitions of integration. Both advocacy and research agendas are needed to address successfully these concerns, aiming toward the goals of a fully integrated and equitable society.

Notes

1. G. Orfield, *Schools More Separate*, 39, 41, 44, 46.

2. Details regarding the study's research design, methods, data, and statistical results can be found in a technical report obtainable from the author.

3. Reddick and Wooster, "Texas."

4. Chipman, "Spanish Texas"; Wright, "Spanish Missions."

5. De León, "Mexican Texas"; Reddick and Wooster, "Texas."

6. In Texas and other parts of the southwestern United States, "Anglo" is the term generally used to refer to white non-Hispanic Americans.

7. T. Carter and Segura, *Mexican Americans in School*; Cruz, "Political Influence."

8. Donato, Menchaca, and Valencia, *Segregation, Desegregation, and Integration*; Laosa, "Social Policies"; U.S. Commission, *Ethnic Isolation*; U.S. Commission, *Excluded Student.*

9. U.S. Bureau of the Census, "Percent of Population, Table 2"; U.S. Bureau of the Census, "Population by Race, Table 1."

10. U.S. Bureau of the Census, "Census 2000 Supplementary Survey Summary Tables."

11. U.S. Bureau of the Census, "2000 Census of Population and Housing: Texas."

12. U.S. Bureau of the Census, "Census 2000 Redistricting Data, Tables PL1, PL2."

13. Texas Education Agency, "Academic Excellence Indicator System."

14. U.S. Bureau of the Census, "Population by Race, Table 1."

15. U.S. Bureau of the Census, "Percent of Population, Table 2."

16. Ibid.

17. As used in this chapter, the term "southern state" refers to Alabama, Arkansas, Florida, Georgia, Louisiana, Mississippi, North Carolina, South Carolina, Tennessee, Texas, and Virginia. U.S. Bureau of the Census, "Population by Race, Table 1."

18. U.S. Bureau of the Census, "Census 2000, Table DP-2."

19. U.S. Bureau of the Census, "2000 Census of Population and Housing, Demographic Profile."

20. Texas State Data Center, *New Population Projections.*

21. Academic performance was measured using the Texas Assessment of Academic Skills (TAAS), a battery of criterion-referenced tests of academic achievement routinely administered to students in the Texas public schools. Texas Education Agency, "Student Assessment Program." In this study I used the schools' passing rates on each of the following TAAS tests, administered in the spring of 2001.

Grade 3—Reading test and mathematics test (English and Spanish versions)
Grade 4—Reading test, mathematics test, and Writing test (English and Spanish versions)
Grade 5—Reading test and mathematics test (English and Spanish versions)
Grade 6—Reading test and mathematics test (English and Spanish versions)

A school's passing rate on a particular language version (English or Spanish) of the test of a particular academic subject (reading, mathematics, or writing) for a particular grade level was computed as the number of students in that grade in that school who passed that language version of that subject's test in that spring divided by the number of students in that grade in that school who took that language version of that subject's test in that spring, multiplied by 100. I analyzed the passing rates of each ethnoracial group separately and analyzed as well the passing rates of the aggregate of these groups. In every instance, I analyzed the passing rates separately by grade level and subject. Each Hispanic/Latino student took either the English- or the Spanish-language version of the tests; I analyzed the passing rates separately for the English and Spanish versions.

22. Laosa, "Intercultural Transitions."

23. The family socioeconomic composition of each school's student body was indexed by the variable *economically disadvantaged*. A school's measurement on this variable is the count or percentage of the school's total students from a family with an annual income at or below the official federal poverty line or eligible for free or reduced-price lunch or for other public assistance. Texas Education Agency, "Public Education Information Management System."

24. See, e.g., Laosa, "School Segregation"; G. Orfield, "Schools More Separate."

PART THREE

The Adverse Impacts of Resegregation

CHAPTER SIX

RUSSELL W. RUMBERGER | GREGORY J. PALARDY

Does Resegregation Matter?

The Impact of Social Composition on Academic Achievement in Southern High Schools

The issue of school segregation came to the forefront of education policy when, in 1954, the U.S. Supreme Court declared that the de jure segregation of schools was unconstitutional because it was "inherently unequal."[1] Subsequent litigation and federal legislation, primarily during the 1960s and 1970s, led to increased racial integration, especially in the South. For example, the percentage of blacks in the South who attended white-majority elementary and secondary schools increased from 2.3 percent in 1964 to 43.5 percent in 1988.[2]

But over the past twenty years, desegregation policies have been largely abandoned because of declining support for desegregation from the executive and judicial branches of the federal government and the growing concentration of minorities in urban school districts that made meaningful desegregation nearly impossible.[3] Instead, many education and government officials have come to believe that integrating schools is less important than providing compensatory funding and setting high standards for all students and schools. As a result, segregation in America's schools is increasing. Between 1988 and 2000, the percentage of blacks in the South who attended white-majority schools decreased from 43.5 percent to 31.0 percent.[4] Nationwide, more than 70 percent of all black and Latino students in the United States attended predominantly minority schools in 2000, a higher percentage than thirty years earlier.[5]

Although segregation has often been viewed in racial terms, racial segregation is strongly related to socioeconomic segregation (see fig. 6.3). Not only are black and Latino students more likely to be poor, they are also more likely to attend high-poverty schools. In 1999, almost one-third of all black and Latino children under the age of eighteen were living in poverty, compared to 13 percent of white children.[6] And in 2000, the average black or Latino student attended a school in which more than 44 percent of the students were poor, whereas the average white attended a school in which 19 percent of the students were poor.[7] To the extent that both individual poverty and school poverty affect academic achievement, black and Hispanic students are doubly disadvantaged.

At the elementary school level, both individual poverty and school poverty affect academic achievement. Recent data from the National Assessment of Educational Progress show not only that poor students have lower math achievement than students who are not poor but also that both poor and nonpoor students have lower achievement in high-poverty schools.[8] In fact, students who are not poor have lower achievement in high-poverty schools than poor students attending low-poverty schools.

But does racial or socioeconomic segregation matter at the high school level? And if so, why? What can be done to overcome any adverse effects of segregation? Finally, do the impacts of and remedies for segregation differ in the South from other parts of the United States? The remaining sections of this chapter address these questions by reviewing existing research evidence and by providing new evidence based on an analysis of data from a large sample of high schools in the South and the rest of the United States.

Previous Research

While research has consistently documented the impact of individual socioeconomic status (SES) on academic achievement, substantial evidence also indicates that the social composition of a school affects student achievement even after taking into account a student's academic and social background. The 1966 Coleman Report was the first major national study to demonstrate that a student's achievement is highly related to characteristics of other students in the school.[9] In fact, Coleman claimed that "the social composition of the student body is more highly related to achievement, independent of the student's own social background, than is any school factor."[10]

Since the publication of that study, a number of studies using a variety of student achievement measures have examined the impacts of school segregation and generally confirmed Coleman's observations.[11] Yet most of the research on the effects of school segregation was conducted in the 1970s and 1980s, and most focused more narrowly on the short-term effects of racial composition and school desegregation on the academic achievement of whites and blacks at the elementary school level.[12]

Based on their review of only three studies that focused on high schools, Christopher Jencks and Susan E. Mayer conclude that "a high school's mean SES has a negligible impact on how much the average student learns in high school,"[13] although they note that one study, recent at the time,[14] found that high school SES did impact twelfth-grade math scores. Yet they did acknowledge some differential effects: (1) a high school's mean SES may have more effect on black students than white students and more effect on high-SES students than low-SES students; and (2) evidence suggests that blacks would probably benefit from attending predominantly white schools in the North, but "we do not know anything reliable about the cumulative impact of desegregated schooling in the South."[15]

Since 1990, a number of studies using more recent data and more sophisticated statistical techniques have demonstrated that both racial and socioeconomic composition relatively strongly affect student achievement in high school. Cross-sectional studies that examine student achievement at one point in time have tended to demonstrate consistently strong effects of both racial and socioeconomic composition.[16] But these studies are less compelling because they do not control or adjust for students' prior academic achievement.

Two earlier studies examined twelfth-grade achievement, but because of the nature of the national data set used, these studies controlled only for prior achievement in tenth grade, two years after most students begin high school. One study found little effect of either racial or socioeconomic composition on twelfth-grade test scores in five subject areas after controlling for tenth-grade test scores,[17] while the other study found very strong effects of school SES but no effect for racial composition on a summary measure of test score gains even after controlling for tenth-grade achievement.[18] Since most students attend high school for four years, both of these studies were unable to assess the impact of segregation over the entire period of high school and to control for the achievement of students prior to entering high school.

Several additional studies have used a more recent and more suitable longitudinal data set that followed a large sample of eighth-grade students through high school. Yet only one of these studies focused specifically on social composition, so determining the effects of social composition on academic achievement is often difficult. Adam Gamoran, for example, examined the effects of school academic climate on tenth grade test scores in public magnet, public comprehensive, and Catholic high schools after controlling for eighth-grade achievement. He found that, collectively, several measures of social composition—percent minority students, percent of students on free or reduced lunch, and percent of students from single-parent families—affected student achievement, but he did not report the size or significance of the three individual measures.[19] In two studies on the effects of school organization and school size on changes in student achievement during high school, Valerie E. Lee, Julia B. Smith, and Robert G. Croninger used two measures of social composition—the mean SES of students in the school and high-minority schools (schools with 40 percent or more black and Hispanic students).[20]

However, the models used and the results reported make it impossible to untangle the individual and contextual effects of SES, so these studies do not reveal whether SES composition by itself matters. Another study examined the effects of teacher characteristics and classroom practices on tenth-grade math scores after controlling for eighth-grade math scores.[21] Of the three social composition variables included in the study—percent white students in the school, percent students from single-parent families, and percent minority students in the classroom—only the third shows a significant yet small negative effect on student outcomes. Finally, after controlling for a host of student background characteristics prior to entering high school (e.g., SES, achievement, college aspirations), we found that the average SES of students' high schools had as much impact on their achievement growth during high school as their own SES.[22]

In summary, existing research suggests that social composition significantly impacts student achievement. The effect is stronger in cross-sectional studies that do not control for prior achievement, but even in longitudinal studies that control for prior achievement, the social composition of students in the school or classroom appears to affect how much students learn in high school. Moreover, socioeconomic composition rather than racial composition is what matters.

But why does social composition matter? Few studies to date have attempted to explain those effects. As Jencks and Mayer point out in their review, "Almost all of it relies on a 'black box' model of neighborhood and school effects that makes no assumptions about how social composition influences individual behavior."[23] Because social composition often correlates with an array of school characteristics from the quality of teachers to organizational features, identifying the causal relationship between social composition and student outcomes is often hard.

Two explanations have been offered for the effects of social composition on student achievement. The first suggests that such effects directly relate to peer influence. Jencks and Mayer suggest that peer effects can be either positive or negative—students with high achievement and motivation levels can help create a "culture of success" in school, while students with low achievement and motivation levels can create a sense of deprivation and despair.[24] Richard D. Kahlenberg reviews evidence to support his contention that the socioeconomic composition of schools directly affects student achievement through three peer mechanisms—influence on learning through in-class and out-of-class interactions (e.g., cooperative work groups, study groups), influence on student motivation and aspirations, and influence on student social behavior.[25]

The second explanation suggests that social composition has indirect effects, operating through social composition's association with resources and the organizational and structural features of schools. For example, minority students are more likely to attend large, high-poverty urban schools with fewer qualified teachers and more traditional organizational features that inhibit student learning.[26] Another study found evidence of ethnic and social inequality with respect to four important educational resources—school disciplinary climate, access to high school algebra, teachers with math backgrounds, and teacher emphasis on classroom reasoning.[27] Social composition may strongly influence one organizational feature of high schools: tracking. Some scholars have argued that racial segregation within schools, also known as second-generation segregation, is as important as segregation between schools in inhibiting the educational opportunities of racial and ethnic minorities.[28]

What is less clear from existing research is whether the effects of social composition are related to school resources, such as teacher quality and class size, or other school characteristics that could be improved directly through increased expenditures or other policy initiatives. If that is the case, then the resegregation of America's schools would not necessarily impair academic achievement, although it could impede race relations and long-term educational and other benefits.[29] Even though schools with high concentrations of poor and minority students often have fewer resources than other schools, those disparities could be reduced by policies designed to reallocate resources and promote school reform without altering the social composition of schools. However, if the effects of student composition cannot be traced to such alterable school characteristics, then attending a school with a high proportion of minority or poor students may itself be problematic. In that case, resegregation could worsen the already large achievement gap between minority and white students in American schools unless new policies are designed to desegregate schools.

The Present Study

This study addresses many of the limitations of past research on school segregation. First, it is based on a national, longitudinal data set—the National Education Longitudinal Study—that tracked a large cohort of eighth-grade students through high school and provides a comprehensive set of controls on the background characteristics of students before they entered high school, allowing much more accurate estimates of the effects of school segregation. Second, the data set provides measures of student achievement at three points in time—eighth grade, tenth grade, and twelfth grade—that can be used to estimate how much students learn (achievement growth) over the entire four years of high school. Third, student test scores cover four academic subjects—math, science, reading, and history—thereby providing a more comprehensive measure of student achievement than tests in a single subject. Fourth, the data include comprehensive information on the characteristics of schools, which can be used to identify how and why segregation affects student learning. Finally, the data include a large number of high schools both in the seventeen southern and border states (N = 325) and in the rest of the United States (N = 588), thereby allowing for regional comparisons of segregation.[30]

How Do Southern Students and High Schools Compare?

Before examining the impacts of segregation, it is useful to see how students and schools in the South compare to students and schools in the rest of the United States. Available achievement data show that student achievement is generally lower in the South than in other regions of the United States. For example, only 26 percent of fourth-grade students in the South scored at the "proficient" reading level on the 2000 National Assessment of Educational Progress, compared to 37 percent in the Northeast, 35 percent in the central region, and 30 percent in the West.[31] Another recent study found that not one southern state had 2002 average college entrance scores in the top ten in the nation and that fourteen of sixteen southern states ranked in the bottom half of the nation.[32]

Data from this study show similar disparities. Both initial average achievement in grade 8 and achievement growth rates between grades 8 and 12 were lower for students attending schools in the South than in other regions of the country during the period from 1988 to 1992 (figure 6.1). The difference in initial achievement on the composite test score (a combined score in math, science, reading, and history) was about 1.5 points, which is equivalent to about three-quarters of an academic year in student learning.[33] In other words, students in the South entered high school about three-quarters of a grade level behind their peers in other parts of the country. By the end of high school, the gap widened to 2.1 points, or about one full academic year.

What accounts for these differences? One factor is demographics. Students in the South are generally more disadvantaged than students in the rest of the United States —in particular in terms of average household income.[34] In our data, the mean SES of students in the South was .12 of a standard deviation lower than in the rest of the United States.[35] The South also has almost twice the proportion of black and Hispanic students—who generally have lower achievement levels—than the rest of the United States.[36]

By controlling for demographic characteristics in our statistical models, we

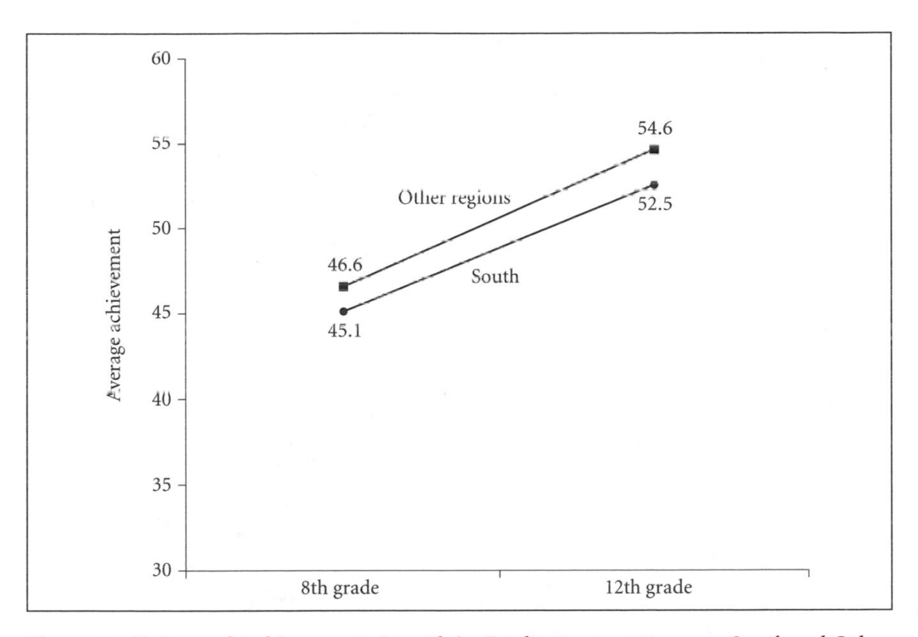

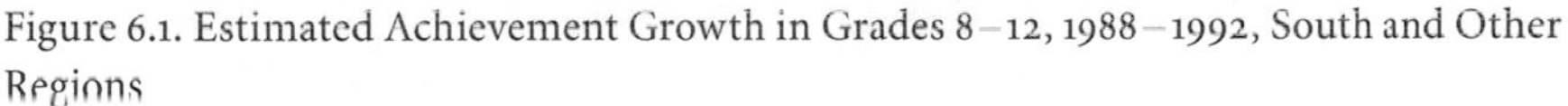
Figure 6.1. Estimated Achievement Growth in Grades 8–12, 1988–1992, South and Other Regions

Source: Estimates based on statistical analysis of data from the National Education Longitudinal Study (Rumberger and Palardy, Technical Appendix, table 3).

compared achievement levels of students in the South with those of students from similar family and academic backgrounds in other regions of the country. These comparisons showed that average achievement levels were lower for all racial groups in southern schools, even after controlling for other characteristics of students that affect achievement, such as SES, family type, and academic background (figure 6.2). For example, middle-class white students in the South began high school in 1988 almost a half year (one point) behind middle-class white students in the rest of the country. And even though their achievement growth (learning) during high school lagged behind other students by only about one month of learning over the four years, they finished high school even further behind their counterparts in the rest of the country.

The achievement gap among racial and ethnic groups was similar in both southern and nonsouthern high schools. Black and Hispanic students began high school with achievement levels considerably lower than those of white students, and, in the case of blacks, the achievement gap widened over the four years of high school. The pattern differed for Asian students—they began high school

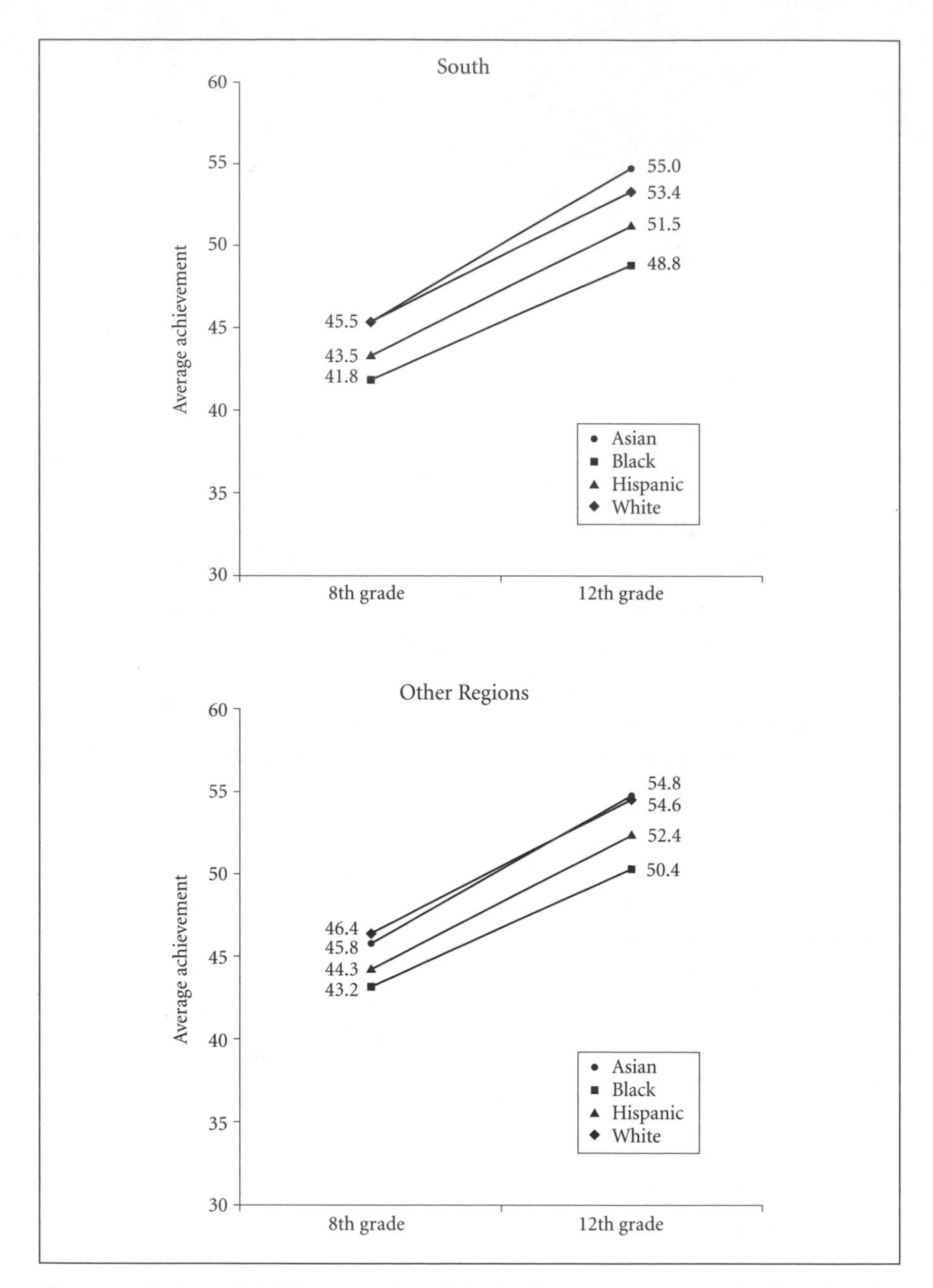

Figure 6.2. Estimated Achievement Growth in Grades 8–12, 1988–1992, by Race, South and Other Regions

Source: Estimates based on statistical analysis of data from the National Education Longitudinal Study that control for other demographic and background variables (Rumberger and Palardy, Technical Appendix, table 4).

with similar achievement levels to white students but exceeded them by the end of twelfth grade, especially in southern high schools.

These data show that considerable differences exist in achievement and achievement growth between students in the South and students in other regions of the country overall as well as among racial and ethnic groups. Our analysis also revealed that most student background characteristics predicted achievement in the South similar to that in other regions of the United States. For example, in both the South and other regions, students' SES was a strong, significant predictor of high school learning.[37] Other student factors that similarly predicted high school learning in both regions were middle school grades, being retained in grade (negative predictor), and having high school friends who had dropped out of school (negative). Only two exceptions arose. Outside the South, coming from a home without two parents was a significant negative predictor of high school learning, while having aspirations to attend a four-year college was a significant positive predictor. In the South, however, neither factor was a significant predictor of high school learning.

Our analysis revealed considerable differences in achievement growth not only among students but also among schools. One way to illustrate those differences is to estimate the range of achievement growth between the highest performing and lowest-performing high schools. Those estimates revealed that differences in achievement growth—the amount of learning that took place during four years of high school—among schools was substantial, ranging from a low of 4.2 points (approximately 50 percent less than the average learning rate in the total population) to a high of 10.8 points (approximately 36 percent more) in the South, and ranging from a low of 4.9 points (approximately 60 percent less) to a high of 11.3 points (approximately 44 percent more) in other regions (figure 6.3). Put another way, students in some high schools learned more than twice as much as students in other high schools. This finding suggests that where students attend high school has a great deal to do with how much they learn.

The extent to which high schools contribute to student learning can be further illustrated by calculating the proportion of the total variability in initial achievement and achievement growth attributable to students and to schools. The results show that about three-quarters of the variability in both achievement and achievement growth resulted from differences among students and about one-quarter resulted from differences among the schools that they attend.[38] Thus, even if differences among schools were completely eliminated, considerable variability would remain in achievement levels and learning rates among students. The 25 percent variability in student achievement growth attributed to schools provides an upper bound on the extent to which school reforms alone could improve educational opportunity for poor, minority students without reforms

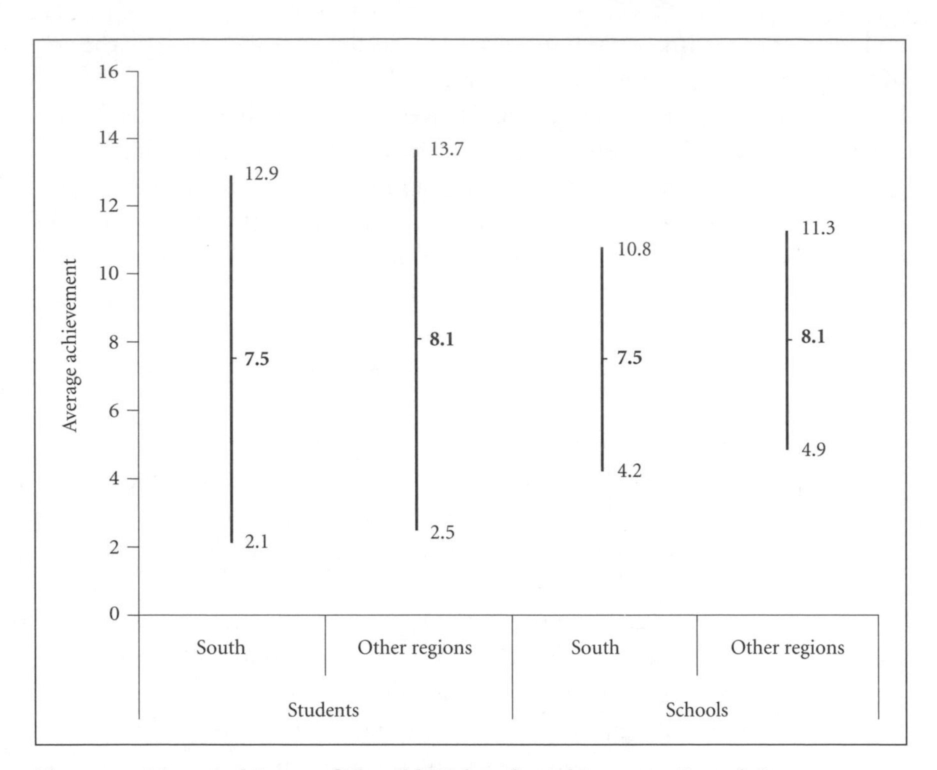

Figure 6.3. Mean and Range of Plausible Values for Achievement Growth Rates among Students and Schools, South and Other Regions

Note: Mean values are in boldface.

Sources: Figures represent the 95% range of expected values based on assumption of normality for variance estimates shown in Rumberger and Palardy (Technical Appendix, table 3) and calculated using the formula presented in Raudenbush and Bryk, *Hierarchical Linear Models*, 71.

in social policy designed to address inequalities in student and family circumstances that contribute to student learning. We discuss this issue further in the chapter's final section.

Although 25 percent of the variability in student achievement occurred at the school level, not all this variability resulted from school characteristics. Some of the variability arose from the differences in the characteristics of students attending schools and the effects of those characteristics on achievement no matter where students attend school. In other words, students from advantaged backgrounds can be expected to do well in school regardless of the school they attend. As a result, schools with more advantaged students will have both higher initial achievement and higher achievement growth than schools with less advantaged students.

Our statistical analysis revealed that differences in the background characteristics of students accounted for almost three-fourths of the initial variability among schools in initial achievement levels and more than one-fourth of the initial variability among schools in achievement growth.[39] Since the initial achievement levels were assessed before entering high school, it makes sense that most of the variability was not related to the high schools that students attend but rather to their background characteristics. In contrast, most of the variability in achievement growth could not be attributed to the background characteristics of students (or at least the characteristics included in our model), so it most likely resulted from the characteristics of the schools that students attended.

Does Segregation Matter?

After adjusting for the background characteristics of students, we then investigated the impact of segregation. We did so by examining whether the average characteristics of students within a school—referred to as compositional or contextual effects —predicted student achievement above and beyond the individual effects of these characteristics. We examined the effects of a number of compositional variables, including the mean SES, the percent of minority students in the school, the mean academic background (grades), and the percent of students who planned to attend four-year colleges. Of course, many of these variables correlate with each other. For example, the racial composition of schools correlates highly with school poverty—students in highly segregated schools are also much more likely be in a predominantly poor school (figure 6.4).

Yet in our analysis, we found only one compositional variable—the average SES of the student body—that significantly affected student achievement. That is, both students' individual SES and the average SES of their schools contributed to achievement growth or learning during high school. One way to illustrate the relative importance of these two factors is by computing the change in achievement growth associated with a change in student and school SES, where the changes are expressed in standard deviations of each respective variable, referred to as effect sizes.[40] One of the benefits of using effect sizes is that it allows comparisons between different sets of data and different studies through the use of a common metric.

The results show that effect sizes for school SES were larger than the effect sizes for student SES in both southern and nonsouthern schools (figure 6.5).[41] For ex-

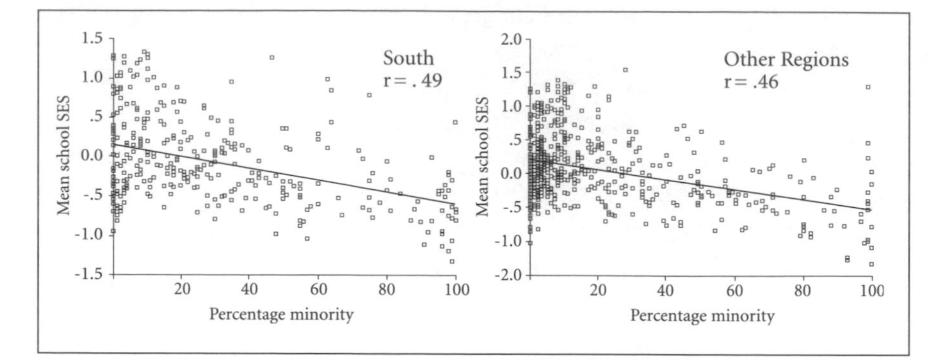

Figure 6.4. Correlation between Percentage Minority and Mean Socioeconomic Status of High Schools, South and Other Regions

Source: Analysis of school-level National Education Longitudinal Study data for schools in the South (N = 325) and schools in other regions (N = 588) (Rumberger and Palardy, Technical Appendix, table 1).

ample, outside of the South, students from families with a 1 standard deviation higher value of SES had average achievement growth rates that were .12 of a standard deviation higher, net of other student factors that also predicted achievement growth rates. That is, the effect size of student SES was .12. In contrast, students attending high schools with a 1 standard deviation higher value of school SES had achievement growth rates that were .14 of a standard deviation higher, an effect size of .14. In the South, the effect size of student SES was .12, almost the same effect as students in other regions of the country. In contrast, the effect size of school SES was .16, about one-third more than the effect size of individual SES.

Although no clear standard exists for how to interpret these values, some scholars have suggested that effect sizes as small as .1 can be considered substantial and meaningful for large populations.[42] Another way to view the magnitude of these effects is to contrast them with what many people consider to be a highly successful school reform program—the Tennessee class-size-reduction experiment—that produced four-year effect sizes of .25.[43] In other words, students who attended more affluent schools in the South—those with a 1 standard deviation higher value of mean SES—improved their achievement growth rates as much as might be expected from almost three years of class-size reduction. Substantial benefits clearly arise from attending a high-SES school, especially for students in the South.

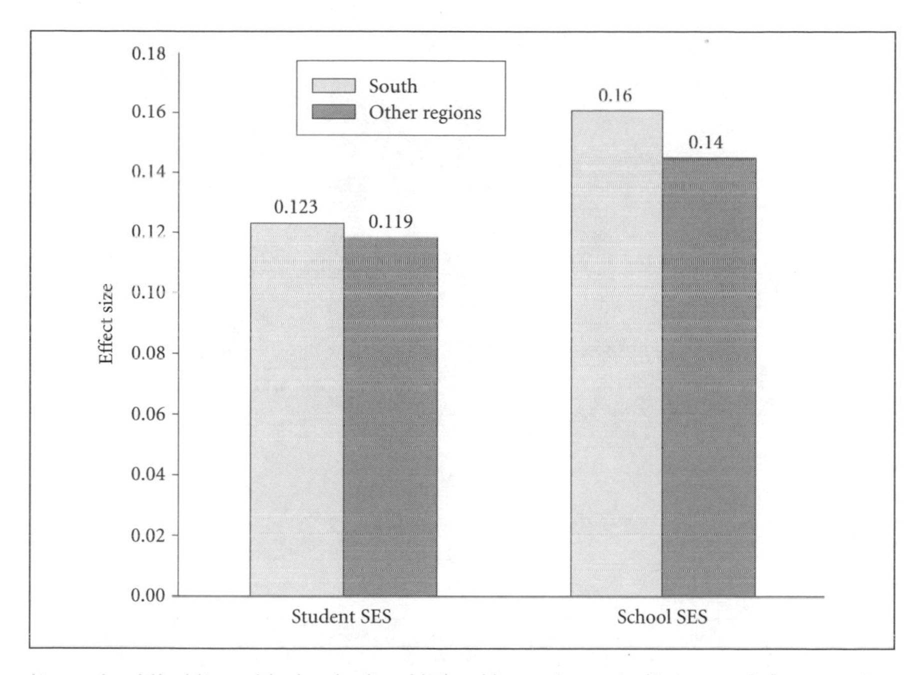

Figure 6.5. Effect Size of Individual and School Socioeconomic Status on Achievement Growth, South and Other Regions

Note: Effect size represents the effect of a 1 standard deviation change in the predictor variables on a 1 standard deviation change in achievement growth at the student level. Effect sizes are computed from parameter estimates based on an HLM model that controls for other student background characteristics (Rumberger and Palardy, Technical Appendix, table 5). All values are statistically significant at .05 level.

Why Does Segregation Matter?

But why does the SES of a school's student body matter? To address this question, we estimated a series of statistical models that introduced a comprehensive series of variables that measured three types of school characteristics: (1) structural features —such as location, size, and control (public/private); (2) school resources—such as student/teacher ratio and credentialed teachers; and (3) school processes —such as academic climate, school safety, and teaching quality.[44] This analysis sought to determine whether any of these school characteristics would render the estimated effect of school SES insignificant. If they did, the results would suggest that school SES indirectly impacted student achievement through association with other school characteristics that could possibly be altered through school reform policies. If they did not, then the results would suggest that the

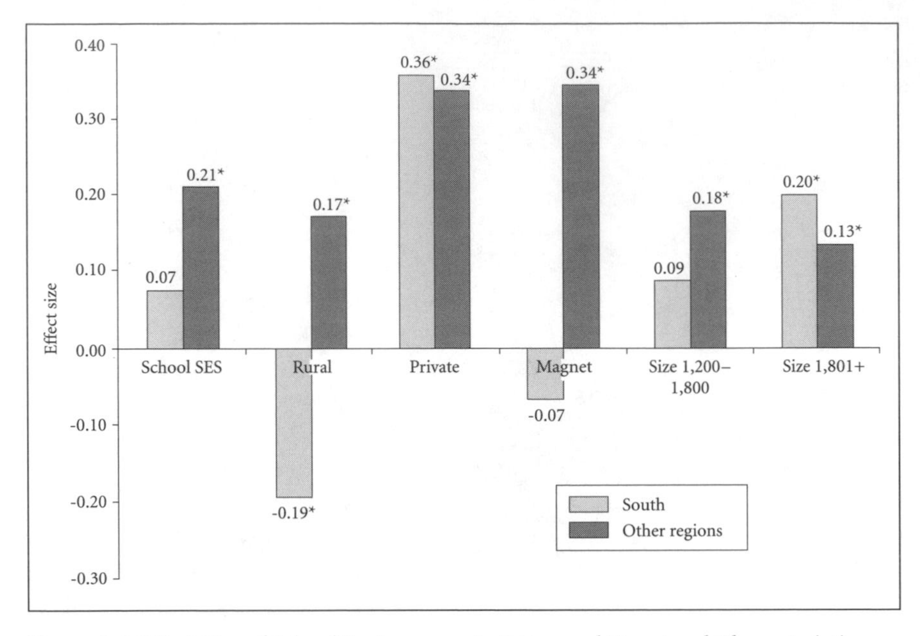

Figure 6.6. Effect Size of School Socioeconomic Status and Structural Characteristics on Achievement Growth, South and Other Regions

*Effect size statistically significant at .05 level.

Note: Effect size represents the effect of a 1 standard deviation change in the predictor variables on a 1 standard deviation change in achievement growth at the student level. Effect sizes are computed from parameter estimates based on an HLM model that controls for student background characteristics and other school variables (Rumberger and Palardy, Technical Appendix, table 6).

characteristics of the student body itself were responsible for the estimated effects of school SES and that the only way to alter such results would be through desegregation policies.

We first examined the impact of structural characteristics. The results of this analysis revealed that several structural features of schools were significant predictors of achievement growth. In the South, these characteristics greatly reduced the effect size of school SES from an initial value of .16 (figure 6.5) to a level of .07 (figure 6.6), rendering it insignificant. In other words, the effects of school SES in the South resulted largely from its association with several structural features of schools—rural (versus urban or suburban), private (versus Catholic, comprehensive public, or public magnet), and school size greater than 1,800 students.

The results differed significantly in other parts of the United States. After introducing the same set of structural variables, the effect size of school SES actually increased from an initial value of .14 (figure 6.4) to a level of .21 (figure 6.6), and it remained statistically significant. Nonetheless, some structural characteristics of schools remained significant predictors of student learning. Some—such as private control and school size—had similar effects on student learning both in the South and in the rest of the United States. Student achievement was generally higher in larger schools than in midsized schools (600–1,200 students), which previous research has suggested are more effective.[45] However, the most effective size varied by region. In the South, schools with more than 1,800 pupils had higher achievement growth, while outside the South schools with 1,200–1,800 students had higher achievement growth.

Other structural features had very different effects in the South and in other areas of the United States. Controlling for school SES, students attending rural schools in the South had significantly lower achievement growth than students attending suburban or urban schools, whereas students attending rural schools outside the South had higher achievement growth. Rural schools in the South enroll a higher percentage of poor and minority students than do other southern schools (as well as rural schools in other regions), but these differences alone do not explain why such southern schools have levels of student learning that are so much lower. Research suggests that southern rural schools have difficulty attracting good teachers because of low salaries and poor working conditions.[46] This is one reason that rural schools in the South may have such low achievement.

Outside of the South, students attending magnet schools had significantly higher achievement growth than students attending public, comprehensive schools. But in the South, students attending magnet schools enjoyed no such educational advantage. Why this is the case remains unclear. The results suggest, however, that magnet schools are an ineffective mechanism for improving student achievement in the South. One recent study also suggests that magnet schools, many of which were created as part of voluntary desegregation efforts, may also increase white flight while failing to introduce any more interracial exposure than do voluntary desegregation plans.[47]

Next we examined the effects of resource variables, including the student-teacher ratio and the proportion of teachers with advanced degrees. After controlling for student background characteristics, school SES, and school structural characteristics, we did not find any resource variables that significantly predicted achievement growth in either the South or the rest of the United States.

Finally, we examined the impact of process variables that reflect the programs, policies, and overall school environment. This analysis revealed that several of these factors predicted student learning above and beyond the factors discussed earlier (figure 6.7). And as we found previously, the effects of these predictors generally differed in southern and nonsouthern schools.

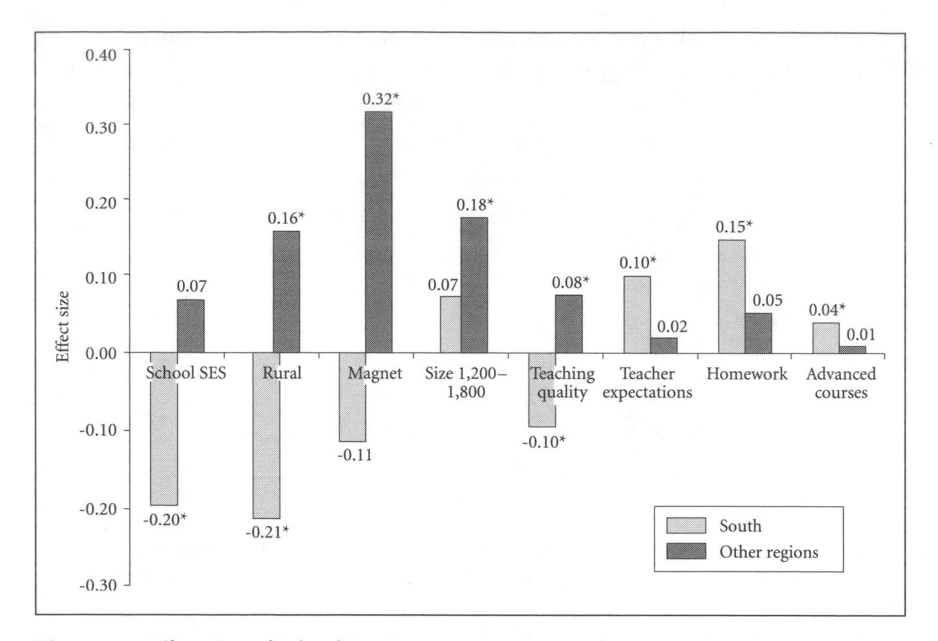

Figure 6.7. Effect Size of School Socioeconomic Status and Structural and Process Characteristics on Achievement Growth, South and Other Regions

*Effect size statistically significant at .05 level.

Note: Effect size represents the effect of a 1 standard deviation change in the predictor variables on a 1 standard deviation change in achievement growth at the student level. Effect sizes are computed from parameter estimates based on an HLM model that controls for student background characteristics and other school variables (Rumberger and Palardy, Technical Appendix, table 7).

Both within and outside the South, teacher quality mattered, but not in the same way. Outside the South, schools in which students rated the quality of teaching higher enjoyed higher achievement growth, controlling for other school characteristics, while in the South the opposite was true. On the face of it, this finding seems puzzling. Why would the same measures of teaching quality have opposite effects? One explanation may be that teachers in some southern schools may treat the students well—generating positive ratings from students—but not be very effective at raising student achievement. This process of demanding less academic work in exchange for cooperative behavior has been documented in other studies.[48] We investigated this issue with our data and found that minority enrollment was positively related to students' rating of teaching quality after controlling for teacher expectations that all students could learn. This suggests that at the same level of teacher expectations, students in high-minority schools rate the quality of teaching higher than do students in low-minority schools even though the higher teacher quality does not translate into improved academic performance, at least in southern high schools.

In the South, both the quality of teaching reported by students and teachers' expectations that all students could learn significantly affected student learning, even after controlling for the previous set of structural variables and school SES. The average amount of homework that students reported and the average number of advanced courses also served as significant predictors of student learning in southern high schools. Yet even after controlling for these other school characteristics, students attending rural schools in the South still had significantly lower achievement growth than students in suburban or urban schools. Interestingly, after controlling for both structural and process variables, school SES became a negative predictor of student learning.[49]

Outside of the South, a different story emerged. None of the measures of teacher quality or academic environment were significant predictors of student learning in high school except for teaching quality, which actually had a small yet statistically positive effect on student learning. As a result, all the structural variables that were significant in the previous model remained statistically significant in this model.

A final issue that we investigated is whether the compositional effects vary among types of students. In other words, did the effects of school SES help or hinder the achievement growth of some students but not others? To address this question, we reestimated the student model to determine whether the effects of SES or minority status varied significantly among schools in each sample. We found that the effects of only one predictor, Hispanic, varied significantly among schools in both the South and in other regions of the country. Even though Hispanics have significantly lower initial achievement levels than whites, Hispanic achievement growth, on average, does not differ from that of whites after controlling for other individual characteristics.[50] But the achievement gap in growth rates between whites and Hispanics does vary among schools. We then investigated whether student composition variables could explain these differences. In the southern sample, school SES did predict the size of the white-Hispanic achievement gap, but in the non-South sample SES did not do so. In the southern sample, the gap in achievement growth between whites and Hispanics was higher in high-SES high schools than in low-SES high schools. So even though, as reported earlier, high-SES high schools have higher achievement growth overall, Hispanic students in southern high schools do not benefit from the compositional effect. This finding could result from increased within-school segregation in higher-SES schools, where Hispanics may be tracked into lower-level classes that compromise that achievement,[51] although it is not clear why this would occur for Hispanics and not blacks.

What Can Be Done about Segregation?

The results of this study confirm a widely held belief of many parents—with whom your children go to school matters. Students who attend high schools with students from higher social class backgrounds learn more than students who attend high schools with other students from low social class backgrounds. In other words, while students' social class background relates to their achievement, so too does the social class background of their peers. These results appeared in both southern and nonsouthern schools, although the effects of social composition were higher in southern than in nonsouthern schools. The results of this study confirm those from earlier studies[52] as well as the original conclusions of the Coleman Report.

But unlike earlier studies, this study also attempted to discover why socioeconomic segregation matters. The study explored three possible causal mechanisms—school structure, school resources, and school processes (policies and practices). These mechanisms, except for school control (Catholic, private) and location (urban, suburban, rural), can be manipulated through policies without attempting to alter the existing socioeconomic segregation of America's schools.

In southern high schools, structural characteristics of schools accounted for almost all of the effects of socioeconomic composition. That is, after controlling for differences in school structure, socioeconomic composition had little direct impact on student learning. This suggests that in the South, where (location, size, and type of school) children go to school matters because that determines with whom they go to school. Outside of the South, structural variables also predicted student learning, but unlike the South, these variables did not mediate the effects of school SES. This suggests that outside the South, with whom children go to school rather than where they go to school matters. School process factors—such as teacher quality—also affected student achievement but did so differently in southern and nonsouthern schools.

The fact that this study found regional differences in the features of schools that predicted student learning has important implications beyond the present study. It suggests that basing school reform policies on research findings conducted on national samples of students and schools or on samples from other regions of the country may not be appropriate for the South. It also suggests the need to conduct more localized studies on school effectiveness.

The study also suggests that overcoming the effects of segregation will require different strategies in the South than in the rest of the United States. Outside of the South, the effects of socioeconomic segregation could be addressed through policies that would change the internal functioning of schools, such as raising teacher quality. In the South, however, the effects of socioeconomic segregation can be addressed only through policies that attempt to redistribute students among schools or improve the quality of schools that students from low SES attend, such as rural schools.

But the analysis also points out a limitation of any school-based reforms as strategies for addressing inequality in educational outcomes. Because most of the variability in student achievement is attributable to the characteristics of students and their families and not to school characteristics, true equality of educational opportunity can be achieved only by directly addressing the pronounced disparities in the backgrounds and circumstances of students and their families, disparities arising from profound differences in jobs, housing, and health care.

Notes

We acknowledge the helpful comments of Jack Boger, Chris Edley, and Gary Orfield in revising this chapter.

1. G. Orfield, *Schools More Separate*, 10.
2. Frankenberg, Lee, and Orfield, *Multiracial Society*, table 10.
3. Ibid.
4. Ibid.
5. Ibid., figs. 6, 8.
6. National Center, *Digest*, table 21.
7. Frankenberg, Lee, and Orfield, *Multiracial Society*, table 8.
8. National Center, *Condition of Education, 2003*, 11.
9. Coleman et al., *Equality of Educational Opportunity.*
10. Ibid., 325.
11. For a recent review of this evidence, see Kahlenberg, *All Together Now.*
12. For two recent reviews of this literature, see Wells and Crain, "Perpetuation Theory"; Schofield, "Review."
13. Jencks and Mayer, "Social Consequences," 144.
14. Bryk and Driscoll, *High School as Community.*
15. Jencks and Mayer, "Social Consequences," 154.
16. See Caldas and Bankston, "Effect of School Population"; Caldas and Bankston, "Inequality of Separation"; Rumberger and Willms, "Impact."
17. Gamoran, "Student Achievement."
18. Chubb and Moe, *Politics, Markets, and America's Schools.* For a detailed critique of the methodology used in this study, see Bryk and Lee, "Is Politics the Problem?"
19. Gamoran, "Student Achievement."

20. Lee, Smith, and Croninger, "How High School Organization Influences the Equitable Distribution"; Lee and Smith, "High School Size."

21. Goldhaber and Brewer, "Why Don't Schools and Teachers Seem to Matter?"

22. Rumberger and Palardy, "Does Segregation (Still) Matter?"

23. Jencks and Mayer, "Social Consequences," 115.

24. Ibid.

25. Kahlenberg, *All Together Now.*

26. National Center, *Condition of Education, 1997.*

27. Raudenbush, Fotiu, and Cheong, "Inequality of Access."

28. Lucas, *Tracking Inequality*; Mickelson, this volume; Mickelson, "Subverting Swann"; Welner and Oakes, "(Li)Ability Grouping."

29. Wells, "Reexamining Social Science Research"; Wells and Crain, "Perpetuation Theory"; Ma and Kurlaender, this volume.

30. A complete description of the data, variables, statistical models, and results of analysis from this study is provided in a technical appendix, which is available at ‹http://education.ucsb.edu/rumberger/›.

31. National Center, *Nation's Report Card*, fig. 2.7.

32. Southern Regional Education Board, *ACT and SAT Scores in the South*, 19.

33. A difference of 1.5 points represents about 19 percent of the average growth rate of 7.85 points for the national sample, which translates into about 6.8 months of the 36 months students attend high school. 6.8 months is about three-quarters of a nine-month school year. The estimates assume that students do not learn tested material over the summer.

34. U.S. Bureau of the Census, *Money Income*, table A.

35. A standard deviation is a common measure of variability in the distribution of social phenomena (J. Cohen, *Statistical Power Analysis*). Many educational outcomes, including SES, are normally distributed in a so-called bell curve. A difference of .12 of standard deviation means that 55 percent of students outside the South had an SES level that exceeded 50 percent of the students in the South.

36. Rumberger and Palardy, "Technical Appendix," table 1.

37. Ibid., table 3.

38. Ibid., table 2. This is in the range first documented by Coleman et al. in their landmark 1966 study of school effectiveness, *Equality of Educational Opportunity.* A recent international study of student achievement by the Organization for Economic Co-Operation and Development (OECD) found that, on average, differences between schools account for 36 percent of the average between-student variation in reading literacy of fifteen-year-olds among the twenty-six countries that participated in the study, including 35 percent for the United States (*Knowledge and Skills*, 60).

39. Rumberger and Palardy, "Technical Appendix," table 3.

40. J. Cohen, *Statistical Power Analysis.* For example, an effect size of .5 represents half of a standard deviation increase in achievement. If achievement is normally distributed, this is equivalent to a person moving from the middle of the distribution, or a point where he or she scores higher than 50 percent of the population, to a point where he or she scores higher than 69 percent of the population.

41. The OECD study found that in most OECD countries, the effects of school SES out-

weigh the effects of individual SES, with the effects of school SES about twice the effects of individual SES in the United States (OECD, *Knowledge and Skills*, 199).

42. Mosteller, "Tennessee Study."

43. Finn and Achilles, "Tennessee's Class Size Study."

44. See the complete list of variables in Rumberger and Palardy, "Technical Appendix," table 1.

45. Lee and Smith, "High School Size."

46. Ballou and Podgursky, "Rural Teachers and Schools."

47. Rossell, "Desegregation Efficiency."

48. Metz, *Classrooms and Corridors*; Sedlak et al., *Selling Students Short.*

49. That is, students in high-SES schools had lower achievement growth, net of all the other predictors in the model.

50. Rumberger and Palardy, "Impact."

51. Mickelson, "Subverting *Swann*."

52. See, e.g., Chubb and Moe, *Politics, Markets, and America's Schools.*

CHAPTER SEVEN

CATHERINE E. FREEMAN | BENJAMIN SCAFIDI | DAVID L. SJOQUIST

Racial Segregation in Georgia Public Schools, 1994–2001

Trends, Causes, and Impact on Teacher Quality

Despite the significant increase in black-white integration in public education between 1954 and 1988, there is evidence that public schools in the southeastern United States are reversing this trend and becoming more racially segregated.[1] Any decrease in integration is problematic, especially if it harms the educational opportunities available to minority students.

This chapter provides analyses of recent trends in black-white segregation across public elementary schools in Georgia, of the causes of this segregation, and of how school segregation affects the characteristics of teachers who serve black students. We find that racial segregation across schools in Georgia is high and that it results largely from segregation between rather than within districts, except in urban school systems. Our results provide evidence that schools with higher percentages of black students have lower-quality human resources. In particular, such schools experience much greater teacher turnover, particularly among white teachers, have fewer teachers with advanced degrees, and have more inexperienced teachers.

This is potentially troubling. Schools that have relatively large yearly teacher turnover may be expected to have more low-performing teachers because high turnover may lead schools to hire and retain less experienced teachers. Several studies find that more experienced teachers are associated with better student performance.[2] Furthermore, differential teacher exit rates may be a good proxy for the quality of the teachers at different schools. This is consistent with the evidence presented by Michael Podgursky, Ryan Monroe, and Donald Watson that average teacher test scores of new teachers in Missouri are lower in the types of schools that have high teacher turnover.[3]

School Segregation

While many southern states experienced large declines in black-white segregation between schools between 1970 and 1980, Georgia did not. Gary Orfield and John T. Yun report that of the thirteen southern states in their analysis, Georgia placed tenth in its increase in black-white integration during the 1970s.[4] In 1970, the typical black student in Georgia went to a public school that had 35.1 percent white students. By 1980, that percentage had increased only to 38.3 percent. Other southern states, including Florida and Tennessee, experienced absolute changes in integration in the 1970s that were more than twice as large as Georgia's. Given this history of relatively stable black-white segregation in Georgia—even during the era of rapidly increasing school integration in most of the United States—we report more recent trends in segregation in Georgia's public schools. We start by considering segregation across all elementary schools, then move to consideration of segregation across school districts, and finally look at segregation within school districts.

School Segregation Statewide and in Urban, Suburban, and Rural Areas

Table 7.1 presents black-white segregation indexes for all elementary schools in selected geographic areas during each of the seven years of our data.[5] We report results for elementary schools only, as our high school results are consistent with the elementary school findings. We focus on segregation between non-Hispanic black and non-Hispanic white students; the implications of our analysis do not differ if we use nonwhite instead of black students. The segregation index we employ is the index of dissimilarity. The possible values of the index range from 0 to 100; higher index numbers indicate greater degrees of black-white segregation.[6] The index reported in table 7.1 was constructed using the population of students in all elementary schools in the geographic area, with the school as the unit of observation.[7]

As the first column of table 7.1 shows, the segregation index for all elementary schools in the state in 2000–2001 was 62.1, which is relatively high and reflects a modest increase over 1994–95.[8] Thus, for the 2000–2001 academic year, 62.1 percent of elementary school students would have had to change schools to have the same black-white racial makeup in each elementary school in the state.

We also calculated the index for elementary schools in three subareas of the state: rural, suburban, and urban areas (columns 2, 3, and 4).[9] Suburban schools are the most segregated, but over the period little change occurred in the segre-

Table 7.1. Segregation Indexes for Elementary Schools, 1995–2001

Year	State	Rural	Suburban	Urban
1995	60.2	47.0	63.4	58.1
1996	60.5	47.1	64.2	57.8
1997	61.2	47.4	64.7	58.7
1998	61.5	48.5	64.6	58.9
1999	62.0	49.0	64.4	59.8
2000	61.9	48.5	64.5	61.4
2001	62.1	49.6	63.9	62.9

gation index. Urban elementary schools experienced a small increase in segregation, and by 2001, the values of the segregation indexes for urban and suburban schools were about the same. Rural schools are less segregated, but these elementary schools experienced an increase in segregation over the seven years.

Table 7.2 presents black-white segregation indexes for elementary school students using school districts rather than schools as the unit of observation. (Georgia has 159 county school districts and 21 city districts, for a total of 180 districts.) The values of the between-district segregation indexes are smaller than the indexes reported in table 7.1 because those indexes reflect both within- and between-district segregation. Consistent with prior evidence from across the nation, most of the segregation at the elementary school level in Georgia results from racial differences between districts rather than within districts. In other words, the observed racial makeup of students differs more when one compares school districts than if one looks across schools within districts.

In rural areas, between-district and between-school indexes are very similar because many rural districts have just one elementary school, in which case school and district are the same. A large difference exists between the between-district and the between-school segregation indexes in urban areas, which suggests that in urban areas substantial black-white segregation occurs within school districts.

Substantial variation in school segregation occurs across Georgia. We find that during the academic year 1994–95, the index of black-white school segregation ranged from a low of 17.9 in the largely rural region in the southern part of the state to a high of 72.5 in metropolitan Atlanta.[10] The wide disparity persisted over time. Broadly speaking, elementary schools in the northern half of the state tend to be the most segregated, while schools in the southern and southeastern portions of the state tend to be the most integrated.

Table 7.2. Between-District Segregation Indexes for Elementary Schools, 1995–2001

Year	State	Rural	Suburban	Urban
1995	50.3	42.2	51.2	28.7
1996	50.6	42.8	51.0	27.9
1997	51.3	43.1	51.6	28.5
1998	51.3	43.8	50.7	27.4
1999	51.3	44.3	49.4	28.4
2000	51.0	43.7	49.0	27.9
2001	50.8	44.7	47.3	27.4

Segregation within Districts

Individual school districts can affect black-white segregation within their borders through the drawing of school zones, decisions about the placement and number of new schools, and other means. Thus, an important question is whether segregation increased among schools within school districts over the period.

In both 1994–95 and 2000–2001, the majority of districts had low segregation indexes. For example, in 1994–95, 59.4 percent of the districts had indexes of twenty or less, and 72.7 percent had indexes of thirty or less. In 1994–95, seventy-eight school districts (43.3 percent) had only one elementary school, and seventy-four (41.1 percent) had only one elementary school in 2000–2001. All of these districts had, by construction, a zero segregation index. In 1994–95 and in 2000–2001, 52.0 percent of districts with a nonzero index had a segregation index of thirty or less.

Between 1994 and 2001, a slight increase occurred in segregation within the state's school districts, reflecting the statewide increase in the segregation index shown in table 7.1. More districts experienced an increase in within-district segregation than experienced a decrease; within district segregation decreased for forty districts, increased in sixty districts, and did not change by more than one point in eighty districts. The unweighted mean value of the indexes across all districts increased slightly, from 18.3 in 1994–95 to 18.8 in 2000–2001. In other words, within-district segregation has been rather stable over the period.

Six school districts experienced large decreases in within-district segregation. Of these, four had fewer than 2 percent black students, so that a movement between schools of a few black students could dramatically change the value of the index. Another district had a reduction in the number of elementary schools, which usually brings more children together and could explain the decrease in the value of the segregation index. The decrease in the index for one district is unexplained. Thus, there was substantial inertia in within-district segregation over the seven-year period.

Causes of School Segregation within Districts

Students in Georgia have almost no options for transferring between school systems without moving their residences; thus, black-white segregation between school systems results largely from residential segregation between systems. Because an individual district has limited ability to alter the racial composition of the student body within the system, we focus on the causes of within-district rather than between-district school segregation. We consider three possible factors:

- If school attendance at elementary schools is based on residential proximity to the school, we would expect that school segregation and residential segregation in a district will be positively related.
- If there are fewer schools in a district, there is less opportunity for racial groups to be segregated into separate schools; therefore, we expect that the fewer schools in the district, the lower the level of segregation.
- If the likelihood increases that white parents will avoid sending their children to school with black students as the proportion of black students increases, we expect that the higher the percentage of the population that is black, the larger the index.

To determine whether these factors are associated with greater segregation, we estimated two regression equations (table 7.3). Column 1 presents a regression equation using the value of the index and the three explanatory variables. The regression lends support to the first two of the expectations—namely, that greater residential segregation and more elementary schools lead to more school segregation within the district. However, the findings do not support the third expectation—that is, that segregation is greater the larger the proportion of black students.

Column 2 reports the regression results using the change in the within-district segregation index and the change in the value of explanatory variables. The results imply that the only variable that has a statistically meaningful effect on the change in segregation is the change in the residential segregation index, which suggests that an increase in residential segregation is a good predictor of an increase in school segregation.[11]

We have seen that within-district school segregation increased and that school segregation within districts strongly relates to residential segregation within those districts. A further question is whether within-district school segregation be-

Table 7.3. Factors Explaining School Segregation, 1995–2001

	Dependent Variable (T-Statistics)	
Explanatory Variable	Within-District Segregation Index, 2001	Change in Within-District Segregation Indexes, 1995–2001
Intercept	−0.380	0.480
	(0.09)	(0.49)
Residential segregation (2000)	0.353* (3.91)	—
Greater number of elementary schools in 2001	0.997* (8.69)	—
Higher percentage of population that is black in 2000	−0.064 (0.91)	—
Change in number of schools between 1995 and 2001	—	3.17 (0.95)
Increase in residential segregation between 1990 and 2000	—	0.213* (2.01)
Increase in percentage of population that is black between 1990 and 2000	—	0.328 (1.36)
R^2	0.436	0.033

* Statistically significant at greater than 5 percent level.

came more closely matched with within-district residential segregation over the 1994–2001 period. Because the courts seem to view school integration as a less pressing legal issue today than in 1994, perhaps the degree of school segregation will more closely match residential segregation today than in 1994. Unfortunately, we do not have residential segregation data for 1995, and thus we are forced to average the 1990 and 2000 residential segregation indexes, implicitly assuming that the trend is linear.

For all 180 school districts, the correlation between school segregation and residential segregation increased from 0.408 in 1995 to 0.440 in 2000, a small but positive change. To control for the effect of a large percentage change in the number of elementary schools on school segregation, we also considered only districts with five or more elementary schools in 1995. For this set of 51 districts, the correlation between residential and school segregation increased from 0.579 in 1995 to 0.773 in 2000. These results suggest that school segregation within districts more closely matched residential segregation in 2000 than in 1995.

As previously stated, there is a concern that granting unitary status to school districts that have fulfilled their obligations under desegregation decrees will lead to more racial segregation within those school districts. We know of four Georgia school districts that achieved unitary status prior to 2003—Chatham, Coffee, De Kalb, and Muscogee Counties. Fulton County was declared unitary in 2003, too recent to allow any analysis.

The Chatham County school district was declared unitary in 1988. We lack information on possible increases in within-district segregation between 1988 and the start of our data; we do know that a substantial increase in school segregation occurred within Chatham between 1994–95 and 2000–2001. During 1994–2001, the segregation index increased from 34.5 to 42.3. During the 1990s, interestingly, residential segregation declined in Chatham County, from 67.5 in 1990 to 61.6 in 2000.

Coffee County, a small county in southeast Georgia, was declared unitary in 1995. During the 1990s the school segregation index increased from 11.2 to 13.3, while the residential segregation index increased from 39.9 to 42.6.

De Kalb County, which lies just east of the city of Atlanta, was declared unitary in 1996, and in 1999 the courts ended its busing program to promote integration. Between 1997–98 and 2000–2001, the school segregation index for De Kalb increased substantially, from 66.6 to 76.4. However, black-white segregation within De Kalb schools began increasing even before the declaration of unitary status. Furthermore, residential segregation was increasing as well, from 68.0 in 1990 to 73.3 in 2000.

Muscogee County public schools were declared unitary in 1997. Between 1998–99 and 2000–2001, within-district segregation increased by 2.2 percentage points, from 58.7 to 60.9, while residential segregation remained largely unchanged in the 1990s. Despite the fact that De Kalb and Muscogee had extremely high levels of within-district segregation before obtaining unitary status, black-white segregation increased after the systems were declared unitary.[12]

Teachers and the Racial Mix of Schools

Strong empirical evidence indicates that teachers are the most important school resource positively affecting student achievement.[13] Therefore, it is important to ask whether greater black-white segregation between schools adversely affects

Table 7.4. Characteristics of Students by Racial Categories, 1994–1995 and 2000–2001

School Classification (Percentage of Black Students)	Characteristics of Students					
	Percentage of Black Students		Poverty Rate[a]		Third-Grade Reading Scores (Iowa Test of Basic Skills)	
	1994–95	2000–2001	1994–95	2000–2001	1994–95	2000–2001
<7	3.1	2.8	21.4	18.6	61.5	59.3
7–25	14.7	15.2	29.4	30.0	59.2	54.7
25–45	34.8	35.1	49.2	47.1	52.3	47.7
45–70	56.9	57.5	61.6	59.5	46.2	43.3
>70	91.6	92.0	79.5	77.0	40.1	38.4

[a] Measured by percentage of students who are eligible for free or reduced-price lunch.

the quality of the teachers who serve black students. In this section we consider how the characteristics of schools and of teachers differ in relation to the schools' black student population.

We placed each school into one of five categories based on the percentage of black students enrolled. The thresholds for each category are round numbers chosen to separate students roughly into quintiles. Table 7.4 illustrates how the characteristics of the students differ across the five categories in the years 1994–95 and 2000–2001. In both years, as the percentage of black students increases, the poverty rate (as measured by the percentage of students eligible for free or reduced-price lunch) increases, while average test scores on the third-grade reading test scores decrease.[14] Thus, schools that serve higher proportions of black students also serve higher proportions of students in poverty and of students who score lower on third-grade reading exams. This pattern existed in both years.

Teacher Characteristics across Categories

Table 7.5 presents the characteristics of teachers in each of the five different categories of Georgia schools for 1994–95 and 2000–2001. The most pronounced difference among the five groups of schools is in the percentage of teachers who are white. In those schools with black student enrollments of 7 percent or less, 97.1 percent of teachers were white in 1994–95. In schools where black students made up 70 percent or more of the school enrollment, by contrast, only 41.7 per-

Table 7.5. Characteristics of Teachers by Racial Categories, 1994–1995 and 2000–2001

School Classification (Percentage of Black Students)	Age		Percentage with Advanced Degrees		Percentage White		Salary (Dollars)		Percentage Certified		Percentage Novice	
	1994–95	2000–2001	1994–95	2000–2001	1994–95	2000–2001	1994–95	2000–2001	1994–95	2000–2001	1994–95	2000–2001
<7	40.8	41.4	45.1	36.8	97.1	96.8	31,253	38,753	95.3	95.3	7.0	7.2
7–25	40.5	41.3	44.2	35.4	91.3	92.1	30,575	38,078	95.0	95.4	7.4	7.3
25–45	40.9	41.5	42.3	34.5	84.1	85.3	30,037	37,107	94.9	94.8	7.4	7.1
45–70	41.1	41.8	42.4	35.3	71.8	72.9	30,320	37,867	94.9	94.9	7.5	7.0
>70	42.3	41.8	41.5	32.2	41.7	38.9	33,589	39,232	95.4	93.3	6.6	7.7

cent of the teachers were white. Between 1994–95 and 2000–2001, the percentage of white teachers remained roughly constant for all categories other than the schools with the highest percentage of black students, which experienced a 6.7 percent (2.8 percentage point) reduction in white teachers.

Schools with higher percentages of black students have teachers with a slightly higher mean age and a lower probability of having an advanced degree, although the differences are small. In 1994–95, teachers in schools with fewer than 7 percent black students were 3.6 percentage points more likely than teachers in schools with more than 70 percent black students to have advanced degrees. By 2000–2001, this difference was 4.6 percentage points. In the 1994–95 academic year, there were no real differences in certification status across the categories of schools—virtually all teachers were fully certified. However, by 2000–2001, students in predominantly black schools had about 2 percentage points fewer certified teachers than students in schools in the other categories. Thus, the No Child Left Behind legislation, which will eventually require all teachers to be certified and to have college degrees, will have only a small positive effect. Unfortunately, Georgia does not maintain or does not make available other information on teachers, such as whether they are teaching in the field of their academic training or what they scored on certification exams.

The percentage of teachers who are novices—that is, who are under age twenty-seven and who have taught for less than two years in a Georgia public school—does not follow a particular pattern either across the categories or between years. The most significant change is the increase in the category for the highest percentage of black students, where the percentage of novice teachers increased from 6.6 percent in 1995 to 7.7 percent in 2001. Exposure to novice teachers is important; Steven G. Rivkin, Eric A. Hanushek, and John F. Kain find that novice teachers generally perform worse than more experienced teachers.[15] This evidence from Georgia is consistent with evidence from New York that schools that serve higher proportions of students who are racial minorities, low income, and have low achievement test scores have teachers with lower average credentials.[16]

Teacher Turnover

Next, we consider the mobility of teachers, both between schools and out of the Georgia teaching force. We define teacher turnover as a teacher leaving his or her current school for any reason—for another school within the district, another school in another district, administration, or out of the Georgia teaching force.

We find that white teacher turnover is much greater in schools with larger percentages of black students (table 7.6). For 1994–95, only 10.7 percent of white

Table 7.6. Teacher Leave Rate by Racial Categories, 1994–1995 and 1999–2000

School Classification (Percentage of Black Students)	Percentage of Teachers Who Left School at End of Academic Year			
	White		Black	
	1994–95	1999–2000	1994–95	1999–2000
<7	10.7	20.4	12.8	24.2
7–25	12.4	18.7	14.3	19.4
25–45	14.7	22.8	12.5	21.2
45–70	15.7	22.1	13.6	18.7
>70	18.2	31.2	13.2	20.6

teachers left schools in the category for low percentage of black students, while 18.2 percent of white teachers left schools in the category for high percentage of black students. A similar pattern exists for 1999–2000, but the percentage of white teachers who left is much higher for all categories.[17] In the intervening years, the rate of departure for white teachers fluctuates from year to year, but the trend is upward.

Black teachers display a markedly different turnover pattern. In 1994–95, the percentage of black teachers leaving their current schools varies little across school racial categories. Although mobility rates are higher in 1999–2000, there is no tendency for higher turnover among black teachers in schools where the percentage of black students is higher. In fact, black teachers who serve in schools with fewer than 7 percent black students have the highest turnover rate (24.2 percent). Thus, we find that white teachers are much more likely to leave schools that serve higher proportions of black students, while no clear pattern exists for black teachers.

In previous work, Benjamin Scafidi, David L. Sjoquist, and Todd R. Stinebrickner have analyzed the turnover of new Georgia teachers, defined as teachers under age twenty-seven who have not taught in Georgia in the past three years.[18] They report that a large proportion of new teachers change schools within the first few years of teaching: 20.9 percent of new teachers move to a new school in the same school district, while another 12.4 percent move to a teaching position in another school district. Large differences exist in the racial composition of the schools of those new teachers who remain in the same schools and those who change teaching jobs. In the 2002 study, teachers who remained at the same school served student populations that were on average 37.2 percent black. Teachers who moved to other schools within the same district left a student population that was on average 39.3 percent black, while teachers who changed districts left a student population that was on average 46.6 percent black. A similar pattern exists in relation to both the students' poverty status and their achievement test scores. These numbers indicate that new teachers who leave their current schools are more likely to serve minority, economically disadvantaged, and lower-achieving students in the year prior to exiting. These findings are consistent with those of Hanushek, Kain, and Rivkin that teacher mobility is strongly related to the characteristics of the students, particularly race and achievement.[19]

Scafidi, Sjoquist, and Stinebrickner also estimated a statistical model of teacher mobility and retention to isolate the independent effect of each of these factors.[20] They found that the race of the student body was the driving factor behind the turnover of white teachers and that student poverty and test scores did not cause attrition of these teachers.[21] Many possible explanations can be suggested for the higher turnover of white teachers at black schools. For example, given widespread residential segregation, white teachers may have longer commutes if they teach at black schools. White teachers may feel unsafe in schools with more black students or unsafe in the neighborhoods where these schools are located. White teachers may deem black students harder to teach or may be averse to teaching black students because of racial prejudice. Teachers may leave because black schools may be more likely to have poor facilities, to lack books and supplies, to have weak administration, and to have large class sizes, although we expect that these factors would cause both black and white teachers to leave such schools.

These patterns of teacher turnover may play an important role in creating racial disparities in educational opportunities. Schools that have relatively large yearly teacher turnover may be expected to have more low-performing teachers. First, high turnover may lead schools to have less experienced teachers. Several studies find that more experienced teachers are associated with better student performance.[22]

Second, evidence indicates that better teachers are more likely to move. In her survey of the literature on attrition and retention, Bonnie Billingsley cites four studies that find that teachers with higher scores on the National Teacher Exam or the SAT were more likely to leave.[23] Melinda Scott Krei reports that better teachers were more likely to transfer from low-income schools.[24] While most of these studies relate to leaves from teaching and not to transfers between schools, and test scores do not imply that a person is an effective teacher, these findings are consistent with a hypothesis that higher-achieving teachers are more likely to transfer.

Third, if school officials can discern, at least partially, the quality of individual teachers, then schools with larger numbers of applications relative to the number of open positions should be able to select better teachers than schools that face a relative shortage of applicants. Thus, schools that face large exoduses of teachers each year will have fewer choices and a more difficult time obtaining quality teachers. Consequently, differential teacher exit rates between schools may be a good proxy for the quality of their teachers. Support for this position is found in Podgursky, Monroe, and Watson's work, which finds that in the types of schools that have higher teacher turnover average, test scores of new teachers are lower.[25]

However, if white teachers are less effective at teaching black students, then the transfer of white teachers from predominantly black schools may be desirable. The only research on this subject of which we are aware found that for the most part, the race, gender, and ethnicity of the teacher did not affect how much students learned.[26]

Conclusions and Policy Implications

In this chapter we provide analyses of recent trends in black-white segregation across public elementary schools in Georgia, of the causes of this segregation, and of how school segregation impacts the characteristics of teachers who serve black students.

The important findings include:

1. Public schools in Georgia have experienced a small increase in black-white segregation in recent years. Between 1994 and 2001, the statewide index of dissimilarity increased from 60.2 to 62.1. About 17.7 percent of students in 1994–95 attended schools with greater than 70 percent black students. This percentage increased to 19.1 percent in 2000–2001.
2. Statewide, most of the segregation between schools results from segregation between school districts. Especially in the suburbs and rural areas, within-district segregation tends to be modest. Urban school districts, however, have substantial within-district segregation.
3. Great heterogeneity exists in segregation across Georgia; the highest segregation between schools occurs in metropolitan Atlanta.
4. School segregation within districts is significantly related to within-district residential segregation, and this relationship has increased over time.
5. Little change has occurred in school segregation from 1994 to 2001 in virtually all school districts that have more than a small number of black students.
6. The four districts that obtained unitary status prior to 2003—Chatham, Coffee, De Kalb, and Muscogee—experienced increases in within-district school segregation in the period after unitary status was granted. In Coffee and De Kalb, at least some of this increase may have resulted from increas-

ing housing segregation, and in De Kalb some of the increase may have resulted from a court-ordered end to its busing program designed to promote integration. The other two districts, however, experienced increasing school segregation at a time when residential segregation was decreasing (Chatham) or flat (Muscogee).

7. Students in schools with larger proportions of black students are much less likely to have white teachers. Students in schools with fewer than 7 percent black students had about a 97 percent chance of having a white teacher. Students in schools with more than 70 percent black students had about a 40 percent chance of having a white teacher.
8. Disparities in other teacher characteristics—age, advanced degrees, certification, and percentage novice—do not appear to be large across school racial categories. However, within-school segregation, which we cannot analyze with our data, could lead to greater disparities in these teacher characteristics.
9. The differences in teacher turnover across school racial categories are immense and have increased over time. In particular, white teachers are much more likely to leave schools that serve higher proportions of black students. In 1994–95, only about 11 percent of white teachers left schools that served fewer than 7 percent black students. In that same academic year, the turnover rate was 18.2 percent of white teachers at schools that served more than 70 percent black students. By 2000–2001, these turnover rates increased to 20.4 and 31.2 percent, respectively.
10. Most white teachers who changed schools moved to schools that served lower proportions of black students, fewer low-income students, and more students who scored higher on achievement exams. This was especially true for teachers who changed school districts.
11. Results adopted from Scafidi, Sjoquist, and Stinebrickner's *The Impact of Wages and School Characteristics on Teacher Mobility and Retention* demonstrate that the race of the students is the most important factor (among those considered) explaining the movement of teachers between schools and out of the Georgia teaching force.[27] This was particularly true for white teachers. Black teachers seemed to have more attachment to schools that serve higher proportions of black students.

These findings suggest that black-white segregation across public schools in Georgia remains a problem early in the twenty-first century, that segregation increased slightly in recent years, that black students are much less likely than white students to have white teachers, and that schools serving higher proportions of black students have much higher turnover rates for white teachers. The large disparity in teacher turnover rates may threaten educational opportunities for black students.

We do not provide any direct evidence that the level of segregation within a school district affects student performance. However, we do show that schools with higher percentages of black students have lower-quality human resources. In particular, such schools experience much higher turnover of white teachers, have fewer teachers with advanced degrees, and have more inexperienced teachers.

Notes

1. G. Orfield, *Schools More Separate.*

2. Ferguson, "Paying for Public Education"; Rivkin, Hanushek, and Kain, *Teachers, Schools, and Academic Achievement*; Krueger, "Experimental Estimates."

3. Podgursky, Monroe, and Watson, "Academic Quality."

4. G. Orfield and Yun, *Resegregation*, table 16, p. 19.

5. We combined data sets in a way that allows us to link teacher characteristics with individual school characteristics. Information on each public school in Georgia for the academic years 1994–95 through 2000–2001 was obtained from the Georgia Department of Education, and information on each public school teacher in Georgia came from the Georgia Professional Standards Commission. Our teacher information includes certification status, educational attainment, race, sex, and age.

6. The segregation index is measured as $(100 \times (Bi/B) - (Wi/W))/2$, where B represents the total number of blacks in the geographic area, W represents the number of whites in the geographic area, and i is the unit of observation (individual school, school district, or census block group) in the geographic area under consideration. We construct segregation indexes for schools and neighborhoods. For schools, the index measures the percentage of students of one racial group that would have to change schools so that all schools in the geographic area would have the same racial makeup.

7. We define an elementary school as a school that has a third grade.

8. In 2000, the median value of residential segregation in U.S. metropolitan areas was 64.8. See Iceland, Weinberg, and Steinmetz, *Racial and Ethnic Residential Segregation.*

9. Urban schools (of which there were 227 in 2000–2001) are those in any school district within a metropolitan statistical area (MSA) surrounding a central city or in the central county if there is no independent city school system. Suburban schools (of which there were 549 in 2000–2001) consist of all schools in an MSA other than urban schools. A rural school (of which there were 338 in 2000–2001) is any school in a district that is not in an MSA.

10. A map of the regions can be found at ‹http://www.georgia.gov/00/article/0,2145,4802_0_11115,00.html›.

11. The coefficients on the two other variables are of the expected sign but are not statistically significant.

12. Reardon and Yun, this volume, find that this phenomenon is occurring elsewhere.

13. Rivkin, Hanushek, and Kain, *Teachers, Schools, and Academic Achievement.*

14. The test score used is the mean percentile rank of third-grade students on the Iowa Test of Basic Skills Reading exam.

15. Rivkin, Hanushek, and Kain, *Teachers, Schools, and Academic Achievement.*

16. Lankford, Loeb, and Wyckoff, "Teacher Sorting."

17. We report mobility rates for 1999–2000 because our data end in 2000–2001. Thus, we do not observe whether teachers leave their schools between 2000–2001 and 2001–2.

18. Scafidi, Sjoquist, and Stinebrickner, *Impact.*

19. Hanushek, Kain, and Rivkin, *Why Public Schools Lose Teachers.*

20. Scafidi, Sjoquist, and Stinebrickner, *Impact.*

21. Although both the student poverty rate and the racial composition of the student body correlate with white teacher turnover, when both variables are included in the regression equation, the race variable is statistically significant, but the poverty variable is not.

22. Ferguson, "Paying for Public Education"; Rivkin, Hanushek, and Kain, *Teachers, Schools, and Academic Achievement*; Krueger, "Experimental Estimates."

23. Billingsley, "Teacher Retention and Attrition."

24. Krei, "Teacher Transfer Policy."

25. Podgursky, Monroe, and Watson, "Academic Quality."

26. Ehrenberg, Goldhaber, and Brewer, "Do Teachers' Race, Gender, and Ethnicity Matter?"

27. Scafidi, Sjoquist, and Stinebrickner, *Impact.*

CHAPTER EIGHT

ERICA FRANKENBERG

The Impact of School Segregation on Residential Housing Patterns

Mobile, Alabama, and Charlotte, North Carolina

A number of recent key school-assignment cases handed down by the U.S. Supreme Court have pointedly declined to address residential segregation when ruling on whether a district has dismantled its system of separate and unequal schools. Schooling and residential patterns of racial segregation, however, are demonstrably interconnected. Segregated neighborhoods often create segregated schools because of a basic feature of many school-assignment policies: schools most commonly draw students from the immediate geographic region. When students are assigned to schools based on neighborhoods, segregated neighborhoods result in segregated schools. Moreover, officials often draw school boundaries (as well as other boundaries, such as city limits) in ways that aggravate already existing patterns of residential segregation. In addition, school board decisions on where to place new schools can have considerable effects on the racial composition of those schools.

Some observers have suggested that the causal relationship might work in the opposite direction as well. Schools can themselves be important in perpetuating residential segregation. Three oft-related school characteristics—racial composition, percentage of poor students, and academic quality—all send important signals to parents and home owners. Schools that are not fully desegregated or whose racial composition varies substantially from that of the district can discourage white and/or middle-class home seekers from buying in the school's vicinity or even prompt white residential flight, which only intensifies the neighborhood racial segregation and consequently the school's racial imbalance.

By contrast, this hypothesis continues, in a district that deliberately promotes desegregated schools, the segregating effect of schools on housing dissipates. If all schools within the district are racially balanced, people will make residential choices without considering the racial composition of neighborhood schools, since their children will be exposed to equal levels of racial integration anywhere in the district. Creation of student attendance zones that produce a thoroughly desegregated district thus ensures balanced schools regardless of neighborhood residential composition. Over time, residential segregation should decrease as people seeking homes have the assurance of stable, mixed-race neighborhoods and schools. If true, these demographic forces operating on a metropolitan level should materially affect both school and residential segregation levels within a school district and between districts.

While within-district segregation has been the focus of most desegregation cases and remedies, between-district segregation is actually a more significant contributor to metropolitan-wide segregation. As the United States changes from a predominantly urban to metropolitan country, a residential move to another school district within the same metropolitan area is an often-used white-flight strategy for those seeking to escape urban school systems. Suburban school systems often function as white enclaves for parents seeking to avoid city schools with growing nonwhite student enrollments. This results in adjacent school systems of vastly different racial composition. Yet the Supreme Court ruled in 1974 that federal courts are normally prohibited from ordering interdistrict, or city-suburban, movement of children to integrate students in predominantly nonwhite central city districts with students in surrounding white suburban areas.[1]

To examine the effect of school desegregation on residential integration, this chapter compares two southern cities: Mobile, Alabama, and Charlotte, North Carolina.[2] Mobile and Charlotte are part of countywide systems that were previously under extensive court-ordered desegregation plans. Before desegregation began in the early 1960s, both Mobile and Charlotte had similar city and school populations and demographic mixes largely of white and black residents. Further, they had very similar levels of residential segregation. Although Charlotte and Mobile have diverged since 1970, their similarities at that time in terms of the racial composition and segregation in their metro areas, in their cities, and in their school systems offer two different contexts in which to examine the effects of school desegregation (or lack thereof) on an area's residential segregation patterns.

My examination of changes in the school-assignment policies and the schooling and residential patterns of these two cities suggests that school desegregation *when fully implemented* can indeed lead to more integrated residential patterns. In contrast, a large proportion of racially identifiable schools in a system can contribute to greater residential segregation.

Background of Desegregation

Because much of the housing market is private and is not a direct governmental responsibility (unlike K–12 education), the government's ability to effectively prevent housing discrimination is not as far-reaching as with school segregation. Yet legal measures to ensure residential segregation—like de jure school segregation—have had a long history. Racial zoning ordinances (limiting neighborhoods to residents of one race) remained legal until 1917, and the courts did not declare restrictive covenants (which forbade whites from selling their property to nonwhites) unenforceable until 1948. Governmental entities such as the Federal Housing Administration and the Veterans Administration for many decades refused to finance housing in some nonwhite areas or established mortgage policies that promoted segregation.[3] Not until 1968 did federal laws begin to prohibit explicit racial discrimination by real estate agents, housing lenders, and builders. In many southern areas, these racially restrictive housing practices—following decades of Jim Crow laws—guaranteed that black and white residents would live in essentially separate spheres. Moreover, increased black migration from rural areas into cities coincided with a growth of white suburbs after World War II, creating a period of increasing residential segregation.

Even after federal courts outlawed formal legal mechanisms that enforced residential segregation, more decentralized and less overt racism continued to operate through price mechanisms and white preferences for living in white areas.[4] Residential segregation has been declining nationally since 1970, primarily because of moves by blacks and other minorities into formerly all-white areas.[5] There are, nevertheless, more all-black tracts in cities than ever before, suggesting that although barriers against black mobility may have lowered, significant segregation remains. Douglas S. Massey and Nancy A. Denton conclude that "when it comes to determining where, and with whom, Americans live, race overwhelms all other considerations."[6] Instead of outright refusal by real estate agents to show houses in white or integrated neighborhoods, black home seekers now face a more subtle process Massey and Denton describe as "discrimination with a smile."[7] These less overt practices have a profound impact on our society: based on 1977 U.S. Department of Housing and Urban Development audits, George C. Galster and W. Mark Keeney found that widespread racial discrimination still leads to residential segregation, which, by restricting black access to both employment and home-ownership opportunities in more prosperous areas, increases interracial economic disparities that only further discrimination and hence segregation.[8]

The legal system has acknowledged the link between residential segregation and school segregation. A unanimous Supreme Court noted in *Swann v. Charlotte-*

Mecklenburg Board of Education in 1971, "[School board decisions] may well promote segregated residential patterns, which, when combined with 'neighborhood zoning,' further lock the school system into the mold of separation of the races."[9] The *Swann* Court added, "People gravitate toward school facilities. . . . The location of schools may thus influence the patterns of residential development of a metropolitan area."[10] *Swann* was monumental in stating in legal terms what had been realized in practice for years—neighborhood schooling perpetuated systems of both residential and schooling segregation.[11] In *Keyes v. School District no. 1, Denver, Colorado*, the Court found that segregated schooling "may have a profound reciprocal effect on the racial composition of residential neighborhoods within a metropolitan area, thereby causing further racial concentration within the schools."[12]

More recently, however, a majority of the Court in *Freeman v. Pitts* found that private choices, not Georgia's history of school segregation, had led to the residential segregation that remained in De Kalb County. The majority further declared that after a school system's initial racial imbalance resulting from prior illegal segregation had been rectified, "the school district is under no duty to remedy imbalance that is caused by demographic factors, because resegregation does not have constitutional implications where it is a product of private choices, rather than state action."[13]

Justice Harry A. Blackmun, in dissent, pointed out that housing choices, though generally considered to be private, might well be influenced by the school district's actions. "This interactive effect between schools and housing choices," he wrote, "may occur because many families are concerned about the racial composition of a prospective school and will make residential decisions accordingly. Thus, schools that are demonstrably black or white provide a signal to these families, perpetuating and intensifying the residential movement."[14] Several decades of demographic change in Mobile and Charlotte seem to provide support for Justice Blackmun's opinion.

Tale of Two Cities

Mobile has had a countywide school system since its inception in 1852, while the city of Charlotte consolidated its school district with that of Mecklenburg County only in 1960. Both districts, however, are the largest school systems in their states. In 1960, several years before any significant desegregation had occurred in most areas of the South, Mobile and Charlotte were similarly sized cities, with relatively equal school enrollments.

Charlotte and Mobile also had similarly sized student populations (about 78,000

Table 8.1. White Percentage of School Population, 1967–2000

	1967	1968	1974	1976	1980	1986	2000
Charlotte	71	71	66	64	60	58	47
Mobile	59	58	55	56	56	55	47

Sources: G. Orfield and Monfort, "Racial Change"; 2000–2001 NCES Common Core of Data.

students) in the mid-1960s, when desegregation efforts began. Following the population trends in their metropolitan statistical areas (MSAs), Mobile's public school population has decreased (to around 65,000 in 2000), while the Charlotte school system continues to grow rapidly (reaching just over 100,000 in 2000 and almost 114,000 in 2004). Until recently, Charlotte had a smaller proportion of minority students than Mobile did (table 8.1).

The legal context of Mobile and Charlotte's school desegregation efforts were also similar through 1971. The Mobile desegregation case was originally filed in 1963. It was combined with the Charlotte case before the Supreme Court in 1971 because the two districts presented similar issues for the Court to decide: namely, what were school districts' responsibilities in designing desegregation plans when, because of residential segregation, a "race-neutral" student assignment plan would result in segregated schools?

Following the *Swann* decision in 1971, the implementation of school desegregation in the two districts diverged. The Charlotte school system undertook a comprehensive, systemwide desegregation effort in 1975. The effectiveness of the desegregation efforts began to erode in the 1990s with the creation of an extensive magnet school system, and in 1999, despite growing segregation, Charlotte-Mecklenburg Schools (CMS) were declared unitary and soon ceased desegregation efforts. By contrast, after implementing a partial school desegregation plan in the early 1970s, Mobile did not even adopt a consent decree to which both the plaintiffs and the school system agreed until 1988. This document acknowledged that a certain number of one-race schools were inevitable given Mobile County's demographics. In 1997, the federal district judge ruled that the Mobile County School System was unitary. Because of the similarities of their demographic and legal contexts before substantial desegregation occurred, the divergent paths trod by these superficially similar districts deserve greater study.

Mobile, Alabama

Alabama's coastal MSA of Mobile consists of Mobile and Baldwin Counties. Mobile, the central city of this MSA, is the county seat of Mobile County. Three other cities in Mobile County had more than 10,000 residents in 2000. Baldwin County, by contrast, has primarily been agricultural, with only two cities with more than 10,000 residents in 2000 (and both with fewer than 17,000 residents).

Schools—Still Separate

The Mobile MSA consists of two countywide school systems. Although Mobile County had a thirty-four-year-old desegregation order, observers question whether meaningful desegregation actually occurred. Whites were rarely bused away from their neighborhood schools and were never bused to minority schools. In 1968, the average black student attended school with a student body that was only 9 percent white. The exposure of black students to white students, or the percentage of white students in the "average" black student's school, increased to more than 30 percent during the late 1970s and 1980s but fell to just 22 percent by 2000 (table 8.2). A 1982 study found that although the Mobile school system had increased districtwide levels of racial balancing, it had taken few steps to reduce the number of racially isolated minority schools.[15] By 2000, the Mobile school system was 47 percent white, 50 percent black, 1 percent Hispanic, and 2 percent Asian. More than half of the district's black students attended racially isolated minority schools.

In 2000, the interracial exposure of white students in Mobile County differed substantially from that of black students. The average white student attended a school that was almost 75 percent white, while the average black student attended a school that was more than 75 percent black (table 8.3). In other words, the average black or white student was in a school where only one-quarter of the students were of other races. There were a large number of intensely segregated minority schools, and few racially balanced schools. In fact, more elementary schools were 99–100 percent minority (fourteen, serving almost 50 percent of black children) than were racially balanced (thirteen).[16] More than one-third of Mobile schools were intensely segregated in 2000–2001: twenty-four schools were 90–100 percent black, and eleven were 90–100 percent white. Taken together, these data point to the continued existence of racial enclaves in Mobile schools.

In Mobile County, the racial composition of schools is closely linked to their location. Of the system's hundred schools in 2000–2001, all twenty-four schools with student bodies that were 90–100 percent minority were located within the

Table 8.2. Isolation of Black Students in Mobile County Schools, 1968–2000

Year	% Black	% White in School of Average Black Student	% Black in 90–100% Minority Schools	% Black in 50–100% Minority Schools
1968	42	9	—	—
1970	44	24	—	—
1978	43	31	—	—
1986	44	30	34	57
2000	50	22	53	85

Sources: Farley, *Recent Trends*; G. Orfield and Monfort, "Racial Change"; 2000–2001 NCES Common Core of Data.

Table 8.3. Racial Composition of Schools in Mobile County Attended by Average Student of Each Race, 2000–2001

Race of Average Student	% White	% Black	% Hispanic	% Asian	Total
White	73.7	23.5	0.6	2.1	99.9
Black	22.2	76.3	0.5	1.1	100.1
Hispanic	53.5	42.5	1.6	2.4	100
Asian	57.7	32.3	0.8	9.2	100

Note: Rows may not add up to 100 percent because of rounding.

Source: 2000–2001 NCES Common Core of Data.

largest cities, Mobile and Prichard (located immediately north of Mobile, 85 percent black, and one of Alabama's poorest towns).[17] Conversely, the eleven schools that had 90–100 percent white student bodies were located in the county.

As discussed later in this chapter, during the 1980s and 1990s an influx of residents —particularly whites—occurred in Baldwin County. Historically, Baldwin County had a small minority population. Mobile residents who sought to avoid integrated schools initially moved to western Mobile County, which was originally not included in court-ordered desegregation plans. Later, a move to Baldwin County became a way to ensure that white students would continue to attend heavily white schools. In 2000, 86 percent of Baldwin County residents

Table 8.4. Population and Racial Composition of Mobile Central City, 1980–2000

Year	% White	% Black	% Hispanic	% Asian	Total
1980	65.2	32.9	1.1	0.5	223,610
1990	58.8	38.8	1.1	1.0	196,237
2000	49.8	46.5	1.4	1.7	198,915

Sources: Lewis Mumford Center for Comparative Urban and Regional Research, *Ethnic Diversity Grows*; Census data.

were white, and more than 81 percent of the 22,000 students in Baldwin County's schools were white in 2000–2001. Ten schools had student bodies that were more than 95 percent white. No schools were predominantly nonwhite, although three schools had only slight white majorities (less than 60 percent white).[18]

Residential Patterns

Mobile's metropolitan area experienced modest population gains during the 1980s, with a larger population increase in the 1990s. Yet the metropolitan area's racial composition remained relatively stable: the white share of the population in 2000 (68.6 percent) was almost identical to the 1980 white percentage (69.8 percent). In the last two decades of the twentieth century, the Mobile area, like many others, experienced significant suburbanization. In 1980, more than half of the metropolitan population lived in the city of Mobile. By 2000, however, the percentage of Mobile city residents in the metropolitan area had fallen to 37 percent. While the city's minority population actually increased during the 1980s, this increase was offset by a nearly 21 percent decrease in white residents. In the 1990s, the city of Mobile's population rose slightly (1.4 percent), entirely because of the increasing minority population: the number of black residents increased 21.3 percent, while the white population declined, comprising less than half of the city's total population by 2000 (table 8.4).

During the 1980s, the suburban areas of Mobile (the part of Mobile County outside the city of Mobile and all of Baldwin County) saw an increase of more than 57,000 white residents (or 35 percent) while gaining fewer than 2,000 new minority residents (3 percent). Overall suburban population growth remained strong in the 1990s (23 percent), and Baldwin County experienced huge population growth during this decade (47 percent). Minorities made only small gains in the absolute number of suburban residents, and the white percentage of the suburban area increased during both ten-year spans (table 8.5). In 1980–2000,

Table 8.5. Population and Racial Composition of Mobile Suburban Area, 1980–2000

Year	% White	% Black	% Hispanic	% Asian	Total
1980	74.5	23.7	1	0.2	219,875
1990	78.7	19.2	0.8	0.5	280,686
2000	79.6	16.5	1.3	1.1	341,343

Sources: Lewis Mumford Center for Comparative Urban and Regional Research, *Ethnic Diversity Grows*; Census data.

the Mobile MSA experienced two opposing trends: the central city became predominantly minority, and the suburban areas remained and even increased their overwhelmingly white composition.

In sum, both the schools and the residential populations in the Mobile metropolitan area have grown steadily more segregated and racially isolated during the past two decades. School data point to the continued existence of racial enclaves within the Mobile school system and an overwhelming white suburban district in close proximity. The central city area has become predominantly nonwhite, and the suburban areas of Mobile and particularly Baldwin County have become overwhelmingly white.

Charlotte, North Carolina

Charlotte Schools—Toward Integration

Half of the students in the Charlotte metropolitan area[19] were enrolled in CMS in 2000–2001. CMS had 140 schools, 44 with some magnet component, to serve just over 100,000 students. The MSA's other five systems averaged 20,000 students, similar to suburban Baldwin County, Alabama. Three-fourths of all students in the suburban systems were white. By contrast, 47 percent of CMS students were white, 43 percent were black, and 10 percent were of other races. Thirty-six percent of CMS students received free or reduced-price lunch in 2000–2001, though the percentage of low-income students has increased since unitary status and the end of desegregation efforts.[20]

Until recently, Charlotte-Mecklenburg has been a model of successful desegregation. Despite significant local conflict over the issue, school segregation levels fell sharply under the supervision of federal district court judge James B. McMillan.

Table 8.6. Isolation of Black Students in Charlotte-Mecklenburg Schools, 1968–2000

Year	% Black	% White in School of Average Black Student	% Black in 90–100% Minority Schools	% Black in 50–100% Minority Schools
1968	29	24	—	—
1970	31	65	—	—
1978	37	59	—	—
1986	39	54	3	35
2000	43	38	6	74

Sources: Farley, *Recent Trends*; G. Orfield and Monfort, "Racial Change"; 2000–2001 NCES Common Core of Data.

By 1970, the average black student in Charlotte-Mecklenburg attended a school in which approximately two-thirds of the students were white (table 8.6). As mandated by the Supreme Court in *Swann*, CMS used mandatory busing and the pairing of schools in noncontiguous geographic zones in a pupil-assignment system aimed at creating schools in which the racial composition of individual schools was within 15 percent of the overall school system average. Although blacks usually were bused further and longer, almost all students at some point under this plan rode buses to schools outside their neighborhoods.[21]

Through the mid-1980s, black student exposure to whites declined somewhat (as the white share of the enrollment in CMS decreased) but remained high. During the 1990s, a system of magnet schools was instituted while the school system remained under a federal desegregation order, and, indicative of the growing segregation in CMS, the percentage of white students with whom the average black student attended school dropped sharply. Further, the percentage of black students in predominantly black schools more than doubled between 1986 and 2000, even though the overall percentage of black students rose only a few points. In 2002–3, the school system began a new, race-neutral assignment plan featuring neighborhood schools and increased parental choice that has further increased school segregation.[22]

CMS students in 2000–2001, on average, attended schools that had substantial percentages of students of other races present.[23] White students attended schools that had a higher white percentage than was present in the schools attended by the average member of any other race (table 8.7). Hispanic students, however, attended schools that were, on average, just over one-third white. Almost uniformly,

Table 8.7. Racial Composition of Schools in Charlotte-Mecklenburg Attended by Average Student of Each Race, 2000–2001

Race of Average Student	% White	% Black	% Hispanic	% Asian	Total
White	55.5	36.1	4.2	4.3	100.1
Black	37.9	51.3	6.1	4.7	100
Hispanic	35.2	48.8	11.1	4.9	100
Asian	43.1	45.2	5.9	5.8	100

Note: Rows may not add up to 100 percent because of rounding.

Source: 2000–2001 NCES Common Core of Data.

the racial exposure for a student of any race differed by less than 10–15 percent from the overall system average, meaning that students had a relatively high level of exposure to students from other racial groups. In CMS, although differences existed in school racial composition, as noted, students attended schools with large percentages of students from other races. White students were the least likely to be exposed to students of other races: 46 percent were nonwhite.

In the past, Charlotte has had a low percentage of racially identifiable schools,[24] although these numbers rose in the 1990s and have soared since the new choice student-assignment plan was implemented in the fall of 2002. During the 1980s, CMS came close to fully complying with desegregation orders requiring the racial composition of all schools to be within 15 percent of the system average.[25] By 2000, however, almost half of CMS elementary schools were not racially balanced.[26] Further, the number of intensely segregated schools had increased to twelve: four 90–100 percent white schools and eight 90–100 percent minority schools (educating 6 percent of all black students). All but one were elementary schools. Elementary schools, to a greater extent than middle or high schools, typically reflect neighborhood racial composition because of their smaller student bodies and thus smaller geographic assignment zone. Racial composition was, moreover, strongly linked to the share of poor students in the school.[27]

Residential Patterns

The Charlotte MSA rapidly expanded from 1980 to 2000, growing more than 25 percent during each decade. In the 1980s, the racial composition of residents remained relatively stable, hovering just under 80 percent white. During the

Table 8.8. Population and Racial Composition of Charlotte Central City, 1980–2000

Year	% White	% Black	% Hispanic	% Asian	Total
1980	66.9	30.7	1.1	0.8	314,445
1990	64.8	31.6	1.4	1.8	395,934
2000	54.5	33.4	7.6	3.7	550,502

Sources: Lewis Mumford Center for Comparative Urban and Regional Research, *Ethnic Diversity Grows*; Census data.

Table 8.9. Population and Racial Composition of Charlotte Suburbs, 1980–2000

Year	% White	% Black	% Hispanic	% Asian	Total
1980	85.7	13.0	0.6	0.2	425,449
1990	87.6	11.0	0.7	0.5	604,615
2000	83.6	11.0	3.4	1.2	749,536

Sources: Lewis Mumford Center for Comparative Urban and Regional Research, *Ethnic Diversity Grows*; Census data.

1990s, the metro area population became slightly less white (71 percent), with strong Hispanic and Asian growth. The central city continued to grow more diverse in the 1990s, with particularly large increases in the number of Asian and Latino residents (table 8.8). In 2000, whites remained a slight majority of the city's residents.

Charlotte's suburbs remained overwhelmingly white through 2000, but the white proportion of the population actually decreased in the 1990s, primarily as a result of the increase of Hispanic and Asian suburban populations (table 8.9). Both the suburbs and central city gained minority residents, although the central cities did so at a more rapid rate. After suburban population growth of more than 42 percent in the 1980s, suburbanization slowed during the 1990s, and the central city area grew at a faster rate than the suburbs.

Given these trends, Dennis Lord's 1999 expert report to the court noted that Mecklenburg County had become more residentially integrated since 1971.[28] Paralleling national trends, the decrease in residential segregation in Mecklenburg County resulted largely from the migration by blacks or other minorities into formerly almost-all white census tracts.[29] Mecklenburg County's overall racial composition has remained relatively stable since 1960: The black percentage was 24.5 percent in that year and by the mid-1990s stood at 26.6 percent.[30] Not surprisingly,

Lord found that residential segregation changed little during the 1960s, a period of little school integration. Since 1970, however, the sharp declines in school segregation as a result of court-ordered desegregation in CMS have been matched by substantial declines in residential segregation in Mecklenburg County.[31]

The Impact of School Desegregation on Housing Patterns

While more cities must be examined before drawing conclusive findings, Mobile and Charlotte seem to exemplify the impact of school desegregation on housing patterns. The promise of school desegregation in both of these metro areas with countywide school systems was great; however, fifty years after *Brown*, the legacy of desegregation is mixed. In Mobile, where school desegregation has been minimal, residential segregation between the suburbs and the city is increasing: Mobile's suburban areas are growing increasingly white and by 2000, the city no longer had a white majority. Charlotte's school system was substantially integrated and through 2000 remained fairly integrated, though the number of racially imbalanced schools was growing. Both Charlotte and its suburbs are growing more racially diverse, and segregation in Mecklenburg County has declined since 1970.

Although residential segregation overall declined in both MSAs, Charlotte's population grew remarkably more residentially integrated between 1970 and 2000 (table 8.10). By contrast, Mobile's population is only marginally more residentially integrated in 2000 than it was in 1970. Further, the city of Mobile's racial composition grew increasingly nonwhite, while the white share of the population in the suburban areas increased during the 1990s.

The average black resident in the Mobile MSA in 2000 lived in a census tract that was almost half black (47.3 percent), while in Charlotte, the average black lived in a far less segregated tract (only 29.9 percent black). In 1970, the two metro areas had similar levels of residential segregation. Measured by the index of dissimilarity, or the percentage of black residents who would need to move for every tract to have the same racial composition as the entire area, segregation in Charlotte fell by nearly one-quarter—from 70.8 in 1970 to 53.7 in 2000. Black isolation fell even more dramatically, from 58.7 to 29.9, an almost 50 percent decrease. Interestingly, the rate of decline in dissimilarity in Charlotte slowed during the 1990s, a decade that also saw increasing school segregation. Dissimilarity in Mobile decreased slightly from 68.3 in 1970 to 61.1 in 2000.[32] From 1970 to 2000, the percentage of black residents in the tract of the average black resident declined

Table 8.10. Dissimilarity and Black Isolation in Selected Southern Metropolitan Statistical Areas, 1970–2000

	Dissimilarity (Black/Nonblack)				Black Isolation			
	1970	1980	1990	2000	1970	1980	1990	2000
Charlotte	70.8	60.6	53.7	50.3	58.7	45.5	37.2	29.9
Mobile	68.3	68.8	65.8	61.1	58.3	57.7	53.3	47.3
Atlanta	82.1	76.8	67.3	61.5	72.4	63.5	53.2	46.1
Birmingham	67.4	72.5	71.9	69.6	51.5	59.9	58.3	56.3
New Orleans	74.2	70.4	67.8	66.5	60.9	57.5	53.9	52.3
Louisville	82.5	73.7	69.4	64.0	66.2	60.1	52.0	45.8
Nashville	77.4	65.5	60.4	55.4	63.0	48.1	43.3	35.2
Raleigh	59.8	53.7	48.2	42.3	44.7	40.8	32.7	24.0
South average	—	—	63.6	59.1	—	—	—	—
National average	—	—	69.5	65.2	—	—	—	—

Sources: Cutler, Glaeser, and Vigdor, "Rise and Decline"; Glaeser and Vigdor, "Racial Segregation."

by only 10 percentage points, demonstrating that black isolation remained high. As a result, any neighborhood school assignment plan will likely result in schools with high levels of segregation.

For comparison, three other large southern MSAs that never underwent substantial school desegregation—Atlanta, Birmingham, and New Orleans—are included in table 8.10; all three have residential segregation figures equal to or higher than Mobile's. This is another indication that areas with segregated schools are likely to also have relatively segregated residential patterns.[35] By contrast, Louisville, Nashville, and Raleigh are three other large MSAs that experienced substantial school desegregation: as table 8.10 shows, their levels of residential segregation all declined sizably after 1970.

The data from Mobile and Charlotte suggest that metropolitan school desegregation—when it results in completely desegregated schools—appears to have a positive effect on residential segregation. Aside from the significant educational benefits of diverse schools, school desegregation helps to lessen the residential segregation of the area by weakening incentives for white parents in particular to relocate to primarily white neighborhoods.

As Mobile shows, partially desegregated schools do not produce residential integration but can in fact increase residential segregation, which then only further segregates schools in the district. Despite a lengthy desegregation case, Mobile

County schools remained racially identifiable. Because the racial compositions of Mobile schools remained quite disparate, parents were still likely to consider school boundaries when choosing where to live. As a result, white residents who sought to avoid integration first moved to West Mobile and later moved to Baldwin County, with its majority-white schools, to escape the Mobile school system altogether.

Conversely, Charlotte until recently maintained an integrated school system in which most schools were racially balanced, leaving very few white enclaves. While Mecklenburg County has seen some demographic shifts during the past three decades of school desegregation (most significantly, white share of population falling from 76 percent in 1970 to 68 percent in 1997 and 61 percent in 2002), it has grown significantly and remains predominantly white, although the school system no longer is. In 1960, more than two-thirds of black residents lived in areas that were more than 75 percent black; by 1990, slightly more than one-third of blacks lived in such tracts.[34] Seventeen of 136 schools were considered imbalanced for at least three years during the 1990s, but all of these schools had previously been balanced for at least sixteen years.[35] Some racial differences existed; for example, some schools in the CMS had larger-than-expected minority populations. In 2000, twelve schools had intensely segregated populations: four 90–100 percent white schools and eight 90–100 percent minority schools. Despite the community's long-term commitment to desegregation, Charlotte's new choice plan has dramatically increased the number of racially imbalanced schools in CMS.[36] It remains to be seen whether, if left unchecked, increasing school segregation will lead to more racially isolated residential patterns, not unlike those in the Mobile area.

School district actions also affect these trends. Most officials in systems with mandatory desegregation plans have realized that coordination is needed between schooling and housing desegregation efforts.[37] In fact, one of the central purposes of a meaningful desegregation plan is to break the connections between demographic trends and racially imbalanced schools that, as segregated housing increases, create more racially isolated schools and concentrate poverty.[38] Remarked a former Charlotte superintendent, "I know of no other way [than busing] to integrate schools until neighborhoods become more integrated."[39] For three decades, Charlotte's leaders and citizens have coordinated housing decisions with schooling patterns to ensure that location of public housing, for example, does not resegregate integrated schools.

Housing and Education: Perpetuating Segregation

A number of factors explain this difference in levels of residential segregation in Mobile and Charlotte. One of the arguments against school desegregation has been that it increases white flight from the public schools. Yet, in 1980, Diana Pearce, citing studies of fourteen cities with varying levels of implementation of their school desegregation plans, argued that white flight could occur only in metropolitan areas in which white enclaves exist.[40] Without such enclaves in the schools, white residents seeking to escape the school system would have nowhere to go. In other words, if school desegregation is fully implemented on a metropolitan level, it actually stems white flight.

Pearce found that school districts with districtwide desegregation usually experienced substantially greater reductions in residential segregation of blacks and whites than urban areas with only partial school desegregation, consequences that often lasted into the second decade of integration. She concluded that school segregation, by supporting housing segregation, is self-perpetuating.[41] By increasing housing segregation, schools become even more racially polarized. Allowing schools to desegregate only partially can result in more segregated housing patterns and white enclaves, creating patterns of segregation that will not easily disappear. In addition to its failure to solve the immediate problem of school desegregation, this partial remedy can result in increasing residential segregation that makes school desegregation even more difficult to accomplish, particularly after the Court's holding in *Freeman* that school systems could disregard continuing racial school segregation that was attributable to private choices (e.g., residential segregation patterns).

Jennifer Jellison Holme substantiates Pearce's argument about the importance of schools' racial composition as a signaling device to parents. She finds that high-status parents (defined as white and wealthy) relied primarily on opinions of others in their social networks in choosing schools for their children. She argues that, contrary to school-choice literature, these parents do not base their decisions on concrete facts about school quality. Instead, these parents tend to move to white districts—or white enclaves within a more racially diverse district—because of their belief that schools in those areas are "better" because of the students they serve—that is, students like their own children—giving little consideration to whether the school or its curriculum are appropriate or best for their child.[42]

School desegregation, of course, was not the sole influence on residential patterns in these two metro areas in the time studied. Charlotte during this time experienced an economic boom as Mobile stagnated, and by 1999, the per capita income of residents of Mobile was much lower than those in Charlotte. Yet as of that year, racial minorities in both cities had far lower incomes than their white neighbors. In Mecklenburg County, the ratio of white per capita income to that of blacks was 2:1; in Mobile County, it was 1.87:1.[43] Thus, no economic explanation, such as higher-income blacks moving to suburban areas of Charlotte, seems sufficient to account for the differences in residential integration in the two areas.

Likewise, although the population in the Charlotte MSA grew at a faster rate than that of the Mobile MSA, this population gain would not be expected to affect residential segregation as long as the growth was proportional. The population in both MSAs was roughly of the same racial composition in 2000 as it was in 1980. In fact, Charlotte's proportion of minority residents grew during the twenty-year span, which, one might speculate, could have led to increases in residential segregation rather than the decreases noted. Finally, other factors such as location of public housing can affect both residential and schooling desegregation. As discussed earlier, Charlotte leaders tried to ensure that such decisions did not subvert the aims of desegregation, which might well have contributed to the lower school and residential segregation the city has enjoyed.

Areas with metropolitan school desegregation plans have experienced both longer-lasting gains in terms of interracial exposure for minority students[44] and decreases in residential segregation that were twice the national average from 1970 to 1990.[45] When school districts are completely desegregated, pressure lessens for whites with children to move out of racially mixed neighborhoods into predominantly white neighborhoods, since racial balance is guaranteed at all area schools.[46] When desegregated districts are organized on a larger scale, as they are in countywide systems, the incentive for white parents to move decreases even more. When the school system is fully desegregated, white or minority parents can move anywhere in the district—even areas where their race is the residential minority—and be assured that their children will not be racially isolated in their new schools.[47] There is no longer the worry that parents must have a certain racial balance in mind when choosing a neighborhood merely to avoid racially isolated schools. Further, if all children in the community attend the same schools, there is a larger incentive for all residents, regardless of race, class, and power, to commit their resources to the success of the school system.[48]

Both of these factors tend to encourage desegregated housing patterns, because home seekers would not need to base their residential choices on schooling considerations. The Jefferson County, Kentucky, school system provides another example of the success that linking housing and school desegregation policies can produce. The Kentucky Human Rights Commission, realizing that the success of school desegregation was tied to housing patterns, counseled recipients of section

8 vouchers to move into the suburbs. The school system, in turn, offered exemptions to busing for these black residents as well as exempted neighborhoods from busing if they achieved a certain level of integration. In the first seven years after the merger of the city and county school systems, the number of black residents in other areas of the city and county tripled, and thirty-two schools were exempted from busing.[49] Today, school composition tends to be uniform across each racial group—that is, a white child in Jefferson County will likely attend a school with a racial composition similar to that of any minority child. Further, as table 8.10 shows, residential segregation levels in Louisville have declined substantially since 1970.

To be effective, however, such a plan must create completely desegregated schools. If pockets of racially identifiable schools remain in a partially desegregated district, the assurance that parents can move anywhere and have their children attend racially balanced schools disappears. Moreover, because heavily minority schools are overwhelmingly more likely to be high-poverty schools,[50] without the assurance of racially balanced schools, racial and economic considerations likely will continue to cause white parents to leave racially mixed neighborhoods.

On a metropolitan scale, the existence of white enclaves that can increase residential segregation across county boundaries produces particularly difficult obstacles to integration. With the legally difficult task of creating remedies across system boundaries and little metropolitan-wide planning, such disparities will only increase the problems of complete school desegregation and consequently of residential desegregation. As courts continue to resist legal efforts to produce desegregated schools, acknowledging the critical impact of school racial composition patterns on housing patterns and focusing on the coordination of schooling and housing policies will be crucial in the continued quest for the still-elusive ideal of an integrated society.

Notes

1. *Milliken v. Bradley.* The impact of this ruling was greatest in metro areas comprised of numerous towns and, more importantly, many separate school systems, commonly found in the Northeast and Midwest.

2. The South has the highest percentage of the nation's black residents and has experienced the greatest extent of school desegregation since the mid-1960s. For further discussion, see Frankenberg, Lee, and Orfield, *Multiracial Society.*

3. For example, neighborhood racial composition was one of the criteria for approval of loan applications by the Federal Housing Administration: areas with a high percentage of black residents were redlined. See G. Orfield, *Must We Bus?*, chap. 13, for further explanation of housing policies that perpetuated segregated residential patterns.

4. Cutler, Glaeser, and Vigdor, "Rise and Decline." White respondents to the 2000 General Social Survey, for example, indicated that they preferred to live, on average, in a neighborhood that was 57 percent white. Further, more than one-fifth of whites described the ideal neighborhood as being composed solely of white residents. See Charles, "Dynamics."

5. Massey and Denton, *American Apartheid*; Glaeser and Vigdor, "Racial Segregation."

6. Massey and Denton, *American Apartheid*, 110.

7. Ibid., 97.

8. Galster and Keeney, "Race."

9. *Swann v. Charlotte-Mecklenburg Board of Education*, 21.

10. Ibid., 20–21.

11. Social scientists have noted that integration might be difficult to achieve in systems utilizing neighborhood schools. Reynolds Farley commented about parents' preference for neighborhood schools, "if the Constitution required integrated schools, then the neighborhoods must be integrated" ("Residential Segregation," 187). Further, he noted that the identification of a school as black or white may increase settlement of families of that race in neighborhoods close to the school (190).

12. *Keyes v. School District no. 1, Denver, Colorado*, 202.

13. *Freeman v. Pitts*, 494–95.

14. *Freeman*, 513.

15. Smylie, "Reducing Racial Isolation." Racially isolated minority schools are those in which 90 percent or greater of the student body is minority.

16. Author's calculations based on data from the 2000–2001 National Center for Education Statistics Common Core of Data.

17. For example, the per capita income in 1999 was just over $10,000 in Prichard but was more than $18,000 in Mobile. Thirty-two percent of Prichard's families fell below the poverty line in 1999, almost twice the percentage of such families in Mobile. Data taken from American Factfinder, Census 2000.

18. Because of the large proportion of white students, the average black had a greater exposure to white students in Baldwin County. As a result, on a metropolitan scale the racial isolation of blacks was slightly lower than in Mobile County, but isolation for white students was higher as a result of the large white share in Baldwin County schools.

19. Charlotte, the largest city in North Carolina, is the major city of this MSA and is in Mecklenburg County. Other medium-sized cities include Gastonia, North Carolina, and Rock Hill, South Carolina. Although York County, South Carolina, is considered part of the Charlotte MSA, it has not been included in most analyses here because it is located in a separate state.

20. Although the racial composition of the two districts is similar, the percentage of poor students in CMS is lower than Mobile County's: in 2000–2001, Mobile County's percentage of students receiving free or reduced lunch was 64 percent. This measure of poverty is inexact—in the 1999–2000 school year, 54.5 percent of Mobile students received free or reduced lunch, a change of 10 percentage points. Nevertheless, the low percentage of students in Charlotte before unitary status was declared indicates that middle-class students remained present in CMS.

21. Mickelson, "Subverting *Swann*." In 1967, before court-ordered desegregation, the level of dissimilarity for the CMS system was .77. Lord, expert report. Lord uses the index of

dissimilarity for his computations of residential segregation levels. This index indicates the percentage of people from one race that would need to move for the area to be perfectly integrated. Zero indicates complete integration, and 1 indicates complete segregation. Only five years later, the index of dissimilarity was .14, an extremely low level. By the 1990s, however, the index of dissimilarity had risen to .27, still fairly low but indicative of growing segregation within the school system.

22. See Mickelson, this volume. In 2003, twenty-five schools had nonwhite enrollments that were 90 percent or greater.

23. Throughout this chapter, these figures consider only segregation at the building level and thus underestimate the actual levels of segregation students experience in their classrooms. Roslyn Arlin Mickelson (this volume) has shown that in Charlotte, within-school segregation creates segregated classrooms even in schools that appear to be desegregated.

24. A racially identifiable school is one in which the school's racial composition differs from the overall system average by more than 15 percent.

25. Mickelson, "Subverting *Swann*."

26. In the *Swann* litigation, the criteria for racially balanced elementary and middle schools was ±15 percent of the district average for each group.

27. The regression model for race regressed on percent free or reduced lunch: $y = -0.8368x + 75.272$ ($R^2 = 0.7476$). A 1 percentage point increase in white percentage is associated with a 0.8 percentage point decrease in share of students receiving free or reduced-price lunches.

28. Lord, expert report.

29. For more discussion of national trends, see Glaeser and Vigdor, "Racial Segregation."

30. Ibid.

31. Lord, expert report.

32. These trends are occurring in Mobile despite the growing disparity between the city and suburban racial compositions.

33. Of course, Atlanta does show a fairly rapid decline in residential segregation, but this results primarily from black suburbanization in the metro area. By 1990, more than half of black residents lived in the suburban areas of this MSA. Several suburban counties around Atlanta are experiencing huge racial change and have predominantly nonwhite populations and school systems. Segregation indexes within the city of Atlanta are much higher than those in the surrounding suburbs.

34. Lord, expert report.

35. *Belk v. Charlotte-Mecklenburg Board of Education.*

36. Using enrollment data from the twentieth day of school in the fall of 2003, 25 of CMS's 133 schools had nonwhite populations that were 90 percent or greater of the total student body. In addition, one school had a student enrollment that was greater than 90 percent white. (*Educate!*, 2 October 2003)

37. G. Orfield, *Toward a Strategy*, 14.

38. G. Orfield and Eaton, *Dismantling Desegregation*, 197.

39. *Three Cities*, 39.

40. Pearce, *Breaking Down the Barriers.*

41. Ibid.

42. Holme, "Buying Homes, Buying Schools."

43. Nationally, the per capita income of whites is 1.66 times that of blacks. Thus, the income differentials by race are greater in both Charlotte and Mobile than they are nationally. U.S. Bureau of the Census, "Income in 1999."

44. Frankenberg, Lee, and Orfield, *Multiracial Society.*

45. See G. Orfield, "Metropolitan School Desegregation," 135.

46. Hawley, *Strategies*, 62.

47. Ibid.

48. G. Orfield, "Metropolitan School Desegregation," 126.

49. G. Orfield and Eaton, *Dismantling Desegregation*, 111.

50. In 86 percent of schools where more than 90 percent of the student body is black and/or Latino, more than half of the students are poor or near poor. Frankenberg, Lee, and Orfield, *Multiracial Society*, table 9.

PART FOUR

The New Pressures from Standardized Testing

CHAPTER NINE

AMY STUART WELLS | JENNIFER JELLISON HOLME

No Accountability for Diversity

Standardized Tests and the Demise of Racially Mixed Schools

Over the past two decades, we have witnessed two overlapping trends in education: an increase in racially segregated schools, and an unprecedented rise in the use of standardized tests to hold both educators and students accountable for higher levels of achievement. While the relationship between these two trends is unclear and may be more coincidental than causal, we argue that the accountability movement, which has mandated more and more student testing and an increased emphasis on school rankings according to test scores, has significantly narrowed the definition of school quality in a way that works against racial diversity in education.

We make this argument based on our in-depth research on six high schools that were racially mixed in the 1970s. Since then, three of these schools have lost virtually all of their white and more affluent student populations. Two additional schools are in the process of losing these students. In all five of these sites, state-mandated tests appear to have played a role in this white and middle- and upper-middle-class flight. As we demonstrate, the flight of white and more affluent families occurred in these schools at a time when mandated tests in each of these five states began to reduce the meaning of a "good school" to a single average test score, obscuring what had once been a broader definition that included such factors as performing arts programs, athletic teams, the number of National Merit Scholars or Ivy League college acceptances, and even the school's diversity.

Over time, these broader measures of school quality have diminished in importance as parents have come to pay more attention to school rankings on state-mandated test scores. According to these rankings, a school cannot be "good" if it is not at the top in terms of standardized test scores, no matter what other programs or accomplishments it boasts. And because schools with more racially and socioeconomically diverse student bodies have, on average, lower overall standardized test scores than do more affluent and predominantly white schools, statewide accountability systems grounded in standardized tests feed perceptions of racially diverse schools as not as good as the schools in more predominantly white and affluent school districts and communities. While we cannot generalize from the experiences of the six school communities we studied to every school across the country, the point of doing this kind of in-depth analysis of those school communities is to better understand how and why phenomena such as white flight occur. These understandings can be generalized to help us make sense of the threat posed by the proliferation of standardized tests and school rankings to student diversity at the school level. This is a general theme about how parents today tend to define "good" and "bad" schools for their children and how too much emphasis on narrow indicators of school quality works against efforts to sustain and maintain diverse schools.

In making this argument we are familiar with claims that these new testing systems may indeed promote more equity because they force schools to be accountable to all families, not just to the high-achieving students who are in the running to be National Merit Scholars and admitted to Ivy League colleges.[1] Indeed, under the federal No Child Left Behind Act, states are required to disaggregate test score data to better understand how students of different racial and social class backgrounds and other characteristics (e.g., limited English proficiency, special education status) are performing on state tests. In theory, such accountability measures could be used to force schools to focus more closely on how they serve *all* of their students.[2]

Yet at the same time, these accountability systems purport to distill the quality of a school down to such a narrow criterion that, given the correlation between test scores and race and socioeconomic status, only the wealthiest schools and those serving very high percentages of white and Asian students tend to consistently rank near the top on average scores. And, we argue, parents who have other educational options are most likely to examine those scores when choosing to flee from or stay in diverse public schools. In other words, our data suggest that affluent parents and/or white parents are less likely to keep their children in diverse public schools that have lower average test scores even if those schools have succeeded in closing much of their black-white test score gap than to move their children to schools with higher overall test scores.

We do not want to claim that the accountability systems in and of themselves created the white and middle-class flight from the schools in our study. Indeed, at each school, other social and political factors contributed to the loss of white and/or more affluent students. Still, test scores lower than those of neighboring districts had become the main rationale for white flight by the 1980s in the three high schools we studied that had lost virtually all of their white and affluent students. In fact, these scores were regularly cited as *the* definitive evidence that these schools were "bad" even though much counterevidence showed that those schools remained strong in several non-test-related dimensions. Too often, however, after the families with resources and political clout left these schools, the self-fulfilling prophecy of these schools as "bad" or "less than" became a reality.

Meanwhile, the state-mandated accountability system and the highly publicized test scores pose the greatest threat to the ability of one of the other racially balanced schools in our study to hold onto white and more affluent students. For another of these still-somewhat-diverse schools, state tests also pose one of many threats as fewer white students enroll each year. In fact, we do not think it is a coincidence that the one high school that has maintained its racial diversity without a major decline in white students over the past twenty-five years was the only site in our study where state accountability measures were less highly publicized and less salient to the way in which interviewees made sense of school quality issues.

And finally, while the issues and concerns about which we write in terms of diversity and accountability systems are not unique to one region of the country, we wanted to emphasize, for the purposes of this particular book, that the public schools in the South have the most at stake here, given how far southern districts have progressed toward desegregating their students and creating more racially diverse schools. Furthermore, many of the southern states led the country in terms of implementing new accountability systems as early as the 1980s.[3] Thus, the South is the region where we can most clearly see the intersection of old school desegregation policies that are being dismantled at a rapid rate and newer accountability systems. The themes raised in this chapter, therefore, may well resonate most strongly with educators, parents, and students in the South.

The Rise of Accountability Policies: Narrowing the Definition of "Good" and "Bad" Schools

Since the 1970s, public schools have been increasingly required to administer state-mandated standardized tests. Beginning with the competency, or basic skills, tests of the late 1970s and early 1980s, until the most recent mandates of the federal No Child Left Behind Act, passed in 2001, schools have been testing their students with greater and greater frequency. While the scope and duration of these exams have varied from state to state, the implications of the expansion of testing policies have not varied as much. Across state contexts, tests initially were used mainly to identify students who failed to achieve minimum competency, yet they have become increasingly rigorous and are now used to measure not only the achievement of individual students but also the performance of schools. More and more, schools are judged, ranked, and defined by the results of these tests.[4]

According to *Education Week*, all fifty states had implemented mandated tests (mostly state tests, but occasionally district tests) to measure student achievement as of the 2000–2001 school year, and, as of 2004, forty-nine states were publishing report cards on individual schools based largely on test scores.[5] Furthermore, eighteen states require students to pass a "high-stakes" test to graduate from high school, and more than half of the states publicly rate schools or at least identify those that are low performing.[6]

And now, with the implementation of the federal No Child Left Behind Act, states are required to identify schools that fail to make "adequate yearly progress" on annual performance levels (as defined by the states) for nine categories of students—for example, different racial/ethnic groups, low-income students, limited English speakers, and special needs students. Report cards on individual schools' and districts' progress toward meeting the state-defined goals for performance are to be made available to the public. By the summer of 2003, all fifty states had submitted plans to the U.S. Department of Education for holding all schools and districts accountable under No Child Left Behind.[7]

From Minimum Competency to the Highest Stakes

The current testing policies are the grandchildren of the minimum-competency-test policies that swept the country in the late 1970s and early 1980s. In fact, by 1983, thirty-nine states had passed bills requiring minimum-competency testing designed to measure students' most basic skills, usually before they could graduate from high school.[8] Jay P. Heubert and Robert M. Hauser note that the minimum-competency-testing movement "gave large-scale, standardized achievement tests a visible and popular role in holding students (and sometimes schools) accountable."[9]

Yet following the landmark 1983 "A Nation at Risk" report and the growing cry for greater "excellence" and accountability in education, many states began to upgrade these "basic skills" tests, moving toward much more rigorous achievement tests even before federal law mandated that they do so.[10] New Jersey—home to one of the six high schools in our study—was one of the states at the forefront of state testing, launching its first statewide assessment system in 1972. This system, known as the Educational Assessment Program (EAP), assessed reading and math skills in grades 4, 7, 10, and 12. By 1976, New Jersey approved a new set of Minimum Basic Skills (MBS) tests for students in grades 3, 6, 9, and 11. By 1983, state officials were rescaling the MBS tests because of charges that they were too easy.[11] A new ninth-grade test was introduced, and by 1986, students had to pass this new test to graduate from high school.[12] Other states, particularly in the South, mirrored New Jersey's pattern of increased testing with increasing consequences.

Aside from New Jersey and California, Tim L. Mazzoni points out that the early to mid-1980s wave of the "educational excellence movement," when one-third of the states enacted sweeping testing and accountability reforms, was far more popular in the South than the North.[13] He credits this southern phenomenon to the more centralized educational systems in southern states and the regional competition for high-technology firms and recognition. We wonder whether the degree of school desegregation—far more prevalent in the South than the North by the late 1970s and early 1980s—may have also played a role. In other words, as students of different racial and ethnic backgrounds were brought together in southern schools for the first time, achievement gaps across racial lines may have become more apparent, fostering reform efforts.

We make this potential link because, in many instances, these early competency and achievement tests were arguably designed to ensure that the lowest-performing students were not being ignored and that schools were providing a minimally adequate education for those students who were not taking SATs, were not finalists for the National Merit Scholarships, and were not enrolled in the growing number of advanced placement (AP) courses.[14] Furthermore, such tests were more likely to be given in schools and districts serving large percentages of low-income students and students of color.[15] These were districts and schools most likely to administer the program evaluations required under Title I of the federal Elementary and Secondary Education Act of 1965, which supported low-achieving students in poor neighborhoods.[16] Heubert and Hauser argue that the minimum-competency tests implemented between 1975 and 1985 were "a response to public concerns about students leaving school without basic reading and mathematics skills, combined with a widespread perception that educational quality had declined."[17]

At the same time, these early testing laws and the subsequent policies of the 1980s and 1990s came to reflect an important shift in the political rhetoric—a shift away from a political focus on equity and equal opportunity issues to a focus on "excellence," "competition," and "accountability."[18] Thus, while many testing proponents have argued that greater "equity" will be a by-product of these new standards and testing reforms—as a rising tide lifts all boats—equalizing opportunities has not been the central focus of the past twenty years of educational policy.[19] A little more than a decade after the release of "A Nation at Risk" and only five years after former president George H. W. Bush met with the nation's governors in Charlottesville, Virginia, in 1989 to proclaim the need for national goals in education, the 1994 federal Goals 2000 legislation required states to establish academic standards as well as tests to measure students' mastery of these standards.[20] At this point, even states that had been less receptive to the standards and accountability movement were forced, under the threat of losing millions of federal education dollars, to jump on the bandwagon. Still, wide variation remained across the states in the types of testing policies that were introduced, with some states implementing more punitive and "high-stakes" measures for students and/or schools.[21] Furthermore, following the theme of "excellence" over "equity," the final Goals 2000 legislation did not include mandated opportunity-to-learn standards that would have prodded states and districts to equalize educational opportunities across schools and districts.[22]

Under the 2001 federal No Child Left Behind law, all state accountability systems must now impose high-stakes consequences on schools whose students perform poorly on standardized tests, regardless of whether those schools or students have access to the resources or teachers needed to facilitate such achievement.[23] While a great deal of attention has been paid to the potentially negative impact on students of punitive, high-stakes testing policies, far less attention has been devoted to such policies' impact on schools.[24] While proponents of such measures argue that dramatic consequences are appropriate for schools that fail to improve students' test scores, others are concerned that these punitive policies ignore not only the gross inequality in the educational system but also the many non-school-related factors—including poverty and cultural biases of tests—that influence students' scores.[25] Thus, to punish schools and educators for low performance on one measure of student achievement may, in some instances, overlook other very positive aspects of those schools.

As Gary Orfield notes, federally mandated state testing and report card programs regularly identify segregated minority schools with concentrated poverty as low performing.[26] Orfield reminds us that there is a very strong correlation between the percentage of poor children in a school and its average test scores.[27] The extent to which this correlation is caused or exacerbated by schools as opposed to other factors, including the impact of poverty on children's development or the inherent bias of the tests, is widely debated.

The question that has too rarely been posed is how these punitive accountability mandates affect efforts to desegregate schools and promote school-level racial diversity. Drawing from more than five hundred interviews of policy makers, educators, and graduates of six racially diverse high schools, we begin to answer that question and thus enter the debate about whether the accountability and testing movement has indeed furthered the cause of greater equal educational opportunity.

The "Understanding Race and Education Study": The Story of Six Racially Diverse High Schools

Our five-year study of racially mixed high schools and their Class of 1980 graduates was designed to answer questions that had nothing to do with twenty-first-century accountability and assessment systems. We wanted to know how graduates of racially mixed schools understand their desegregated school experience and its effect on their lives—that is, their racial attitudes, educational and professional opportunities, personal relationships, and social networks. We also wanted to know how the policy context of their experiences shaped these understandings.

To answer these questions, our team of researchers from Teachers College, Columbia University, and the University of California at Los Angeles selected as the focus of our study six towns and school districts and then six high schools within those districts. In conducting case studies on these school sites, we developed a three-tiered data-collection strategy: tier one consisted of historical case studies of the six high schools; tier two entailed interviews of a diverse sample of forty to fifty graduates of the Class of 1980 from each school; and the third tier involved in-depth "portraits" of about four of the graduates interviewed in tier two.

Overall, we conducted a total of 540 interviews with people in these six communities who were involved in desegregation efforts, including policy makers, high school teachers, and 242 students who graduated in the spring of 1980 from one of the six high schools we selected. Twenty-six of these graduates were interviewed a second time for a more in depth portrait interview.

Sampling Six Racially Diverse Schools

After conducting extensive research into the history of about twenty potential cities and the racial balance of their schools, we chose the following six cities/towns to study: Austin, Texas; Charlotte, North Carolina; Englewood, New Jersey; Pasadena, California; Shaker Heights, Ohio; and Topeka, Kansas. Not only do these cities vary in their geographic locations—one each in the Northeast, South, Southwest, and West and two in the Midwest—but also in how and why the public schools became racially diverse. In all but one of these districts, some of the schools were desegregated via court-ordered mandatory student reassignments. In the sixth, the schools were racially balanced via the creation of diverse attendance zones or residential areas. But each of these six towns and school districts had at least one high school that was racially mixed[28] during the late

1970s and early 1980s, even when the high schools were not part of the mandatory student-reassignment plans.

The six high schools we chose to study in depth are Austin High School, Dwight Morrow High School in Englewood, Muir High School in Pasadena, Shaker Heights High School, Topeka High School, and West Charlotte High School (see table 9.1). Interestingly, both Muir and Dwight Morrow had enrollments that were less than 50 percent white by the late 1970s. Both of these schools, along with West Charlotte High School, have experienced massive white flight since the Class of 1980 graduated, and they are presently predominantly African American and/or Latino. Austin High School, Shaker Heights High School, and Topeka High School have remained somewhat more stable over the past two decades, although both Austin and Shaker Heights are steadily losing white students as well as many middle-class black and Latino students. This leaves only Topeka High School promising to maintain some white-black-Latino diversity for the next several years.

Through our data collection for the first phase of the study—the historical case studies—we came to learn a great deal about the schools' "reputations" and, in many instances, about what role past and present state accountability measures had played in the formation and evolution of these reputations. The interviews with graduates of the Class of 1980 from each school also helped us understand how the students themselves made sense of their schools' reputations and how that related to measures such as test scores, racial diversity, and white flight.

In other words, much of what we found ourselves documenting in this study was the resegregation of these schools. We argue that state policies mandating standardized tests and comparisons of test scores across schools played a role in this resegregation process in every school except Topeka High School, where test scores appear to not have played as large a role and white and middle-class flight has been less dramatic.

Defining "Good Schools" before and after State-Mandated Tests: The Role of Diversity

In the following sections of this chapter, we present evidence from our study to explore the relationship between state-mandated tests and accountability systems and the racial demographics of the six high schools in our study. To do so, we first provide a brief overview, in table 9.2, of the state testing mandates for each of the six states in which these schools are located. This table provides the time frame for the state testing polices. The following two sections describe, through our interview data from these six sites, the "then" versus "now" perspective on the important characteristics of each school's reputation. This analysis demon-

Table 9.1. Racial Demographics Then and Now: Six High Schools

	Late 1970s		Late 1990s/Early 2000s	
High School	Race	%	Race	%
Austin High School, Austin, Tex.	African American	15	African American	8
	Hispanic	19	Hispanic	37
	White	66	White	54
			Asian/Pacific Islander	2
Dwight Morrow High School, Englewood, N.J.	African American	57	African American	65
	Hispanic	7	Hispanic	32
	White	36	White	1–2
			Asian/Pacific Islander	2–3
John Muir High School, Pasadena, Calif.	African American	50	African American	49
	Hispanic	11	Hispanic	40
	White	35	White	9
	Asian/Pacific Islander	5	Asian/Pacific Islander	1
Shaker Heights High School, Shaker Heights, Ohio	"Minority" (mostly African American)	39	African American	52
			Hispanic	1
	White	61	White	43
			Asian/Pacific Islander	3
Topeka High School, Topeka, Kans.	African American	20	African American	20
	Hispanic	8	Hispanic	15
	White	69	White	61
			Native American	3
			Asian/Pacific Islander	1
West Charlotte High School, Charlotte, N.C.	African American	48	African American	75
	White	52	Hispanic	10
			White	10
			Asian	5

strates the growing importance of standardized test scores in defining "good" versus "not good" schools. And for these racially diverse schools, table 9.2 shows that this shift has a negative impact on the schools and their ability to maintain diversity.

Thus, all six of the schools we studied are now subject to a set of accountability measures dominated by standardized tests that were not in place when the Class

Table 9.2. Overview of School-Level Accountability Mandates for Six States

State	Date State Policy Is Effective	School-Level Accountability
New Jersey: Dwight Morrow High School	1972—New Jersey launched its statewide assessment system with the Educational Assessment Program (EAP). Assessed reading and math skills in grades 4, 7, 10, and 12.	District-level data (not school-level data) were returned to districts and were to be made public, but only for those items that measured the skills districts had taught. Had limited impact on students or schools.
	1976—New Jersey legislature passed a law ending EAP and creating the Minimum Basic Skills (MBS) test to measure students' proficiency in minimum reading and math skills in grades 3, 6, 9, and 11. MBS was administered for the first time in the spring of 1978. In 1979 a law was passed making passage of the test a graduation requirement beginning with the Class of 1985.	While EAP reporting was left to the districts and based on selected items, the MBS aggregated scores—e.g., the percentage of students passing by district—were reported to the public. Districts were publicly compared based on these scores.
	1983—The new High School Proficiency Test (HSPT) was designed to measure higher-level skills than MBS. For two years, 1983–85, ninth-graders took both tests. By 1985, the MBS was phased out.	New Jersey School Report cards included scores on state assessments, enrollment, language, diversity, attendance, class size, student mobility rates, student/faculty ratio, etc.
	2001–2—HSPT was replaced by the High School Proficiency Assessment (HSPA).	Test scores are listed on school and district report cards mandated by the federal No Child Left Behind law.

Table 9.2. (continued)

State	Date State Policy Is Effective	School-Level Accountability
California: John Muir High School	1972—California instituted its first testing program, the California Assessment Program (CAP), which was designed to measure achievement of schools and districts rather than students. 1975—California also created an optional proficiency test for sophomores to verify their competency in basic skills.	The CAP required schools to administer multiple-choice tests for four grade levels. Schools were then graded based on their test score results, which were then compared to predicted scores based on the socioeconomic background of the students in the school.
	1997—California began using the Stanford-9 test (SAT-9) to measure student learning as part of the new Standardized Testing and Reporting (STAR) Program.	Academic Performance Index (API) provided a single index to rate the performance of all schools on several indicators, including the SAT-9 portion of the STAR tests as well as a high school exit exam.
	1999—California instituted a new accountability system, the Public Schools Accountability Act (PSAA), which relied further on the SAT-9 scores. California also authorized the California State High School Exit Exam (CASHEE) but delayed this as a requirement for graduation until 2006.	By 1999, California school boards were required to issue a School Accountability Report Card for each school in the jurisdiction. Information on the report cards includes most recent three years of data for each area of student assessment, high school dropout rates, and high school students' SAT scores.
	2002—The SAT-9 was replaced by the California Standards Tests (CSTs) and the California Achievement Test (CAT-6).	Test scores are listed on school and district report cards mandated by the federal No Child Left Behind law.

Table 9.2. (continued)

State	Date State Policy Is Effective	School-Level Accountability
North Carolina: West Charlotte High School	Late 1970s—North Carolina began administering the California Achievement Test (CAT) to assign students to different level tracks.	Students were assigned to "skills," "regular," and "advanced" tracks based on these test scores.
	1992—The statewide testing program in North Carolina was implemented, with state tests measuring competency in reading, math, and writing.	A system of school building improvement reports for each school was developed.
	1995—Legislators passed a new state accountability program, the ABCs of Public Education. The program included annual tests in math and reading in grades 3–8; a writing assessment in grades 4, 7, and 10; a computer-skills exam for eighth-graders; and a high school exit test.	Data reported by high schools included gains in competency test passing rates, percentage of students completing college prep courses, and student results for the North Carolina High School Comprehensive Tests in reading and mathematics. Test score data were used in the school accountability process as well as the school improvement plans. Incentive awards were offered to educators in high-performing schools. Low-performing schools worked with assistance teams.
	1999—The North Carolina State Board of Education established the Students Accountability Standards, which includes a requirement that students pass an "exit exam of essential skills" to graduate.	Test scores are listed on school and district report cards mandated by the federal No Child Left Behind law.

Table 9.2. (continued)

State	Date State Policy Is Effective	School-Level Accountability
Texas: Austin High School	1979—Texas established the first state mandated testing program, the Texas Assessment of Basic Skills (TABS), for ninth-graders.	TABS scores and passage rates were made public by school and district.
	1984—Texas replaced TABS with the Texas Educational Assessment of Minimum Skills (TEAMS).	School- and district-level data were made public for TEAMS scores.
	1990—The Texas Assessment of Academic Skills (TAAS) was instituted.	TAAS was tied to school report cards with passing rates by student subgroup and average rates for state, district, and school.
	2003—The Texas Board of Education replaced the TAAS test with the Texas Assessment of Knowledge and Skills (TAKS).	TAKS scores are listed on school and district report cards mandated by the federal No Child Left Behind law.
Ohio: Shaker Heights High School	1987—The Ohio State Board of Education recommended the establishment of proficiency tests for ninth-graders, required to graduate from high school. The assembly required graduates of the Class of 1994 to pass proficiency tests in reading, writing, math, and citizenship.	School building report cards include enrollment; per-pupil spending; state assessment results by grade, subject, etc.; attendance; graduation rates; and number of graduates with state honors.
	1997—Ohio legislation eliminated the requirement for ninth-grade proficiency tests and instead enacted a requirement that all tenth-graders (beginning with the Class of 2004) pass proficiency tests for graduation. Ohio Proficiency Tests (OPTs) are administered in grades 4, 6, 10 and 12.	Test scores are listed on school and district report cards mandated by the federal No Child Left Behind law.

Table 9.2. (continued)

State	Date State Policy Is Effective	School-Level Accountability
Kansas: Topeka High School	1995—The state legislature directed the State Board of Education to provide statewide assessments in core academic areas. Under this assessment system, high school students are tested in various subjects in either grade 10 or 11, but there is no high school exit exam that students must pass for graduation.	Each school must prepare a report card that includes demographics, attendance, dropout rates, violent acts against students and teachers, and state assessments by grade in reading, math, writing and science. According to the Center for Policy Research in Education's Web-based report on state assessment and accountability, "Kansas officials strongly discourage the use of assessment data for purposes such as promotion, retention or accountability." Test scores are listed on school and district report cards mandated by the federal No Child Left Behind law.

of 1980 entered high school. The rise of the accountability systems in these states clearly has had implications for these six high schools. In the late 1970s, North Carolina's use of the California Achievement Test to assign students to track levels no doubt contributed to the resegregation of students within the desegregated schools that we and other researchers have documented.[29] Furthermore, we do not think it is pure coincidence that the two states that were the first of the six to implement statewide testing programs—New Jersey and California—were the sites of the two schools in our study that had, by the mid-1980s, lost much of their white student populations. These tests clearly played a major role for the school in New Jersey. Furthermore, we wonder to what extent Topeka High School managed to remain the most racially diverse of the schools because it is in a state in which officials have strongly discouraged the use of assessment data for accountability purposes. In the next two sections, we examine this confluence of factors.

Back Then—Defining "Good Schools" Prior to State Testing

We have learned from our hundreds of interviews in these communities that the reputation of each high school has changed and evolved over time. And in only one case—Topeka High School—is the reputation of the school better today than it was in the mid-1970s, according to many people we interviewed. Overall, we see a trend in our data from earlier assessments of school reputations as "good" based on a broad array of factors—such as curriculum, teacher quality, athletics, theater, band, curriculum, diversity, National Merit Scholars, college acceptance of graduates, and student diversity—to much more narrowly defined reputations based primarily on standardized test scores. In this section, we provide some of the many quotations from our interviews that illustrate these earlier definitions of school quality—definitions that were sometimes less grounded in hard, "scientific" or "objective" data and more grounded in people's memories and emotional bonds to a place. These perceptions of school quality were very important in making students feel loyal to their racially diverse schools because their personal experiences were generally very positive.

One of the most robust findings to emerge from our data was the pride that both graduates and educators had in the drama and music departments in their schools in the 1970s. And many of these quotations indicate that these high schools had good reputations in part because of these strong performing arts programs and consequently that students of very different racial and ethnic and socioeconomic backgrounds wanted to attend. As one white 1980 graduate of Muir High School in Pasadena noted, "I had heard that [Muir] was a good school. . . . I knew it had a strong music and . . . drama department, . . . good athletics. . . . I know within the music department . . . it had a really good reputation for high-quality, you know, education as well as . . . really a program that got students out of the mainstream."

Although each of the six schools in our study had different strengths and weaknesses, quotations such as this one are not unusual. A teacher at Austin High School, the flagship school of the Austin Independent School District, noted, "This was an old school with lots of tradition[;] it had a very excellent reputation in athletics as well as in speech and theater. It was pretty well known across the state as an outstanding school, just across the board."

Meanwhile, Dwight Morrow High School in Englewood, New Jersey, which, like Muir in Pasadena, had lost most of its white student population by the early 1980s, was known across predominantly white Bergen County not only for its performing arts but also for its fine arts program, as an art teacher who had been there for thirty years recalled: "I was offered a position in two other communities . . . and

I chose [Dwight Morrow] over them because not only did I want to work with my friends but I knew that at the time the school had a fabulous reputation, especially in the art department but not limited only to the art department."

In addition, many students, educators, and community members from our six sites noted that college admissions officers at top universities thought highly of their schools. Students and faculty from Dwight Morrow boasted that even as fewer white students were choosing to enroll by the late 1970s, their school's college-going rate remained between 85 and 90 percent. Indeed, many of the people we interviewed in Englewood commented on the large number of students—white and African American—who went on to Ivy League universities from Dwight Morrow.

In fact, these issues were highlighted during a ninety-day trial in a court case between Englewood and Englewood Cliffs, the small K–8, predominantly white neighboring school district. In the early 1960s, the Englewood Cliffs School Board asked to send its eighth-grade graduates to Dwight Morrow for high school in the absence of a high school in the Cliffs. By the late 1970s, as Dwight Morrow's African American enrollment increased and its white enrollment decreased, Englewood Cliffs school board members sought to end this sender-receiver relationship and to reassign their students to a predominantly white high school a few miles to the north. The Englewood Cliffs School Board claimed that the quality of the education at Dwight Morrow was so poor that their children needed to attend a different school. The lawyers for Englewood Cliffs cited Dwight Morrow's MBS test scores, which were lower than those at the high school to the north.

The Englewood lawyers set out to demonstrate other important measures of school quality and to show that Dwight Morrow remained a "good" school. One of the witnesses for the Englewood Board of Education was an admissions officer from Yale University who testified that many Dwight Morrow graduates had been admitted to Yale and had done very well there—they were strong academically, well rounded socially, and prepared to live in a diverse society. In the end, Englewood won the court case, proving that measuring school quality required more than looking at test scores, but it lost all of its white students anyway as Englewood Cliffs students began attending private high schools.

Still, the argument that there is more to a good school than just test scores echoed across the sites in our study, especially among respondents who recalled the late 1970s, when fewer states or districts used these narrow measures. A white graduate of West Charlotte High School from a very affluent family noted that it was not a sacrifice for her to travel from her very wealthy neighborhood to West Charlotte—a historically black community—because the high school there was strong in many different dimensions at that time: "We felt truly we were at the finest high school period. There was not a question that West Charlotte was not the best high school. We had the most pride, we had the best teams, and we had the best teachers."

An African American classmate noted that at that time, West Charlotte had "a really good reputation and it was a good ratio [of black to white]. There was a lot of, during that time period, students that received scholarships from prestigious colleges. So at that time I think it had a pretty good reputation and a lot of kids from all over Charlotte—[West Charlotte] wasn't their assigned school [but they] were driving across town and making other kinds of arrangements to attend the school. So at that time it had a pretty good reputation. . . . Academically it had great programs and also sports were pretty good."

In fact, many graduates of formerly all-black West Charlotte High School noted the high quality of the teachers and the curriculum, especially the AP courses offered, at their school. But they also talked about how strong the theater and music programs were. A white graduate recalled that "we thought at the time—and I have, you know, I have no idea if this is true—but we thought at the time that we had the most AP programs of any school in the system. . . . We had a theater department that . . . was just unbelievable. I mean, we basically had professional staff on our theater."

In Pasadena, one white community activist and parent of a former Muir High School student recalled that in the 1960s, Muir had a lot of parental support and was a strong school in terms of athletics and academics. Thus, he stated, Muir was one of the schools to which competitive colleges looked for prospective students: "We just couldn't say enough about it. And interestingly enough, some of the kids that had been pulled out into private schools, but were not top students, you know, they just got along in private school, but their parents wanted them to go to Stanford, . . . they would come back and do their senior year at Muir, because Stanford especially used to pay real attention to schools like Muir, and they had a better chance of getting in."

Another powerful theme to emerge from our data was that the racial diversity of these schools and the interactions between students of different racial backgrounds added yet another dimension to their quality. A longtime English teacher from Dwight Morrow High School in Englewood commented, "I guess through the '70s [Dwight Morrow] was at its very best. You had kids who lived together, who learned together, or listened to the same kinds of music together, they all listened to Motown together, I remember. . . . When it came to soul and Motown, kids would listen to one another's music. It's just that it was, I guess, a laboratory representing what an interracial society could be. It was very, very nice. It was a very nice and wonderful thing."

Indeed, in only one of the six high schools we studied—Topeka High School—were the student, educator, and community member reflections on the reputation of the school back in the 1970s more consistently negative than they are today. There, many of the interviewees noted that the school was known as a pretty "tough" school, in part because there had been some black-white fights—some called them "riots"—there in the early 1970s. Ironically, this is the only school that is currently stable in terms of its racial balance. It is also the school in our study that seems to be least affected by its state's testing system, which was not established until 1995 and restricted in its use as a measure of school or student accountability. Yet for three of the other five high schools in our study, the statewide testing systems appear to have proved far more problematic, as we discuss below.

Since Then—Defining "Good" Schools via Tests and How That Relates to Diversity

Our data also clearly demonstrate that the relatively new accountability systems implemented over the past twenty-five to thirty years in all six states where these schools are located have changed the playing field for five of these schools. Basically, in every state except Kansas, where very little mention occurred of the relatively new and less consequential accountability system, standardized test scores have become the most important markers of "good" and "bad" schools over the past several decades. Because students of color and lower-income students tend to score more poorly on these tests, the diverse schools we are studying generally have lower average scores than do nearby schools that are more affluent and have higher percentages of white students.

For three of the sites we studied in particular—Englewood's Dwight Morrow High School, Shaker Heights High School, and West Charlotte High School—these tests have clearly played (or are currently playing) a central role in promoting white and middle-class flight from these schools. While the tests were not the only factors influencing the flight, the timing of their implementation was extremely problematic for these schools as they struggled to maintain what had been strong reputations in the face of average test scores that were lower than those of less racially and socioeconomically diverse neighboring schools. For Dwight Morrow, the role that the well-publicized test scores played in encouraging and legitimizing white flight was highlighted in the Englewood Cliffs court case. Indeed, as we noted, New Jersey began statewide competency testing in the early 1970s, and the implementation of these policies coincided with the early and subsequent waves of white flight from Dwight Morrow in the 1970s and 1980s. Meanwhile, the flight of white students from Shaker Heights High School and West Charlotte High School occurred much later—becoming more noticeable during the 1990s—as the statewide testing systems in Ohio and North

Carolina were being instituted and beginning to have an impact. Other factors certainly have played a role in the flight of white and affluent students from these schools—particularly in Charlotte, where the school district's once-comprehensive school desegregation plan languished in the 1990s and then ended in 2002. Still, the timing of the implementation of state tests apparently could not have been worse for these three schools.

The relationship between testing and white and middle-class flight from Austin High School and Muir High School is, as we note, less clear. While the tests seem to matter in both of these states, many confounding variables exist for these two sites, and we have less evidence that the timing of new state tests was as critical. Muir High School lost much of its white population when a section of the Pasadena school district seceded. This school district was also embroiled in a very volatile school desegregation court order that many white parents strongly resisted. And in Austin, the school district tried for many years to assist its flagship high school in maintaining its white and more affluent student population and relatively higher test scores by redrawing the attendance boundaries. Thus, at Topeka High School—the one school in our study that has not lost a large portion of its white student population—the state tests and the high schools' average scores are not yet as salient in the way that interviewees define "good" schools.

In this section we discuss the relationships between the state test policies and the enrollments of these six schools. As we note in table 9.2, California and New Jersey were the first states in our sample to implement state tests. In New Jersey this initial test, the EAP, was by the mid-1970s already being updated and made more rigorous and consequential with the introduction of the MBS test. This test, a precursor to the current generation of accountability tests, was designed to identify those students who lacked basic minimum skills that state officials thought high school graduates should possess.

In the late 1970s, as these new tests were implemented, the Englewood Cliffs School Board first attempted to sever the sending-receiving relationship that assigned the white and more affluent Cliffs students to Dwight Morrow. As we noted earlier, Dwight Morrow students' scores on this MBS test played a central role in the lawsuit that Englewood Cliffs brought against the Englewood Public Schools in the mid-1980s on the basis that the quality of education at the high school was inferior. As one of the main lawyers representing Englewood and Dwight Morrow noted,

> I think that's really when it started, you know, the late '70s is when the racial composition started to really shift. I'm a little hazy on exactly the timing of this, but I think also what began to loom large was the state test scores, because it was true even back in the middle, the late '80s and probably had started to

> become true before, that relative to other communities in Bergen County the standardized test scores [at] Dwight Morrow were low. You know, I think we all know that the extent of the socioeconomic status is a factor, and although Englewood had lots of middle, upper-middle-income people they also had some lower-income people. . . . I think as the state testing program took hold, and the results [were] circulated and published in the paper and, you know, Englewood starts showing up at or near the bottom of the list.

Similar comments about the importance of state tests and the high schools' average scores were heard in Shaker Heights, where these issues became much more salient during the 1990s as the state accountability system became more established. Indeed, in the past decade, Shaker Heights High School has watched its white and upper-middle-class student population shrink. The impact of the Ohio state tests on the school's once-stellar reputation is especially acute. A marketing teacher who has been at the high school for many years said that an influx of poor students from Cleveland into Shaker Heights has resulted in an increase in the number of students who failed the Ohio proficiency test. This has caused backlash and discontent in the Shaker Heights community, even though the high school continues to produce as many or more National Merit Scholars as in the past: "Shaker gets seventeen out of twenty-seven [points on the state test]. This community goes nuts. They want to know why we're doing so poorly on all these proficiency tests, and yet [we are] number 1 in the state of Ohio in National Merit semifinalists. How can you be teaching them and not teaching them? Well, we're teaching 'em all, but you got to take who comes through the door."

A man who taught for many years at Shaker Heights High School recognized the contrast between high-achieving students who were faring well at high school and the average test scores for the school as a whole. In comparing Shaker Heights to a neighboring predominantly white school district, he noted, "The [state] proficiency test judges the school district. The National Merit test judges the students within the school district. So the City of Beachwood, where I live, gets twenty-seven out of twenty-seven on proficiency tests and the best [college any graduate of Beachwood High has] ever gone to is like Duke or Northwestern. Shaker Heights sends kids to Brown, Harvard, Cornell, Yale, Dartmouth in addition to schools like Duke or whatever else you want to say. So, to me, the proficiency tests are nothing more than another one of those man-made business games set up by bureaucracy."

Similar contrasts between the high-achieving white and affluent students and the lower-achieving students of color and low-income students existed at Dwight Morrow High School back in the days when the school was losing many white and middle-class students each year. As one white graduate explained, Dwight

Morrow had a very mixed reputation because "a lot of people ended up going to top schools out of there, but also we had probably the worst test scores in the state. You know, we had this very big paradox at Dwight Morrow."

An argument could be made that state-mandated tests were an improvement because they forced these high schools, which were in many ways racially segregated within their own corridors through tracking and within-school segregation, to focus more intently on the students at the bottom of the academic achievement ladder—students who may well have been overlooked by schools chasing records on AP tests and National Merit Scholars. Indeed, as a former English teacher at West Charlotte noted, when the state measures for accountability were instituted in the early 1990s, emphasis was placed on closing the gap between the black and white scores.

Furthermore, in the high school's defense, several educators in Shaker Heights point out that when test scores are broken down by race, Shaker Heights students consistently outscore students of the same race from other high schools. Yet too often, the scores for the school as a whole are averaged together, and Shaker Heights has a lower ranking overall than high schools that enroll only white and more affluent students. The educators and graduates we interviewed recognized the connection between demographic shifts and schools' rankings on the state tests.

An African American graduate of West Charlotte High School noted that her alma mater has a good history because "it was originally an all-black school and integration really worked there." But she added that she is embarrassed about West Charlotte now because the test scores are "awful." She explained these low test scores as the result of the transferring in of students who were not doing well academically.

Yet people—particularly white and more affluent parents—too often decide not to enroll their children in these racially diverse high schools solely on the basis of *average* test scores. A white graduate of Shaker Heights High School articulated this view, noting that, "If proficiency scores didn't come down the blacker the schools get, then white people wouldn't run away from it."

The consequences of a tarnished academic reputation may be most devastating for the students who remain in these schools—those who lack the option to flee. Thus, perhaps the most frustrating aspect of these narrow test-based perceptions of the quality of these racially diverse schools is the extent to which the perception becomes the reality well after the fact. In other words, it is not simply that these schools have fewer white and affluent students that matters. Rather, it is the self-fulfilling prophecy of the bad reputation that most bothers the educators and graduates of these high schools. In their eyes, these schools had so many things going for them before being labeled as failing schools as a consequence of their average test scores and their demographics. But as more and more white and middle-class students flee them, they are—or are becoming—less competitive, with fewer resources and a diminished curriculum.

As a longtime guidance counselor from Dwight Morrow High School explained, "it was like a self-fulfilling prophecy. Once people did leave, then things really did start to go down—you know, the perception from the community went down, academics went down as all these good kids left, and our SAT scores were down."

Similarly, everyone interviewed who was asked about the present state of West Charlotte High School—formerly the jewel in the district's crown and the symbol of the success of the school desegregation plan there—cited the most recent state test scores and the sharp decrease in white students at the school as the key indicators that the school was not what it had been during the heyday of desegregation. One former principal of the high school commented that parents and students had started asking, "Why should I go there? It's not as strong a school as it used to be. It's low-performing now. It's on the state list. It has a team of state people . . . sent there by the state to say, 'Get this school out of this trap.'"

Interestingly, Austin High School—seated in the capital of a state well known for its comprehensive testing and accountability program—seemed less directly impacted by state-mandated testing than Dwight Morrow, Shaker Heights High School, West Charlotte High School, or even Muir High School. The issue of Austin High School's test scores and how they compared to other nearby schools did not emerge in our interviews as one of the most salient themes for this school. Some of our district-level interviews shed some light on this phenomenon. A former school board member noted that the board had made several boundary line changes for Austin High School over the years, thereby excluding many Latino and African American students who would have otherwise been assigned to the school: "Austin High was on the verge of almost becoming a minority school, and Austin High was not going to have that to happen to it, particularly by being in West Austin. . . . The test scores . . . would have gone down, the rating of the school was gonna go down . . . so therefore boundary lines were redrawn so that we could ensure the fact that the test scores would remain where they are and even escalate. And I'm giving you the long and short of it. And that's straight up."

The other interesting theme to emerge from Austin was that most interviewees were more focused on the quality of the Austin Independent School District as a whole and less focused on individual schools within the city. This may be because these respondents, many of whom were whites who graduated from Austin High but now live in more suburban school districts, were more focused on choosing a school district than an individual school when they purchased their homes.

The high-profile nature of the Texas tests contrasts with the Kansas accountability measures, which were rarely discussed at all in our interviews in Topeka. As we note in table 9.2, Kansas came later to the statewide testing movement, and after the state's policy makers implemented a testing system, they discouraged the use of assessment data for purposes of accountability.

Within this less-test-crazed context, Topeka High School is, as noted earlier, the only school in our study that appears to have a stronger reputation today than it did in the 1970s. Of course, this is not true across every interview, but the vast majority of respondents see Topeka High as strong or stronger academically than it was twenty-five years ago. Such an attitude is reflected in the response of one graduate to the question of how the school differs today from when she attended in the late 1970s: "I think education is number 1; it's not partying. I think it's number 1 now to get your education, to get your scholarships and to be recognized. I would say that's the difference."

In this way, Topeka High School—the only school in our sample that has neither lost the majority of its white and middle-class students nor is on the verge of doing so—has managed to avoid being labeled and evaluated according to its average state test scores.

Summing It All Up: Where Accountability and Diversity Collide

Heubert and Hauser note that whether tests are used for high- or low-stakes purposes, "the information they provide will feed public debate about the educational goals and curricula and about whether schools are accomplishing their mission."[30] We have demonstrated in this chapter, however, that the state tests do *not* feed public debate about the educational goals and curriculum. In fact, in at least five of these states, they appear to stifle such a debate because they narrow the understanding of what constitutes a "good" school. Such understandings work against racially diverse schools in ways that are unfair and erroneous, at least prior to the self-fulfilling prophecy.

Still, as we have noted throughout this chapter and as we have learned from prior research,[31] test scores may sometimes legitimize decisions that white and more affluent parents would make anyway. In other words, the real issue here may be that the perceived quality of these schools has more to do with the race and social class of the students within them than with any supposed objective measure of student achievement.[32] In this way, the test scores of racially diverse schools only legitimate what parents were planning to do all along. In fact, in an article written as the latest versions of the state testing regimes were being implemented, Richard F. Elmore and Susan H. Fuhrman foreshadowed this possible consequence: "Since prior student academic achievement and students' social class are still the strongest predictors of how well a given school will do on academic achievement measures, focusing state policy on student performance might simply concentrate high-achieving students in a few schools, thereby aggravating current disparities in the racial and socioeconomic composition of schools."[33]

Despite the accuracy of Elmore and Fuhrman's hypothesis, the data from our study also demonstrate that at one time, racially mixed schools could and did have "good" reputations. Our research demonstrates, however, that these reputations are incredibly fragile and need to be bolstered—not undercut—by state policies intended to hold schools accountable. Indeed, given everything that racially diverse schools have working against them in a racially segregated and unequal society, such policies should support these schools rather than contribute to their demise.

Thus, we call on state and federal policy makers to consider accountability measures that more accurately reflect the range of experiences of students within racially diverse schools. Devising policies that would ensure that we do not either forget about improving or stop working to better the education of *all* students in racially diverse schools will also ensure that these schools are not punished simply for being diverse.

Notes

1. See Riley, "Reflections on Goals 2000."
2. See L. Olson, "Final Rules."
3. Mazzoni, "State Policy-Making."
4. Linn, *Reporting School Quality.*
5. See Doherty, "Accountability."
6. Ibid.; Heubert and Hauser, *High Stakes.*
7. L. Olson, "All States."
8. Feldman, "N.J. Plans More Rigorous Competency Testing"; Mazzoni, "State Policy-Making."
9. Heubert and Hauser, *High Stakes*, 15.
10. Mazzoni, "State Policy-Making."
11. Feldman, "N.J. Plans More Rigorous Competency Testing."
12. Ibid.
13. Mazzoni, "State Policy-Making."
14. Lemann, *Big Test.*
15. Bishop and Mane, "Impact."
16. Ibid.
17. Heubert and Hauser, *High Stakes*, 38.

18. Petrovich and Wells, *Bringing Equity Back.*

19. Heubert and Hauser, *High Stakes*; Kornhaber and Orfield, "High-Stakes Testing Policies."

20. L. Olson, "Final Rules."

21. Goertz and Duffy, "Assessment and Accountability."

22. Riley, "Reflections on Goals 2000."

23. Elmore, "Testing Trap"; Linn, *Reporting School Quality.*

24. See McNeil and Valenzuela, "Harmful Impact."

25. See Heubert, "High-Stakes Testing."

26. Orfield, "Schools More Separate."

27. Ibid.

28. By "racially mixed," we mean between 40 and 75 percent of any one race and no more than 25 percent off the racial balance of the city or town for any one race.

29. See, e.g., Mickelson, this volume.

30. Heubert and Hauser, *High Stakes*, 47.

31. See esp. Holme, "Buying Homes, Buying Schools."

32. Ibid.; Saporito and Lareau, "School Selection."

33. Elmore and Fuhrman, "Opportunity-to-Learn Standards," 448.

CHAPTER TEN

JAY P. HEUBERT

High-Stakes Testing, Nationally and in the South

Disparate Impact, Opportunity to Learn, and Current Legal Protections

This chapter focuses on "high-stakes" tests, defined here as tests that states and school districts use in deciding whether individual students will receive high school diplomas or be promoted to the next grade. It places the South's graduation and promotion test programs into the context of such testing nationally. It also considers how federal law, including the No Child Left Behind Act of 2001 (NCLB) and the Individuals with Disabilities Education Act of 1997 (IDEA), both of which emphasize *system* accountability (for states, school districts, and schools), may influence state and district assessment programs that instead have high stakes for individual students.

Large-scale assessment, including testing for high-stakes purposes, has changed in important ways since the minimum-competency test (MCT) programs of the 1970s and 1980s. First, most current tests embody much higher academic standards. Second, chiefly because of changes in federal law, including NCLB and IDEA, many more low achievers, especially students with disabilities and English-language learners (ELLs), are now included among those tested. Third, while state graduation testing has increased somewhat, state- and district-level promotion testing has grown rapidly.

Other important changes are less widely recognized. For example, recent changes in federal law have weakened important civil rights protections, even in situations where students of color, students with disabilities, and ELLs fail high-stakes tests at rates far higher than in the 1970s and 1980s. Also, legal standards developed in older cases involving MCTs, though useful, do not take into account the current standards movement, which, in seeking to educate all students to high standards, places heavy new demands on assessments, schools, and students. The results are (1) a changed legal climate in which to evaluate current graduation tests and promotion tests, and (2) a more complex educational context that educators and researchers may need to help courts understand and that may call for refinement in the standards that courts developed decades ago in MCT cases.

The sections that follow (1) describe the current nature and scope of graduation and promotion testing in the United States, both of which are particularly prevalent in the southern states; (2) examine empirical evidence on the current disparate effects of such testing on minority students, students with disabilities, and ELLs; (3) consider varied evidence now available about whether states, school districts, and schools are teaching all students the kinds of knowledge and skills they need to pass high-stakes tests; and (4) examine the current status of federal law concerning high-stakes testing, pointing out changes in the law, limitations in the law's current treatment of high-stakes tests, and shortcomings in existing mechanisms for enforcing broadly accepted norms of appropriate test use.

The Nature and Extent of High-Stakes Testing in the United States

The Extent of Graduation Testing

As part of the "back to the basics" movement in the 1970s and early 1980s, seventeen states adopted MCTs, which students had to pass to receive standard high school diplomas, even if they had completed satisfactorily all other requirements for graduation.

In the past five years, the number of states with graduation tests remained fairly constant at eighteen, rising to nineteen in the spring of 2003.[1] Graduation testing has always been especially popular in the southern states; this was true in the early days of minimum-competency testing and remains so today: eleven of the current nineteen graduation test states are defined in the Census as "southern states."[2] Nationally, about five more states are now planning to adopt graduation tests between now and 2008.[3] As discussed subsequently in this chapter, however, some factors may lead states to reconsider or postpone such requirements.

Equally important is the changing nature of large-scale assessments. While earlier exit tests focused on minimum competencies, more than two-thirds of the current tests embody standards at the tenth-grade level or higher,[4] and an increasing number reflect "world-class" standards such as those embodied in the National Assessment of Educational Progress (NAEP), a highly regarded assessment administered nationally to representative samples of students. This trend reflects the emphasis, in the standards movement and in state and federal laws, on helping all students reach high standards of achievement.

Little debate occurs on the desirability of teaching students high-level knowledge and skills: higher expectations and improved instruction lead to improved achievement.[5] At the same time, where standards are high and large numbers of students start out at low achievement levels, the gaps in teaching and learning that must be closed are greater than where standards reflect only basic skills. The gaps are greatest in schools where instruction is weak and resources are inadequate, conditions that are common in many southern states and, more generally, in schools serving large numbers of low-achieving students.

As discussed subsequently, student failure rates on newer, more demanding exit tests are much higher, more persistent, and more persistently disparate for different groups than on MCTs, when failure rates and group disparities typically declined quickly to low levels. Even after initial test implementation, some groups fail particular graduation tests at rates of well over 50 percent.

In recent years, at least two states have withdrawn exit exam requirements, and four have postponed them,[6] while others have lowered passing scores or allowed students to substitute scores on other tests for graduation purposes.

Several factors seem to be involved. One is the continuing evidence of high and disparate failure rates, which raises educational as well as political questions. In 2003, for example, California postponed until 2006 the date by which students would have to pass a state graduation exam to receive a standard diploma. The State Board of Education acted in the face of predicted statewide diploma-denial rates of about 20 percent; evidence of far higher failure rates for African American students, Latino students, ELLs, and students with disabilities; and indications that many students were not yet being taught the knowledge and skills that the graduation tests measure.[7] Similarly, in 2003, when 13,000 Florida students failed that state's graduation test, the state allowed students to substitute scores from the SAT, ACT, and other standardized tests and granted waivers to some students with disabilities.[8]

Declining state revenues, currently a serious problem in almost every state,[9] including those in the South, is a second factor that could slow the growth of graduation testing. The budget situation may also explain the apparent decline in the number of states providing special funding to help low-achieving students meet state test standards.[10]

Last but not least, both Georgia and North Carolina have postponed implementation of new versions of their graduation exams out of concern that the tests might not conform to NCLB requirements.

Two other developments have affected the scope of high-stakes testing: the rapid growth of promotion testing and the inclusion of students with disabilities and ELLs in large-scale assessments, some of them high-stakes tests.

The Extent of Promotion Testing

Promotion testing has grown very rapidly in response to concerns about social promotion. In 2001, seventeen states (including nine in the South) required or planned to require students to pass standardized tests as a condition of grade-to-grade promotion, a rise of eleven states since 1999. Thirteen states (including Florida, Louisiana, Mississippi, North Carolina, South Carolina, Texas, and Virginia) administered promotion tests at both the elementary and middle school levels or planned to do so.[11]

Students of color are likelier than white students to live in states that administer graduation tests[12] and promotion tests.[13] In addition, many urban school districts, including those in the District of Columbia, New York City, Boston, and Chicago, have adopted promotion test policies even where states have not. Thus, many of the nation's minority students and immigrant students—and increasing numbers of all students—must pass promotion tests.

NCLB, which requires end-of-year testing for students in grades 3–8 as of 2005–6, also seems to be fueling further growth in promotion testing. Neither NCLB nor any other federal statute requires promotion testing or any other kind of high-stakes testing. But North Carolina is already using for promotion purposes the new tests that NCLB mandates, and other states that administer promotion tests will probably do likewise.

Students with Disabilities, ELLs, and High-Stakes Testing

Since 1994, federal laws have required states and school districts to include students with disabilities and ELLs in large-scale assessments, to report disaggregated scores for these and other groups, and to give all students access to high-quality instruction.[14] Many such students had previously been exempted from testing.[15]

This chapter deals less with system accountability than with tests that have high-stakes consequences for individual students, and on this question federal laws are silent. Thus, NCLB and IDEA require system accountability but leave states and school districts to decide whether students with disabilities or ELLs who fail such tests will be subject to individual high-stakes consequences such as retention or denial of a standard diploma.[16]

This decision is complex, and states have approached it differently. Some authorize individual education plan (IEP) teams to decide individually whether a student with disabilities who fails a promotion test will nevertheless be promoted. In other states, promotion test requirements apply fully to students with disabilities. States differ in similar ways on graduation testing.

In some states, students who fail state exit tests are eligible for alternative diplomas or certificates. Some, such as IEP diplomas, are available only to students with disabilities, while others, such as certificates of completion or attendance, may also be available to other students. Unfortunately, to this point, little research has examined the value of such certificates and alternate, nonstandard diplomas in terms of a student's future opportunities for education or employment. The only alternative certificate on which extensive research exists is the General Equivalency Diploma (GED), and evidence suggests that GED holders are more like high school dropouts than like the holders of standard diplomas in terms of future educational and employment opportunities.[17] Students with disabilities who do not receive standard diplomas have a right to special education and related services until the age of twenty-one or twenty-two.[18] Policy makers should therefore proceed cautiously with alternatives to standard diplomas.

From Minimum Competencies to World-Class Standards: Pass Rates, Disparate Impact, and Other Effects of High-Stakes Testing

A central objective of standards-based education reform is "systematically to improve learning for students who have done poorly in the past,"[19] to reduce inequality in educational achievement by helping all students reach high standards. Indeed, many people believe that "[c]urrent versions of standards-based reforms will have their greatest impact on children at the bottom of the achievement distribution."[20]

Some observers believe that standards-based reform will especially benefit low-achieving students; as attorney William Taylor writes, "When schools and districts are held accountable for the achievement of all students, the means are at hand to force them to improve the quality of schooling provided for previously neglected students."[21] Taylor speaks here of system accountability. There is broad agreement both (1) that accountability for improved educational achievement should be widely shared[22] and (2) that accountability for improved educational achievement should be based on school performance.[23]

Though "accountability for adults is in its infancy,"[24] accountability is expanding for individual students, who are increasingly subject to the serious and well-documented harms associated with being retained in grade or denied standard high school diplomas. In our society, for example, not having a standard high school diploma is associated with much lower income, diminished opportunities for employment and further education, higher risk of criminal incarceration, and greater likelihood of dysfunction in family life.[25] Concerns have arisen that low-achieving students, including many minority students, students with disabilities, and ELLs—who typically rely heavily on their schools for academic knowledge—may be failing increasingly demanding high-stakes tests because their schools do not yet expose these students to the knowledge and skills needed to pass the tests.[26]

What is known, then, about the pass rates and group disparities on high-stakes tests? This section compares empirical evidence for early MCTs and for current tests that embody higher standards.

State Pass Rates and Disparate Impact

Even on basic-skills tests, minority students, students with disabilities, and ELLs typically fail at higher rates than other students, especially at first. For example, 20 percent of African American students but only 2 percent of white students initially failed Florida's MCT.[27] And although most students with disabilities and ELLs were exempted from early exit tests, those who were tested failed at higher rates.

For a variety of reasons, failure rates typically decline among all groups in the years after a new graduation test is introduced.[28] This held true for early MCTs: within a few years, failure rates declined substantially for all groups.[29]

This pattern—high initial failure rates that decline over time—apparently continues for graduation tests adopted more recently, but important qualifications exist. First, where high-stakes tests embody demanding standards, initial failure rates are much higher than for earlier tests. Second, group disparities on high-standards tests are typically quite high—well beyond the requirements for showing "disparate impact" under federal law. A test is considered to have adverse impact when a statistical analysis shows that one group's pass rate is significantly lower than another's[30] or when one group's pass rate is less than four-fifths of another's.[31] Third, both failure rates and group disparities on high-standards tests typically decline more slowly. The following discussion illustrates how failure rates and group differences can change as tests become more demanding.

Texas's graduation test, the Texas Assessment of Academic Skills (TAAS), is set at the seventh- or eighth-grade level, higher than earlier MCTs but lower than current standards in most states.[32] Texas reports that pass rates for African Americans and Latinos roughly doubled between 1994 and 1998 and that the gaps in failure rates for whites, African Americans, and Latinos narrowed considerably during that time—conclusions that scholars have since questioned.[33] Texas data for 1998 nonetheless show continuing disparities: cumulative failure rates of 17.6

percent for African American students, 17.4 percent for Hispanic students, and 6.7 percent for white students.[34] Thus, even on fairly low-level exit tests, failure rates for African Americans and Hispanics remain higher in Texas than was true for early basic-skills exit tests, and a court found that TAAS has adverse impacts.[35]

The same pattern is evident in Florida, where the Florida Comprehensive Assessment Test was introduced in 1998. Pass rates for all groups have increased over time. As noted previously, however, when the graduation test requirement took effect in the spring of 2003, some 13,000 seniors were denied standard diplomas, including about 5.2 percent of white seniors, 19.1 percent of African Americans, and 11.9 percent of Latinos.[36]

Moreover, these statistics for Texas and Florida understate minority failure rates and group discrepancies since they do not account for students who were not tested because they had dropped out, been retained in grade, or been excluded improperly from the test-taking population—all categories that disproportionately include minority students, students with disabilities, and ELLs.[37]

California's English and mathematics exit tests, first administered in the spring of 2001, reflect ninth-grade standards.[38] According to data from the California Department of Education through May 2002—the most recent administration for which the state posts data on the rates at which groups passed both tests needed for graduation—failure rates for students in the class of 2004 were far higher than those of the early basic-skills tests: only 48 percent of all test takers had passed both tests, and African Americans, Hispanics, students with disabilities, and ELLs had far lower pass rates: 28 percent of African Americans and 30 percent of Hispanics in the class of 2004 had passed both tests, compared with 65 percent of whites. Students with disabilities and ELLs also had passed both tests at far lower rates: 13 percent and 19 percent, respectively.[39] Spring 2003 data for the class of 2004[40] show improved subtest pass rates for all groups, but faced with the prospect of denying diplomas to more than 20 percent of all students in the spring of 2004, the state postponed until 2006 the date by which receipt of standard high school diplomas will become contingent on passage of both tests.

Failure rates are typically highest on exit exams that embody "world-class" standards such as those of NAEP assessments. About 38 percent of all students would fail tests that reflect such standards, and failure rates would be about twice as high for minority students.[41] Careful multistate studies show students with disabilities failing various state tests at rates 30–40 percentage points higher than those for other students.[42]

In Massachusetts, where current "world-class" examinations were introduced in 1999 and the graduation test requirement took effect in the spring of 2003, pass rates for the class of 2003 increased between 2001 and 2003:

- As tenth-graders in 2001, 71 percent of white students had passed both tests needed for graduation, compared with 18 percent of African American students, 14 percent of Hispanic students, and 9 percent of ELLs. Thirty percent of students with disabilities passed, compared with 61 percent of nondisabled students.[43]
- By the spring of 2003, the following percentages of twelfth-graders had passed both tests needed for graduation: 97 percent of whites, 86 percent of African Americans, 83 percent of Hispanics, 82 percent of ELLs, 80 percent of students with disabilities, and 97 percent of nondisabled students.[44]

These are substantial gains. At the same time, five years after initial test implementation, these data show high and disproportionate failure rates for students of color, ELLs, and students with disabilities. Moreover, because the reported pass rates are for seniors, they do not take into account members of the 2003 cohort who had dropped out, had been retained in grade, or for other reasons had not reached twelfth grade by the spring of 2003. Calculations by Anne Wheelock of Boston College suggest that graduation rates would be much lower if they accounted for nearly 17,000 additional students who were part of the 2003 cohort as ninth-graders but not as twelfth-graders three years later.[45]

New York received national publicity when it reported that nearly twice as many students with disabilities passed the state's new Regents English Exam in 1998–99 as had taken the exam two years earlier.[46] This information is factually correct, but the state's pass-rate data suggest somewhat less dramatic changes. Between 1997–98 and 1999–2000, the percentages of twelfth-grade students with disabilities who passed New York's Regents English exam increased from 5.1 percent to 8.0 percent.[47] In other words, the percentages of twelfth-graders who had not passed the Regents Exam declined from 94.9 percent to 92.0 percent over two years—and these figures exclude dropouts, students previously retained, or students absent on test day; Daniel Koretz and Laura Hamilton estimate that only about half the students with disabilities were present for a Regents Exam administration they studied.[48]

These data, while limited, suggest that where high-stakes tests embody higher content and performance standards, (1) initial failure rates are higher than for earlier tests, (2) group disparities are typically quite high and legally "disparate," and (3) both failure rates and group disparities typically decline more slowly than for earlier MCTs.

Evaluating State Pass-Rate Data

State data on high-stakes tests understate low achievement and group disparities for two reasons.

First, NAEP data, which researchers consider more reliable than state test reports, consistently show much less gain in student performance than do state test results. This held true during the 1980s, when most states reported sharply increased student achievement even as aggregate NAEP data showed little or no gain, and it remains true today.

At the same time that many states report higher pass rates on more demanding graduation tests, national NAEP results for 2000 show that the math achievement of twelfth-graders has declined since 1996, with significantly more students in the "below basic" category and significantly fewer students demonstrating "basic mastery."[49] While NAEP scores have improved for fourth- and eighth-grade students, nationally and especially in some states, twelfth-graders are likelier to be affected by state graduation test policies.

A study of the Texas achievement gap is noteworthy.[50] A court there strongly emphasized state data showing that the achievement gaps among white students, African American students, and Latino students had closed dramatically between 1994 and 1998 on the TAAS.[51] Using NAEP data, however, Stephen P. Klein and colleagues showed that the achievement gaps between white students and other groups in Texas had actually increased slightly during this period. For Robert Linn, this evidence "raises serious questions about the trustworthiness of the TAAS result for making inferences about improvements in achievement in Texas or about the relative size of the gains for different segments of the student population."[52]

National NAEP math results for 2000 also suggest widening racial achievement gaps among thirteen- and seventeen-year-olds.[53] The racial gap is widening most at higher performance levels,[54] an obvious concern as more states' tests emphasize high-level skills. NAEP does not yet include enough students with disabilities (or ELLs) in its samples to provide meaningful state-level performance scores for these groups, but future NAEP results should help assess state data that suggest improvements for these groups.

Second, as discussed earlier, the meaning of state pass-rate data depends on what proportion of all students took the test. Apparently good news—that 100 percent of eleventh-graders passed a graduation test, for example—means something quite different if three-fourths of all students dropped out before eleventh grade or if many students with disabilities or ELLs did not take the test. Since the standards movement is concerned with all students, an assessment of the disproportionate impact of high-stakes testing should consider the many individuals who do not take such tests with other students their age.

As noted earlier, state test data rarely include information on dropouts, students previously retained in grade, students improperly exempted or excluded from testing, or students absent on test days. Even NAEP results do not account for these students. At the grade levels where states administer exit tests, however, these students often represent a substantial portion of the cohort. If these students were included in the denominators when states calculated pass rates, those rates would be much lower, especially for minority students, students with disabilities, and ELLs.

A closely related question is whether exit testing or promotion testing causes increased dropout rates or retention in grade. The effects of graduation testing are debated. Walt Haney argues that the Texas graduation test does increase retention and dropout, especially for African Americans and Hispanics, while Martin Carnoy and colleagues claim that high retention and dropout rates for these groups do not result from TAAS.[55] A 2001 California survey indicates that 80 percent of principals and 61 percent of teachers in the state believe that graduation tests there will have "a strongly negative or negative impact on student dropout rates" and that 55 percent of principals and 32 percent of teachers think the tests will have "a strongly negative or negative impact on student retention rates."[56] The most carefully designed national longitudinal study to date tracked high school students who were eighth-graders in 1988 and seniors in 1992 and found no general relationship between basic-skills graduation tests and dropout rates but concluded that students in the lowest quintile are "25% more likely to drop out of high school than comparable peers in non-test states."[57]

There is less debate about failing promotion tests. Decades of research show that students required to repeat a grade are much worse off than similar low-performing students who are instead promoted to the next grade. A committee of the National Research Council found that low-performing elementary and secondary school students who are held back do less well academically, are much worse off socially, and are far likelier to drop out than are equally weak students who are promoted.[58] Other studies conclude that retention in grade is the single strongest predictor of which students will drop out.[59] The evidence on simple retention in grade is so compelling that a committee of the National Research Council concluded that it constitutes inappropriate test use for states or school districts to use test scores for this purpose.[60]

Thus, unless schools rely on early intervention rather than retention to reduce the number of low achievers, the proliferation of promotion testing is likely to increase significantly the numbers of minority students, students with disabilities, and ELLs who suffer the serious economic, educational, and other harms associated with dropping out. And, as noted earlier, NCLB will probably lead to more promotion testing even though the legislation does not require it. It would be unfortunate—and hardly evidence of success—if states, school districts, or schools achieved high graduation test pass rates because large numbers of low achievers had already left school and were no longer among the test takers.

Evidence That Students Are Being Taught the Requisite Knowledge and Skills

The standards movement rests on the premise that virtually all students can reach high levels of achievement if they receive high-quality curriculum and instruction. This premise rests, in turn, on dramatic recent research findings in such areas as brain development, early childhood education, and effective pedagogy. In three federal statutes, Congress has accepted this premise and the research supporting it.[61]

Standards on the appropriate use of high-stakes tests are consistent with the standards movement's central premise. Under applicable legal standards and psychometric norms, states may administer tests that all students must pass as a condition of receiving standard high school diplomas—*if* states and schools first give students an adequate opportunity to acquire the knowledge and skills that such tests measure. Courts have ruled for two decades that graduation tests must be a fair measure of what students have been taught.[62] The measurement profession, the National Research Council, and the American Educational Research Association (AERA) all say that results of large-scale tests may be used in making individual promotion or graduation decisions only after students have had an adequate opportunity to acquire the knowledge and skills that such tests measure. These standards apply to all students, including ELLs and students with disabilities. This "prior opportunity to learn" requirement does not apply to the use of student test information to improve schools.

It is far harder today than in the MCT days to ensure that all students have had a meaningful opportunity to learn the knowledge and skills that tests measure. Standards have gotten much higher, and they now apply to many more low-achieving students, who start out behind and often must also overcome barriers related to disability, English proficiency, or poverty. Moreover, the school districts and schools that serve large numbers of needy students often must operate with less money and fewer certified teachers than other school districts and schools, even though NCLB requires that all eligible students be taught by teachers who are certified in the subjects they teach.

Criteria by Which to Evaluate "Opportunity to Learn"

Different types of evidence exist by which to determine whether students are being taught the knowledge and skills that tests measure.

Perhaps the most straightforward approach is to examine actual indicators of student achievement, such as test scores and grades. As Lauress Wise and his colleagues suggest in evaluating California test results, "the best evidence that a school system is providing its students adequate opportunity to learn the required material is whether most students do, in fact, learn the material."[63] And even if "most students" are learning well, there are usually subgroups that have low achievement and that may not have received an adequate opportunity to learn. Indeed, what constitutes adequate opportunity to learn for some students may be inadequate for others.

A second broad approach, which federal law employs, is to see whether states have met system accountability standards that are intended to gauge how well schools are serving different kinds of students and to ensure that states and school districts set high standards for all students. A third broad approach focuses on whether states have adopted demanding content and performance standards; on whether curriculum, instruction, and large-scale assessments are properly aligned with those standards; and on whether schools and teachers possess the capacity to deliver high-quality instruction to all students. This approach is based on the logic of the standards movement, under which improved capacity and alignment are the principal means to improved student achievement.[64] It is also a requirement of NCLB.

Evidence That Schools Are Teaching Students the Knowledge and Skills That Tests Measure

Research evidence shows that achievement, especially for younger students, has improved in some states and schools. Other evidence demonstrates, however, that many schools do not yet give all students an opportunity to acquire the knowledge and skills they need to pass increasingly demanding high-stakes tests.

Consider state pass-rate data of the kind discussed previously. While pass rates continue to rise, many states, especially those with more demanding exit tests, continue to show disproportionate and unacceptably high failure rates for minority students, students with disabilities, and ELLs. If virtually all children can learn to high standards, such high failure rates must result at least in part from insufficient high-quality instruction.

The good news is that more states now meet current federal system accountability requirements than was previously the case.[65] Despite the requirements of NCLB and IDEA, many states do not yet include all students with disabilities or ELLs in their assessment systems, and many do not yet properly disaggregate achievement information for various student populations.[66] Without such data, states and school districts lack basic information about how well low-achieving groups perform and about how to serve them more effectively. Such information is a precondition for improved achievement.

And what evidence illustrates that curriculum and instruction are aligned with high-stakes assessments? Eva Baker and Robert Linn describe alignment as "the linchpin of standards-based accountability systems" and express the view that "in many parts of the country . . . alignment is weak."[67] Evidence shows that such alignment is increasing[68] as well as that alignment—and the improved capacity that alignment requires—is still more aspiration than reality in many schools.

Empirical research supports such expressions of concern. One line of research, by Andrew Porter, John Smithson, and others, studies eleven states and finds only modest overlap between a state's tests and what teachers in that state say they teach. For example, in fourth-grade mathematics, reports from five states showed overlaps ranging from a high of 45 percent to a low of 23 percent; in eighth-grade mathematics, reports from six states showed overlaps ranging from a high of 35 percent to a low of 5 percent.[69] Other subjects showed comparable or even lower overlap. Other studies find low overlap and "instructional content . . . not very well aligned with . . . the state test."[70]

Despite limitations, these studies suggest that many states and schools have not yet reached the point where they are teaching students all or even most of what state tests measure. This poses a serious problem where tests are used to make high-stakes decisions about individual students, as is true in some states Porter and Smithson studied. In such circumstances, close alignment should precede the use of test scores for high-stakes purposes.

Alignment is closely linked with capacity. According to Richard Elmore, the "work of turning a school around entails improving the knowledge and skills of teachers—changing their knowledge of content and how to teach it—and helping them to understand where their students are in their academic development." In many places, the necessary investments have yet to be made: "Low-performing schools, and the people who work in them, don't know what to do. If they did, they would be doing it already." "[W]ithout substantial investments in capacity, [the increased pressure of test-based accountability] is likely to aggravate the existing inequalities between low-performing and high-performing schools and students."[71]

Indeed, a central objective of education reform efforts since at least the 1950s has been to attract strong teachers to schools that serve large numbers of low-achieving students. Reversing traditional teacher mobility patterns, in which experienced, well-regarded teachers gravitate toward wealthier suburban schools, "is a necessary condition for standards-based reform to improve educational outcomes for children of color."[72] According to Richard Murnane and Frank Levy,[73] however, and to Helen F. Ladd,[74] current standards and accountability mechanisms may increase the incentives for marketable teachers to avoid or leave schools with high proportions of low-achieving students.

Long-standing problems of alignment and capacity also exist between "general education" and programs for students with disabilities or ELLs, both of which also serve large minority populations. For example, while some studies document real progress in reducing barriers between general education and special education,[75] others raise serious concerns. Case studies at high schools in three states found that many special education teachers "lacked guidance about how to align IEPs with the standards," that they were "by and large . . . not involved in school-wide discussions about standards," that special education teachers "tended to use the IEPs rather than the standards as a guide for instruction," that "most IEPs were not aligned with the standards," and that many special education and general education teachers "tended to have a 'wait and see' attitude about exposing students with disabilities to and engaging them in standards-based instruction."[76]

Taken together, such studies suggest improvement coupled with major continuing problems of capacity and alignment. State test score data, studies of system accountability under federal law, state-specific studies of alignment, and studies of standards-based reform for students with disabilities all indicate that many schools are not yet teaching students the full range of subject matter and skills that high-stakes tests measure. It therefore seems problematic that so many states and school districts are already administering or moving forward with high-stakes graduation and/or promotion tests.

Federal Law on High-Stakes Testing

Under what circumstances will the federal government or other entities intervene where some student groups fail high-stakes tests at substantially higher rates than other students or where there is evidence that states and schools do not yet teach students the knowledge and skills that graduation or promotion tests measure?[77]

Despite the fact that the standards of the measurement profession contain clear "opportunity to learn" language covering both promotion tests and graduation tests,[78] the measurement profession itself will not intervene. There is no mechanism by which the testing profession investigates complaints or enforces its standards.[79] Thus, legal action may be the likeliest mechanism for challenging inappropriate use of high-stakes tests.

Legal protections, however, may be less extensive than many educators, parents, and students think. In 2001, the U.S. Supreme Court held that private individuals could no longer bring "disparate-impact" cases under Title VI of the Civil Rights Act of 1964, the federal civil rights statute that most strongly protects minority groups and ELLs. Similarly, most graduation test cases were decided in the days of minimum-competency testing and suggest a judicial reluctance to probe deeply whether schools are teaching what exit tests measure. And in the relatively few cases involving promotion test policies, courts have tended to assume that students benefit from retention in grade and have no legal interest in avoiding it.

Changed conditions in education argue for more sensitive judicial inquiry. Even if it was appropriate to assume that most schools taught students basic skills, recent research suggests that problems arise in assuming that all students are being taught the knowledge and skills that current "high standards" exit tests measure, especially as students with disabilities and ELLs increasingly take part and as researchers document continuing problems of alignment and school capacity. Similarly, court opinions on promotion testing do not refer to strong research on grade retention's harmful effects.

It may be possible to resolve concerns over high-stakes testing through the policy process. But if judges are to play a role in protecting equality of opportunity, they will need help from educators, researchers, and lawyers in understanding the current policy context, the current educational realities, and the complex issues surrounding high-stakes testing.

Disparate-Impact Claims

Since the early 1970s, most cases alleging discrimination in education have been brought under federal civil rights statutes and their accompanying regulations. The regulations forbid federal fund recipients from engaging in policies or practices that, although not overtly discriminatory, produce disparate impact and have the effect of discriminating unless the defendant can show that the policies or practices advance a substantial, legitimate objective.

Thus, in *Lau v. Nichols* (1974), a case brought by parents of children who had recently arrived from China, the U.S. Supreme Court ruled that San Francisco's failure to make any provision for the students' language needs had the effect of discriminating against them in violation of Title VI regulations. Similarly, when private citizens challenged the Texas graduation test, the court explored whether TAAS had disproportionate, adverse impact on African American and Hispanic students. Concluding that it did, the court nonetheless ruled for Texas because the court accepted the state's asserted justifications: that TAAS provided a uniform, objective standard for high school diplomas in the state and that group disparities were being reduced.

In 2001, however, in *Alexander v. Sandoval,* the U.S. Supreme Court ruled, 5–4, that only the federal government, not private individuals, may invoke the Title VI regulations that allow "disparate-impact" claims. If *Sandoval* had been decided thirty years ago, hundreds of discrimination cases—many successful—could never have been brought, including the *Lau* case and the Title VI part of the 2000 TAAS case. Since *Sandoval,* numerous discrimination cases have been dismissed.

What can private individuals do? They can file complaints with the U.S. Department of Education or the U.S. Department of Justice, which can still bring disparate-impact cases, administratively or in court. In the current climate, however, these agencies are less likely than private individuals to challenge testing programs.

Private individuals can also file lawsuits but must prove that educational policies or practices having adverse impact were motivated, at least partly, by intent to discriminate. This standard is very hard to meet, and "intent" claims have consistently been rejected in cases challenging exit tests. Thus, unless Congress overrules *Sandoval,* which is unlikely in the present climate, this decision substantially reduces the likelihood of successful discrimination cases against high-stakes testing programs.

Graduation Testing and Opportunity to Learn

Relying on due process provisions in the U.S. Constitution, federal courts have ruled that students have a legally protected "property interest" in receiving standard high school diplomas if they have completed their other graduation requirements. Where this property interest exists, courts then examine (1) whether students received sufficient advance notice of the exit test requirements and (2) whether the exit test is a fair measure of what students have actually been taught.

In the early graduation test cases, which involved basic-skills tests, most courts did not inquire deeply into whether students were being taught the requisite knowledge and skills. In *Anderson v. Banks* (1981), where a school official acknowledged that there had been no effort to determine whether students were being taught what the district's exit test measured, the court ruled without discussion that the district could rectify the situation within two years, given the availability of remedial programs and multiple test-taking opportunities. In *Debra P.* (1983), a statewide case in Florida, the court concluded after four years had passed that the test was a fair measure of what students were taught based on (1) evidence that the test measured skills included in the state curriculum, (2) a survey showing that most teachers considered the skills to be ones they should teach, and (3) evidence that teachers were actually teaching the requisite knowledge and skills in Florida's classrooms.

It would be problematic today, however, for judges to assume that the gaps could be closed so quickly when the gaps are often far greater, when historically excluded groups are increasingly included in high-stakes testing, when numerous indicators show that many states do not yet provide adequate opportunities for students to learn the knowledge and skills they need, and when profound "capacity" problems have been well defined and documented. And while courts are usually inclined to defer to educators' judgments, some high-stakes testing programs appear to lack a firm foundation in educational research or practice. As Elmore points out, "State policies require proficiency levels for grade promotion and graduation for students . . . without any empirical evidence or any defensible theory about how much it is feasible to expect students to learn over a given period of time or what types of instruction have to be in place in order for students to meet expected rates of improvement."[80] These matters call for careful scrutiny.

It is therefore noteworthy that two recent court decisions, both involving students with disabilities, did not explore more thoroughly the issues surrounding whether students had been taught what a state exit test measures.

Rene v. Reed (2000) arose in Indiana, which announced in 1997 that most learning-disabled students would have to pass the state's exit exam in the spring of 2000 to receive standard diplomas. Previously, students with disabilities had received diplomas if they met their IEP requirements, which often did not track the state standards. In the spring of 2000, more than 1,000 learning-disabled students failed the test. The students sued in state court, arguing that their IEPs had not been modified in time for them to learn the knowledge and skills on the graduation test, particularly since they had been behind in 1997. The state argued that students had had sufficient time to prepare in light of remedial programs, opportunities to retake the exam, and the option to remain in school for further instruction after the senior year.

While recognizing Indiana's legal duty to test only what students had been taught, the judge found it "implausible" that the learning-disabled students had not been exposed to the subjects on the exit test. In reaching this conclusion, the opinion showed little evidence that the court had considered the difficulty of the exit test, students' prior achievement levels, or whether schools had the capacity to provide students with the necessary instruction. The court encouraged students to remain in school after their senior year to receive additional instruction and retake the test.[81]

In California, students with disabilities filed a lawsuit challenging the state exit test, which was first administered in the spring of 2001 and which, at the time, all students in the class of 2004 needed to pass to graduate.[82] (As noted earlier, California subsequently extended this deadline until the spring of 2006.) Before the trial began, the students sought a preliminary injunction (an emergency court order) on several matters that they said could not wait until after the trial. One claim was that students with disabilities would not have sufficient time before the spring of 2004 to learn what the exit test measures.

In February 2002, the court issued detailed orders on issues of testing accommodations and alternative assessments. The court declined, however, to act immediately on the "opportunity to learn" claim, saying only that "the present state of the evidence does not reveal an asymmetry between what students are taught and [the exit test]."[83]

Because only 10.3 percent of all students with disabilities who took both state tests in the spring of 2001 passed,[84] some evidence appears to show "asymmetry" between what students had been taught and what the exit test then required them to know by the spring of 2004. The Court of Appeals for the Ninth Circuit was therefore correct when it affirmed this decision, not because there was no "asymmetry" but because possible delays in the 2004 deadline made the claim premature.[85]

More thorough consideration of "opportunity to learn" issues would not be without precedent. Early cases held that students with disabilities, like their nondisabled peers, could be denied standard high school diplomas if they failed exit exams as long as they had received sufficient advance notice and as long as they had already been taught the knowledge and skills that the exam measured.[86] These courts also recognized that students with disabilities would probably need more time than other students to master the requisite knowledge, both because some "learn at a slower rate than regular division students"[87] and because students whose IEPs did not yet reflect the content of the state exit test would have to be taught a substantially different curriculum before they could be expected to pass the state test.

In other words, these courts saw even in the early 1980s that for students with disabilities, "opportunity to learn" issues could be complex, requiring an inquiry into how far behind students were at the outset, what measures would be needed to align IEPs and instruction with state standards and tests, and how much time these students would need to master the requisite knowledge and skill after schools were equipped to provide the necessary instruction. Similar logic would apply to ELLs and low-socioeconomic-status students, who must also acquire increasingly high-level knowledge and skill while overcoming different barriers and whose schools often have limited capacity to provide high-quality instruction to these students.

Promotion Testing and Opportunity to Learn

According to the standards of the testing profession, promotion tests (like graduation tests) should cover only the "content and skills that students have had an opportunity to learn."[88] The AERA agrees,[89] as does the U.S. Department of Education's Office for Civil Rights.[90]

Nonetheless, most courts that have evaluated promotion tests under the Constitution's Due Process Clause have taken a different view. As noted earlier, the due process claims recognized in *Debra P.* and other cases rest on the view that students have a property interest in receiving a high school diploma. Without this property interest, students would have no claim to remedies such as advance notice of testing or a test that measures only what students have actually been taught.

Few reported federal cases have involved promotion test policies, and in each the court has upheld promotion testing. Two related rationales emerge. First, courts have drawn a distinction between graduation testing and promotion testing, declining to recognize a property interest in being promoted. As one federal appeals court said about a classroom-based promotion test, "We conclude that *Debra P.* is distinguishable and hold that plaintiffs had no property right [that would justify judicial intervention]."[91] The decision rested, in part, on the court's view that retention in grade is beneficial for low achievers: a "program of retention for students who do not perform satisfactory work is both acceptable and desirable."[92] A more recent decision used similar language in upholding a statewide retention test policy: the policy "is designed to help the retained students: a student who is not promoted is given what is, in effect, a remedial year which should allow the student to catch up on the skills that he is lacking and perform better in the future."[93]

Such views are understandable, particularly considering the bipartisan calls to end social promotion. As discussed previously however, powerful social science evidence demonstrates the harmful effects of retention. Students who are retained are likely to have lower academic achievement, less social development, and a much greater likelihood of dropping out than similar low-performing students who are promoted.[94] Moreover, some critics of social promotion are equally critical of retention in grade, finding early intervention strategies preferable to both.

Courts presented with this research might conclude that a student does have a property interest in avoiding retention. A student's interest in avoiding retention is certainly greater than the interest in avoiding a short-term suspension from school, in which courts have long recognized a property interest. If such a property interest in avoiding retention were recognized, students presumably would also have a right to advance notice and a test that measures only what they have been taught. At present, however, students probably cannot count on courts to support them in opportunity-to-learn cases involving promotion tests.

Conclusion

Evidence presented here shows that minority students, students with disabilities, and ELLs are failing some state tests, especially those that reflect high standards, at rates higher than 50 percent, that "disparate impact" often declines slowly, and that failure rates would be higher if states took into account students who have dropped out, been retained, or been excluded improperly from testing. This chapter also presents powerful evidence from leading scholars that many students are not yet being taught the knowledge and skills that current high-stakes tests measure.

Low-achieving students need high-quality instruction more than anyone else, and there is little question that data from large-scale assessments, if used properly, can help improve instruction, hold schools accountable for improved achievement, and identify and address students' learning needs. It is a tragedy that so many of these students have been ill served by their schools for so long, and it is a welcome change when states and schools aspire to educate all students to high standards.

At the same time, where demanding tests have high stakes for individual students, minority students, students with disabilities, ELLs, and low socioeconomic status students are at heightened risk of suffering the serious, well-documented harms associated with grade retention and denial of high school diplomas. It would be a great loss if high-stakes testing policies operated to deny diplomas to large numbers of these students or to subject them to the serious harms of retention. It would be unfortunate if states and schools used high-stakes tests in ways that punished students for not knowing what their schools had never taught them.

Principles of law and measurement hold that high-stakes tests should measure only what students have already been taught, and there should be ways of ensuring that high-stakes tests are used properly. But the measurement profession does not enforce its own rules of appropriate test use, and the law is limited in the protections it affords. The U.S. Supreme Court has closed off for now the chief route by which individuals have challenged educational policies and practices that have adverse impact by race, national origin, and language. Federal courts have thus far been unsympathetic to lawsuits challenging promotion testing, perhaps because they are unfamiliar with powerful research, now widely accepted, on the negative effects of grade retention.

In reviewing future legal challenges, courts will have to evaluate circumstances markedly different from those associated with the early MCTs. Fortunately, much more is understood today about the human and social consequences of inappropriate test use, about what school improvement requires, and about how educators can help all students acquire high-level knowledge and skills. Educators and researchers who understand these complex issues can help judges as they attempt to apply and modify legal precedents and principles in light of dramatically changed educational objectives and of realities that have been slower to change.

Notes

This chapter is a revised and expanded version of "High-Stakes Testing in a Changing Environment: Disparate Impact, Opportunity to Learn, and Current Legal Protections," in *Redesigning Accountability Systems for Education*, ed. Susan Fuhrman and Richard Elmore (New York: Teachers College Press, 2004), 220–44;

The author is grateful to the Carnegie Scholars Program of the Carnegie Corporation of New York, which supported this research, and to Erica Frankenberg and Rebecca High, who provided first-rate research and editorial support. The views expressed are the author's.

1. Gayler et al., *State High School Exit Exams.*

2. The eleven southern states with exit exams in 2003 were Alabama, Florida, Georgia, Louisiana, Maryland, Mississippi, North Carolina, South Carolina, Tennessee, Texas, and Virginia. Ibid.

3. Ibid.

4. American Federation of Teachers, "Making Standards Matter 2001."

5. No Child Left Behind Act; Elmore, *Building*; Individuals with Disabilities Education Act.

6. Gayler et al., *State High School Exit Exams.*

7. Wise et al., *Independent Evaluation: AB 1609 Study Report*; Wise et al., *Independent Evaluation: Analysis of the 2001 Administration.*

8. Gayler et al., *State High School Exit Exams.*

9. Gehring, "States Open Fiscal Year"; Zehr, "Once 'Sacred,' School Aid Falls."

10. American Federation of Teachers, "Making Standards Matter 2001."

11. Ibid.

12. Gayler et al., *State High School Exit Exams.*

13. Reardon, "Eighth-Grade Minimum Competency Testing."

14. Individuals with Disabilities Education Act; Improving America's Schools Act.

15. Thurlow, "Biting the Bullet."

16. Heubert, "Disability, Race, and High-Stakes Testing of Students."

17. Beatty et al., *Understanding Dropouts.*

18. Individuals with Disabilities Education Act.

19. Baker and Linn, "Validity Issues," 49.

20. Murnane and Levy, "Will Standards-Based Reforms Improve," 401.

21. Taylor, "Standards, Tests, and Civil Rights," 56.

22. Heubert and Hauser, *High Stakes.*

23. No Child Left Behind Act; Elmore and Rothman, *Testing, Teaching, and Learning.*

24. Fuhrman, Goertz, and Duffy, "Slow Down," 269.

25. Heubert and Hauser, *High Stakes.*

26. Elmore, "Problem."

27. *Debra P. v. Turlington.*

28. Linn, "Assessments and Accountability."

29. Jacob, "Getting Tough?"

30. U.S. Department of Education, Office for Civil Rights, *Use of Tests.*

31. *G.I. Forum v. Texas Education Agency.*

32. Schrag, "Too Good," 46.

33. Klein et al., *What Do Test Scores*; Linn, *Design and Evaluation.*

34. Natriello and Pallas, "Development and Impact."

35. *G.I. Forum.*

36. Florida Department of Education, *School Diploma.*

37. Natriello and Pallas, "Development and Impact."

38. Fuhrman, Goertz, and Duffy, "Slow Down."

39. California Department of Education, *Class of 2004.*

40. Wise et al., *Independent Evaluation: AB 1609 Study Report.*

41. Linn, "Assessments and Accountability."

42. Ysseldyke et al., *Educational Results*; Thurlow et al., *Where's Waldo.*

43. Massachusetts Department of Education, *Spring 2001 MCAS Test.* I am grateful to Jeffrey Nellhaus of the Massachusetts Department of Education, who graciously provided data on students with disabilities and ELLs.

44. Massachusetts Department of Education, *Progress Report on Students Attaining the Competency Determination.*

45. Using state enrollment figures, Wheelock estimates an overall "on-time" graduation rate of 73.3 percent rather than the state's reported 95 percent and the following "on-time"

graduation rates for different groups: for whites, 78.1 percent rather than the state's reported 97 percent; for African Americans, 60.9 percent rather than 86 percent; for Latinos, 46.2 percent rather than 83 percent. Wheelock, e-mail to author, 6 October 2003. How important a role the graduation test plays in such attrition is the subject of debate.

46. Keller, "More New York Special Education Students," 33.

47. New York Department of Education, *2000 Pocket Book*; New York Department of Education, *2002 Pocket Book*.

48. Koretz and Hamilton, *Performance*.

49. "NAEP Achievement."

50. Klein et al., *What Do Test Scores*.

51. *G.I. Forum*.

52. Linn, *Design and Evaluation*, 28.

53. National Center, *Condition of Education, 2001*.

54. J. Lee, "Racial and Ethnic Achievement Gap Trends."

55. Murnane and Levy, "Will Standards-Based Reforms Improve."

56. Wise et al., *Independent Evaluation: Analysis of the 2001 Administration*, 45.

57. Jacob, "Getting Tough?" 116.

58. Hauser, "Should We End"; Heubert and Hauser, *High Stakes*.

59. Goldschmidt and Wang, "When Can Schools"; Lillard and DeCicca, "Higher Standards."

60. Heubert and Hauser, *High Stakes*.

61. Improving America's Schools Act; Individuals with Disabilities Education Act; No Child Left Behind Act.

62. *Debra P.*; *G.I. Forum*.

63. Wise et al., *Independent Evaluation: Analysis of the 2001 Administration*, 93.

64. Fuhrman, "Conclusion"; Elmore and Rothman, *Testing, Teaching, and Learning*.

65. Thurlow, "Biting the Bullet."

66. Citizens' Commission, *Closing the Deal*; M. Cohen, *Review*; Robelen, "States Sluggish."

67. Baker and Linn, "Alignment," 2.

68. Wise et al., *Independent Evaluation: Analysis of the 2001 Administration*; McLaughlin, *Reform*.

69. Porter and Smithson, "Alignment," tables 5–6.

70. Blank, Porter, and Smithson, *New Tools*, 26.

71. Elmore, "Unwarranted Intrusion," 13–14.

72. Murnane and Levy, "Will Standards-Based Reforms Improve," 411.

73. Ibid.

74. Ladd, "Briefing."

75. McLaughlin, *Reform*; Thurlow, "Biting the Bullet."

76. Dailey, Zantal-Wiener, and Roach, *Reforming*, 8–9.

77. Other legal issues, while important, are beyond the scope of this chapter.

78. American Educational Research Association, American Psychological Association, and National Council on Measurement in Education, *Standards*.

79. Heubert and Hauser, *High Stakes*.

80. Elmore, "Problem," 278.

81. Since this litigation involved a request for a preliminary injunction—a court order issued before a full hearing in court—the Indiana courts could still reach a different result after trial, though that is unlikely given the strong language in which the courts rejected students' due process claims. An Indiana appeals court affirmed the decision.

82. *Chapman v. California Department of Education.*

83. Ibid., 9.

84. Wise et al., *Independent Evaluation: Analysis of the 2001 Administration.*

85. *Smiley v. California Department of Education.*

86. *Brookhart v. Illinois State Board of Education*; *Board of Education v. Ambach.*

87. *Brookhart*, 187.

88. American Educational Research Association, American Psychological Association, and National Council on Measurement in Education, *Standards*, 146.

89. American Education Research Association, "AERA Position Statement."

90. U.S. Department of Education, Office for Civil Rights, *Use of Tests*, 20.

91. *Bester v. Tuscaloosa Board of Education*, 7.

92. Ibid., 7.

93. *Erik V. v. Causby*, 388–89. Another circuit court, in an apparently unpublished opinion, recently rejected due process claims in connection with a Louisiana state promotion test; Thevenot, "Students."

94. Hauser, "Should We End"; Heubert and Hauser, *High Stakes.*

The Uncertain Future

CHAPTER ELEVEN

JACINTA S. MA | MICHAL KURLAENDER

The Future of Race-Conscious Policies in K–12 Public Schools

Support from Recent Legal Opinions and Social Science Research

As other chapters of this book have discussed in greater detail, racial patterns in the public schools have changed dramatically since the U.S. Supreme Court's decision in *Brown v. Board of Education*. We are more than a decade into a period in which federal courts are declaring many school districts unitary and dismantling long-running and very successful desegregation plans. The massive gains in racial integration at public schools that have occurred across the South are indeed at great risk. Although evidence demonstrates that the public schools in the South are rapidly resegregating—even as segregation continues to grow in other areas of the United States—segregated schools are far from inevitable.

The trend toward unitary status challenges people committed to racial and ethnic equity in our schools to find legally permissible ways to keep our schools diverse and to obtain the political support for such means. The theory driving the declaration of unitary status is the inherent value of local governmental control of the schools. Courts analyzing whether a school district has achieved unitary status generally have given local school officials considerable deference. Ironically, school boards wishing to voluntarily maintain racially and ethnically diverse schools, including at least one southern district that was declared unitary, have been prevented from exercising local control by extremely skeptical courts striking down race-conscious student-assignment and admissions policies. However, at the same time federal courts are increasingly abandoning mandatory desegregation, a strategy that has resulted in decades of racially integrated schools, the judicial system (as the Supreme Court's decision in *Grutter v. Bollinger* portends) and social science evidence on the benefits of a racially and ethnically diverse student body will likely continue to support the use of race as a tool for creating diverse schools.

This chapter analyzes the judicial system's treatment of one strategy for achieving racially integrated schools—the voluntary use of race by school boards in K–12 school assignment and admissions. It is important to distinguish this approach to student assignment from those desegregation remedies mandated by federal courts. Led by three 1990s Supreme Court decisions that relaxed the standards required of districts to prove that they had desegregated their schools, many districts have been declared unitary, and voluntary race-conscious plans are currently the most effective means for maintaining the racially diverse schools created by desegregation plans. In the past decade, uses of this voluntary strategy have been increasingly challenged and in some cases struck down, with no clarification from the Supreme Court. The recent cases of *Grutter v. Bollinger*, *Comfort ex rel. Neumyer v. Lynn School Committee*, and *McFarland v. Jefferson County Public Schools*, as well as recent social science research on the educational benefits of a diverse student body, provide new support for the legality of these types of race-conscious policies. Whether voluntary race-conscious plans ultimately are allowed is important because even these recent cases will have no impact on slowing, much less reversing, the judicial trend toward declaring school districts unitary.

First, we discuss the issue of diversity in higher education and K–12 education law. Then we argue why voluntary race-conscious student-assignment and admissions policies in K–12 public schools serve a compelling state interest in having diverse student bodies. Finally, we discuss "narrow tailoring" and why it is likely that race-conscious policies will meet that standard.

Legal Analysis

Traditional Fourteenth Amendment Equal Protection Clause principles require courts to examine public school officials' actions and policies in which students are classified by race under a "strict scrutiny" standard. Under strict scrutiny, school officials' actions must first demonstrate a "compelling state interest"—a very important or compelling purpose for taking race into account in making decisions. Second, these actions must be "narrowly tailored," or closely tied to accomplishing their very important purpose.

In this section, we begin by examining a line of cases that allowed race to be considered voluntarily as part of the admissions process in higher education and then turn to more recent cases in the South that limited the voluntary use of race. Finally, we consider the Supreme Court's *Grutter v. Bollinger* and *Gratz v. Bollinger* decisions and discuss the implications of those decisions on the use of race-conscious policies in the K–12 context.

Affirmative Action Cases

Until the University of Michigan cases (*Grutter* and *Gratz*), the case of *Regents of the University of California v. Bakke* was the most well known education case addressing race-conscious admissions policies. In that case, a rejected white applicant challenged the admissions policy of a medical school. The Supreme Court held in *Bakke* that colleges and universities could take race into account as one factor in their admissions process because obtaining the educational benefits of diversity is a compelling state interest. The interest articulated by Justice Lewis Powell in *Bakke* is one of creating a diverse student body that would foster a robust interchange of ideas. That ruling remained essentially undisturbed for more than fifteen years and was generally understood to allow colleges and universities to take account of race in creating a diverse student body.

Affirmative action policies in employment and contracting were increasingly questioned in the 1990s,[1] and it was only a matter of time before questions about affirmative action in education followed suit. The first constriction on the ability of public education officials to consider race positively in situations other than those designed to remedy past racial discrimination occurred in the South. In 1996, the Fifth Circuit (the federal appellate court for the states of Texas, Louisiana, and Mississippi) ruled in *Hopwood v. Texas* that the University of Texas Law School's race-conscious admissions policy was unconstitutional because promoting educational diversity was not a compelling interest. The *Hopwood* court held that Justice Powell's opinion in *Bakke* was no longer binding precedent and that more recent Supreme Court decisions suggested that only a government's interest in remedying the present effects of its own past discrimination was sufficiently compelling to justify a race-conscious policy.

Three years later, the Fourth Circuit struck down a magnet school admissions program considering race in Virginia and cast doubt on the viability of that type of policy in all the states in the Fourth Circuit (Maryland, North Carolina, South Carolina, Virginia, and West Virginia).[2] In 2001, in *Johnson v. Board of Regents of the University of Georgia*, the Eleventh Circuit (which oversees the states of Georgia, Alabama, and Florida) struck down a diversity-based admissions policy as unconstitutional. Similar to the Fifth Circuit Court in *Hopwood*, the Eleventh Circuit Court suggested that Justice Powell's *Bakke* opinion was no longer binding precedent and expressed doubt about whether diversity in higher education would be a compelling state interest. These cases made it increasingly unclear whether school officials could voluntarily employ race in implementing educational policies.

A New Turn: Impact of University of Michigan Cases

Around the same time that the federal courts were considering those cases, *Gratz v. Bollinger* and *Grutter v. Bollinger* were making their way through the courts of the Sixth Circuit. In *Gratz*, plaintiffs challenged the University of Michigan's undergraduate admissions policy, which gave certain underrepresented racial groups an automatic 20-point "plus" factor in a 150-point allocation system. The plaintiffs in *Grutter* challenged the University of Michigan Law School's admissions policy, which viewed race as one plus factor in an individualized, whole-file review system.

In June 2003 rulings on these cases, the Supreme Court made three significant clarifications of the law. First, it declared that school officials can consider race voluntarily and not only in situations in which they need to remedy past discrimination. Second, the Court held that racial and ethnic diversity can be a compelling interest justifying the consideration of race in higher education admissions. Third, it clarified the framework for determining whether a compelling interest in diversity has been implemented in a narrowly tailored manner.

The Supreme Court in *Grutter* held specifically that Michigan's "Law School has a compelling interest in attaining a diverse student body" because "such diversity is essential to its educational mission."[3] It found that the law school's interest lay not merely in obtaining certain percentages of particular racial and ethnic groups but in obtaining a critical mass defined "by reference to the educational benefits that diversity is designed to produce."[4]

The Supreme Court further explained its holding by reviewing the benefits of a diverse student body. Primarily relying on social science evidence introduced at the trial level and presented in amicus briefs, it stated that the benefits included promoting cross-racial understanding, breaking down racial stereotypes, enabling students to better understand people of different races, encouraging better classroom discussions, promoting learning outcomes, and better preparing students to live and work in an increasingly diverse society.

The Court also pointed to the importance of education in "sustaining our political and cultural heritage" and stated that "effective participation by members of all racial and ethnic groups in the civic life of our Nation is essential if the dream of one Nation, indivisible, is to be realized."[5] Furthermore, the Court explained that universities, especially highly selective law schools, train a significant number of the country's leaders and that "to cultivate a set of leaders with legitimacy in the eyes of the citizenry, it is necessary that the path to leadership be visibly open to talented and qualified individuals of every race and ethnicity."[6]

In large part, the Supreme Court based its holding on the deference owed to universities under the First Amendment of the Constitution in their exercise of their right to academic freedom and educational autonomy, which includes selecting a student body. The Supreme Court also deferred to the expertise of the university in making educational judgments.

In evaluating the second part of the strict scrutiny test—whether the compelling state interest is narrowly tailored—the Supreme Court found that the law school's admissions policy was narrowly tailored because there were no quotas for certain racial groups and because applicants from particular racial groups were not insulated from competition for admission. "In other words, an admissions program must be flexible enough to consider all pertinent elements of diversity in light of the particular qualifications of each applicant, and to place them on the same footing for consideration, although not necessarily according them the same weight."[7]

Grutter contrasted illegal quotas, defined as "a fixed number or percentage which must be attained or which cannot be exceeded," with a permissible goal that represents an "effort . . . to come within a range demarcated by the goal itself."[8] The Court emphasized the importance of the law school's individualized review of each applicant's file, which prevented any applicant's race or ethnicity from becoming the defining feature of his or her application. It praised the law school's policy because it did not limit the broad range of qualities and experiences that could be considered to contribute to student body diversity and did not automatically assume that a single characteristic would always have a specific and identifiable contribution to a university's diversity.

In *Gratz*, the Supreme Court stated that while attaining a diverse student body of undergraduates was a compelling state interest, the University of Michigan's undergraduate admissions policy was not narrowly tailored because there was no individualized review of student applicants during the admissions process and because all factors contributing to diversity were not meaningfully considered alongside race.

How the University of Michigan cases will affect policies in K–12 education remains to be seen. The standards and principles applied in college and university admissions are relevant to race-conscious student-assignment and admissions policies in K–12 public schools but should not be applied in a wholesale manner that fails to address the specific context and purpose of K–12 schools. *Grutter*'s recognition of colleges' and universities' compelling interest in attaining a diverse student body should translate positively to the K–12 context, while the narrow-tailoring analysis may not be as relevant, as we discuss later in the chapter.

Mission of K–12 Education Differs Significantly from Higher Education

Although some overlap in their missions exists, elementary and secondary public schools generally differ significantly from institutions of higher education. K–12 education is targeted toward and available to all students and is compulsory in most states until at least age sixteen. These differences present an even stronger case for the use of race-conscious policies in K–12 education.

Legal and education literature make clear that the primary mission of K–12 education is to provide children with basic knowledge, values, and social skills so that they can participate in and maintain a complex democratic society.[9] In a 1988 decision, *Hazelwood School District v. Kuhlmeier*, the Supreme Court cited its opinion in *Brown* and quoted its opinions in *Ambach v. Norwick* (1979) and *Board of Education v. Pico* (1982), holding, "Public education serves vital national interests in preparing the Nation's youth for life in our increasingly complex society and for the duties of citizenship in our democratic Republic. . . . The public school conveys to our young the information and tools required not merely to survive in, but to contribute to, civilized society. It also inculcates in tomorrow's leaders the 'fundamental values necessary to the maintenance of a democratic political system. . . .' All the while, the public educator nurtures students' social and moral development by transmitting to them an official dogma of 'community values.'"[10]

Both K–12 schools and institutions of higher education have missions that include developing leaders and educating students to live and work in an increasingly diverse society. K–12 education, however, is concerned primarily with instilling basic, general knowledge, unlike institutions of higher education and particularly university graduate programs, which provide students with more specialized information and training.

The government interest in fostering a racially desegregated or integrated environment is especially important in a K–12 setting. First, K–12 schools reach more students and thus have more opportunities to influence race relations. Not all individuals go on to college, while K–12 education is compulsory. In addition, K–12 schools have an opportunity to influence very young children's views on race. Social science evidence shows that children are aware of visible difference at a very early age and that it is easier to overcome racial stereotypes in children than adults.[11]

Moreover, K–12 schools have a long history of trying to address segregation that, especially in the South, has required them to create desegregated schools and transform their missions to reflect this challenge. Such efforts are directed not merely at improving test scores and educational opportunities for African

American and other minority students but also at changing historical relationships among different racial groups.[12]

Compelling Interests Justifying Race Conscious Policies in K–12 Education

Both the diversity interest clearly affirmed by *Grutter* and the other diversity interests present in K–12 education have been discussed in most of the few lower court cases addressing race-conscious policies in K–12 education. Some of these cases have carefully refined the definition of "diversity" in a K–12 context and upheld related additional interests. We should consider carefully how these lower courts have defined diversity as we evaluate the likelihood that K–12 race-conscious programs will ultimately be upheld by the Supreme Court.

Although K–12 schools share the diversity interest established in *Bakke* and upheld and clarified in the University of Michigan cases, some diversity interests are distinct in the K–12 context. While it is important in higher education to expose students to a wide range of ideas, the desirability of enhancing classroom discussion and preparing students to work and lead in an increasingly diverse society extends to K–12 schools as well. In fact, for primary and secondary schools, it may be even more important to expose students to others who look different to break down racial stereotypes, promote cross-racial understanding, and better understand people of different races.

Moreover, the distinct K–12 interests in preventing segregation and racial isolation have been found to be compelling.

Court Cases Questioning Race-Conscious Policies

Prior to *Grutter* in 1998 and 1999, three federal cases addressed race-conscious admissions and transfer policies in K–12 schools that asserted a compelling interest in "diversity."[13] These cases arose after the outcome in *Hopwood*, which emboldened those who oppose race-conscious policies to extend their challenge to K–12 education. One of these cases involved a highly academically selective high school, often referred to as an exam school, in Massachusetts; the other two cases involved magnet schools, one in Maryland and one in Virginia.

In *Wessman v. Gittens*, the First Circuit Court of Appeals addressed the constitutionality of a race-conscious admissions policy used at the Boston Latin School, a prestigious institution whose selective admissions policy was based on a mathematical formula that combined grades and test scores as well as race. The school committee argued that the policy furthered an interest in promoting *Bakke*-type educational diversity.

In *Tuttle v. Arlington County School Board*, a school board employed a race-conscious admissions policy in assigning students to its alternative schools, citing an interest in (1) preparing students to live in a diverse, global society and (2) serving the needs of the district's diverse students. A Maryland transfer policy that took race into account in deciding whether a student could transfer to a different school was challenged in *Eisenberg v. Montgomery County Public Schools.* Despite school officials' assertions that avoiding racial segregation was their compelling interest, the Fourth Circuit equated that interest to an interest in diversity.

In all these cases, the courts simply assumed a compelling interest in "diversity" yet struck down the challenged policies as insufficiently narrowly tailored. The outcomes in *Grutter* and *Gratz* support these courts' assumptions that attaining a diverse student body in K–12 education is a sufficiently compelling interest to justify the consideration of race in these admissions and assignment policies. *Grutter* and *Gratz,* however, cast into serious question the grudging interpretation of "narrow tailoring" employed by these courts.

However, at least one case decided since *Grutter* has adopted a similar approach. In *Parents Involved in Community Schools v. Seattle School District no. 1* (July 2004), the Ninth Circuit Court of Appeals recently addressed the Seattle School District's student-assignment plan, in which race was used as a tie-breaker factor to correct significant deviations between a school's racial composition and the overall racial composition of the school district. The court agreed that an interest in diversity as articulated in *Grutter* is also a compelling interest at a K–12 level. In applying the narrow-tailoring analysis set forth in *Grutter* and *Gratz,* however, the court found that the school district failed every factor.

Court Cases Favorable to Race-Conscious Policies

The cases addressing nonremedial race-conscious K–12 school-assignment policies more favorably have generally conducted thorough analyses taking account of the storied desegregation history of K–12 public schools. In these cases, courts have considered the compelling state interests of mitigating the effects of de facto residential segregation and preventing "racial isolation," a term that has long been associated with segregated schools. The courts viewed the cases from a lens cognizant of desegregation and affirmative action law and at times attempted to reconcile the two lines of cases.

Some cases addressing mandatory desegregation plans have suggested that voluntarily maintaining desegregated schools can be a compelling interest. The first, most significant mention by the Supreme Court of the use of race in school assignment specifically addressing a nonremedial K–12 situation occurred in *Swann v. Charlotte-Mecklenburg Board of Education,* the seminal 1971 desegregation case. The Court stated, "School authorities are traditionally charged with broad power to formulate and implement educational policy and might well conclude . . . that in order to prepare to live in a pluralistic society each school should have a prescribed ratio of [African American] to white students reflecting the proportion for the district as a whole. To do this as an educational policy is within the broad discretionary powers of school authorities."[14]

In *Brewer v. West Irondequoit Central School District*, the Second Circuit found in May 2000 that reducing racial isolation resulting from de facto segregation can be a compelling interest. At issue in that case was a voluntary interdistrict transfer program whose primary purposes were reducing racial isolation within the participating school districts and eliminating de facto segregation. The program allowed minority students to transfer from city schools to suburban schools and nonminority students to transfer from suburban schools to city schools. The school district asserted that reducing racial isolation would help prepare students to function as adults who could interact with people from different backgrounds and make students more tolerant and understanding of others throughout their lives. In finding that reducing racial isolation can be a compelling interest, the court drew on previous desegregation cases in the Second Circuit, which held that voluntary efforts by school authorities to remedy de facto segregation are a compelling interest and that integration serves important societal functions.

In *Comfort* (June 2003), a federal district court in Massachusetts soundly upheld a voluntary desegregation plan with a race-conscious transfer policy. Broadly, the plan guarantees every child a space in his or her neighborhood school, but if the child wishes to transfer to another school, school officials will consider whether the transfer would improve or worsen either school's proportion of minorities to nonminorities relative to the proportion of minorities and nonminorities in the school district. The court found a compelling state interest in (1) preparing students to be citizens in a multiracial society, (2) reducing racial isolation resulting from de facto segregation, and (3) fulfilling the promise of *Brown v. Board of Education* by eliminating school segregation. While a three-judge panel of the U.S. Court of Appeals for the First Circuit reversed the district court's holding, that panel decision has itself been withdrawn so that the full First Circuit can consider these issues.

In *McFarland v. Jefferson County Public Schools* (June 2004), the first K–12 decision applying the *Grutter* decision, the federal district court strongly upheld a Kentucky county's consideration of race in its student-assignment plan.[15] The court relied heavily on *Grutter* and found that the interests the school district asserted "overlap with those of Michigan Law School at the individual student level"[16] but also considered the different mission of K–12 education. The court found that the school district's interest in having integrated schools is compelling. It noted the important role of local school boards in crafting educational policy and the deference courts should give to these elected officials, and the court viewed voluntary school integration policies as a logical extension of desegregation jurisprudence. Moreover, the court found that the school board had valid reasons to believe that integrated schools lead to better academic achievement, increased racial tolerance and understanding, and a better educational setting for all students and parents. It found that the school board was sincerely motivated, not just engaging in racial balancing, as a result of all the evidence the school board presented on the benefits of having integrated schools. In addition to these court cases that support race-conscious policies for assigning students to K–12 schools, social science research provides strong evidence that having racially and ethnically diverse schools is compelling.

Research Evidence about the Benefits of a Racially and Ethnically Diverse Student Body

Social science research suggests that clear educational benefits result from racial and ethnic integration and diversity in K–12 public schools. Specifically, social science evidence suggests that racially isolated and segregated schools pose clear harms for minority students. Moreover, minority students who attend desegregated schools display, on average, higher academic achievement and hold greater educational and occupational aspirations than do students in segregated minority schools. In addition, desegregated schools increase social interaction, comfort levels, and friendships among peers of different racial and ethnic backgrounds and promote civic engagement across racial/ethnic lines.[17] These benefits and the prevention of these harms support the mission of K–12 public schools and enrich the learning experiences of their students.

Preventing Harms of Racial Isolation and Segregation

The harms of racial isolation and segregation for minority students are threefold. First, the existing patterns of income distribution and residential segregation make it extremely difficult to disentangle race and poverty in American schools. Despite varying beliefs about the benefits or costs of desegregated schooling, consensus exists that racial segregation closely relates to economic segregation.[18] Schools with large concentrations of poverty offer less in the way of educational preparation, fewer resources, and access to informal networks necessary for education and social mobility.[19] Moreover, minority students tend to be concentrated in schools with fewer educational offerings and substantially lower overall achievement levels.[20] Thus, the benefit that accrues to a minority student from attending a desegregated school often results in large part from the wealth of resources and the overall school quality that usually exist in integrated or predominantly white schools.[21]

In addition, because many minority groups have historically been afforded fewer educational opportunities, the parents of minority students often lack familiarity with the norms and procedures of our K–12 educational system and may have difficulty effectively navigating the system. Research shows that such familiarity is closely tied to students' educational success.[22] As a result, some research suggests that when isolated from white students, minority students are prevented from absorbing the dominant group's cultural and behavioral norms.[23] Yet this "assimilation" model has also been criticized for its assumption that minority students need to conform to the dominant white culture. Other researchers conclude that the structural barriers of discrimination in fact cause the denial of equal opportunities for minorities and that racial isolation prevents access, specifically for African American students, to broader social networks that provide contacts necessary for career and educational advancement.[24]

Finally, evidence shows that to obtain any of the benefits of school desegregation, schools must enroll a critical mass of students from any one particular racial group. Early research on school desegregation noted that approximately equal proportions of whites and African Americans are ideal for maximizing the benefits of desegregation. Because many schools are far from this ideal racial composition as a result of a fear of white flight,[25] increased suburbanization, and a growing number of schools with student bodies composed of a number of racial groups, the number necessary to reach critical mass remains somewhat vague in the social science literature. Several researchers, however, have developed theories of what would constitute a critical mass. For example, some consensus exists in K–12 school desegregation research that if one group in a school represents more than 70 percent of the population, that group will dictate the school's norms and behaviors.[26] Moreover, evidence also shows that too few minority students can result in "tokenism"[27] and in great discomfort and insecurity.[28] Thus, we can conclude that critical mass lies somewhere between the optimum of equal proportion and the feared tokenism as a result of racial isolation.

Benefits of Promoting Diversity

One of the benefits of promoting racial and ethnic diversity is that it ends the self-perpetuation of the impact of racial segregation that tends to occur.[29] Perpetuation theory and the contact hypothesis have often been applied to school desegregation studies and suggest that only when students are exposed to sustained desegregated experiences will they lead more integrated lives as adults.[30]

From a review of twenty-one studies applying perpetuation theory, Amy Stuart Wells and Robert L. Crain concluded that desegregated experiences for African American students lead to increased interaction with members of other racial groups in later years. Results from these studies indicate that school desegregation had positive, albeit modest, effects—both blacks and whites who attended desegregated schools were more likely to function in desegregated settings later in life.[31] These later desegregated environments include workplaces, neighborhoods, and colleges and universities.

Although some of the earlier social science literature has focused on the impact of desegregated schooling on the experiences of African American students and on the short-term gains of blacks attending desegregated schools, more recent studies have documented that all students, including whites, benefit from racially and ethnically diverse schools.

White students in integrated settings exhibit more racial tolerance and less fear of their black peers over time than their peers in segregated environments.[32] In addition, classroom racial composition and racial composition of academic as well as social activities have been found to affect the stability of interracial friendships between whites and blacks, with the effect being stronger for white students.[33] In their longitudinal study of 375 fourth- to seventh-grade students in sixteen desegregated classrooms, Maureen T. Hallinan and Richard A. Williams found that the classroom climate, in particular, influences the stability of interracial friendships of black students.[34] Thus, the exposure to diverse peers and the potential for cross-racial friendships suggest that diverse settings can reduce stereotypes and promote racial understanding.

In addition to cross-racial friendships, other important attitudinal and behavioral outcomes can occur as a result of attending diverse schools. Specifically, a more recent set of studies on attitudes of students toward their peers of other racial groups found that students of all racial/ethnic groups who attend more diverse schools have higher comfort levels with members of racial groups different from their own and have an increased sense of civic engagement and a greater desire to live and work in multiracial settings than do their more segregated peers.[35] The importance of interracial contact for whites is also evident in surveys of students attending schools with varying racial compositions.[36] For example, a study of more than 8,000 students attending thirty-three different schools in Miami–Dade County, Florida, showed that whites who attend more diverse schools have a stronger desire to live and work in multiracial settings than their white counterparts at more segregated schools.[37] The educational and democratic benefits that arise for all students in more heterogeneous settings result from the complexity of interactions in diverse schools that lead to a greater ability to work with and understand people of different backgrounds and to more fully participate in a rapidly changing democratic society.[38]

Although additional social science research about the benefits of having a racially and ethnically diverse student body would be useful, the benefits already found clearly support the legal finding that achieving racial and ethnic diversity could be a compelling interest for any school. Recent examples include the Supreme Court in *Grutter* citing social science evidence in its analysis of whether diversity could be a compelling state interest; the Washington State Supreme Court citing social science evidence to support its decision that the Seattle school district's race-conscious assignment policy is not prohibited by its state statute prohibiting racial preferences;[39] and the federal district court in *Comfort* relying heavily on social science evidence to support its holding that attaining a diverse student body is a compelling state interest.

This social science evidence, in combination with the current legal standards, particularly after *Grutter*, makes it seem likely that the Supreme Court ultimately will find that reducing racial isolation, preventing segregation, and attaining a diverse student body to prepare students to live and work in an increasingly diverse society are compelling state interests justifying race-conscious policies.

When Are Race-Conscious Policies Narrowly Tailored to the Stated Interest?

The legal standard for the second part of the Equal Protection Clause's strict scrutiny test—whether a policy is narrowly tailored—is less clear in the K–12 context. Only a few race-conscious policies have been found constitutional, and the Supreme Court's recent guidance on narrowly tailored programs in *Grutter* and *Gratz* creates some confusion because, in most K–12 situations, the Supreme Court's reasoning should not apply.

Whether a policy is narrowly tailored depends, of course, on the interest being served. Even if K–12 schools rely on diversity interests identical to those articulated in *Grutter* and *Gratz*, it is unclear whether a K–12 school-assignment program would have to be implemented in the same manner as a higher education admissions policy because of the differences in the institutions. It is even less clear what policies will be considered narrowly tailored if a court accepts different K–12 interests as compelling, such as interests in reducing racial isolation, combating the effects of de facto segregation, or obtaining a diverse student body to prepare students to live and work in a multiracial society.

In determining whether a policy is narrowly tailored, courts have generally followed the framework set forth in *United States v. Paradise*, an employment case dealing with a remedial affirmative action plan. That framework requires an examination of (1) the necessity of the policy, (2) the burden of the policy on innocent third parties, (3) the efficacy of race-neutral alternatives, (4) the duration of the policy, (5) the flexibility of the policy, and (6) the relationship of numeric goals to the relevant population. Subsequent cases have modified this framework to better address the distinct issues raised in the education context.[40] The Supreme Court in *Grutter* did not expressly adopt the *Paradise* standard and in fact stated that an inquiry into whether a policy is narrowly tailored "must be calibrated to fit the distinct issues raised by the use of race to achieve student body diversity in public higher education."[41] However, the actual factors the Court looked at in *Grutter* resembled those enumerated in *Paradise* and included consideration of the flexibility of the program to look at each individual's merit, the basis for the numeric goal set by the law school, race-neutral alternatives, burden on nonminority applicants, and the duration of the policy. This approach suggests that although courts examining race-conscious policies in K–12 education will not need to adhere strictly to a *Paradise* standard, courts are likely to apply some *Paradise*-like factors in their analysis of narrow tailoring. For example, in *McFarland*, the district court examined only four of the factors based on those articulated in *Grutter*: (1) whether individualized review occurs for each student; (2) whether the student-assignment plan constituted a quota; (3) whether the school board considered race-neutral alternatives; and (4) whether the plan "unduly harms members of any racial group."[42] If the courts acknowledge compelling state interests in a K–12 context, such as attaining a diverse student body, reducing racial isolation, preventing de facto segregation, and preparing students to live and work in a multiracial society, they will likely find that these policies meet the tailoring requirements of a *Paradise*-type standard. By definition, compelling state interests that are racially explicit require a certain number of students from different races to be at a school and require that contact occur among people from different racial groups.

If courts consider the burden on innocent third parties,[43] they will likely find that race-conscious K–12 student-assignment policies pose little or no burden because a school district will be able to show that no student is denied an elementary or secondary school placement and will likely be able to show based on social science evidence (and ideally with some evidence from the school district in question) that all students—that is, students from every race—benefit from a racially and ethnically diverse student body.[44] Race-conscious policies in K–12 education often boil down to the issue of whether a parent should have the right to choose among arguably comparable schools; in higher education, in contrast, the issue is whether a highly coveted opportunity is being completely denied. The court in

McFarland relied on exactly this rationale in finding that no student is denied a benefit because of race. Courts have never recognized a right of K–12 students or their parents to insist on a particular school; any student who challenged a denial to attend a specific K–12 school would in essence be challenging the educational judgment of school officials that it is more important for that student and all students to attend racially and ethnically diverse schools than for that student to attend any particular school.

To satisfy any race-neutral alternatives requirement, school authorities would need to consider potentially viable race-neutral alternatives, which may include lotteries, policies based on socioeconomic status, and percent plans.[45] Officials would need to determine whether the race-neutral strategies would be as successful as a race-conscious plan in achieving the benefits of a racially diverse student body. What constitutes "sufficient consideration" is ambiguous—the Supreme Court emphasized in *Grutter* that it does not mean school authorities need to implement all possible race-neutral alternatives to see if any work, although officials must undertake a serious, good-faith consideration of these alternatives. In addition, the Supreme Court makes clear that these race-neutral strategies do not have to be pursued to the detriment of the quality of the schools or other important educational values. Nor must a school district adopt a race-neutral alternative that runs counter to a cornerstone of the institution's educational mission.

In *McFarland*, in determining whether the school board had looked at race-neutral alternatives, the court held that the board had considered and implemented a variety of race-neutral strategies to achieve its goals. The court found that a number of students are not governed by the racial guidelines and that voluntary school choice and geographic boundaries account for most of the student assignment. Guided by *Grutter*, the court also noted that the school board did not have to exhaust every race-neutral alternative and stated that an alternative such as a lottery system was not required because it "would require a 'dramatic sacrifice' in student choice, geographic convenience and program specialization . . . at a huge financial cost."[46]

Analyzing race-neutral alternatives, school authorities are likely to determine that they would not produce results similar to those of race-conscious policies in creating a racially and ethnically diverse student body. Social science evidence clearly supports this conclusion, showing that significant residential segregation remains and pointing to the difficulties of creating racially and ethnically diverse schools without affirmative race-conscious efforts.[47] Moreover, one education study shows that some educational benefits are directly tied to the racial and ethnic composition of the student bodies. This finding supports an argument that race-conscious student-assignment policies are inherently narrowly tailored because having a racially and ethnically diverse student body is the only means to produce the end benefits sought.[48] Furthermore, preliminary social science research suggests that school-assignment plans based on socioeconomic status do not result in as racially and ethnically diverse schools as those implemented through a race-conscious plan.[49]

In *Grutter*, the Supreme Court, ostensibly following *Paradise*, required that a race-conscious policy could not continue indefinitely. The Supreme Court likely reasoned that some people gained while others lost because of race-conscious policies. Courts considering this requirement may find it inapplicable in the K–12 context because scarce resources such as a job or admission to an elite university are not being denied and because all students benefit from racially and ethnically diverse schools. Even if courts apply this part of *Grutter*'s reasoning to K–12 education, school authorities could meet the requirement by including a sunset provision (as long as twenty-five years later) and periodically reviewing the policy. Logic suggests that school authorities could revise the sunset date if the periodic reviews indicated that the goal had or had not been met or if their goal changed. Imposing a sunset requirement would not alter the importance of a compelling interest but would acknowledge that the school officials believe a time will come when the compelling state interest could be achieved without considering race.

The thorniest issue in determining whether a race-conscious policy in K–12 education would be narrowly tailored appears to be the flexibility and relationship of the numeric goals-type requirements. The holdings in *Wessman*, *Tuttle*, and *Eisenberg* indicate that courts may be most critical in this part of the legal standard.

However, for several reasons, the narrow-tailoring analyses in these cases are unlikely to be the future trend for race-conscious policies in K–12 education. First, the outcomes of these K–12 cases did not rest on a determination of whether diversity could be a compelling state interest. In bypassing the question of whether diversity is a compelling state interest, the judges were not required to perform a detailed analysis of the benefits the school district was trying to seek through "diversity." This omission resulted in a less rigorous analysis of whether a program was narrowly tailored than was conducted in some of the more recent cases upholding race-conscious policies in K–12 schools. In fact, in *Eisenberg*, the court equated "diversity" with an interest in "avoiding racial segregation," which other court cases have established as two different interests.

Second, these challenges were directed at selective or specialized school-admissions policies that differ significantly from general school-assignment policies. As discussed previously, most K–12 schools do not select and create student bodies in the same way institutions of higher education do, nor are the goals of the two types of schools entirely comparable; thus, individualized review generally is inapplicable to K–12 education. In addition, a public school system must serve a defined community and must serve all the students in that community with limited public resources. The requirement of an individualized review may be appropriate in situations in which selective admissions occurs in specialized K–12 schools such as the Boston Latin School in *Wessman*. It is not likely to be appropriate when a school district is simply trying to maximize racial and ethnic diversity as one of a number of educational goals for the maximum number of children in the district. It would be reasonable simply to examine whether the policy is flexible enough to accommodate a school district's other priorities—for example, avoiding individual hardships and providing a preference for siblings to attend the same school.

However, the district court in *McFarland* awkwardly applied this factor by distinguishing the K–12 student-assignment plan from the law school admissions process. Thus, the court found that the school board's assignment process focused on "individual characteristics of a student's application, such as place of residence and student choice of school or program." It stated that many factors determine student assignment and that race acted as one possible factor among many and occasionally as a permissible "tipping" factor.[50]

A third reason why the *Wessman*, *Tuttle*, and *Eisenberg* narrow-tailoring analysis will not likely apply to future cases is the three cases' discredited reasoning on racial balancing.[51] Although the Supreme Court reiterated in *Grutter* that quotas—reserving a fixed number or percentage for members of minority groups—is impermissible, it simultaneously differentiated the University of Michigan Law School's attempt to achieve a critical mass from racial balancing and a quota because it set goals for minority enrollment with no specific number firmly in mind. The Supreme Court stated that attention to numbers does not automatically turn a goal into a quota. The courts in *Wessman*, *Tuttle*, and *Eisenberg* did not seem to recognize this distinction. In addition, *Grutter* found that the law school's reasoning for obtaining a critical mass was connected to the benefits of a diverse student body that the university hoped to achieve. The decision also lends support to the argument that establishing a critical mass of groups of students is necessary, contrary to the findings of the *Wessman* court.

Several lower court decisions have already moved decisively in this direction. In *McFarland*, the district court found that the school-assignment plan did not constitute a quota because it had a goal of a racial mix of between 15 and 50 percent of African American students at each school, while the actual percentage ranged between 20.1 and 50.4 percent. The court also found that the process did not insulate students from competition with other applicants because all students were subject to the same criteria.[52]

Seemingly anticipating the *Grutter* decision, the court in *Comfort* upheld the school committee's racial percentage goals and found that they were not static because they varied based on the city's demographics. In addition, the court found that the school committee's goal of creating a critical mass was supported by social science evidence presented at trial showing the benefits of a diverse student body when a critical mass of minority students are present.

Student-assignment plans will more likely be upheld when school authorities clearly articulate a rationale and provide evidence for why they are seeking certain numeric or percentage goals—whether to have a critical mass to combat stereotypes as in *Grutter*, to provide the optimum amount of intergroup contact for racial tolerance as in *Comfort*, or to achieve another purpose. These rationales will need social science research support and will be stronger if also supported by evidence from the specific school district. More research in these areas is still needed.[53]

The issue of whether a policy is narrowly tailored is the most unpredictable aspect of the legal standard because it depends significantly on the specific facts at issue in a school district. In this discussion, we have attempted to clarify some of the critical issues and to show why in many cases a well-reasoned race-conscious policy should withstand constitutional scrutiny.

Conclusion

Although the trend toward more school districts being declared unitary seems certain, the future of voluntary race-conscious policies in K–12 education is promising but uncertain. It is unclear whether the reasoning in *Grutter* will ultimately result in the upholding of voluntary considerations of race in the K–12 context. Having racially and ethnically diverse schools is arguably even more important in the K–12 context, however. Because the consideration of race was upheld in higher education admissions, reason suggests that courts ultimately will uphold the voluntary use of race in K–12 education as well.

Lawsuits challenging the constitutionality of race-conscious student-assignment policies are currently proceeding. Cases that have strongly supported race-conscious policies have not yet withstood appellate review or have been overturned on appeal:[54] *Comfort* is on appeal, and *McFarland* will likely be appealed. The outcome of these cases will provide additional guidance about whether and under what circumstances race-conscious policies can be used in K–12 education, but some uncertainty will continue until the Supreme Court rules on a K–12 education case.

After the legal parameters for achieving diverse schools become clearer, we will need people of good will and hard work by community activists and education leaders in southern communities—indeed, across the nation—to make political choices and take affirmative steps to create racially and ethnically integrated schools. Only then can the South succeed in its quest for racial and ethnic equity in K–12 education.

Notes

The authors thank Jim Freeman for his research assistance. Thank you also to Angelo Ancheta, Jack Boger, Erica Frankenberg, Rebecca High, Gary Orfield, and John T. Yun for their helpful comments on earlier versions of this chapter.

1. See, e.g., *Wygant v. Jackson Board of Education*; *City of Richmond v. J. A. Croson Co.*; *Adarand Constructors, Inc. v. Peña.*
2. *Tuttle v. Arlington County School Board.*
3. *Grutter v. Bollinger*, 328.
4. Ibid., 330.
5. Ibid., 332.
6. Ibid.
7. Ibid., 334.
8. Ibid., 335, citing *Sheet Metal Workers v. EEOC.*
9. See, e.g., the following Supreme Court language: "Public education, like the police function, 'fulfills a most fundamental obligation of government to its constituency.' *Foley v. Connelie*, 297 (1978). The importance of public schools in the preparation of individuals for participation as citizens, and in the preservation of the values on which our society rests, long has been recognized by our decisions." *Ambach v. Norwick*, 76. "The role and purpose of the American public school system were well described by two historians, who stated: '[P]ublic education must prepare pupils for citizenship in the Republic. . . . It must inculcate the habits and manners of civility as values in themselves conducive to happiness and as indispensable to the practice of self-government in the community and the nation.'" Beard and Beard, *New Basic History*, 228; *Bethel School District no. 403 v. Fraser*, 681.
10. *Hazelwood School District v. Kuhlmeier*, 278.
11. Killen and Stangor, "Children's Social Reasoning."
12. Institutions of higher education also have a history of trying to address segregation. Because of the selective nature of institutions of higher education that use race-conscious admissions policies, the large differentiation among particular colleges and universities, and the significant role of individual choice in determining the student composition of institutions of higher education, institutions of higher education generally have focused on ensuring equal access to their own institutions (or set of institutions) rather than on desegregating schools in a geographical region.
13. A 1996 federal district court decision held that preventing racial isolation was not a compelling state interest because the school district's concerns about preventing racial isolation were based on a projection of future trends. The court questioned the legitimacy of the interest and did not address whether preventing racial isolation could be a compelling state interest. It held that the school district needed to show that preventing white students

from taking advantage of an open transfer policy was actually necessary to prevent extensive "white flight." The court rejected the school district's articulated interest in preventing the worst-case scenario. *Equal Open Enrollment Association v. Board of Education of Akron City School District.*

14. *Swann v. Charlotte-Mecklenburg Board of Education*, 16.

15. This outcome is not surprising given the district court's June 2000 desegregation decision in *Hampton v. Jefferson County Board of Education*, which found that maintaining a desegregated school system is a compelling interest. The court ratified the constitutional authority of school boards to voluntarily take race into account to prevent resegregation. In dissolving a twenty-year-old desegregation decree, it recognized that it would be "incongruous that a federal court could at one moment require a school board to use race to prevent resegregation of the system, and at the very next moment prohibit [the voluntary implementation of] that same policy." *Hampton*, 379.

16. *McFarland v. Jefferson County Public Schools*, 849.

17. Wells and Crain, "Perpetuation Theory."

18. G. Orfield and Yun, *Resegregation*; Massey and Denton, *American Apartheid*; Wilson, *Declining Significance of Race.*

19. Anyon, *Ghetto Schooling*; Braddock, "Perpetuation of Segregation"; Dawkins and Braddock, "Continuing Significance."

20. R. Carter, "Unending Struggle"; Natriello, McDill, and Pallas, *Schooling Disadvantaged Children.*

21. Wells and Crain, "Perpetuation Theory."

22. Lareau, *Home Advantage.*

23. Gordon, "Assimilation in American Life."

24. Dawkins and Braddock, "Continuing Significance."

25. Rossell, "Desegregation Plans."

26. McConahay, "Reducing Racial Prejudice."

27. The social science research on tokenism originates from the work of Rosabeth Moss Kanter in the context of gender in the workplace. Kanter, *Men and Women*, found that "skewed" groups engendered distinctive dynamics between men and women, labeling men as dominants (comprising approximately 85 percent) and women as tokens (approximately 15 percent). Kanter noticed that women in skewed groups were perceived as highly visible and different, which resulted in a tendency to be stereotyped. Kanter described stereotyping as an act in which the "familiar generalizations about a person's social type" (211) are overemphasized while their other personal attributes are often ignored. Kanter's study revealed that within skewed groups populated predominantly by men, women were viewed as symbolic representatives of their social type rather than as individuals and that they often experienced performance pressures as a result of their high visibility. Based on her observations of skewed groups with men as dominants and women as tokens, Kanter suggested that her findings could be applied to any group composed of two significant social types as long as the ratio was approximately 85:15. Moreover, she asserted that tokens in all contexts would suffer from similar aspects of tokenism: high visibility, exaggeration of difference, and stereotyping. For a more detailed discussion of tokenism, see Kanter, *Men and Women*; G. Smith, "As Few Become Many."

28. Eaton, *Other Boston Busing Story.*

29. Braddock, "Perpetuation of Segregation"; Braddock and McPartland, "Social-Psychological Processes."

30. Crain, "School Integration"; Braddock, "Perpetuation of Segregation"; Braddock and McPartland, "Social-Psychological Processes"; Braddock and McPartland, *More Evidence*; Wells and Crain, "Perpetuation Theory"; McPartland and Braddock, "Impact of Desegregation."

31. Wells and Crain, "Perpetuation Theory"; Kurlaender and Yun, "School Racial Composition."

32. Schofield, "Uncharted Territory."

33. Hallinan and Williams, "Interracial Friendship Choices"; Hallinan and Williams, "Stability"; Jackman and Crane, "'Some of My Best Friends.'"

34. Hallinan and Williams, "Stability."

35. Kurlaender and Yun, "School Racial Composition"; Kurlaender and Yun, "Is Diversity a Compelling Educational Interest?"

36. The past lack of focus on outcomes that look beyond standardized test results and at racial interactions beyond blacks and whites are slowly being addressed. One of the latest efforts is by researchers at The Civil Rights Project at Harvard University, who developed the diversity assessment questionnaire, a seventy-item student survey developed by researchers at The Civil Rights Project in collaboration with the National Education Association and the National School Boards Association's Council of Urban Boards of Education. This classroom-administered questionnaire asks students about their experiences in their school and classrooms and includes questions about students' future goals, educational aspirations, attitudes, and interests. It has been administered in seven school districts around the country, providing the local evidence district leaders need to make important decisions about the effectiveness of school-assignment policies based on more than standardized test scores.

37. Kurlaender, "Impact of School Racial Composition."

38. Gurin et al., "Diversity and Higher Education."

39. "Most students educated in racially diverse schools demonstrated improved critical thinking skills—the ability to both understand and challenge views that are different from their own. *PICS I,* 137 F.Supp.2d at 1226; see also Erica Frankenberg & Chungmei Lee, *Race in American Public Schools: Rapidly Resegregating School Districts* (The Civil Rights Project, Harvard Univ., Aug. 8, 2002); Gary Orfield, *Schools More Separate: Consequences of a Decade of Resegregation* (The Civil Rights Project, Harvard Univ., July 2001); Janet Ward Schofield & H. Andrew Sagar, *Desegregation, School Practices, and Student Race Relations* (1985). Research has also shown that a diverse educational experience improves race relations, reduces prejudicial attitudes, and achieves a more democratic and inclusive experience for all citizens, *PICS I,* 137 F.Supp.2d at 1226; see also Frankenberg & Lee, *supra*; Irons, [*Jim Crow's Children*]; Michal Kurlaender & John T. Yun, *Is Diversity a Compelling Educational Interest? Evidence from Metropolitan Louisville* (The Civil Rights Project, Harvard Univ., August 2000); Orfield, *supra*; Ward Schofield & Sagar, *supra.*"

40. In *Johnson v. Board of Regents of the University of Georgia* the court looked at whether (1) race was used in a rigid or mechanical way that does not take sufficient account of the different contributions to diversity, (2) the policy fairly takes account of race-neutral factors

that may contribute to a diverse student body, (3) the policy provides arbitrary or disproportionate benefits to members of the favored racial groups, and (4) university officials genuinely considered and rejected as inadequate race-neutral alternatives.

41. *Grutter*, 334.

42. *McFarland*, 856, quoting *Grutter*, 341.

43. In fact, there is an argument that race-conscious school assignment policies do not rise to the level of a strict scrutiny analysis because the "racial classification" does not confer a benefit or a burden on a particular racial or ethnic group. Members from every racial and ethnic group may be denied a particular school choice. See *Comfort ex rel. Neumyer v. Lynn School Committee*, 244–46.

44. Although more research in this area is clearly necessary to bolster this argument, enough social science research already exists to support making this type of argument before a court.

45. A percent plan in a K–12 context might take the form of taking only a certain percentage of students from the surrounding district.

46. *McFarland*, 861.

47. See, e.g., Reardon and Yun, this volume.

48. Kurlaender and Yun, "School Racial Composition."

49. Although Kahlenberg, in *All Together Now*, argues that socioeconomic integration can produce racial/ethnic integration because many minority students come from lower socioeconomic backgrounds, this is not inherently true because there are still many more lower-income whites, given their proportional share of the population. Furthermore, this assertion has not been fully examined by researchers. For additional work on this topic, see Flinspach and Banks, this volume; Reardon, Yun, and Kurlaender, "Limits."

50. *McFarland*, 859.

51. "Racial balancing" has generally referred to achieving specific predefined percentages or numbers of members of different racial and ethnic groups.

52. The court did strike down the school board's admissions policy for its "traditional" schools because students were placed on separate lists according to race and gender, which the court found was unconstitutional because it put students from different racial groups on different admissions tracks.

53. For example, an examination of whether there is a racial and ethnic composition at which the benefits of a diverse student body begin to decline and case studies of the effects of critical mass in K–12 education settings would help in determining whether a compelling interest is narrowly tailored.

54. See *Parents Involved in Community Schools v. Seattle School District no. 1.*

CHAPTER TWELVE

SUSAN LEIGH FLINSPACH | KAREN E. BANKS

Moving beyond Race

Socioeconomic Diversity as a Race-Neutral Approach to Desegregation in the Wake County Schools

This chapter draws on a study of diversity and achievement in the Wake County Public School System (WCPSS).[1] The school system has a reputation for high-quality, high-achieving schools and, following an era of race-based school desegregation, for preserving school diversity through a race-neutral approach to student assignment. The Wake County district includes Raleigh, the capital of North Carolina. A metropolitan area with cities, suburbs, and farms, Wake County is 72 percent white and has mostly middle-class families.[2] In 2002–3, its school system was the twenty-seventh largest in the nation, 67 percent larger than the Boston Public Schools and 78 percent larger than San Francisco Unified School District. The WCPSS served more than 104,000 students in seventy-nine elementary schools, twenty-five middle schools, sixteen high schools, and five special or alternative schools.[3] In addition, it is one of the fastest-growing districts in the country, having increased by roughly 3,300 students over each of the past seven years.[4]

Wake County has a history of maintaining diverse schools through student assignment by race and a large magnet program. School desegregation in Wake County was board initiated rather than court ordered, as in many other southern districts. On 10 January 2000, however, the Wake County school board, spurred by court decisions against the use of race in school assignments elsewhere, eliminated all references to race and ethnicity from its assignment policies and adopted a race-neutral strategy for student assignment based on family income and student achievement. That action prompted the three-year study that included the historical records, system documents, longitudinal school data, and interviews used in this chapter. The chapter describes how the Wake County leaders use race-neutral student assignment to sustain school diversity and to support achievement. Although the evidence is preliminary, the race-neutral strategy appears to be maintaining a level of racially balanced schools in the district and may be a factor in raising achievement and narrowing the income achievement gap.

Desegregation—A Waning Local Priority

Wake County's commitment to school diversity stands out because school desegregation has been a waning priority in many school systems. Throughout the past decade, an unfavorable policy climate and legal uncertainty about the constitutionality of using race to diversify schools have deterred officials from continuing to desegregate their schools. More recently, increasing district responsibility for achievement and the growth of parental and governmental support for public-school choice have further discouraged system leaders from working for school diversity. Fewer and fewer districts include balancing school enrollments among their top goals.

In *Dismantling Desegregation*, Gary Orfield describes the increasing judicial hostility throughout the 1980s and 1990s toward the principles underlying earlier school desegregation decisions. He also discusses the impact of the antidesegregation politics that held sway during the Reagan–George H. W. Bush years, including the symbolic triumph of labeling school desegregation as a failed reform.[5] He argues that decades "of intense attacks on school desegregation have made proposals for resegregation sound reasonable to many Americans."[6] Erwin Chemerinsky describes the later politics of school desegregation as inert rather than defeated.[7] Jeffrey A. Raffel agrees, noting that the "public rejection of de jure segregation, at least by the public in the North and progressive areas of the South, has not developed into a political force for racial balance. The political will to challenge demographic forces and suburban enclaves is simply not there."[8] All of these descriptions characterize the recent policy climate as negative, leaving school officials in the early twenty-first century with little popular support for continuing past policies of school desegregation.

A second factor that works against school desegregation is the uncertain legal standing of race in student assignment. Federal courts have not ruled consistently on this issue.[9] Some, such as the Fourth Circuit Court of Appeals, which has jurisdiction over North Carolina and its neighboring states, have very narrow interpretations of acceptable race-based strategies: "In essence the new [Fourth Circuit] decisions forbid all school boards (unless they are operating under federal desegregation decrees) from considering race or ethnicity as they assign children to public schools. The prohibition holds even if it leads to resegregated schools, even if most parents desire their children to attend racially diverse schools, and even if the school boards are acting in good faith to ensure that students receive the educational benefits that may come from a diverse school environment."[10]

In some school systems under court order to desegregate, like the district including Charlotte, North Carolina, the use of race as a criterion for making school placements has also been disapproved.[11] A 2002 guide published by the National School Boards Association to help district officials decide whether to use race in student-assignment plans goes to the heart of the matter: "This uncertainty is one of the hardest conditions for an attorney advising school districts, because the natural instinct in many cases is to counsel the client to safety. From that instinct flows the kind of commentary that many school boards and administrators have heard in recent years, such as 'Is it really worth it?' or 'Let someone else get sued!'"[12]

The Supreme Court's spring 2003 decision in *Grutter v. Bollinger* does not remove this legal uncertainty because of its unclear application to the K–12 level.[13] Despite the risk, some local officials continue to diversify schools by race because they believe the benefits of desegregation outweigh the costs in their school systems.[14] Many others do not.

The recent federal and state accountability focus has obliged many local leaders to put achievement ahead of school diversity and other goals. State mandates governing testing and reporting[15] and the requirements of the No Child Left Behind Act[16] have moved achievement gains into the limelight as never before. Amy Stuart Wells and Jennifer Jellison Holme propose that preserving school diversity is a task made more difficult by the state accountability movement because the definition of a "good school" has increasingly come to rest exclusively on test scores.[17] Similarly, the growing state and federal accountability mandates work against school diversity as a district priority. Local goals such as diversity bend or change to accommodate demands to raise test scores as district officials face increasing responsibilities for the regulation and monitoring of intergovernmental achievement policies.[18] Under this combined scrutiny from the public, the state, and the federal government, raising achievement has unseated goals like preserving diverse schools in districts across the nation.

Finally, recent shifts toward public-school choice may further discourage efforts to maintain school diversity. Frances C. Fowler notes that at least on its surface, the school-choice debate concerns the public funding of schools and how students are assigned to schools.[19] As choice options increase, the capacity of school leaders to assign students to schools (for diversity or other reasons) decreases. In general, officials cannot assign charter school students, students selecting interdistrict transfers, or students making use of interdistrict open enrollment. Under the No Child Left Behind Act, administrators are not able to control fully the assignment of students from schools that have failed to achieve "adequate yearly progress" for two consecutive years.[20] So, particularly in school systems with low-performing schools, the pool of students that the board can reliably assign to diversify school memberships is diminishing.[21]

Supporting Diversity and Achievement in the Wake County Schools

All of these factors have affected the WCPSS, yet local officials have recently crafted a response that supports both their achievement goals and a commitment to school diversity that was born with the merger of the Raleigh Public Schools and the previous county school system in 1976. In 1975, the Raleigh Public Schools served 19,796 children in the capital city, and the county system educated 33,929 students from the surrounding area. In the late 1960s and early 1970s, the Raleigh system was censured for maintaining separate schools for whites and for African Americans. Raleigh was becoming increasingly residentially segregated and was experiencing white flight from the central city into county suburbs. Under pressure from the Department of Health, Education, and Welfare (HEW) and from disgruntled local constituencies, the Raleigh school board took real steps toward school desegregation in 1971.[22] By that date, however, white flight from downtown Raleigh presented school leaders with demographic challenges in balancing school enrollments, and officials began to discuss merging the city and county school systems.[23]

The merger was not easily won. By a ratio of more than two to one in the early 1970s, Wake County citizens expressed their disapproval of merging the two school systems.[24] Yet the Wake County commissioners, some school leaders, and the Raleigh business community believed that a single county district of high-quality, integrated schools would help stem the downtown area's economic decline. In an interview commemorating the twenty-fifth anniversary of the merger, current superintendent Bill McNeal, then a teacher at a Raleigh school, noted that the "business community was worried about economic development, economic vitality, and what was in the best interest of the school districts."[25] The General Assembly of North Carolina passed "enabling legislation for consummating merger," and during the 1975–76 academic year, both school boards voted in favor of unifying the systems. On 1 July 1976, the two systems merged and became the WCPSS.[26] McNeal recalled, "It was a time of upheaval, and there was strong leadership. . . . When we talk about bold leadership—it would have been easy to fold your hand. But there were some people who climbed out on a limb and said,

'This is a good thing.' And it was not a popular limb. Had they not done that, I'm not quite sure what this district would look like today."[27]

HEW's civil rights enforcement officials continued to scrutinize the new school system for evidence that it was eliminating Raleigh's racially segregated schools. The district responded with a student-assignment plan designed to balance the student racial composition in the majority of its eighty schools to reflect the enrollment of the system as a whole. About 28 percent of the district's students were African American and 71 percent were white. Because of Wake County's patterns of residential segregation, many African American students who lived in central Raleigh were bused to formerly all-white county schools. In an effort to distribute the busing burden between the races, the plan included a few sixth-grade centers in African American neighborhoods to which white Raleigh students were bused. The first WCPSS student-assignment plan satisfied HEW's Office of Civil Rights, and the unified school board implemented the plan in the fall of 1977.[28]

School desegregation and the underutilization of schools in the central city were difficult issues for the new school system. The first magnet schools, geared to serve the academically gifted, opened in 1977 to draw white families voluntarily into downtown schools. In 1981, the school board chose Walter Marks, an administrator with a track record of building effective networks of magnet schools, as the second superintendent of the merged system. The following year, Superintendent Marks redesigned the magnet program to serve a broader range of student interests and opened twenty-seven new magnet schools. Although controversial, the magnet schools quickly became popular, and white students from both Raleigh and the county enrolled in the specialized programs, most of which were housed in central-city schools.[29]

Although a few of the early magnet schools were short-lived, the magnet program itself gradually expanded. As the business community had hoped, the ongoing popularity of magnet schools helped to put empty or underutilized central-city buildings back into use as racially diverse schools. Given the program's success, the school board tried other school-choice strategies to complement the traditional magnet program. First, some board members felt that students at the far edges of the county lacked access to the enriched curricula offered in magnet schools. These members convinced the board to locate "equity magnet schools" far from downtown Raleigh to give students in those areas the opportunity to attend a magnet without riding a bus for more than two hours daily. The equity magnets had little to do with school desegregation, instead addressing unequal geographic access to enrichment programs. Second, the board discussed setting up "reverse magnets" to attract African American students to schools in white residential areas. The notion of reverse magnets emerged from a desire to provide the most frequently bused students with choices. The reverse-magnet idea generated little interest among its target communities, however, and was never implemented.[30]

The board's other choice strategy was to offer year-round magnet schools. In 1989, the Wake County Schools opened the country's first such school.[31] Not wishing to force the year-round calendar on families, district officials assigned no base populations from surrounding neighborhoods to the year-round schools; all students attended by choice. The year-round schedule has evenly spaced, three-week breaks that demand alternative (usually hard-to-find and expensive) child-care arrangements. Because of the schedule and the schools' locations in mostly white neighborhoods, the year-round magnets became predominantly white schools. One school official commented, "We created a monster when we put all those year-round schools out there, because [white students] want to stay in those [year-round schools] instead of going down to the [traditional] magnets."[32] At one point, the school board assigned minority-dominant base populations to all the year-round schools. Still not wishing to force that calendar on families, however, the board allowed the base-population students to attend other schools if they could provide their own transportation. Most of the assigned students opted out of the year-rounds, leaving the white students in relative racial isolation.[33] Finally in 2001, the board reassigned low-income, high-minority base populations to three year-round magnet schools. Because school officials were imposing the year-round calendar for the first time, they also arranged to help the families with child-care coverage.[34] The year-round schools are popular with neighborhood families and with some local officials concerned with fiscal efficiency. However, a former board member said that the schools remain problematic because most families choosing them are white and because they do not coordinate well with the system's overall objectives (table 12.1).[35]

In 2002–3, the WCPSS magnet program included twenty-two elementary schools, eight middle schools, three high schools, and the twelve year-round schools. The academic performance of the magnet schools is competitive with that of the system's other schools,[36] and since 2000, Magnet Schools of America has recognized five of the traditional magnets for their national excellence. This strong magnet program has helped the district create and maintain diverse schools and improve student achievement.

In the 1980s, district leaders also developed student-assignment policies to desegregate the schools. They moved away from the initial WCPSS desegregation goal of having every school reflect the racial balance of the system as a whole; that type of desegregation was difficult in a residentially segregated, countywide school system. Instead, they adopted the "15–45 percent rule," a standard setting

Table 12.1. Concentration of White Students in the Wake County Schools, 2002–2003

School	Total	<25% White	25–50% White	50–75% White	>75% White
All schools[a]	123	4	34	73	12
Magnet schools (excluding year-round magnets)	33	0	13	20	0
Year-round magnets	12	0	1	6	5

[a] Includes elementary, middle, high, and special schools but excludes two alternative schools

Table 12.2. Compliance with the 15–45 Percent Rule, 1980–2001

	1980–81	1985–86	1990–91	1995–96	2000–2001
% Total minority enrollment[a]	29.7	29.1	30.5	31.4	36.8
Total schools[b]	80	76	82	94	117
Schools with <15% minority enrollment[a]	2 (2.5%)	4 (5.3%)	1 (1.2%)	4 (4.3%)	5 (4.3%)
Schools with >45% minority enrollment[a]	11 (13.8%)	7 (9.2%)	6 (7.3%)	17 (18.1%)	40 (34.2%)
Schools in compliance with the 15–45% rule	67 (83.8%)	65 (85.5%)	75 (91.5%)	73 (77.7%)	72 (61.5%)

[a] Twentieth day enrollment or membership.
[b] Excludes special and alternative schools.

minority enrollment between 15 percent and 45 percent in all schools. Table 12.2 examines compliance with the 15–45 percent rule in five school years from 1980 to 2000. In general, compliance increased throughout the 1980s and declined during the 1990s, even as the proportion of minority students remained stable through the mid-1990s. The 15–45 percent rule was the Wake County school desegregation standard for nearly two decades.[37]

As Wake County school leaders weighed student assignments explicitly for their impact on the racial and ethnic composition of the schools, these officials often considered the schools' socioeconomic status as well. One school official commented, "When the court handed down the *Brown* decision, nobody was thinking about Japanese Americans. But I think early on, people who were concerned about this issue and committed to the idea that the schools ought to reflect the society as a whole and ought to be diverse, saw the issue was really not just race. Race certainly was an issue. How could it not be in this country? It's been an issue since the seventeenth century—always. But the issue of poverty and of disadvantagement from various socioeconomic problems which correlate with race, but are not the same thing, that was always [what mattered]. There was always a concern about the socioeconomics. So, over time, race was always sort of . . . a proxy for socioeconomic status."[38] The development and annual approval of student-assignment plans provided school leaders with repeated opportunities to reflect on the importance of racial and ethnic diversity, socioeconomic status, and achievement in the WCPSS. With the passage of each plan, they renewed their predecessors' commitment to sustain a system of desegregated schools in Wake County.

Legal uncertainties about the 15–45 percent rule, which depended on racial minority enrollment, mounted in the late 1990s. The long and contentious battle over school desegregation in Mecklenburg County, the largest school system in North Carolina, was coming to an end. The Charlotte-Mecklenburg Schools had been under court-ordered desegregation since 1971, but a lawsuit, *Capacchione et al. v. Charlotte-Mecklenburg Schools*, challenged the use of race to maintain desegregated schools. In addition, the Fourth Circuit Court of Appeals was hearing two cases of race-based assignments, *Tuttle v. Arlington County School Board* and *Eisenberg v. Montgomery County Public Schools*. The fate of school desegregation in North Carolina rested uneasily in the hands of the courts, and Wake County administrators began to think about alternatives to race.[39]

Socioeconomic status and achievement were informal policy factors in diversifying school enrollments prior to the adoption of the race-neutral assignment strategy. In the late 1990s, though, school administrators started routinely to incorporate these factors into student assignments. The 1999–2000 WCPSS student-assignment plan listed socioeconomic indicators, academic achievement, and racial diversity as three of the five diversity components used in assignment decisions that year. The magnet program selection criteria for 1999–2000 dropped race entirely.[40] A school official commented on the changes, "we set criteria for magnet selection based upon [North Carolina's four-tiered measure of academic achievement] level 1, 2, 3 and 4.[41] And I knew we were looking at maps based on the academic level of a child. How many [level] 1s, [level] 2s were being moved? . . . And we were actually really more concerned about that [achievement] than the race at that point, or even than the economic status of the child. We were really more concerned about . . . how many challenges you had in a classroom."[42]

In 1998, the school system and the Wake Education Partnership, an advocacy organization for the district, hosted a community summit to help the system establish priorities for the next five years.[43] Based on input from the summit and from local leaders, parents, and staff, school officials adopted Goal 2003: by 2003, 95 percent of students tested will be at or above grade level as measured by the state accountability tests in grades 3 and 8.[44] As in many other districts, raising achievement—measured by state tests—became the school system's first priority. One factor distinguished the Wake County experience, however: setting a single, overarching priority unified the school community and created a wellspring of support for meeting the goal. County, community, and school leaders stood firmly behind Goal 2003, and they realigned existing resources and recruited new ones to help raise test scores.[45] District officials began to employ Goal 2003 as a filter for their decisions, including decisions about school diversity.[46]

School officials considered changes to the 15–45 percent rule that would serve both diversity goals and Goal 2003. In March 1999, the district's evaluation and research staff published a brief on the impact of poverty on schools. It summarized current research and concluded, "Students are most likely to be successful when they are in heterogeneous classes in socio-economically diverse schools in which the concentration of poverty is kept as low as possible."[47] Board members and administrators began to discuss the relationship between socioeconomic status and achievement. The Office of Student Assignment prepared materials for the school board using socioeconomic status, achievement levels on the state accountability tests, and minority status. Although the first version of the 2000–2001 student-assignment plan included minority enrollment, school officials were prepared to look at diversity in other ways.

A federal district court ruled against race-based assignments in Charlotte-Mecklenburg in September 1999. In September and October of that year, the Fourth Circuit Court of Appeals struck down the use of race and ethnicity in two Virginia and Maryland student-assignment cases. According to legal experts, these decisions directly challenged Wake County's 15–45 percent rule.[48] In late fall, four new members took their seats on the nine-member Wake County school board. The staff presented this new board with the 2000–2001 student-assignment plan on 6 January 2000, and board members began to discuss the legal situation, asking about alternatives. One board member recalled, "And we talked about that briefly, and we didn't take long to say, 'Okay, let's move away from race, and let's use low SES [socioeconomic status].'"[49] The school board then directed administrators to prepare a new student-assignment policy and a plan that excluded race and ethnicity.

Administrators had to revise the policy quickly to construct another student-assignment plan for 2000–2001. They felt that the new policy should clearly link diversity to academics. One administrator who helped draft the race-neutral policy commented that the "earlier version [of the policy] dealt with race but implied in the issue was socioeconomic status."[50] He also felt that achievement was implicit in the 15–45 percent rule but needed to be spelled out clearly in the new version. He argued, "It is not true that all kids who are on free and reduced lunch do poorly in school. That is not true. And it's not true that all the kids who are black do poorly in school. So, with that in mind, we said it would be better to put a performance piece in [the new policy] because we may deal with the issue of [socioeconomic status], and a school still may have an abundance of [level] 1s and 2s [below-grade-level performers on the state accountability tests]."[51] Four days after the board request, key staff members presented the school board with new draft policies on student assignment.

On 10 January 2000, the board amended its student-assignment policies, removing all racial references, eliminating the 15–45 percent rule for minority enrollment, and adding school-level caps on the enrollment of low-income students and of low achievers (figure 12.1). It waived the customary second public reading of policy changes and voted unanimously in favor of the amendments that night. The WCPSS had linked its pursuit of diverse schools to raising achievement and had moved from race-based desegregation to race-neutral student assignment.

A legal challenge to the new assignment policy soon followed. In a letter to Superintendent McNeal, an official from the U.S. Department of Education's Office for Civil Rights wrote, "complainants claimed that the District adopted student socioeconomic status (SES) as a discriminatory proxy for race and national origin in the assignment of students to schools and in selection of students for magnet/year-round programs."[52] After investigation, however, the Office for Civil Rights agreed that socioeconomic status was not a proxy for race in WCPSS policy or practice and cleared the system of all charges.[53] Wake County's commitment to diverse schools was preserved through its race-neutral assignment strategy.

Socioeconomic Diversity, Racial Diversity, and Achievement: Assignment Policy in the Wake County Schools

Wake County policy 6200 (see fig. 12.1) depends on an annual process for student assignment. Staff members juggle a matrix of school variables that affect the assignment of students—facility capacity, instructional program, the enrollment of low-income and low-performing students, and other factors. To build district compliance with the diversity caps, administrators initially identify schools that exceed the low-achievement cap (more than 25 percent of students below grade-level on the state reading test, with these scores averaged over two years) or the low-income cap (more than 40 percent of students receiving free or reduced-price

The Wake County Public School System believes that maintaining diverse student populations in each school is critical to ensuring academic success for all students, and this belief is supported by research. The school system also must consider such factors as cost effective use of facilities.

Each student enrolled in the Wake County Public School System shall be assigned to the school of his or her grade level serving the attendance area in which that student's parents or court-appointed guardian lives. Exceptions will be made as necessary to limit enrollment of a school due to overcrowding or for special programmatic reasons; e.g., special education, English as a Second Language, or alternative school programs. Each student will have the option of applying for admission to one of the magnet educational programs or year-round programs, which will be offered in designated schools.

All of the following factors, not in priority order, will be used in the development of the annual student assignment plan:

A. Instructional program; e.g., magnet programs, special education, ESL, etc.
B. Adherence to K–5, 6–8, 9–12 grade organization.
C. Facility utilization, including crowding (projected enrollment should be between 85 percent and 115 percent of approved campus capacity). New schools may operate with less than 85 percent of capacity enrolled if some grade levels will not be assigned during the first year *or* if significant growth is anticipated in the following years.
D. Diversity in student achievement (percentage of students scoring below grade level should be no higher than 25 percent, averaged across a two-year period). Schools with more than 25 percent of students below grade level will receive an instructional review to ascertain the reasons for the low achievement; improvement trends will be considered in deciding whether to address this issue in development of the assignment plan.
E. Diversity in socioeconomic status (percentage of students eligible for free or reduced price lunch will be no higher than 40 percent). Schools with more than 40 percent of students eligible for free or reduced price lunch will receive an instructional review; improvement trends will be considered in deciding whether to address this issue in development of the assignment plan.
F. Stability (the percentage of students who will remain at the same school).
G. Proximity (no student will travel more than the maximum time established by board policy).

Beginning in the fall 2000, the board will review and approve the factors to be considered in developing the student assignment plan and will approve the list of factors and ways to measure those factors by their first meeting in October each year.

Revised: January 10, 2000

Figure 12.1. Wake County Policy 6200, Student Assignment

Source: Wake County Public School System Board Policy.

lunch). They review instructional programs in the identified schools and consider other assignment-related factors affecting each one. The decision to reassign students also depends on the status of similar schools within a bus ride of the identified school (e.g., overcrowding, other planned reassignments, exceeding the same diversity cap, and so forth) since one or more of those schools would be involved in the exchange of students. When administrators decide that reassigning students is the best option for an identified school, it is added to the student-assignment plan as a school that will send or receive students.

Nodes have been the basis for school placements since the development of the first WCPSS student-assignment plan.[54] A node includes all students within a relatively small geographic area, and the district maintains various types of student and family data by node. The map of the school system is divided into nodes. A school's attendance area usually includes many nodes, and its attendance boundaries overlap with node boundaries. The students living in a node receive the same school placements; feeder patterns are set by node. Nodes are reassigned from one school to another, thus ensuring that students attend school—and change schools—with at least some of their closest neighbors. Nodes also allow administrators to present student-assignment data in the aggregate (at the node level), rather than revealing information about the achievement or income of individuals or their families.

When staff members recommend the reassignment of a node from one school to another, they intend to create conditions in both schools where all the students, reassigned or not, are better able to reach their full educational potential. In theory, nodes of students at any performance level or from any income group may be reassigned to improve system compliance with the two diversity enrollment caps. The Wake County school board reviews the staff plan, and public hearings are held. Public input and board preferences modify the staff proposals, and the school board approves the final student-assignment plan.

Socioeconomic Diversity and Achievement

The race-neutral policy establishes explicit connections between diverse schools and academic performance, beginning with the opening sentence: "The Wake County Public School System believes that maintaining diverse student populations in each school is critical to ensuring academic success for all students, and this belief is supported by research." The two enrollment caps also recast the former desegregation policy in terms of achievement. Wake County school officials contend that the diversity caps help teachers by limiting the number of high-needs students in their classes. Teachers then can better serve all of their students.[55]

As the policy states, educational research supports the school leaders' contention about school poverty and lower achievement. For almost forty years, researchers have found that the academic performance of individual students directly relates to their families' wealth.[56] In addition, schools that enroll a high proportion of low-income students have an additional negative academic effect. Studies show that all students, regardless of income level, generally have less success in high-poverty schools than their peers in other schools.[57] Consequently, schools with high concentrations of poverty are often low-performing schools.

From 1992 to 2002, the poverty rate in the Wake County Schools remained stable: 18–21 percent of enrolled students received free or reduced-price lunch. As research predicts, student performance on the state accountability tests was directly related to family income[58] and, given large variations, also directly related to the school concentration of poverty.[59] Consequently, Wake County school officials expected the race-neutral policy to help raise achievement, and achievement did improve. In six years, the school system made considerable progress toward the 95 percent targets of Goal 2003 (figure 12.2). Many factors affected the gains achieved under Goal 2003, and one likely contributor, especially to the dramatic improvement of low-income students, was the explicit focus on income and achievement in the assignment policy. The Wake County income achievement gap in reading for grades 3–8 narrowed 8.5 percentage points from 2001 to 2003, whereas the state income achievement gap decreased 6.6 percentage points during the same period. For WCPSS third- through eighth-graders, the income achievement gap in reading shrank from a 35.2 percentage-point difference in 1998 to 20.6 percentage points in 2003 (figure 12.3). From 2001 to 2003, the Wake County Schools also reduced the income achievement gap in third- through eighth-grade math (down 8.0 percentage points) faster than the state as a whole (down 6.5 percentage points). The income achievement gap in math for Wake County's third- through eighth-graders narrowed from 34.9 percentage points in 1998 to just 16.4 percentage points in 2003.[60] Regulating the concentration of low-income and low-achieving students in some schools and classrooms may have enabled teachers and administrators to work more effectively.[61]

Socioeconomic Diversity and Racial Diversity

The Wake County student-assignment policy is crafted to make diversity for diversity's sake secondary to academic success, as indicated by the language in the policy's initial sentence. The commitment to desegregated schools has disappeared, but Wake school leaders still want diverse schools. They certainly value diversity in achievement and socioeconomic status for its anticipated effects on academic performance. They may also value diversity in achievement and socioeconomic status as social differences that enrich students' education. Legally

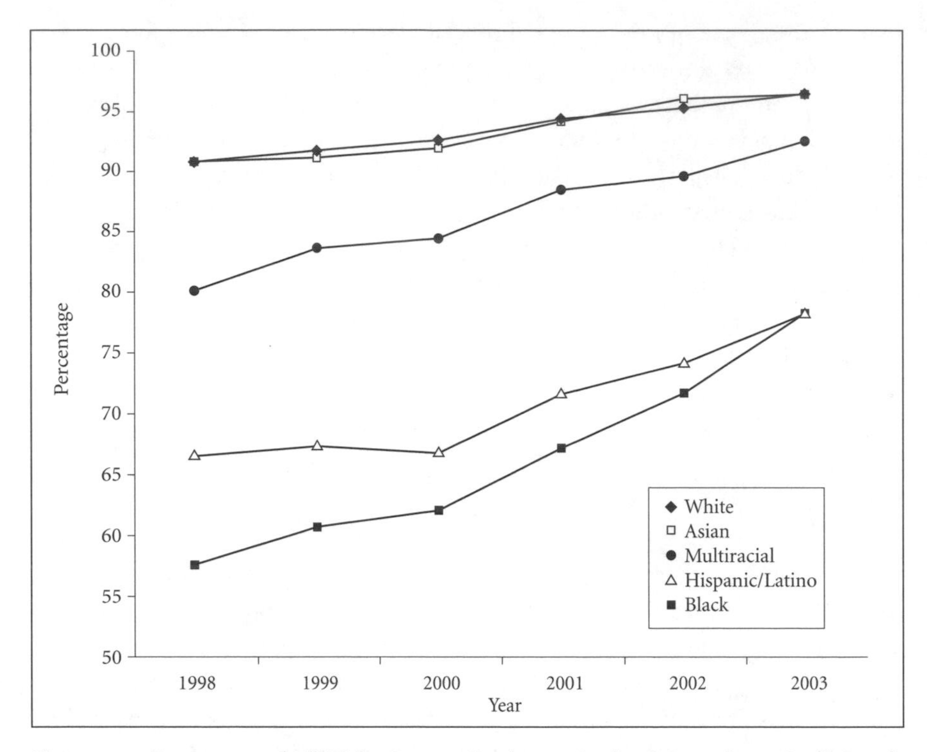

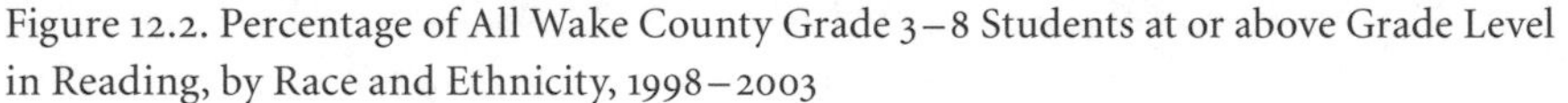

Figure 12.2. Percentage of All Wake County Grade 3–8 Students at or above Grade Level in Reading, by Race and Ethnicity, 1998–2003

Source: Flinspach, Banks, and Khanna, "Socioeconomic Integration Policy."

safe,[62] the new policy's emphasis on achievement does not deny that diversity, defined in various ways, is itself an important value in the school system.[63]

Student-assignment approaches that center on socioeconomic status are often called race-neutral desegregation strategies. Wherever income categories and racial/ethnic groups overlap sufficiently, income-based student assignment may preserve racially desegregated schools—either by design or as a by-product of other goals. Nationally, there is a moderately strong correlation (r = .61) between the percent of African American and Latino enrollment and the percent of low-income enrollment in schools. During the 2000–2001 academic year, the average African American and the average Latino student attended schools with more than 44 percent low-income students, whereas the average white student's school had fewer than 20 percent low-income students.[64] School systems that reflect these national trends could theoretically adopt income-based assignment strategies and achieve significant racial desegregation.

Achievement also reflects racial and ethnic differences nationally,[65] which

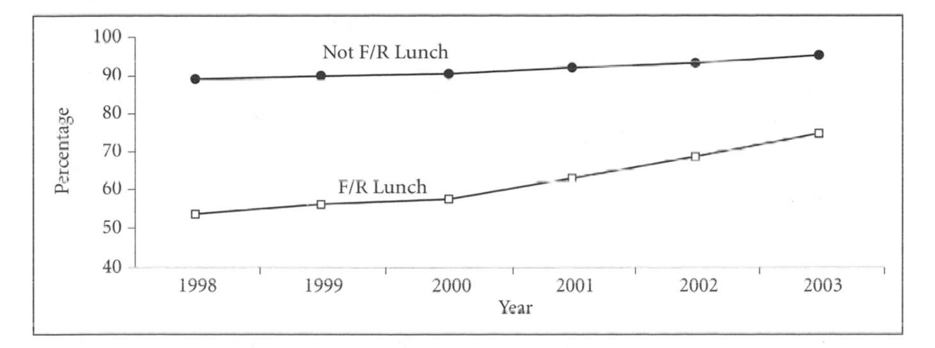

Figure 12.3. Percentage of All Wake County Grade 3–8 Students at or above Grade Level in Reading, by Free or Reduced-Price Lunch Status, 1998–2003

Source: Flinspach, Banks, and Khanna, "Socioeconomic Integration Policy."

makes achievement another possible race-neutral criterion. Although African American and Latino achievement has improved on the National Assessment of Educational Progress, for example, it still lags behind that of whites and Asians in reading, science, and math.[66] In theory, districts with racial/ethnic achievement gaps could assign students to school by achievement variables to help preserve desegregated schools.

These national correlations are reflected in Wake County's student population as well. In 2001–2, 21 percent of all Wake County students came from low-income families. That figure included just 5 percent of the white students but 50 percent or more of the African American and the Latino students. Similarly, achievement is linked to racial-ethnic status in the school system.[67] Under Goal 2003, African Americans and Latinos had much higher gains than did whites and Asians on the state accountability tests, but African Americans' and Latinos' overall performance still lagged behind (see fig. 12.2).[68]

Wake school leaders no longer monitor the schools' racial and ethnic enrollments, but an outside analysis indicates that the WCPSS's race-neutral policy has preserved a moderate level of school desegregation thus far.[69] During the first two years of the new policy, 2000–2001 and 2001–2, more than three-quarters of the Wake County schools had enrollments below 40 percent low-income and 25 percent low-achieving students as prescribed by the diversity caps. The percentage of racially desegregated schools in Wake County dropped in 2000–2001 (from 64.6 percent to 60.0 percent) but then increased (to 63.3 percent) the next year. The analysis found that the 15–45 percent rule and the diversity caps identify many of the same schools for reassignment, thus providing continuity across the two standards. Although the full relationship between race-neutral and race-based assignment will not be known for years, these early observations suggest that Wake County's race-neutral strategy is maintaining a system of racially desegregated schools, albeit at a lower rate than before.[70]

The WCPSS is one of a growing number of districts that rely on socioeconomic status to diversify school enrollments. Two others that also have long desegregation histories are the Cambridge Public Schools in Massachusetts and the San Francisco Unified School District. Local officials in Cambridge apply both race and socioeconomic status as diversity criteria,[71] whereas school leaders in San Francisco have created a diversity index based on six variables about each student: socioeconomic status, academic achievement, mother's educational background, proficiency in English, home language, and prior school's academic performance.[72] The effects of the Cambridge policy on racial diversity remain unreported. San Francisco Unified experienced a two-year hiatus between racial desegregation and race-neutral desegregation, during which time the schools underwent considerable resegregation. Two studies have found that based on the early implementation of the diversity index following that hiatus, race-neutral desegregation has not yet helped San Francisco schools move back into racial balance.[73]

Fighting for Diverse Schools

Wake County officials have traditionally employed a powerful tool to maintain school-board support for the WCPSS student-assignment policy: "in-service" education. Long-serving Wake County board members help orient new members, sharing arguments about school diversity's importance for the system's excellence and for the desirability of the county as a place to live. As one board member described it, "Those board members nurtured me, to understand why the decisions . . . were made, why it was important that those stay in place, and what the community would look like if we didn't [keep them in place]. And we know that in communities where the schools have become segregated again, they're just—they are not healthy communities or healthy school systems."[74] This practice of educating new board members about school diversity has helped change more than one board member's stance toward the assignment policy[75] and has passed the responsibility for a system of "healthy" schools down from one Wake County school board to the next.

A veteran board member commented on the never-ending political fight for school diversity: "You've got to really believe that what you're doing is the right thing to do. Otherwise, it would be intolerable. Student assignment is not pleasant."[76] After school desegregation became accepted district policy in the 1980s, the people who objected to diversifying the schools through student assignment generally were the individual families or groups of neighboring families slated for reassignment. They lobbied to change their children's new bus ride or school placement, but they did not organize to oppose the policy itself or other aspects of its implementation.[77]

In the late 1990s, a second type of political battle emerged in the town of Garner, where some parents and community leaders felt that too many students from nearby low-income areas of Raleigh were being assigned to Garner schools. This situation triggered the flight of middle-class Garner parents from their local schools, greater concentrations of poverty in the Garner schools, and increasing community dissatisfaction. The Wake County school board and representatives of Garner held annual retreats to discuss this issue, and the administration has been cautious about further reassignments to Garner schools.[78] With the goal of encouraging middle-income Garner parents back into the public system, the school board has converted the high school and both middle schools to magnets.[79] The community has worked to resolve this conflict through policy implementation rather than policy change.

In 2002, a third sort of political opposition organized expressly for the purpose of policy change—to end diversity-related student assignment in Wake County. A group supporting neighborhood schools and public-school choice, Assignment by Choice, is "a united, county-wide effort to reform student assignment policies of the Wake County Public School System."[80] Assignment by Choice quickly entered school politics in Wake County, endorsing four candidates for the five open seats on the Wake County school board in 2003.[81] Two were elected (one running unopposed), but the election also returned strong proponents of diverse school enrollments to the board. Mirroring the national struggle, the political battle between local control of student assignment and school choice continues in Wake County.

Since the merger of the city and county school systems, Wake County leaders have been committed to providing a system of diverse schools. They have weathered storms that led many others to abandon school diversity goals—a policy climate unfavorable to school desegregation, legal uncertainties about student assignment by race, increasing intergovernmental responsibility for other goals, the erosion of local control over student assignment, and political controversies. After twenty years of countywide racial and ethnic desegregation that successfully integrated most schools, Wake school officials moved from race-based to race-neutral desegregation without resistance and within an established pattern of metropolitan integration. Resistance soon developed, but given the system's legacy, Wake school leaders should be prepared to continue the fight for diverse schools against their newly organized challenger, public-school choice.

Notes

1. The Spencer Foundation generously funded the data collection for this study.
2. U.S. Bureau of the Census, *United States Census 2000.*
3. WCPSS, "WCPSS Overview."
4. WCPSS, "Superintendent's Budget Message 2003–04."
5. G. Orfield and Eaton, *Dismantling Desegregation*, 18.
6. Ibid., 335.
7. Chemerinsky, this volume.
8. Raffel, "History of School Desegregation," 36.
9. R. Jones, "Defining Diversity."
10. Boger and Bower, "Future," 3.
11. The Charlotte-Mecklenburg Board, aware of the district judge's hostile views, decided voluntarily to abandon its former use of race as a factor in making student assignments. The district judge thereafter held, in his 1999 opinion, that any use of race in making assignments after the district had been declared unitary and released from its affirmative duty to eliminate segregation to the greatest extent possible would be unconstitutional, and he enjoined "any future use of race-based lotteries, preferences, and set-asides in student assignments." *Capacchione v. Charlotte-Mecklenburg Schools*, 292. The Fourth Circuit, sitting en banc, narrowly reversed this part of the judge's order, not because it disagreed with his legal position but because it concluded that no injunction was appropriate since the Charlotte-Mecklenburg Board had neither taken any action to employ racial criteria nor suggested that it might do so in the future.
12. Darden, Coleman, and Palmer, *From Desegregation to Diversity*, 2.
13. Ma and Kurlaender, this volume.
14. R. Jones, "Defining Diversity."
15. Boser, "Pressure without Support."
16. Kim, "Initial Response."
17. Wells and Holme, this volume.
18. Sunderman, "Implementing"; Hardy, "New Federal Role"; Harrington-Lueker, "States Raise the Bar."
19. Fowler, "Great School Choice Debate," 4.
20. Kim and Sunderman, "Findings."
21. An additional wrinkle in maintaining school diversity is the overrepresentation of certain racial or ethnic groups among the students who choose their schools. Three recent studies—Weiher and Tedin, "Does Choice Lead to Racially Distinctive Schools?"; Rickles and Ong, "Integrating (and Segregating) Effect"; and Frankenberg and Lee, *Charter Schools and Race*—find that charter schools are more segregated than the public school systems from which they draw their students. Thus, in districts where public-school choice restricts the number of students that can be assigned, the disproportionate exit of assignable students from particular racial and ethnic groups may make it impossible to diversify schools through student-assignment practices.
22. Slate, "Inertia of Moderation," 90.
23. C. Jones, *History*, 22.

24. Ibid., 10.

25. Quoted in WCPSS, "From 1976 to 2001."

26. C. Jones, *History.*

27. Quoted in WCPSS, "From 1976 to 2001."

28. C. Jones, *History*, 26–28.

29. WCPSS, Community Services, *Resource Guide*; WCPSS, "From 1976 to 2001"; WCPSS, "Senior Director."

30. Interviews, 30 June 2002, 11 July 2002.

31. WCPSS, "Year Round Education."

32. Interview, 11 July 2002.

33. Interviews, 14 June 2002, 30 June 2002, 1 July 2002, 11 July 2002.

34. Hui and Perez, "Education."

35. Interview, 1 July 2002.

36. Penta, "Comparing Student Performance."

37. Interview, 14 June 2002.

38. Ibid.

39. Interview, 11 July 2002.

40. Interview, 30 June 2002.

41. These levels are categories for reporting student achievement on North Carolina's state accountability tests. Levels 1 and 2 indicate that the child has performed below grade level. Level 3 is grade-level performance, and level 4 is above grade level.

42. Interview, 30 June 2002.

43. Information about the organization and the annual education summits are available at ‹http://www.wakeedpartnership.org/index.html›, 13 October 2003.

44. WCPSS, "Goal 2003."

45. WCPSS, "Superintendent McNeal"; WCPSS, "Schools Cheer."

46. Interview, 10 July 2002.

47. WCPSS, Department of Evaluation and Research, *Impact of Poverty.*

48. Boger and Bower, "Future."

49. Interview, 26 June 2002.

50. Interview, 10 July 2002.

51. Ibid.

52. U.S. Department of Education, Office for Civil Rights, Muhammad to McNeal.

53. Ibid.

54. Interview 14 July 2002; C. Jones, *History.*

55. Interviews, 24 June 2002, 28 June 2002, 30 June 2002, 10 July 2002, 11 July 2002.

56. Coleman et al., *Equality of Educational Opportunity*; Mosteller and Moynihan, "Pathbreaking Report"; Kennedy, Jung, and Orland, *Poverty, Achievement, and the Distribution*; Judith Anderson, Hollinger, and Conaty, "Re-Examining the Relationship."

57. Coleman et al., *Equality of Educational Opportunity*; Mosteller and Moynihan, "Pathbreaking Report"; Meyer and Levine, "Concentrated Poverty"; Kennedy, Jung, and Orland, *Poverty, Achievement, and the Distribution*; Myers, *Relationship*; Orland, "Demographics of Disadvantage"; Judith Anderson, Hollinger, and Conaty, "Re-Examining the Relationship"; Lippman, Burns, and McArthur, *Urban Schools*; Schellenberg, "Concentration of Poverty";

U.S. Department of Education, Planning and Evaluation Service, *High Standards*; Helms, "High-Poverty Schools."

58. Dulaney and Burch, *2000–2001 End-of-Grade Multiple-Choice Test Results*; Dulaney and Regan, *2001–2002 End-of-Grade Multiple-Choice Test Results*; Dulaney and Regan, *End-of-Grade Multiple-Choice Test Results: 2002–03.*

59. Banks, *Effect.*

60. Dulaney and Regan, *End-of-Grade Multiple-Choice Test Results: 2002–03*; North Carolina Department, "Reports."

61. The authors are now investigating how the race-neutral strategy affects achievement.

62. U.S. Department of Education, Office for Civil Rights, Muhammad to McNeal.

63. R. Jones, "Defining Diversity"; Darden, Coleman, and Palmer, *From Desegregation to Diversity.*

64. Frankenberg, Lee, and Orfield, *Multiracial Society*, 35.

65. See, e.g., Jencks and Phillips, *Black-White Test Score Gap.*

66. Hoffman and Llagas, *Status and Trends*, 48–53; Llagas, *Status and Trends*, 48–53.

67. WCPSS, Department of Evaluation and Research, *Gaps, 2000–01*; WCPSS, Department of Evaluation and Research, *Gaps, 2001–02.*

68. Dulaney and Regan, *End-of-Grade Multiple-Choice Test Results: 2002–03*; WCPSS, Department of Evaluation and Research, *Gaps, 2001–02.*

69. Flinspach, Banks, and Khanna, "Socioeconomic Integration Policy."

70. Ibid., 13–16.

71. See the link to the Cambridge Public Schools' Controlled Choice Policy at ‹http://www.cpsd.us/pubinfo/›, 10 November 2003.

72. See the link to "Process and Methodology for Student Assignment" in San Francisco's comprehensive plan, *Excellence for All*, at ‹http://portal.sfusd.edu/template/default.cfm›, 10 November 2003.

73. Flinspach, Banks, and Khanna, "Socioeconomic Integration Policy"; Biegel, *Report.*

74. Interview, 11 July 2002.

75. Interviews, 30 June 2002, 11 July 2002.

76. Interview, 14 June 2002.

77. Interviews, 13 June 2002, 14 June 2002.

78. Interviews, 29 April 2002, 9 May 2002, 22 May 2002, 24 June 2002.

79. Hui, "Magnet Schools Work."

80. Assignment by Choice, "About ABC."

81. Assignment by Choice, "Home."

CHAPTER THIRTEEN

JOHN A. POWELL

A New Theory of Integrated Education

True Integration

Fifty years ago, *Brown v. Board of Education* recognized public education as fundamental to good citizenship. More recently, the U.S. Supreme Court acknowledged it as "pivotal to 'sustaining our political and cultural heritage' with a fundamental role in maintaining the fabric of society."[1] Every state makes education compulsory, and it is usually the largest single item in a state's budget, for what other institution plays such a vital role in preparing individuals, workers, and citizens for life in our complex and diverse nation? This role is radically undermined, however, by racial and economic segregation. Indeed, it is not an overstatement to suggest that segregation creates not just an unequal education but also a *mis*education for all isolated students, both white and nonwhite. The role of education in a democracy is not to reproduce family, community, class, and racial hierarchies but instead to reduce these social constraints in favor of equal opportunity and democracy.[2] So often, however, low-income students of color, living in impoverished neighborhoods, are consigned to high-poverty schools with inadequate resources and very limited access to real opportunity.[3]

Though our schools today are more equitable along some indexes than they were before *Brown*, they have never been truly integrated and are currently re-segregating at alarming rates, both racially and economically. When we consign students to these apartheid-like conditions, we make a mockery of democracy. It is hardly an adequate response to simply assert that the current arrangement of segregated schools is achieved through housing choices or the drawing of school boundaries. Both our history and our collective future demand more: they demand that we initiate a discussion of what constitutes *true integration*, how it relates to the goals of public education, and how it contrasts with segregation.

"Segregation" and "desegregation," despite their popular usage, have both legal and social science meanings that are often at odds with one another. The legal meaning of "segregation," which, because it allows courts to act to end racial isolation, is arguably the most important, is also the narrowest. For several decades, the Supreme Court has recognized legal segregation only when there is provable, intentional, state-sponsored segregation:[4] if legal barriers are removed, desegregation has been legally achieved. This standard did not flow directly from *Brown* and was strongly opposed by a number of justices when it was adopted. In decisions that adhered to *Brown*, the Court clearly rejected mere "choice," placing an affirmative duty on school districts to eliminate segregation to the greatest extent possible. Yet today, unless there is proof that the state actions that produce segregation were intended to have such effects, the federal courts do not recognize the results as segregation for purposes of legal remedy—even if whites and nonwhites are completely separated.

The social science meaning and common understanding of "segregation" is the occurrence of racial isolation or separation without focus on whether it results from intended state acts. Drawing a distinction between segregation "by law" (de jure) and segregation "in fact" (de facto) is troubling, especially when one considers that the Court in *Brown* recognized that segregation causes harm even if it is not state mandated. As used here, then, "segregation" simply describes situations in which a disproportionate number of white students or students of color attend a school or school system.

Desegregation efforts, even in the educational settings in which they have been implemented, have mostly been limited to moving and mixing racial populations to end racial isolation. So desegregation has generally required students of the nondominant group (most often nonwhite) to adapt to schools created for and controlled by the dominant group (most often white) no matter how inappropriate or even hostile the result. Curricula, level of instruction, and institutional culture have rarely been addressed under this process;[5] rather, nonwhite students are expected to assimilate to the existing culture and structure. This limited notion of "desegregation," which is often inappropriately used as a synonym for "integration," has made many African American scholars and parents suspicious of integration.[6] Consequently, even desegregated schools are a limited and incomplete response to the problem of segregation.

What We Know but Refuse to Accept about Segregation, Resegregation, and Desegregation

At least partly because we have focused on desegregation rather than true integration, leaving important structural and cultural work undone, we have seen a reassertion of the separate-but-equal doctrine originally overturned in *Brown*.

The assumption in this argument is that if there is equality in resources, it does not matter if students are racially isolated. Segregation, however, negatively affects not only our students but also our democratic structure, reifying racial subordination in employment, health, wealth access, and political participation. We also find ourselves today having to defend the principles of *Brown* against arguments that segregation has been disestablished or that its persistence is merely a matter of choice. Focusing on choice misconstrues racial separation as symmetrical, as if whites and blacks choose to be exclusive in the same fashion. Segregation, however, has historically been and remains today a reality imposed by those with power and privilege on those without. In the end, both of these arguments uncritically accept the limited, legal concept of segregation and ignore or misread the meaning of *Brown*.

The claim that segregation is neutral is exposed as dangerously wrong when we think of the educational goals of citizenship in a diverse nation or even of employment in a diverse workplace. As the military brief explained in the 2003 case affirming the importance of diversity at the University of Michigan Law School, *Grutter v. Bollinger*, the need for diversity in our institutions of higher learning is a matter of national security, not because students cannot learn to read and write in a segregated setting but because of what such a setting conveys in terms of stereotypes, racial subordination, and racial hierarchy.[7] If this is so, what does this tell us about the widespread segregation in our nationwide system of compulsory education?

One may question why we refuse to accept what we know about these issues. In *The Possessive Investment in Whiteness*, George Lipsitz answers this question: the costs, real or perceived, associated with what we know are such that we are unwilling to accept the implications of that knowledge. Similarly, we often feel that the response needed is collective, while we, at best, have control over only our individual lives.[8] We feel collectively disempowered to do what we know individually to be right.

Education is critical to solving this problem. Education is the site of the constitution of the self and the basis for the creation of a more equitable multiracial and multiethnic democracy. In 1916, John Dewey wrote that it is the role of our schools "to balance the various elements in the social environment, and to see to it that each individual gets an opportunity to escape from the limitations of the social group in which he was born, and to come into living contact with a broader environment."[9] Leading educational institutions, businesses, and military officials validated and perhaps expanded this imperative in friend of the court briefs seeking to preserve diverse educational settings today, reminding the *Grutter* Court that "numerous authorities concur that '[c]rosscultural competence' is 'the most important new attribute for future effective performance in a global marketplace.'"[10] This competence, the Court agreed, "can only be developed through exposure to widely diverse people, culture, ideas, and viewpoints."[11]

If our schools are the laboratories in which we reinvent and renew our changing society, pushing aside these important interests in favor of the current focus on testing reflects goals that are far too narrow and shortsighted. Moreover, as the *Grutter* case made clear, segregated schools do not well serve even limited testing goals. We need to prepare students for an increasingly diverse society to the maximum extent feasible not only at the university level but also in the context of K–12 education. It is critical that we provide these opportunities to children during their formative years and beyond, since public school will constitute the greatest part of most students' educational experience.

The Realities of Residential and Educational Segregation

Despite the importance of cross-cultural competence and despite our nation's increasing diversity, data from the 2000 Census show that intense racial separation persists in our metropolitan areas. Residential segregation remains high in both cities and their suburbs. And although residential segregation by race declined slightly, racial and economic segregation in schools increased during the 1990s.[12] While people of color are moving from cities to suburbs in increasing numbers, they are often resettling in largely nonwhite neighborhoods.[13]

We continue to segregate not only by race but also by income. In spite of research clearly demonstrating the harms associated with concentrated poverty, we experienced a threefold increase in the number of such communities through the 1980s.[14] This concentration of poverty disproportionately affects communities of color.[15] Of those living in concentrated poverty in 1990, 74 percent were nonwhite—half were black and one-fourth were Latino.[16] In 2000 this number had increased to 76 percent.[17] In fact, 33 percent of all blacks in the United States live in neighborhoods of concentrated poverty.[18] We know that this level of neighborhood poverty functions differently from and more destructively than individual poverty and results in multifaceted harm to entire communities, yet our policies favor its proliferation.

Suburban sprawl and metropolitan fragmentation, along with concentrated poverty and concentrated wealth, are the counterparts to segregation and present perhaps the greatest obstacles to achieving a more racially just society. Manning Marable has argued that residential segregation is the most important factor today in reproducing racial hierarchy and undermining racial justice.[19] Francis

Cardinal George refers to our present arrangement as spatial racism.[20] As people and businesses with the economic means sprawl away from central cities, they settle into developing suburban jurisdictions, leaving behind low-income minorities in high-need, resource-depleted central cities. Home values are lower, employment opportunities are limited, and the ability to move into stable areas is hindered by lack of accumulated assets.[21]

Because of these realities and because education is, despite increasing state participation, still funded largely through local taxes, segregated areas of concentrated poverty offer significantly diminished educational opportunities. Moreover, although the role of federal, state, and local governments in the creation of housing segregation is well documented, it is most often unacknowledged.[22] Much school segregation is directly attributable to this residential segregation,[23] yet the Supreme Court severely limits plaintiffs' ability to challenge school segregation on this basis.[24] Our society must acknowledge and begin to dismantle the forces, past and present, that shape the neighborhood patterns that deny equal educational opportunity to so many children.

The Harms of Segregation and Concentrated Poverty

Educational disadvantage is closely linked to poverty—both the poverty of individual students and that of the schools they attend.[25] Educational disadvantage is particularly pronounced where poverty is concentrated. We know that students do better when their individual families' circumstances improve, but we also know that impoverished students do better if they live in middle-class neighborhoods or attend more affluent schools.[26] Persistent resource disparities in public education track the concentration of poverty, however.[27] So does race. Students of color are far more likely than whites to attend schools with larger proportions of students in poverty. The average white student in 2000 attended a school in which 19.1 percent of students were impoverished; in contrast, 44.1 percent of the classmates of the average Latino student were impoverished, as were 44.8 of the average black student's peers.[28]

Compared to desegregated schools, racially isolated schools with high proportions of low-income students of color more often rely on transitory teachers, have curricula with greater emphasis on remedial courses, have 15 percent larger class sizes overall, experience higher rates of tardiness and unexcused absence and lower rates of extracurricular involvement, and have far less access to technology and the resources available through the Internet.[29] Given these inequalities, racial segregation in public schools has devastating implications for the educational environment in which many students must attempt to prepare for meaningful futures.

The Role of Segregation in Perpetuating the Achievement Gap

Brown looked to a future free of racially imposed limitations on learning, but the harms caused by our failure fully to employ the means necessary to overcome the educational legacy of legally segregated housing and schools are compounded daily. Indeed, far from functioning as an equalizer among citizens, public education as measured by achievement is highly stratified by race.[30] On average, black students still score below 75 percent of whites on standardized tests.[31] This achievement gap begins before kindergarten and persists into adulthood. Black and Latino students obtain college degrees at half the rate of white students nationally.[32] And although a U.S. Department of Education study found that the gap between black and white students narrowed during the 1980s, it widened in the 1990s as our schools resegregated.[33] The intergenerational nature of segregation and concentrated poverty also affects student achievement, with students of all races performing better if their parents have more education.[34] The average 2003 SAT scores of students whose parents were at the top and bottom levels of income and education clearly demonstrate this pattern.[35]

Conservative explanations for the achievement gap tend to attribute these differences to genes, the "culture of poverty," single parenthood, or a lack of will—all of which, argue Christopher Jencks and Meredith Phillips, fail to find support in the available evidence.[36] A more viable explanation, documents Linda Darling-Hammond of Stanford University, is unequal access to key educational resources.[37]

The unequal access to educational opportunity of previous generations and the ongoing maintenance of educational inequality are thrown into high relief in the area of student placements. Nationally, black and Latino students are underrepresented in gifted and talented and advanced placement programs, and blacks are overrepresented in special education programs.[38] One of the most pernicious forms of segregation in our schools, tracking or ability grouping, is not necessarily destructive in theory but is often used to create segregated classrooms within outwardly desegregated schools. Even putting aside the contested educational value of such practices, having white children in advanced placement classes and black students in remedial classes not only fails to overcome family and neighborhood differences but in fact builds on them in ways that magnify existing racial and economic inequalities.

And can it be a coincidence that our fascination with tracking and ability groups occurred as we moved to desegregate the schools after *Brown*? We need to be sure that tracking that produces substantial racial disparities in the sorting of students is required to bear a heavy burden of justification, and school districts, schools, and teachers should make careful use of quantitative and qualitative data to avoid the kind of racial effects in course access that have been well documented by Roslyn Arlin Mickelson and others.[39] Indeed, the segregative effect of tracking that has racially unequal classroom-assignment consequences can be challenged under federal law, although a plaintiff challenging such inequity under the Fourteenth Amendment or Title VI would need to show that school officials intended to discriminate.[40] Even though courts frequently defer to educators on issues of what constitutes sound educational policy, the Applied Research Center and other researchers and advocates report that a more widespread awareness of the negative implications of tracking has resulted in a more conciliatory judiciary.[41]

Challenging standardized testing, however, is practically futile under current law.[42] Intended to equalize opportunity, improve achievement, and increase educational opportunities, high-stakes testing in fact often punishes students of color who attend inferior segregated schools. As the focus on testing grows, in addition to keeping our emphasis on accountability *to* students, we need to be clear about what we are measuring and deliberate about finding appropriate measurement tools. To be able to do basic math and reading is certainly important, but so are critical thinking and the ability to engage and interact with those different from oneself. Having perhaps finally realized that students must become culturally and racially fluent, how do we teach and test for this fluency? And how can we do so in schools that maintain rigid racial and class segregation?

Transforming Public Discourse on Race

Much of the legal language on the issue of segregation has been unhelpful in addressing these important issues. For example, the doctrine of color blindness as adopted by the courts has masked and tolerated extreme racial segregation through the use of legal fictions that ignore the injuries of the past and the goals necessary for a better future. The color-blind position legitimates and maintains the social, economic, and political advantages that whites hold over others. It is driven by a legal skepticism of racial categories and classifications; claims that all persons should be treated equally without reference to context, history, or culture; and assumes that the law recognizes only individuals, not groups, and should therefore not take race into account.

Color blindness at best conflates process with outcome. It focuses on the elimination of racial categories rather than of racism or racial hierarchy. It falsely propagates the idea that to talk about race is to perpetuate racism. To move beyond color blindness to racial justice, then, requires challenging the public story that racism is a thing of the past and that other battles have been or are being won—for example, the "war on drugs," welfare reform, equal opportunity in employment, and of course, integrated housing and education.

The first step we must take in achieving a transformation of this public discourse is to recognize race as a social construct. Race has no scientific reality, but it does have a powerful social reality: it orders and affects our real-life experiences. White America has always signified who is entitled to privilege, as we see so clearly in the case of educational disparities.

The second step we must take is to expose the institutional, structural, and systemic nature of racism. Laws and institutions need not be explicitly racist to disempower communities of color but need only produce or perpetuate unequal racial conditions.[43] In the context of education, while de jure segregation has disappeared, de facto segregation and resegregation persist, fueled by continued residential segregation, unequal educational funding, and other racialized institutional arrangements. In this way, while neutral on its face, the entire education system functions in racist ways.

Consequently, despite the courts' reluctance to acknowledge the role of racism in education and society and despite high poverty rates' strong effects on student outcomes, socioeconomic integration is not an adequate substitute for racial integration. There is good reason to support integrating schools economically: there is a high correlation between racial and economic isolation for Latino and black students. Race functions, however, in a way that is related to but different from class. As Gary Orfield explains, "Middle-class blacks and Latinos face discrimination on racial grounds, poor blacks and Latinos face dual discrimination, and even upper-class blacks tend to live in segregated patterns and experience differential treatment on the basis of race."[44]

In addition, addressing class without race might well meet with resistance equal to that against racial integration, intensify white flight, and increase housing segregation. Effective race-conscious plans, however, like Chicago's *Gautreaux* remedy,[45] demonstrate the dramatic improvements in employment and educational levels that can be achieved by families given no more than access to middle-class communities. Finally, socioeconomic remedies are not enforceable by law, which leaves persons of color dependent on political rather than civil rights remedies.

So color-blind control of discourse is not benign, and color-blind remedies to segregation are not adequate. They allow structural racism to go unacknowledged, which in turn allows whites to retain their oversubscription to resources and opportunities. We must, then, transform our ways of thinking and talking about race to acknowledge publicly that institutional, structural, and systemic racism implicates us all.[46]

Transforming Public Discourse on Choice

Another neutral-sounding phrase that limits important discussion is "public-school choice." Choice has been marketed very effectively in recent years in the form of vouchers, charter schools, and neighborhood schools (the most common form)—even to the point of equating it, and the free market system generally, with democracy itself. Choice is publicly discussed as a private act, although choices are in fact relational, with social consequences. If one is permitted to choose to maintain a school district as white and economically exclusive, for example, then the choices of nonwhite low-income students will necessarily be constrained. Fundamentally, transforming choice discourse requires that we recognize education as an important social good rather than as a mere private commodity. But even as "private" choices, the major innovations proffered by the choice movement are problematic from a social justice perspective.

Vouchers, for example, though touted as a tool to increase equity for low-income families, fail to address the subtle realities of racial and economic disparities that accompany school choice. These programs provide parents with a certain amount of tuition to use at schools of their choice. Yet voucher plans are often structured in such a way that they can be effectively used only within struggling school districts. Academically successful suburban schools can functionally opt out of these plans. Indeed some plans require that the vouchers be used inside urban school districts. Even where vouchers can be used outside central cities, acceptance of vouchers remains optional for receiving schools or districts, so suburban schools may be unwilling to participate for fear of becoming failing schools. A study by the Applied Research Center showed that California's voucher proposition would increase racial inequality, give false hope to those in need of education reform, and allow the persistence of practices that have a racist impact.[47]

Like vouchers, charter schools provide more educational choices but fail to deracialize choice or disturb racial hierarchy. "Race neutral," they have the potential to perpetuate racial hierarchies because of their regulatory freedom, which allows them to admit students selectively. And because their admissions practices are often not race conscious, charter schools increase segregation at the school level and may even provide school officials with a means to resegregate. Some charter schools will attract a large proportion of high-achieving students (partly because parents with resources have more choices), while others will enroll disproportionate numbers of students of color and low-income, high-needs, and limited-English-proficient students.[48]

Another "choice" for students of color, neighborhood schools, perpetuates the color-blind position by claiming to offer parents a natural and neutral choice of attending the closest school while masking the fact that parental choices will be skewed because of residential segregation. James Ryan notes that the larger choice plan in the country is the purchasing of housing, and it is structured to maintain racial and economic isolation and "good" schools.[49] As with other choice options, opportunities and constraints differ for whites and nonwhites. In terms of housing choice, even middle-class blacks have far fewer real choices than do whites, and only part of this difference can be explained by income. Low-income blacks often have little choice at all.[50]

Neighborhood schools, then, generally work this way: The highest bidders (i.e., parents with the greatest resources to investigate and select schools or parents who live in suburbs that can attract a substantial tax base) get to "choose" the best schools. The lowest bidders (i.e., parents who lack time, education, and resources or who live in the inner cities) get to "choose" the struggling schools. And, although they may be closer to home, struggling neighborhood schools by no means automatically increase parental involvement in communities and families where poverty is high. In fact, these schools most often firmly reinforce racial and economic isolation in housing, employment, and education.[51]

Structuring Choice

The reality of choice is that it is a racialized system that reproduces the inequity it is supposed to address. Effective responses to persistent segregation and concentrated poverty cannot be furnished by purely individualistic solutions such as letting students choose their schools one by one. The Supreme Court considered this approach after *Brown* and rejected it as inadequate.[52] The *Brown* Court noted that choice is not an end in itself and must not be used to perpetuate segregation. This is as valid today as it was fifty years ago. The rights of our children to a truly integrated education cannot be fully achieved in isolation from what happens to other children. We must, therefore, coordinate and structure choices to foster integration and safeguard against white supremacy. This requires talking about how racism compromises real choice. If students and parents of color were allowed to participate meaningfully in the creation of school and educational goals and practices, all students and parents would have a different set of choices.[53]

Transforming the discourse on choice may even result in more individual educational decision making. But in any case, allowing communities or individuals to subvert the need for broad social integration in the name of choice or local control is an outdated model that fails to take into consideration the fact that in economic terms, the viability of the entire community, whether metropolitan or global, depends on an educated citizenry, not a perpetual underclass.[54] It is in our self-interest to choose what is good for the whole, rather than just for our individual selves.[55]

Seeing Education as a Public Good

Given the important role that education plays in our democracy and given that the government already has its distributive hands on a good portion of public education, legal scholar James Liebman urges that we look to the communal nature of our rights under the Equal Protection Clause to help promote a view of education less as a private right that desegregation dislocates than as a public good that is appropriate for governmental and constitutional distribution: "Rather than being portrayed or vilified . . . as the redistribution of resources from 'innocent' whites to 'unjustly enriched' blacks . . . [a]n effective remedy . . . induce[s] . . . empathy by making each person recognize the interests she potentially shares with all other persons. . . . Once advocates give up arguing that desegregation corrects imbalances in the distribution of private rights when it palpably does not, they are free to point out that the rearrangement of private rights that *Brown* incidentally does effect is relatively inconsequential and clearly worth the politically reconstructive candle."[56]

Desegregation of public education, Kevin Brown has argued, should be viewed in light of its socializing function, its role in inculcating "fundamental values necessary to the transmission of our democratic society."[57] For example, "education must both foster individual self-determination, but at the same time attempt to constrain the choices individuals make in order to allow others the same ability for self-determination." Since desegregation clearly furthers the values of tolerance of racial and ethnic diversity, it should survive strict scrutiny analysis when examined from a value-inculcating perspective.[58]

The Supreme Court validated these ideas in *Grutter*. Even in dissent, Justice Antonin Scalia noted that "cross-racial understanding" and the ability to work with diverse groups are facets of good citizenship that should be learned in "public-school kindergartens,"[59] seemingly implying that the K–12 support structure for higher education is broken and that it is racially broken. Scalia argued that cross-racial understanding and the ability to work in a diverse society are not educational benefits but rather facets of "good citizenship." In the majority opinion,

Justice Sandra Day O'Connor adopted language from *Brown* in reminding us that "education . . . is the very foundation of good citizenship."[60]

This line of reasoning, with its emphasis on the communal values underlying public education and its broad social goals, has more recently been extended to K–12 school-assignment plans in districts that consider race among other factors to ensure that all students have access to well-supported, diverse public schools. Most recently, a federal court upheld the Louisville school district's managed-choice plan, which strives to keep schools integrated. The court acknowledged that the plan serves several compelling interests, among them the improved educational experiences of and benefits for all students attending diverse schools.[61] A similar case in Lynn, Massachusetts, upheld a policy that took race into account when considering student transfers out of neighborhood schools. Although a First Circuit Court of Appeals panel subsequently struck down the policy, the case is scheduled for rehearing before all of the judges.[62] Another federal Court of Appeals panel, this time in the Ninth Circuit, struck down a Seattle assignment plan that used race as a tiebreaker in assigning students to oversubscribed high schools. The extent to which public school districts can consider race in their assignment plans, therefore, has yet to be fully resolved at the federal level.[63]

Renewing Legal Strategies under Federal Law

Given the new support that *Grutter* provides for decreasing racial isolation and increasing opportunities for integrated education in our central social enterprise, what can we do to move more rapidly toward those goals? A number of strategies have proved or might prove useful in advancing true integration, but a very important caveat must be taken into account before considering these and other strategies: we must hold fast to the goals we are trying to achieve and measure progress by outcomes, not simply by adherence to process.

The exact constellation of strategies that will work will vary based on context. Consider the limitations of school desegregation in areas where there are multiple and fractured school districts or the limitations of funding redistribution where there are a number of schools with concentrated poverty and high-poverty neighborhoods. Moreover, even if one were sure which procedures would produce the desired outcomes in a given context, the context might change, either because of unforeseen developments or because of white resistance and retrenchment. It is impossible to fully anticipate the next challenges, but if we focus on outcomes, not just procedures and process, and remain clear about the goal, we can ask the questions that will move us forward.

Some have argued that from a legal standpoint, *Brown* has run its course,[64] that the Supreme Court will eventually rule, as have the Second and Fourth Circuits, that race neutrality is required in K–12 student assignments except where race is used as a remedy for past discrimination. To be sure, there is a basis for this claim. During the past decade, courts have been rapidly declaring that school districts have achieved unitary status, effectively reversing the twenty-five-year-old standard requiring affirmative behavior to eliminate racially segregated schools.[65] Current federal jurisprudence provides limited avenues for effecting positive change in the racial makeup of schools or school districts. Since *Keyes v. School District No. 1, Denver, Colorado* and *Washington v. Davis*, to prove that a school policy or practice violates the Fourteenth Amendment, a plaintiff must demonstrate that the policy was enacted with the specific intent to discriminate against a class of students based on their race, ethnicity, or national origin. This is an extremely difficult standard to meet.[66] Private suits under Title VI can also be brought only for intentional discrimination.

Grutter, however, made some important contributions to the federal law on education. It established nonremedial interests that justify the use of race,[67] holding that advancing educational diversity is a forward-looking interest[68] necessary to develop a broadly accepted leadership class, combat stereotypes, acknowledge our diverse society, and prepare students for diverse workplaces. The language seems to allow educational institutions to decide for themselves whether student body diversity is important. How best to encourage school boards and districts to voluntarily integrate then becomes a question of some urgency, and conducting research and disseminating information on the value and success of diversity in education become much more important. Although some time is always needed for the full meaning of a decision to emerge, *Grutter* signals the country's willingness to reexamine race and racial inequality, and it should also refocus our attention on the way we are handling these issues in K–12 education.

Renewing Strategies under State Law

More than just the federal courts have begun to reengage with the imperative of integrated education. Virtually all states have provisions in their constitutions guaranteeing an efficient or adequate education, and over the past twenty years, lawsuits under these provisions have successfully challenged racial and economic segregation of students as well as school finance policies. All state constitutions guarantee protections similar to those of the Fourteenth Amendment, and the state courts have the authority to interpret these protections more broadly than the protections under the U.S. Constitution—allowing actions based on racially disparate impact, for example.[69] All state constitutions also recognize education as a function of the state: some explicitly prohibit discrimination or the implementation of educational policies with discriminatory effects, and others guarantee a certain minimum level of education to all students.

State court litigation to date has largely challenged the equity or adequacy of state public school funding mechanisms. Equity suits assert that state constitutions (through their equal protection or education clauses) guarantee some degree of equality in school funding across districts. Adequacy suits assert that these provisions require the state to provide some minimum quality of education to all students and that an adequate education, in turn, requires a basic level of funding.[70]

Remedies under adequacy suits vary greatly. In *Rose v. Council for Better Education*, the court invalidated Kentucky's entire public school system and required the state legislature to implement a detailed instructional plan that placed responsibility on the state. In *Sheff v. O'Neill*, a state court found that extreme racial and ethnic isolation in public schools had resulted from a merely voluntary interdistrict desegregation effort and placed an affirmative duty on the Connecticut legislature to remedy school segregation, regardless of whether it arose de jure or de facto. In *Hoke County Board of Education v. State of North Carolina* ("*Leandro*"), the state supreme court upheld orders requiring the state to provide services and other resources necessary to assure that low-performing students receive a sound basic education. The court explicitly stated that these constitutional rights are vested in the state's children not only in their school years but as early as infancy and that young children at risk of academic failure could receive services before entering school to ensure that they arrive at kindergarten ready to learn. These cases are concerned both with inputs—what resources go into educating students—and, equally importantly, with the outcomes of the states' educational processes. They ask, What are the minimum educational requirements for preparing students to function in society? and What is required to meet the need for students to function in a diverse society, especially when that need is undermined by racial segregation and isolation?

Since *Grutter* established that diversity is a compelling state interest in the context of educating students, in a state with a fundamental right to education, one could argue that diversity (integration) is required wherever practicable and that failure to implement it is a denial of adequate education. Such a finding would require that states seriously address the social goals found compelling in *Grutter*. A court would likely find reasonable efforts to achieve diverse public schools to be narrowly tailored, since the tailoring requirement is designed to protect innocent parties from race-based denial of public benefits. In the K–12 public education context, there is no issue of scarcity—all students are guaranteed an education—so this issue is muted, leaving opponents with the dubious argument that they are getting a lesser education because they were denied the right to attend racially segregated schools.

Pursuing Integration beyond Jurisdictional Borders

Education is a state function, and the drawing of school district as well as municipal boundaries is subject to the rule and purview of the state. The widespread practice of allowing fragmented zoning at the jurisdictional level encourages racial and economic segregation between districts, yet the Supreme Court talks about this fragmentation as it would some impenetrable natural barrier. It is anything but.[71] Moreover, a growing body of research demonstrates that the more fragmented a region, the more likely that there will be racial and economic segregation at the jurisdictional level. It makes little sense to reward cities for engaging in exclusionary zoning practices that keep out students of color and students from low-income families, yet that is exactly what we do. Then, after we allow zoning to separate our students, we often allow funding and local property taxes to segregate the money for students.

Some state courts have been willing to challenge the notion of immunity that school districts or municipalities invoke in this context, but federal courts since *Milliken v. Bradley* (1974) have been protective of this arrangement. Strategies of reinvestment in inner cities offer some amelioration of conditions and are meritorious, but a regional approach to policy making is required to significantly reduce polarization, stabilize urban cores, and equalize educational opportunity throughout metropolitan areas.[72]

Because the real city is the total metropolitan area—city and suburb—the surest way to avoid or reverse patterns of racial and economic segregation is to create effective, visionary metropolitan governments or, if the metro area is too large, to ensure that all local governments pursue common policies that foster integration and diminish segregation. Myron Orfield calls this process of achieving regionalism "metropolitics."[73] Effective regional governments require the building of enduring political coalitions, and such coalitions are often formed between the urban core and the inner-ring suburbs. Progressive business leaders like those who created Chicago Metropolis 2020 also promote regionalism because it is the most effective strategy for maintaining economic viability.[74]

A regionalist approach most often includes (1) land-use reform that stems urban sprawl and provides adequate funding to older areas with aging infrastructure; (2) opportunity-based housing policies that encourage or, better yet, require the construction and maintenance of low- and moderate-income housing in all jurisdictions associated with opportunity, such as good schools; (3) fair employment and fair housing policies; (4) tax-sharing arrangements that offset tax-base disparities between the central city and its suburbs; (5) welfare reform that focuses on job readiness and creation in core poverty neighborhoods and tackles the related issues of transportation, child care, and health care; and (6) until affordable housing is available across the region, lawsuits calling for adequate education in the inner-ring schools and metropolitan-wide desegregation.[75]

Federal and state governments can foster reform through regionalism by providing bonuses in grants-in-aid formulas and incentives to promote the formation of forward-looking metropolitan governments.[76] State governments can facilitate city-county consolidation, create housing policies that require affordable housing to be built in opportunity-rich areas, utilize state aid as a revenue-equalizing mechanism, and require a minimum guaranteed income or minimum living wage.

Regionalism has sometimes met with resistance from people of color because of the perception that it could fragment their communities. Deconcentration of persons of color is seen as resulting in both their assimilation into more affluent areas and the dilution of their culture and political power in areas where white flight and poverty persist.[77] Far too often, when low-income people are forced to move, they are displaced to low-opportunity areas. People are much less likely to resist moving if they are given both a voice in the process and a chance to move to greater opportunity. And although moving can be stressful and larger political and cultural issues such as vote dilution merit attention, ways exist to address these concerns, and the potential gains from moving to opportunity are large in both economic and educational terms.

Attempting to solve the problems of concentrated poverty through the infusion of new resources can be much more challenging. Money invested in segregated schools yields far lower results than the same money invested in metrowide desegregation. Segregated schools in Kansas City, Missouri, for example, underwent a $1.4 billion court-ordered lowering of class sizes, renovation of severely deteriorated facilities, and initiation of the most extensive magnet school plan in the nation. The court-appointed monitoring committee has reported very limited gains.[78] By contrast, as Susan Leigh Flinspach and Karen E. Banks have noted, Raleigh, North Carolina, acted in the mid-1970s to stop school segregation and the emptying out of its urban areas, and its economy has prospered as its schools thrived.[79] Stories from other cities support the effectiveness of interdistrict efforts and caution against fragmentation and its accompanying segregation.

Metropolitan-wide planning should be incorporated into student assignment through district consolidation (combining urban and suburban districts) whenever possible. Where there is the political will, districts can be dissolved or consolidated by the state. District boundaries can also be redrawn within a metropolitan area into fewer, larger, more racially balanced districts, or inner-ring suburban districts can be merged with those in the inner city. More than thirty years of court-ordered school desegregation has confirmed that the most extensive desegregation plans are the most effective both in terms of achieving desegregated schools and in maintaining stable levels of enrollment metrowide.[80] Among states with the largest average size of school districts, none report much more than one-third of black students in intensely segregated schools, whereas states with relatively small school districts and fragmented district patterns have experienced the highest levels of segregation of black students.[81]

What *True* Integration Requires

Education is our most important public resource for overcoming family socioeconomic disparities, enhancing life opportunities, developing citizens, and promoting a genuine multiracial and multiethnic democracy. Racially segregated education negatively impacts all citizens and undermines the goal of constructing a multiracial and multiethnic democracy. We need to provide all children with a truly integrated education. As Dr. Martin Luther King Jr. wrote in *The Ethical Demands for Integration,*

> Integration is creative, and is therefore more profound and far-reaching than desegregation. . . . Integration is genuine intergroup, interpersonal doing. Desegregation then rightly is only a short-range goal. Integration is the ultimate goal of our national community.
>
> Thus as America pursues the important task of respecting the letter of the law, i.e., compliance with desegregation decisions, she must be equally concerned with the spirit of the law, i.e., commitment to the democratic dream of integration.[82]

Desegregation is only the first step in eradicating segregation. It must be followed by the transformative and inclusive goal of true integration. Nowhere is the task more essential than in our nation's public schools. Never was the timing more urgent than it is now, as our schools resegregate and as we abandon what are admittedly limited desegregation efforts, donning the color-blind mask of school choice and accountability instead.

True integration moves beyond desegregation—beyond removing legal barriers and simply placing together students of different races. It means bringing students together under conditions of equality, emphasizing common goals, and deemphasizing interpersonal competition. Because segregation creates a culture of racial hierarchy and subordination, true integration requires community-wide efforts to dismantle that culture and to create a more inclusive educational system and a more inclusive society in which all individuals and groups have real, equal opportunities to build and participate in the democratic process.

True integration in our schools, then, is transformative rather than assimilative. That is, while desegregation assimilates minorities into the mainstream, true integration transforms the mainstream. It does not assume that blacks will benefit if they sit next to whites and some of their whiteness rubs off. Rather, it recognizes that cultures are not static but are constantly evolving and that all students benefit from a truly equal and just system of education. Integration is inclusive, placing value on all groups' historical, intellectual, and cultural contributions. As a result, truly integrated schools are creative and are best equipped to prepare students for life in our changing, pluralistic democracy.

To achieve this result, true integration addresses the issues of achievement, opportunity, community, and relevancy at a systemic level. In this process, institutions, communities, and individuals are fundamentally changed to foster multiracial and multiethnic social interaction and to provide equal opportunities for students of all colors.[83] Mandatory, interdistrict desegregation or consolidation is just an initial and temporary step in this structural transformation. We must then link housing, school, economic, political, and cultural opportunities and spread accountability throughout entire metropolitan areas via regional planning.[84] Only then can the changes we make within the school take on new meaning for students. Integration is a process; the nature of the experience is, therefore, crucial.[85]

A truly integrated school must employ teaching techniques that address the multitude of student learning styles and utilize learning materials fashioned by and about people of diverse racial and ethnic backgrounds in more than an "add-on" fashion. In addition, a truly integrated school must create a supportive atmosphere to improve student self-esteem and motivation and encourage positive interactions both in the school and beyond. This requires transforming accountability measures, tracking, discipline policies, curricula, and the entire school environment, including extracurricular activities.

As the U.S. Supreme Court recognized in *Grutter*, students who find themselves in a distinct minority within a school can withdraw or be excluded. Teachers may not respond to their needs. The establishing of status can have powerful positive or negative effects on student achievement outcomes depending on what capital the groups bring and on the approaches adopted by teachers.[86] But at the most basic level—whatever the racial or socioeconomic ratio of students—coherent, purposeful efforts must be made at the district, school, classroom, and student levels to carry out the mandate of *Brown* as rearticulated in *Grutter*.

There is much to gain. Increasing access to the best teaching and curricula for students of differing abilities can encourage teachers to develop more inclusive teaching strategies that benefit all children.[87] And mixed-ability-level classes can markedly reduce the number of discipline problems that are natural outgrowths of the low expectations and sense of failure common in lower-track classes.[88] Racially balanced classes also often produce positive interracial attitudes and behaviors—influencing, for example, students' choices of lunchtime companions.[89] Moreover, multiple studies show that enrollment in higher-level, challenging classes increases test scores and college attendance rates for low-income black and Latino students just as surely as it does for higher income and white students.[90]

The goals of truly integrated schools must go beyond educating students in an inclusive and multicultural environment. If we are partially constituted by our environment, then the injury of segregation cannot be fully measured by an achievement gap. Our very humanity is compromised. Toni Morrison has captured this in her observation that we have considered how our history of racial hierarchy has distorted the lives of blacks but have devoted very little thought to what this system has done to the lives of whites.[91] Integration then is both an external and an internal process; we need to integrate not only the students inside the building but the hearts and minds of the students as well.

These changes must be made in holistic or "integrated" efforts rather than in piecemeal, individualized, or compartmentalized ones, and the efforts of the larger community must include legal, legislative, and educational approaches. To be effective, these approaches require an accompanying reconfiguration of our collective understanding and political will, particularly when we talk about education as a public good or the need for regional strategies such as fair-share housing. Districtwide, school site, and individual classroom efforts are all essential, and we must develop an evaluative template to help us determine how well schools are meeting these integrative goals.[92]

Taking Enough Time to Integrate

True integration, like democracy, is a process that must be constantly practiced and may never be fully achieved. It is what Jurgen Habermas calls a regulative ideal.[93] It is an ongoing engagement rather than an event. Its evolution requires us to look at other interactive structures, such as housing, in addition to education efforts and at the larger structure of opportunity that supports or retards human and social development. Some observers will claim that desegregation and—by extension and confusion—integration have already been tried and have failed. But while reasons for concern exist, powerful reasons also exist to reject every part of this claim: that we have tried as a nation to desegregate, that desegregation is the same as integration, and that we have failed. Although many of our efforts have been fraught with compromise and ambivalence, we have made some progress and done some things right.

Justice O'Connor in *Grutter* shared a hope that in twenty-five years we would no longer need remedial or nonremedial race-conscious approaches to school inclusion and student assignment. Hers is a good hope to hold onto, yet stark temporal facts remain: twenty-four years after *Brown*, the integrated education debate entered the courts via *Bakke*, and almost fifty years after *Brown*, the debate went to court in *Grutter*. While it is important to understand our past, it may be more important to look—as the *Grutter* Court does—to our future. Students must be involved not only in critical thinking but also in critical imagining. Our future depends on a positive vision of a diverse democratic society, and we have neither the luxury of deferral nor justification for failure.

The myriad initiatives required to achieve true integration in our communities and schools must not deter us from the task. Rather, we must undertake a massive campaign to educate the public about the necessity of these initiatives, to determine the scope of the task, and to insist that these measures be fully implemented—immediately or certainly within Justice O'Connor's stated goal of twenty-five years. Armed with the knowledge that segregation harms our children as well as our democracy and ready to admit that we have not done desegregation well enough, we can combat the color-blind position and the predominance of school-choice and accountability measures by advocating a transformation of our educational system into a vividly multiracial and multiethnic one. To achieve such a transformation, however, we must first take off our individualistic blinders and see the connections among who we are and where we live and what we want for our children and our nation. That is, we must integrate our lives with our efforts. Only then will we be able to truly integrate our schools.

Notes

1. *Grutter v. Bollinger*, 334 (quoting *Plyler v. Doe*).
2. Unger, *False Necessity*.
3. Boger and Wegner, *Race, Poverty, and American Cities*; G. Orfield, *Schools More Separate*.
4. For a discussion of the legal meaning of "segregation" and the problems with it, see powell, Kearney, and Kay, *In Pursuit*.
5. See L. Ware and M. Ware, "*Plessy*'s Legacy."
6. See Bell, *Race, Racism, and American Law*.
7. Brief of Lt. Gen. Julius W. Becton Jr. et al., 27.
8. Loury, *Anatomy of Racal Inequality*.

9. Dewey, *Democracy and Education*, 20.

10. Brief of Amicus Curiae General Motors Corporation, 4.

11. *Grutter*, 334.

12. G. Orfield, *Schools More Separate*.

13. Civil Rights Project, "2000 Segregation Levels for U.S."

14. Jargowsky, "Ghetto Poverty."

15. Civil Rights Project, "2000 Segregation Levels for U.S."

16. Jargowsky, "Ghetto Poverty."

17. The federal government defines concentrated poverty as a census tract with 40 percent or greater of its residents living below poverty level. As of 1990, close to 2,800 of the nation's 45,000 census tracks experienced concentrated poverty, compared with only 1,000 in 1970. Civil Rights Project, "2000 Segregation Levels for U.S."

18. Ibid.

19. Marable, *Great Wells of Democracy*.

20. George, "Dwell in My Love."

21. Oliver and Shapiro, *Black Wealth/White Wealth*. The per capita wealth differential between blacks and whites is 1:11, with the net worth of blacks, measured in terms of home equity and financial assets, remaining at more than $40,000 less than that of whites.

22. From the earliest zoning laws to racial covenants, from redlining and discrimination in mortgage lending to exclusionary zoning, housing choices for black families have been limited by both public and private agents. The struggle to establish housing rights preceded and was integral to the push for desegregated schools. See generally Massey and Denton, *American Apartheid*.

23. Massey and Denton, *American Apartheid*; Denton, "Persistence." For a detailed discussion of the link between housing and education, see powell, "Living and Learning"; powell, Kearney, and Kay, *In Pursuit*.

24. *Keyes v. School District No. 1, Denver, Colorado*.

25. G. Orfield, *Schools More Separate*.

26. Schellenberg, "Concentration of Poverty," 130, 137; Rosenbaum et al., "Can the Kerner Commission's Housing Strategy Improve Employment?" 1519.

27. Education Trust, *Other Gap*.

28. Frankenberg, Lee, and Orfield, *Multiracial Society*.

29. National Commission, *What Matters Most*; Council of Chief State School Officers, *Helping Students*.

30. By the end of the fourth grade, students in poverty as well as African American and Latino students are already two years behind other students; by the eighth grade, three years behind; and by the twelfth grade, four years behind. See Haycock, Jerald, and Huang, *Closing the Gap*.

31. Ibid.

32. Ibid.

33. G. Orfield, *Schools More Separate*.

34. Belluck, "Reason Is Sought." Segregation and the lack of cultural fluency may also play a larger role than has yet been acknowledged. See Freedle, "Correcting the SAT's Ethnic and Social-Class Bias"; Mathews, "Bias Question."

35. The average scores were 444 for students with family income levels under $10,000

but 568 for those over $100,000; 443 for children of high school dropouts but 569 for students whose parents had attended graduate school. College Board, "2003 College Bound Seniors."

36. Jencks and Phillips, *Black-White Test Score Gap.*

37. Darling-Hammond, "Unequal Opportunity."

38. See data from the Education Trust at ‹http://www2.edtrust.org/edtrust›, 3 March 2004.

39. Mickelson, this volume. See also Welner, *Legal Rights, Local Wrongs.*

40. Losen, "Silent Segregation," 518.

41. See, e.g., Welner and Oakes, "(Li)Ability Grouping."

42. See Heubert, this volume.

43. Ford, "Boundaries," 449–50.

44. G. Orfield, "Response."

45. See Rosenbaum et al., "Can the Kerner Commission's Housing Strategy Improve Employment?"

46. Even if there is agreement about education reform and about institutional arrangements that burden students of color, it is doubtful that this will produce the policy changes necessary for transformation. Because powerful whites apparently benefit from the existing arrangement, they have resisted any change that will disturb what Lipsitz has called their possessive investment in whiteness. See Lipsitz, *Possessive Investment.* But this does not suggest leaving such arrangements unchallenged. Instead, it suggests a strategy that can transform and realign some of these interests. An example of this would be some of the suggestions regarding equalizing funding, in which whites see themselves as winning.

47. T. Johnson, Della Piana, and Burlingame, "Vouchers."

48. The proportion of black students attending intensely segregated charter schools (70 percent) is twice that of black public school students in general (34 percent). Frankenberg and Lee, *Charter Schools and Race,* 7.

49. Ryan and Heise, "Political Economy."

50. See, e.g., Massey and Denton, *American Apartheid.*

51. This problem was documented in the study of the *Gautreaux* remedy mentioned earlier. See Rosenbaum et al., "Can the Kerner Commission's Housing Strategy Improve Employment?"

52. *Green v. County School Board of New Kent County.* Indeed, tuition vouchers, charter schools, and choice plans all emerged as possible tools for maintaining racially segregated schools in the wake of the *Brown* decision.

53. For a review of research on increasing parent involvement in schools, see, e.g., Boethel, *Diversity.*

54. Much about schools is not and probably should not be local. Most states and school districts have some form of state-equalized funding. The curriculum is often set by the state. School district boundaries are determined by the state, and now accountability and testing processes are set by the state and the federal governments. After graduating, students often will not stay in a given community for work or further schooling. So what is the reason for the strong claim for local control? My point is not to abandon local control but to challenge its segregative function in our society. This is part of a much larger issue. Roberto Unger urges that institutional arrangements in society are never neutral. See, e.g., Unger,

False Necessity. This in itself is not a problem, but when the institutional arrangements consistently distribute benefits along racial lines, it is a problem, and such arrangements must be on the table for consideration, whether or not racial motives have been enunciated.

55. Indeed, there is good reason to take a global view of this issue, drawing on international human rights law in seeking support for equity and integration in our public schools. See, e.g., the United Nations General Assembly, *Universal Declaration*, *International Covenant on Economic, Social, and Cultural Rights*, and *International Covenant on Civil and Political Rights*; see also the General Assembly's *Convention on the Rights of the Child*, *International Convention on the Elimination of All Forms of Racial Discrimination*, *Convention against Discrimination in Education*, and *Declaration*. Although these standards are not binding on our courts and cannot be the basis for legal action, our courts do turn to them for guidance in defining rights provided under U.S. law. For example, the West Virginia court in the adequacy case *Pauley v. Kelly* cited the importance of education in international human rights documents, recognizing education to be a "fundamental right of everyone." *Pauley v. Kelly*, 863–64 n. 5 (quoting *Universal Declaration of Human Rights*).

56. Liebman, "Implementing *Brown*," 362–363.

57. K. Brown, "Implications," 1002.

58. Ibid., 1003. Brown also argues that as long as the use of racial classifications to bring about integrated student bodies furthers the internalization of the importance of treating all as individuals, then their use is also narrowly tailored enough to meet that compelling interest (1006).

59. *Grutter*, 344–45 (Scalia, dissenting in part).

60. Ibid., 334 (quoting *Brown v. Board of Education*).

61. *McFarland v. Jefferson County Public Schools*.

62. *Comfort ex rel. Neumyer v. Lynn School Committee* also upheld the Massachusetts Racial Imbalance Act.

63. *Parents Involved in Community Schools v. Seattle School District No. 1*.

64. See Kahlenberg, "Socioeconomic School Integration."

65. See M. Ware, "School Desegregation," 465–66. As G. Orfield and Yun, *Resegregation*, document, school districts recently ending or phasing out desegregation plans include Buffalo, New York; Broward County (Fort Lauderdale), Florida; Clark County (Las Vegas), Nevada; Nashville–Davidson County, Tennessee; Duval County (Jacksonville), Florida; Mobile, Alabama; Minneapolis, Minnesota; Cleveland, Ohio; San Jose, California; Seattle, Washington; and Wilmington, Delaware. A number of other major districts are now in litigation over the issue, with some of them struggling to be permitted to continue their desegregation plans.

66. Courts look less favorably on school systems that remain under desegregation orders. For example, Fourteenth Amendment challenges to tracking policies that negatively impact students of color have succeeded against school districts that already have been ordered to remedy the effects of past discrimination.

67. Joint Statement, *Reaffirming Diversity*.

68. Civil Rights Project, *Overview*.

69. *Jackson v. Pasadena City School District*.

70. See, e.g., *Campaign for Fiscal Equity, Inc. v. the State of New York*, in which the Court of Appeals ordered the state to determine the cost of providing a sound basic education to

all of the state's students; to reform the funding system in such a way that all schools would have the resources necessary to provide such an opportunity; and to implement accountability measures to ensure that the reforms work.

71. Massey and Denton, *American Apartheid.*

72. M. Orfield, *Metropolitics.*

73. Ibid.

74. See Chicago Metropolis 2020, "One Region, One Future."

75. See M. Orfield, *Metropolitics*, 11, 87–90; Rusk, *Inside Game, Outside Game*, 85–87, 123.

76. Rusk, *Inside Game, Outside Game*, 90–115.

77. West, *Keeping Faith.* Cornel West has argued that the dispersion of black professionals and entrepreneurs into predominantly white communities does little to change the culture and values of the white opportunity structure.

78. G. Orfield and Thronson, "Dismantling Desegregation," 782.

79. Flinspach and Banks, this volume.

80. G. Orfield, "Metropolitan School Desegregation."

81. Ibid., 839–42.

82. King, "Ethical Demands," 118.

83. powell, "Tensions," 695.

84. powell, "Is Racial Integration Essential?"

85. Schofield, "Promoting Positive Intergroup Relations."

86. For a study of how teaching styles affected the success of integration in the wake of the economic desegregation of public schools in La Crosse, Wisconsin, see Plank, *Finding One's Place.*

87. Ibid.

88. See Welner, *Legal Rights, Local Wrongs*, 170. Intriguing new studies have recorded marked drops in IQ and achievement scores as well as increased apathy and hostility among adults randomly chosen for exclusion or rejection. See Twenge and Baumeister, "Social Exclusion."

89. Sagar and Schofield, *Peer Interaction Patterns*; Sagar and Schofield, *Classroom Interaction Patterns*; Sagar and Schofield, "Interracial Interaction."

90. R. Johnson, *Using Data.*

91. Morrison, *Playing*; Stowe, "Uncolored People."

92. The diversity assessment questionnaire discussed in Ma and Kurlaender's chapter in this volume provides an example of a tool districts can use to assess their inclusiveness in regard to course taking, counseling, and climate. For a sample analysis, see Civil Rights Project, "Impact."

93. Habermas, *Moral Consciousness and Communicative Action.*

CONCLUSION

JOHN CHARLES BOGER

Brown and the American South

Fateful Choices

The Supreme Court's unanimous decision in *Brown v. Board of Education* has prompted five decades of intense struggle over the future of American public education and, more deeply, over the meaning of the nation's commitment to equality under the law. Despite subsequent disappointments, failures, and partial measures in implementing *Brown*, nothing has diminished either its central insight that "separate educational facilities are inherently unequal" or its implicit holding that African Americans and other nonwhites are constitutionally entitled to and must be afforded the full measure of American citizenship from the nation's courts and other public institutions.

Yet many of the authors who have contributed to this volume are profoundly troubled about the future of racially integrated public education fifty years after *Brown*, and nowhere more so than in the American South, where *Brown* worked its greatest social transformation and had its greatest educational successes. Some of these authors feel a professional obligation as legal scholars, empirical analysts, and students of public policy to document the reemergence of school resegregation, to warn about the vast potential costs if racially integrated schools disappear, and to plead subtly with public officials and citizens alike, as Justice Robert Jackson wrote in another context, "to be last, not first, to give them up."[1]

At stake are the accomplishments of a painstaking political, social, and educational reform, carried out by a broad, often uneasy coalition of civil rights advocates, federal judges, governmental officials, and educators who worked throughout the latter half of the twentieth century, sometimes against overwhelming odds, to end the dual system of white and black schools and fashion its replacement.[2] It is vital to remember that in so doing, these men and women faced and overcame something far more unyielding than a system of school segregation. Their deepest and most formidable opponent was America's mid-twentieth-century political regime, which accepted white supremacy as official policy in most southern states and as daily practice in many others.[3]

Thanks to extraordinarily brave public and private efforts, not only the widespread, state-mandated segregation of the nation's schools but this broader "American apartheid" was repudiated both in law and in fact. Laws and customs that had long authorized the segregation of courtrooms, public theaters, restaurants, city parks, playgrounds, and, indeed, all public and private employment—interwoven systems of racial oppression that had been universally accepted as a commonplace of American life—were gradually dismantled. African Americans and Latinos fought to free themselves from official subordination and to widen access to the American political process, taking their rightful places as voters, candidates, officeholders, and judges.[4]

Ironically, although these principles of nondiscrimination have steadily gained acceptance in American law and polity, the racially segregated schools that *Brown* condemned have gradually reappeared across the educational landscape, as the empirical contributions to this volume reveal (Reardon and Yun; Clotfelter, Ladd, and Vigdor; Mickelson; Laosa; Frankenberg).[5] While no school districts today are segregated in obedience to formal constitutional or statutory decrees, the emerging demographic realities are just as powerful, their effects on the education and socialization of America's children just as devastating—especially since racial segregation tends to go hand in hand with isolation by social class, as other contributors to this volume suggest (Rumberger and Palardy; Laosa; Heubert; Freeman, Scafidi, and Sjoquist; Wells and Holme).

How can we reconcile two contradictory developments, America's increasingly bipartisan commitment to oppose racial injustice and its widespread acquiescence in the resegregation of public schooling across much of the South—the region that, by the 1970s, possessed the most racially integrated schools in the nation?

Clear evidence for our national commitment to fight racial injustice begins in the political sphere: both major political parties employ a rhetoric that explicitly affirms the value of racial diversity.[6] Colleges and universities demonstrated their support for these principles in "friend of the Court" briefs filed with the Supreme Court in 2003, defending affirmative action admissions policies that would ensure the continuance of racially diverse student bodies.[7] Hundreds of public and private institutions throughout the nation worked in 2004 to commemorate and celebrate the fiftieth anniversary of the *Brown* decision. Yet as contributors to this volume have also documented, widespread public indifference has greeted the reemergence of school segregation. Indeed, many communities have demonstrated hostility toward the student-assignment policies needed to preserve meaningful racial integration in our public schools.

Unless and until we uncover the root causes of this apparent contradiction, there seems little prospect that the drift toward school resegregation will abate or that john a. powell's "true integration" will receive a broad educational test.

White Support for Public School Integration: Why Has It Waned?

One plausible source of this contradiction might lie in continuing (though unspoken) racial prejudice. The advances of the *Brown* era, this hypothesis would suggest, were more illusory than real. Whites cracked open their schoolhouse doors under compulsion from the Warren Court, but only as wide as federal courts required and not an inch further. When the federal judicial commitment to the *Brown* imperative began to wane in the mid-1980s and 1990s, those doors began to close again, though by subtler means, with the result that nonwhite elementary and secondary students again find themselves set apart in racially separate schools. While the Supreme Court was politically unable to repudiate the formal commitments made by the Warren Court, the more conservative Burger and Rehnquist Courts have silently assured whites that no further judicial intervention will impose practical equality. In this altered legal climate, traditional southern majorities have begun to reassert their preference for white exclusivity in their public schools, as Erwin Chemerinsky discusses in this volume. This hypothesis is consistent with Derrick Bell's argument for the "permanence of racism" in American life.[8]

Yet although a significant minority of white Americans doubtless still retain some sense of white superiority and although many more silently harbor uneasiness in mixed-race settings, numerous reliable surveys of American attitudes reveal that white racial prejudice has abated significantly in the past three decades (if so, almost certainly as a consequence of *Brown* and the broader civil rights movement of the 1950s and 1960s).[9] Far more has changed, moreover, than just attitudes. Whites have altered their behavior in everything from home-buying choices to decisions on employee hiring and promotion in ways that suggest lessened prejudice against African Americans and other nonwhites.[10] If these behavioral changes really do reflect an underlying shift in racial attitudes, the question becomes even more puzzling: what explains the current drift toward school resegregation?

john a. powell has suggested that many people who resist mandatory integration believe that since racial segregation has been legally vanquished as state policy, any residual segregation is the product of individual choice. This focus on the "educational choice movement" offers a crucial insight. In every generation, Americans struggle to mediate between and accommodate two fundamental political and social ideals, each with deep roots in America's past. Abraham Lincoln named both in his immortal address at Gettysburg, where he spoke of "a new nation, conceived in Liberty, and dedicated to the proposition that all men are created equal." Americans in every generation must prioritize these two venerable values, weighing their desire for individual freedom against their commitment to equal opportunity and collective responsibility.[11]

Measured on that scale, many Americans in this first decade of the twenty-first century have opted for liberty—some beguiling amalgam of individualism, libertarianism, and market theory. Whites who live in the South and West appear especially likely to have cherished liberty over equality.[12] In the area of public education, this preference translates into a demand for greater "freedom of choice" in selecting their children's schools. Many such parents view schools as consumer goods, understand their children and families as consumers of those goods, and consider their exercise of personal choice among competing educational products to be an inherent right.[13]

Wealthier parents have, for better or worse, long enjoyed considerable flexibility in making educational choices, since their financial resources give them multiple options in selecting or changing their community of residence. Yet many nonwealthy parents now insist that they too should be entitled to significant discretion in choosing their children's school placements even within local school districts; in consequence, local school boards have lost much of their prerogative to assign children for a variety of social ends.[14] The shift in the role of magnet schools illustrates this transformation in public attitudes. Initially designed as a tool to encourage racial desegregation, each magnet school adopted some special educational emphasis (e.g., science, the arts, Montessori methods) to entice students voluntarily to cross racial lines.[15] Yet in recent years, the magnet idea has been decoupled, in the popular mind, from its original desegregative function. Many parents today see magnet schools solely as avenues to serve their children's special interests; indeed, some decry any school board efforts to consider student racial composition to maintain diversity in magnet schools.[16]

The charter school movement, less than fifteen years old, offers willing parents and disgruntled educators still other choices—quasi-independent schools paid for with public funds that can operate independent of local public school bureaucracies and educational priorities except for their "charter" obligations negotiated with local or state school boards in exchange for their freedom.[17] The school voucher movement (recently given constitutional support by a narrowly divided Supreme Court) permits parents a still more radical choice—to leave the public schooling system altogether, with a state voucher sufficient to purchase educational options in the private market.[18]

Many parents imbued with values of educational choice bristle at the suggestion that their support for these choices and their relative indifference to racial integration amounts to racism. Instead, they see themselves as supporting an opportunity open to all parents—black, white, Latino, Asian, Native American, and others—to exercise greater guidance over their children's futures. Viewed through this lens, any measure to promote racial and ethnic integration can appear as meddlesome "social engineering" that unjustifiably interferes with parents' valid liberty interests.

By contrast, those whites and nonwhites who begin with an emphasis on equal opportunity tend to view education as among society's most important collective enterprises. Through education, they observe, society is constantly re-forming itself in every generation, simultaneously educating children about shared political and social values and advancing our society's potential for economic and scientific growth through the transmission of crucial knowledge and skills to each new generation. Society transmits its values, they suggest, not only by deciding what we teach but also by determining whom we choose to gather together in particular educational settings. Bringing together children of different racial and ethnic backgrounds to learn from one another, they contend, is a central objective of American education, especially important in a new century during which nonwhites will become a majority of the nation's citizens and residents.[19]

Proponents of this view insist, moreover, that to ensure equality of educational opportunity, citizens must delegate strong, implementing authority to school officials. It is naive at best, they believe, to hope that genuine racial equality might emerge on its own through the working of some "invisible educational hand," the product of every parent's individual choice. Even in purely private markets, they note, society has learned that it must impose detailed centralized regulation of consumer goods to ensure product safety, avoid fraud, and prevent market domination by unscrupulous forces.

Jennifer Hochschild has characterized this divide over race and public education as pitting "the competing values of diversity and freedom of movement," on the one hand, against "liberalism and democracy" on the other. Those drawn to diversity, as she defines it, seek to live grounded in their "cultural distinctiveness and racial separation." Freedom of movement is a complementary value for these citizens, at least "in the context of American race and ethnic relations," since it embodies "the classic liberal promise of individual opportunity," which includes "the right to pursue happiness wherever and however one desires." In contrast, Hochschild characterizes those who opt for "liberalism and democracy" as tending "to endorse school desegregation, because it is the method in which our nation has invested the most effort in seeking to grant equal protection of the laws."[20]

While one camp of white Americans focuses on liberty and individual choice as prime values, the other emphasizes equality of educational opportunity and the need for community. In consequence, the two camps talk past each other, mutually baffled that others seem so bereft of defensible first principles.

Nonwhite Support for Public School Integration: Why Has It Waned?

To add to the current confusion over educational objectives, some African Americans, long at the forefront of public education's civil rights advances, have lost their earlier zeal for desegregated schooling. The black majorities that Thurgood Marshall commanded in support of school desegregation following *Brown* no longer rally quite as quickly and confidently to preserve integrated schooling. Some disillusioned former supporters lament the loss of black schools, which often provided social and intellectual nourishment to black communities during decades of segregation. Others cite bitter encounters with whites during the battles over desegregation, the frequent loss of jobs experienced by African American principals and teachers as dual, segregated school systems merged, or the disproportionate burden of transportation that fell on black children, who were typically bused far longer and farther than whites were to desegregated schools.[21]

Still others know from personal experience what Roslyn Arlin Mickelson and Charles T. Clotfelter, Helen F. Ladd, and Jacob L. Vigdor have documented in this volume: within nominally desegregated schools, many black children have routinely been assigned to largely nonwhite classrooms, often classes with less well qualified teachers and lower educational goals. Moreover, while African American students have experienced steady growth in academic achievement, school desegregation has not lifted all black children to educational parity with whites. The substantial "academic achievement gap" that remains in 2005 undercuts, in the minds of some black parents, the most important promise of school desegregation: that desegregated schools would substantially improve black children's educational performance.[22]

Thus, some black parents and other first- and second-generation veterans of school desegregation no longer share the belief that racial integration is indispensable or even desirable. One frequently hears the objection, "My child doesn't have to sit next to a white child to learn. Give my child an all-black school, with a black principal and teachers, and with equal educational resources, and she will do just fine." Of course, most of these parents and their children have never experienced the "true integration" that powell urges here, yet some might view his proposal as utopian or doubt whether it will ever be implemented.

Moreover, others within the nation's burgeoning Latino community view the debate over school desegregation as a relic of an earlier time. Latino students were an infinitesimal fraction of the student population in most southern states during the 1960s, and the desegregation of Latinos played an insignificant role in earlier policy debates. Moreover, the special language needs of many limited-English-proficient students prompted widespread support for separate bilingual education programs, which take precedence over the goal of increasing classroom diversity for many Latinos.[23]

As Sean F. Reardon and John T. Yun, Luis M. Laosa, and Russell W. Rumberger and Gregory J. Palardy have shown in this volume, however, ethnic isolation is increasing faster in the South for Latino students than for any other racial or ethnic group. Consequently, whites, African Americans, and Latinos—all who would abandon the struggle for racially integrated public schooling—need to pay close attention to pertinent lessons from America's educational past as well as to contemporary social scientific research. That evidence cautions that the consequences of a return to ethnic and racial resegregation could ultimately prove disastrous to children's educational futures.

Cautionary Lessons from Southern History and Contemporary Social Science

America's Unhappy History of Segregated Public Education

The current drift away from integrated public schooling and the deeper loss of urgency about integrated public institutions bear an unsettling parallel to the nation's more drastic late-nineteenth-century repudiation of the post–Civil War efforts to assure civil and economic rights to African Americans. For nearly a decade after 1865, a remarkable series of legal and social reforms went forward in the American South, prompted by a national congressional leadership that demanded a new legal order in slavery's aftermath. The Thirteenth Amendment abolished slavery; the Fourteenth Amendment guaranteed federal and state citizenship to ex-slaves and forbade states to deny any person either "due process of law" or "the equal protection of the laws"; the Fifteenth Amendment forbade any racial distinctions in eligibility to vote or hold public office, effectively extending the franchise to black men throughout the nation.[24]

Beyond these constitutional provisions, Congress passed a sweeping Civil Rights Act in 1866, extending to blacks the same civil rights in property, contracts, and the civil and criminal justice system as were enjoyed by whites. The Freedmen's Bureau Act created a temporary federal bureaucracy in southern states that assisted blacks in obtaining fair employment opportunities, strove for equal justice in the courts, and encouraged the provision of schools for black children and their parents, eager to seize the long-denied chance for literacy. Under the Reconstruction Act of 1867, southern state constitutions were rewritten to permit black participation in the political process, and many states soon initiated universal systems of public (though still racially segregated) education. For a short period, African Americans took a substantial part in public life in the South. Indeed, two states, South Carolina and Louisiana, had black electoral majorities. Under the watchful supervision of federal troops, black leaders and their white political allies adopted a remarkable series of legal reforms that broadened public commitment to social institutions such as schools, hospitals, and charitable facilities for the disabled; shared political participation widely in local governance; and tipped the balance of economic laws toward small farmers and laborers and away from large landowners. Not only did black literacy, landownership, and small business flower, but blacks found political allies among middle- and lower-income whites who had endured decades of political indifference and dismal public services under white-planter-controlled legislatures.[25]

As the southern white elite reassumed political control, however, many of these reforms were gradually—and sometimes abruptly—repudiated. By the late 1890s, state and local power were concentrated in white elite hands. As national congressional attention shifted from the plight of African Americans and as federal courts abandoned their constitutional obligation to enforce the promises of the post–Civil War amendments (epitomized by the Supreme Court's 1896 decision in *Plessy v. Ferguson*, acquiescing in Louisiana's regime of racially "separate but equal" transportation services), blacks found their political, economic, and social world shrunken to an extent that would have astonished those who fashioned the constitutional and statutory protections of a generation earlier.[26]

Booker T. Washington helped smooth the way for this retrenchment. In his famous 1895 "Atlanta Compromise Speech" before a southern white audience, Washington proposed that blacks "acquiesce in disfranchisement and some measure of segregation, at least for the time being, in return for a white promise to allow blacks to share in the economic growth that northern investment would bring" to the South.[27] After this speech, white elites lionized Washington and soon implemented some version of this compromise throughout the South and nationally. Indeed, by 1899, the Supreme Court felt sufficiently free to declare in *Cumming v. Board of Education* that a Georgia school board might properly provide publicly funded high schools for white students in Augusta, with no comparable funding for a black high school, "except in the case of a clear and unmistakable disregard of rights secured by the supreme law of the land."[28]

What followed *Plessy* and *Cumming* proved a decades-long disaster for black public education. Throughout the South, state legislatures and local school authorities neglected or cut funding for black elementary and secondary education even as state support for white education soared. By 1915, leading cities of the South—such as Atlanta, Charleston, Charlotte, Jacksonville, Mobile, New Orleans, and Roanoke—could boast multiple public high schools for their white student populations but not a single public high school for black students.[29] Indeed, the federal government reported in 1917 that in "the entire South, there were only sixty-four high schools for black children." Racial inequities were not confined to high school students: data reveal that in 1935 South Carolina, Georgia, Alabama, Mississippi, and Louisiana each spent less than twenty dollars per year on the average black pupil, 30 percent or less of the public support provided for white children's schooling in those states.[30]

As economic historian Robert Margo concludes,

> During the first half of the twentieth century, the South failed to abide by the equal part of the separate-but-equal doctrine, as established in the Supreme Court's 1896 case, *Plessy v. Ferguson*. It was demonstrated that separate-but-equal provision of public schools in the South retarded black educational achievement. Had the schools been separate-but-*equal*, southern black children would have attended school more frequently, achieved higher literacy rates earlier in the century, and had higher scores on standardized tests. However, separate-but-equal would not have compensated for aspects of family background—poverty and adult illiteracy—that hindered black educational achievement. This "intergenerational drag" was a major factor behind the persistence of racial differences in schooling before World War Two.[31]

African Americans and Latinos in 2005 are, to be sure, far better positioned than they were in 1900 to resist the official depredations of the Jim Crow era. The Supreme Court's *Brown* decision and the congressional legislation of the "Second Reconstruction"—principally the Civil Rights Act of 1964 and the Voting Rights Act of 1965—offer more express protection for racial equality than was available in 1877. Moreover, there are today thousands of highly trained, economically secure African Americans and Latinos in positions of local, state, and national leadership, in both the public and the private spheres, who would assuredly resist any thoroughgoing retrenchment on legal, economic, and political rights if one were initiated.[32]

Yet in 2005, the potential threat comes less from overt, intentional racism than from policies, race-neutral on their face, that work to the systematic disadvantage of nonwhites. The Supreme Court in the early 1970s repudiated any federal constitutional claim to equal educational funding. Soon thereafter, it held that even governmental actions with severely adverse racial effects do not violate the federal constitution, absent proof that government actors intended to discriminate. More recently, the Supreme Court drastically curtailed citizens' legal right to enforce the many federal regulations that bar governmental actions with racially adverse effects unless the petitioners can meet the heavy burden of proving intentional discrimination. James Ryan has shown that, for whatever reason, school finance lawsuits have failed more often when the apparent beneficiaries would be nonwhite students and their parents. Finally, the Voting Rights Act will expire in 2007 unless it is reauthorized at that time, a most uncertain prospect as of this writing.[33]

In sum, African American and Latino parents who now hope to focus primarily on the quality of their children's schools, even while acquiescing in racial resegregation, risk the prospect that future legislators might turn sharply against their children, who could find themselves consigned to inadequately funded schools with fewer well-trained teachers, inferior scientific and technical equipment, and fewer course offerings—and with far weaker legal tools with which to challenge these inequities.

The Educational Challenge of High-Poverty Schools

Beyond this sobering historical evidence—that without public commitment to full equality, schools drift toward racial segregation, which relegates nonwhites to schools with substantially inferior resources—both whites and nonwhites must also weigh another powerful body of research. According to 2002 Bureau of the Census data, more than twice as many African American families (27.1 percent) and Latino families (24 percent) live in poverty as do white families (11 percent). Consequently, if and as southern schools resegregate by race, their black and/or Latino schools will simultaneously become "high-poverty" schools, in which more than 40 percent of all students will come from poor families.

Contributors to this volume report that attendance at high-poverty schools tends to depress the academic performance of all students who attend them (Rumberger and Palardy; Laosa; Heubert; powell). The adverse effects of a high-poverty environment operate independently of a family's wealth or poverty. In other words, both middle-class and poor children tend to perform worse in high-poverty schools, just as both poor and middle-class students tend to perform better in middle-class schools. These adverse academic consequences have been well documented in a wide variety of school settings for nearly forty years.[34]

The advent of state and federal accountability testing programs raises the stakes still higher because parents, teachers, and administrators now use these tests to chart the progress of every school and district on an annual basis. Accountability supporters obviously hope that this testing regime will force teachers and administrators to redouble their efforts, thereby raising all students' performance. Yet

Amy Stuart Wells and Jennifer Jellison Holme caution that this emphasis on statewide test results has had a distressing unintended consequence: many middle-class white (and nonwhite) parents have fled from formerly successful, integrated public schools, where more nuanced measures of school success (strong choral and dramatics programs, Ivy League acceptances by top graduates, outstanding athletic teams) have been overshadowed by the narrow results on end-of-grade accountability scores. Catherine E. Freeman, Benjamin Scafidi, and David L. Sjoquist, moreover, report that Georgia's white teachers tend to leave majority nonwhite schools far more rapidly than they do majority white schools, and others have reported that better-trained teachers of all races tend to flee lower-performing schools.

The Inescapable Truth about Twenty-first-Century Public Schooling

Two challenges confront all who would preserve racially diverse schooling. The first is to convince those parents for whom liberty and parental choice are prime values that their children's individual interests will be best served by receiving public education in racially integrated settings. The second is to persuade these parents to look for a moment beyond their children's best interests and to consider the broader, long-term public interest in common schooling.

The argument that school integration serves the best interests of these parents should focus on the upside gains racial integration can bring to their children. Nowhere have those reasons been stated more forcefully than in briefs filed in *Grutter v. Bollinger*, the University of Michigan Law School affirmative action case, by America's leading corporate, academic, and military leaders. Together, such international powerhouses as 3M, General Electric, Intel, Merck, Microsoft, and more than sixty other major multinational corporations voiced their need for college graduates with educational experiences that teach them to work comfortably across racial lines. As their joint brief stated,

> For these students to realize their potential as leaders, it is essential that they be educated in an environment where they are exposed to diverse people, ideas, perspectives, and interactions. In the experience of the *amici* businesses, today's global marketplace and the increasing diversity in the American population demand the cross-cultural experience and understanding gained from such an education. Diversity in higher education is therefore a compelling governmental interest not only because of its positive effects on the educational environment itself, but also because of the crucial role diversity . . . plays

> in preparing students to be the leaders this country needs in business, law, and all other pursuits that affect the public interest.[35]

Echoing that imperative, the nation's military leaders, including a former secretary of defense; three former chairmen of the Joint Chiefs of Staff; the former superintendents of West Point, Annapolis, and the Air Force Academy; and other highly ranked officers from every branch of military service underscored that "a highly qualified, racially diverse officer corps educated and trained to command our nation's racially diverse enlisted ranks is essential to the military's ability to fulfill its principal mission to provide national security."[36] Scores of colleges and universities also joined to affirm the value they have found and seek to preserve in racially diverse public education.

In short, American children who attend predominantly one-race schools in the twenty-first century—whether those schools are white, or black, or Latino—will operate at an increasingly significant lifelong disadvantage as they move into the postschool worlds of business, the military, politics, and private life. Just as many corporations and other businesses now count the knowledge of a second language a significant plus factor in employment decisions, so too will these institutions demand interracial experience as a necessary precondition for personal advancement in a multiracial society. While some few students may obtain this experience in their residential neighborhoods or in other settings, public schools, where students are required to spend a preponderance of their waking hours between ages five and sixteen or seventeen, are the most obvious and effective settings in which to forge these indispensable interracial relationships. Parents who put their children's interests first—in short, parents who want the liberty to make individual choices—need well-supported systems of racially integrated public schools to meet their children's long-term educational objectives.[37]

This key insight about the future educational demands on America's students should provide new common ground for those American parents who value educational choices and those whose first priority is to strive for equality. In this century, both the personal interests of individual students and the nation's collective interests will depend on maintaining a nationwide system of equal-opportunity, racially diverse public schools. Yet this is not an insight new to the twenty-first century. John Dewey, perhaps America's greatest educational theorist, wrote in 1900, "What the best and wisest parent wants for his own child, that must the community want for all its children. Any other ideal for our schools is narrow and unlovely; acted upon, it destroys our democracy."[38]

What is the collective interest in avoiding the reemergence of segregated schools? The finest investigators have concluded that even if racial resegregation were otherwise a neutral educational policy (and it is not, for reasons explored subsequently), even if it did not threaten to saddle many nonwhite schools with inferior physical and human resources (which it does), it inexorably leads toward high-poverty schooling for many, which in turn will multiply the problems of delivering a sound education to every child. In other words, student-assignment policies that are designed solely with the aim of furthering individual choice will almost certainly create clear "winner" and "loser" schools, separated by wide spread disparities in teacher quality and physical resources and with wide variations in student performance. At first, this might seem to pose little real risk to better-educated and more affluent parents, who can simply use their resources to ensure that their children attend "winner" schools. Yet such systems tend to be unstable over time, since the supply of "best schools" is always limited and alert parents must constantly watch to be sure that their children are assigned to those schools. Their understandable vigilance, ironically, can make this inherent instability far worse, since any slight decline in a school's performance—or any increase in its number of low-income, low-performing, or nonwhite students—can easily be interpreted as the first signal of a downward demographic trend, which can then induce the educational equivalent of panic selling, with irrational and educationally disastrous results.

Parents motivated primarily by their children's self-interest, in sum, need to recognize that a winner-loser game in public education comes with downside consequences for all, not simply for the poor. If student assignments are determined principally by parental choice, the cumulative effect will likely be to accelerate the trend toward public school resegregation already under way throughout the South and the nation. Very few schools will experience stable, meaningful levels of racial diversity, and thousands of schools will become overwhelmingly nonwhite and poor even as others become overwhelmingly white. Students in both settings will be deprived of crucial interracial learning and lifelong friendships that could enrich their lives. By contrast, if educators are permitted to craft educational policies that ensure integrated schooling, the South's school systems can deliver more meaningful long-term educational options for all their students because stable, racially integrated public schooling will continue to be available for students throughout every school district.

How can such schools be created and maintained? Our final section begins to address that important question.

Toward the Preservation of Integrated Public Education

Race-Conscious Student Assignments

The most straightforward way to ensure racially integrated public schooling certainly would be for local school boards to adopt integration as a chief educational priority and then to devise student-assignment policies to assure its attainment. Yet certain lower federal court decisions in the late 1990s cast doubt on the constitutionality of this approach; these cases strongly suggested that any use of race-conscious student-assignment policies—even by willing school boards acting in good faith to further racial diversity—might violate the Equal Protection Clause.[39]

Their rationale depends on a narrow reading of earlier Supreme Court cases that demanded "strict judicial scrutiny" of any race-conscious governmental actions. To survive such scrutiny, such government actions must further "compelling government interests," and any race-conscious methods must be "narrowly tailored," both to ensure that the racial preferences are no wider than necessary to attain the government's compelling ends and to avoid unnecessary injury to innocent third parties. When the Court struck down racial preferences in a very different sphere—government contracting programs that favored minority subcontractors—some federal courts concluded that racial diversity could never be a sufficiently compelling educational interest to survive this review.

As Jacinta S. Ma and Michal Kurlaender have suggested in this volume, however, the Supreme Court's 2003 decision in *Grutter v. Bollinger* places the constitutionality of race-conscious public school assignments in a new and far more favorable light. Not only did Justice Sandra Day O'Connor's opinion for the Court in *Grutter* uphold the explicit consideration of race by universities as a "plus factor" in making admissions decisions, but the Court expressly acknowledged that the University of Michigan School of Law had "a compelling interest in attaining a diverse student body," noting that "numerous studies show that student body diversity promotes learning outcomes, and 'better prepares students for an increasingly diverse workforce and society, and better prepares them as professionals.'" In addition, the Court expressly approved the university's objective of enrolling "a critical mass" of minority students (defined as "'meaningful numbers' . . . that [encourage] underrepresented minority students to participate in the classroom and not feel isolated"), as long as the university used means to obtain that critical mass that fell short of "outright racial balancing" or "a quota system."[40]

If we project the new constitutional teachings of *Grutter* forward, toward ordinary student-assignment decisions in K–12 public school systems, several points seem to emerge. First, federal courts are likely to conclude that racial diversity is a "compelling end" that will survive "strict scrutiny" in the public elementary school setting as well. As Ma and Kurlaender point out, some of the principal compelling ends the Court recognized in *Grutter* translate easily to the public school context, and K–12 public schools may indeed demonstrate additional interests unique to their setting. In addition, student assignments to most elementary and secondary public schools are not based on merit (except in a few competitive schools) or indeed on individual student characteristics at all—except for race and ethnicity. Instead, student assignments are typically made on a neighborhood basis, irrespective of the many individual differences among the children residing within that neighborhood.[41] Moreover, in contrast to highly competitive universities like Michigan's law school, public school assignments are not zero-sum games. No student "applicants" are ever denied all admission; every student is "admitted" to the fourth grade in some local school; each receives a homeroom assignment and a full year of instruction. To that extent, *Grutter*'s concern that schools tailor their race-conscious programs "to assure that [they] will work the least harm possible to other innocent persons competing for the benefit" or "not 'unduly to burden individuals who are not members of the favored racial and ethnic groups'" simply has no public school relevance. While some students may be disappointed if they do not receive a particular school or teacher, there are no "innocent victims" in the eyes of the law, and most race-conscious programs simply do not "favor" one race over another because some students of different races will be present in every school.

Nor would race-conscious student-assignment programs spell a necessary end to parental choice. Many racially desegregated school systems have successfully followed "controlled choice" models created by Charles Willie and others that set floor and ceiling goals to ensure some critical mass of students from different racial backgrounds at each school while continuing to provide parents real choices among various schools.[42]

The first two post-*Grutter* decisions by lower federal courts concluded that willing school boards may constitutionally consider race to ensure that our nation's public schools remain racially diverse. The first decision, announced in the fall of 2003, upheld a voluntary desegregation plan adopted by the Lynn, Massachusetts, school board. The court observed that to "say that school officials in the K–12 grades, acting in good faith, cannot take steps to remedy the extraordinary problems of *de facto* segregation and promote multiracial learning, is to go further than ever before to disappoint the promise of *Brown*. It is to admit that in 2003, resegregation of the schools is a tolerable result, as if the only problems *Brown* addressed were bad people and not bad [educational] impacts. Nothing in the case law requires that result."[43] Subsequently, a second federal district court, considering a student-assignment plan authorized by the Jefferson County (Louisville), Kentucky, school board, held that the board "meets the compelling interest requirement [under the Equal Protection Clause] because it has articulated some of the same reasons for integrated public schools that the Supreme Court upheld in *Grutter.* Moreover, the Board has described other compelling interests and benefits of integrated schools, such as improved student education and community support for public schools that were not relevant in the law school context but are relevant to public elementary and secondary schools."[44]

Subsequently, however, two federal appellate panels—one in the First Circuit, the other in the Ninth Circuit—have read *Grutter* very narrowly. One struck down the assignment policies upheld by the federal district court in the Lynn, Massachusetts, case discussed earlier, and the second overturned a high school assignment system in Seattle that used race as one factor in assuring diversity in each high school. However, the appellate panel's *Lynn* decision was quickly vacated by the full First Circuit, which has ordered that all of its judges will hear and pass on the issues en banc.[45] It is almost certain that the ultimate constitutionality of the voluntary use of race by school boards will be decided by the Supreme Court in some future case, not by the lower federal courts. Unless the Supreme Court retreats from its *Grutter* decision, school boards should be encouraged that the educational undertaking sanctioned by *Brown v. Board of Education*—bringing together schoolchildren formerly separated by race so that they might learn together in common schools—is and will remain a constitutionally permissible road toward the American future.

Assigning Students by Student Performance and/or Family Income

For those school districts that remain concerned, even after the Supreme Court's *Grutter* decision, about race-conscious student assignments, other race-neutral student-assignment plans exist that will ensure some degree of racial diversity. Susan Leigh Flinspach and Karen E. Banks report in this volume on the experience of Wake County, North Carolina, where the school board decided in 1999 to abandon racial considerations in favor of two alternative assignment criteria, student academic performance and family income. The Wake County School District policy now limits the percentage of low-achieving students in any one school to 25 percent and limits the percentage of lower-income children in each school to 40 percent.

Wake County's reliance on these factors is backed by strong pedagogical research. Policies that cap the percentage of low-income children in each school prevent the development of high-poverty schools, which, as we have seen, can significantly depress student performance. In addition, by limiting the percentage of low-performing students, Wake County avoids the emergence of academic "problem schools" that might prompt parental or teacher flight.[46]

Moreover, because higher percentages of African American and Latino students come from low-income families and more frequently fail statewide performance tests, these student-assignment policies will reduce the overall racial resegregation of minority students. Indeed, Flinspach and Banks report that in 2001, more than 60 percent of all Wake County schools had nonwhite populations of between 15 and 45 percent (although that percentage is down from 91 percent of all schools in 1991, when the school district consciously assigned students by race).

Yet the effects of the Wake County approach are not identical to race-conscious assignment policies, as powell notes, since the plan provides a ceiling but not a floor for the percentage of struggling students. All-white schools, filled with upper-middle-income students who perform well, might well meet Wake County's current achievement and socioeconomic criteria despite their evident lack of racial diversity. Moreover, allowing these "white enclave" schools to persist almost certainly increases the pressure on some other schools, elsewhere in the system, to become disproportionately nonwhite. To assure the distinctive educational benefits of racial diversity, in short, most school districts will need to keep racial diversity goals clearly in mind even if they choose to emphasize performance, as Wake County has.

Making Integrated Schooling Work

White and nonwhite parents alike naturally share concerns about the quality of education their children receive in integrated schools. Nonwhites have special apprehensions that their children will be relegated to second-tier classes in nominally desegregated schools, will be assigned to the least experienced teachers, will be unfairly diagnosed as special needs students, or will face excessive rates of suspension and expulsion. Prior experiences during three decades of desegregation fully justify African American and Latino concerns about these prospects. White parents may also have apprehensions that their children's academic progress will be impeded by slow learners or that classes will be disrupted by unruly students from dysfunctional family backgrounds.

What powell's chapter urges, and what any meaningful recommitment to common public schools will require, is first that parents and educators concerned about equity or the quality of public education channel their concerns into meaningful, shared efforts to make racially integrated public schooling work rather than resort to socially destructive fixes based on unfettered choice and parental flight (for those who are able). However initially attractive the road out may appear in the short term, however politically easy its initial implementation, the message of this book is that the long-term consequences of abandoning a commitment to integrated public schools will prove disastrous for our schools and for our nation's future.

Second, the future of "truly integrated" education depends upon a fresh reconsideration by principals and teachers of ways to bring our children together within the walls of our schoolhouses so that they can learn from each other across racial lines. This goal, we must hope, is not an exercise in utopian impracticality. The future of our multiethnic population of 295 million people, drawn together from every nation on earth, depends almost entirely on our capacity to accomplish just that task: to look beyond race and culture for common values we can pursue, to nurture in all children the talents and motivation that await the touch of gifted teachers, to forge an ever-changing national culture and identity that will allow us to surmount the next generation of social, economic, and geopolitical challenges.

Public education, Chief Justice Earl Warren wrote in *Brown*,

> is perhaps the most important function of state and local governments. . . . It is required in the performance of our most basic public responsibilities, even service in the armed forces. It is the very foundation of good citizenship. Today it is a principal instrument in awakening the child to cultural values, in preparing him for later professional training, and in helping him to adjust normally to his environment. In these days, it is doubtful that any child may reasonably be expected to succeed in life if he is denied the opportunity of an education. Such an opportunity, where the state has undertaken to provide it, is a right which must be made available to all on equal terms.

Justice Thurgood Marshall, who led the legal campaign in the 1940s and 1950s that brought forth *Brown*, subsequently worked to implement its decrees throughout the South, and later joined the Supreme Court as an associate justice, warned in 1974 about the long-term consequences of any weakened judicial or executive commitment to *Brown*'s ultimate goals as the Court confronted the challenge of large-scale urban school segregation in the metropolitan northeast and north-central states:

> Desegregation is not and was never expected to be an easy task. Racial attitudes ingrained in our Nation's childhood and adolescence are not quickly thrown aside in its middle years. But just as the inconvenience of some cannot be allowed to stand in the way of the rights of others, so public opposition, no matter

how strident, cannot be permitted to divert this Court from the enforcement of the constitutional principles in this case. . . . In the short run, it may seem to be the easier course to allow our great metropolitan areas to be divided up each into two cities—one white, the other black—but it is a course, I predict, our people will ultimately regret.[47]

This book addresses a prospect that Justice Marshall never contemplated: that the South—the region most profoundly touched by *Brown*'s decrees, where the schools had become the nation's most thoroughly desegregated by the 1970s, where African American students made greater gains in academic achievement than in any other region—would begin to undo the handiwork of *Brown* itself. If that lamentable unraveling continues, if those prior gains are truly lost, then future commemorations of *Brown* and its legacy should surely cease. Either *Brown* is alive in the schools of the nation, or it is a useless historical relic. We profoundly hope it will be the former.

Notes

1. *Youngstown Sheet and Tube Co. v. Sawyer*, 655 (Jackson, J., concurring).

2. G. Orfield, *Reconstruction* (examining the political and administrative struggle to desegregate southern schools after the passage of the Civil Rights Act of 1964, noting the obstacles imposed by the decentralized federal system, and focusing on the role of the different federal branches, particularly administrative agencies); Wilkinson, *From Brown to Bakke* (exploring the Supreme Court's role in the racial integration of the American education system from elementary to graduate levels); Bass, *Unlikely Heroes* (profiling the federal judges who led the lower court efforts to implement *Brown* in the South); Peltason, *Fifty-eight Lonely Men* (recounting how federal judges in the southern states, charged with implementing *Brown v. Board of Education*, enforced that ruling in the face of strong white resistance); Payne, *I've Got the Light* (examining the voter registration movement by "ordinary people" in rural Mississippi and elsewhere in the during the 1960s); Gaillard, *Dream Long Deferred* (detailing the struggle to desegregate the Charlotte–Mecklenburg County public schools); Kluger, *Simple Justice*, 751–89 (reflecting on the many gains but continued frustrations during this fifty-year struggle between 1954 and 2004).

3. Myrdal, *American Dilemma*, 50–80, 452–520 (discussing the racial theories that underlay political discrimination against African Americans in the 1940s, with references to the South's political history and black disenfranchisement); Woodward, *Strange Career*, 139–68 (examining the "Second Reconstruction" of the 1950s and the role of the Supreme Court and the federal government in ending Jim Crow laws). See generally James Anderson, *Education of Blacks*, 2 (noting that "[s]oon after the 1870s, Blacks were ruthlessly disenfranchised; their civil and political subordination was fixed in southern law, and they were trapped by statutes and social customs in an agricultural economy that rested heavily on coercive control and allocation of labor. From the end of Reconstruction until the late 1960s, black southerners existed in a social system that virtually denied them citizenship,

the right to vote and the voluntary control of their labor power. They remained an oppressed people").

4. Branch, *Parting the Waters* (recounting the tumultuous early struggles of the post-*Brown* civil rights movement, with particular focus on Dr. Martin Luther King Jr. and the Southern Christian Leadership Conference); Branch, *Pillar of Fire* (carrying the story of civil rights era forward into the 1960s); Fairclough, *Better Day Coming* (chronicling civil rights efforts between 1955 and 1965); Carson, *In Struggle* (documenting the Student Nonviolent Coordinating Committee's role in the civil rights movement of the 1960s).

5. See generally Clotfelter, *After Brown* (describing these changes in detail).

6. See "America 2004" (affirming, "We support affirmative action to redress discrimination and to achieve the diversity from which all Americans benefit"). In 2003, many Democrats in Congress joined in an amici curiae brief supporting the University of Michigan's affirmative action admissions policies; see Brief of John Conyers Jr. et al. Republican President George W. Bush has agreed that diversity is an important interest in schools: "America is a diverse country, racially, economically, and ethnically. And our institutions of higher education should reflect our diversity. A college education should teach respect and understanding and goodwill. And these values are strengthened when students live and learn with people from many backgrounds." Bush Administration Statement.

7. Brief of Amici Curiae Harvard University et al.; Brief of Amici Curiae Columbia University et al.; Brief of Amici Curiae Amherst et al.; Brief of Amicus Curiae the School of Law of the University of North Carolina.

8. Bell, *Faces.*

9. The February–March 1996 issue of the Roper Organization's *Public Perspective* magazine reported on a February 1995 survey by Princeton Survey Research Associates that found that 93 percent of blacks and 91 percent of whites believed that "white students and black students should go to the same schools." The same article reported on an April 1994 Gallup Poll that found that 74 percent of blacks and 62 percent of whites "feel that school integration has improved relations between whites and blacks" (40). See also Kahlenberg, *All Together Now,* 159 (pointing to a 1998 Public Agenda survey in which 66 percent of white parents said it is very or somewhat important to have their children educated in a racially integrated school and a 1996 *Phi Delta Kappan* poll "finding that 83 percent of the public view interracial schools as desirable").

10. Residential segregation between blacks and whites declined between 1980 and 1990 and again between 1990 and 2000. See Glaeser and Vigdor, *Racial Segregation,* 3–4, fig. 1; Lewis Mumford Center, *Ethnic Diversity Grows,* 4 (reporting that while residential segregation remained high in ten "Rust Belt" metropolitan areas of the Northeast and Midwest, it had fallen into "the moderate range" by 2000 in some midsized metro areas, especially in the South and West).

11. Lincoln, "Address," 536. See also Wills, *Lincoln at Gettysburg.*

12. See generally E. Black and Black, *Rise of Southern Republicans,* 224–25 (reporting that "[c]onservative whites now also dominate the mass base of the modern Southern Republican party. Accounting for 64 percent of the region's white Republicans in 1996, [their] worldview starts with a highly developed sense of personal responsibility for one's own economic well-being. The vast majority think that individuals themselves—acting alone or as part of a family—should be mainly responsible for finding employment and provid-

ing a good standard of living for themselves and their families. . . . Eighty-one percent of the region's conservative Republicans place responsibility for 'getting ahead' on the individuals themselves. . . . The overarching appeal . . . for many conservative southern whites is grounded in its rhetorical insistence upon minimizing the scope of the federal government to regulate the activities of law abiding citizens and businesses"). See also Viteritti, *Choosing Equality*, 210 (observing that the "distinct political perspectives of contemporary liberals and conservatives [can be explained] by their differing definitions of equality. In the general realm of public policy, conservatives (once referred to as classical liberals) tend to favor a more neutral state role in resolving social equities. Ever protective of individual freedom, conservatives are more comfortable with a conception of equal opportunity that restricts the role of government in intervening on behalf of the less fortunate"); D. Olson, "Dimensions," 237, 240.

13. Chubb and Moe, *Politics, Markets, and America's Schools*, 35, 207 (noting that "[s]urveys reveal that the vast majority of public school parents want to choose the schools their children attend—and that, when choice plans are implemented and people have a chance to exercise their newfound freedom, popular support for choice grows").

14. See, e.g., Hendrie, "Panel" (reporting on a two-year study by the National Working Commission on Choice in K–12 Education, sponsored by the Brookings Institution, which concluded that in education, "[c]hoice is here to stay,—like it or not" and that "[t]oday's public education system encompasses a large and growing number of options providing significant choice to American parents with regard to their children's education. As a consequence, the discussion about 'choice' is not about 'whether,' but rather is about 'what kind' and 'how much?'"

15. In fact, many conservative educational policy analysts originally promoted magnet school-assignment systems as superior to forced school assignments in assuring racial diversity in public schools precisely because of the greater choice provided to parents. See, e.g., Armor, *Forced Justice*, 223–25 (stressing the advantages of voluntary magnet school programs); on the same theme, see Rossell, *Carrot or the Stick*, 209–11.

16. See, e.g., *Belk v. Charlotte-Mecklenburg Board of Education*, 316–17 (opinion of Traxler) (noting that plaintiff William Capacchione sued the Charlotte-Mecklenburg School Board in 1997 when it denied his daughter a place in a Charlotte magnet school to maintain the school's racial balance under its districtwide assignment policy); *Eisenberg v. Montgomery County Public Schools*, 125 (upholding a claim by Jacob Eisenberg that his daughter was entitled to consideration for admission to a public magnet school without any administrative consideration of her race); see also Godwin, Kemerer, and Martinez, "Comparing Public Choice," 296 (observing that "[b]etter educated parents tend to select magnet schools because of perceived academic excellence. Even when a student's past academic performance is not a selection criterion, magnet schools tend to underrepresent low income, African American, Latino, bilingual, and low-test-score students").

17. Viteritti, *Choosing Equality*, 64–72 (describing the basic legal, fiscal, and administrative relationships between authorizing public school authorities, which issue the charters, and charter school officials and teaching staffs).

18. In *Zelman v. Simmons-Harris* the Supreme Court upheld, against federal Establishment Clause challenge, a Cleveland, Ohio, voucher program that provided financial vouchers to low-income parents, noting that the low-income parents, not the state itself, would

be directing state funds to religious educational institutions wholly as a result of genuine and independent private choices.

19. See, e.g., Gutmann, *Democratic Education*, 286 (citing Aristotle for the idea that education "cannot be left, as it is at present, to private enterprise, with each parent making provisions privately for his own children, and having them privately instructed as he himself thinks fit. Training for an end that is common should also itself be common").

20. Hochschild, *New American Dilemma*, 198–200; see generally Hochschild and Scovronik, *American Dream*.

21. See Cecelski, *Along Freedom Road*, 34; Vickerstaff, "Getting off the Bus," 159. See also Bell, "*Brown v. Board of Education*," 531–32 (discussing the ostensible failure of the integration promised by *Brown v. Board of Education* and contending that "[s]uch racial balance measures have often altered the racial appearance of dual school systems without eliminating racial discrimination. Plans relying on racial balance to foreclose evasion have not eliminated the need for further orders protecting black children against discriminatory policies, including resegregation within desegregated schools, the loss of black faculty and administrators, suspensions and expulsions at much higher rates than white students, and varying forms of racial harassment ranging from exclusion from extracurricular activities to physical violence"); see generally Bell, *Silent Covenants*.

22. See generally Jencks and Philips, *Black-White Test Score Gap* (thoroughly examining factors—biological, familial, economic, social—that could contribute to the racial gap in test scores and tracing changes in the gap over time). The Bush administration has identified the achievement gap as a major justification for imposing its federal accountability program, the No Child Left Behind Act. See U.S. Department of Education, "Closing the Achievement Gap" (creating a "blueprint" for an accountability system that will close the achievement gap).

23. For a look at the educational status of Hispanics in the United States, see Llagas, *Status and Trends* (examining trends and problems in the education system for Hispanics in the United States). For a more general look at the problems facing Hispanic students, see President's Advisory Commission, "From Risk to Opportunity."

24. See generally Foner, *Reconstruction*, 66–67, 251–61, 446–49; Franklin, *From Slavery to Freedom*, 290–302 (both describing the political and social forces that led to the adoption of the Thirteenth, Fourteenth, and Fifteenth Amendments).

25. See Foner, *Reconstruction*, 346–411 (detailing the political, economic, and social components of southern reconstruction); Franklin, *From Slavery to Freedom*, 302–19 (analyzing the economic and political realities for African Americans after the Civil War, with a focus on African American political participation); see generally Du Bois, *Black Reconstruction*.

26. See Foner, *Reconstruction*, 564–601 (discussing the collapse of Reconstruction and its consequences); Franklin, *From Slavery to Freedom*, 320–38 (analyzing the shift to white supremacy and the eventual disenfranchisement of African Americans); Woodward, *Strange Career*, 31–109 (offering a classic account of this shift). See also Margo, *Race and Schooling*, 68–86 (exploring the effect of the separate-but-equal doctrine on African Americans' educational opportunities).

27. Harlan, *Booker T. Washington*, vii.

28. *Cumming v. Board of Education*, authored by Justice John Marshall Harlan, the only justice who had dissented when *Plessy* was decided three years earlier.

29. James Anderson, *Education of Blacks*, 194–95, table 6.3.

30. Margo, *Race and Schooling*, 20, 21, table 2.5.

31. Ibid., 130.

32. See generally Farley and Allen, *Color Line*, 409–19 (analyzing 1980 Census data that document "a group of highly educated blacks [who] have found unprecedented opportunities for occupational mobility").

33. See *San Antonio Independent School District v. Rodriguez* (rejecting a claim that state school funding inequities should receive "strict judicial scrutiny" under the Equal Protection Clause of the Fourteenth Amendment); *Alexander v. Sandoval* (restricting prior cases, which had permitted aggrieved parties to enforce federal regulations implementing the Civil Rights Act of 1964, to instances in which the parties demonstrate intentional discrimination by state actors). See also Ryan, "Influence" (suggesting that racial considerations may well explain the fact that nonwhite plaintiffs have fared significantly worse than have white plaintiffs in seeking judicial or legislative assistance with school financing inequities).

34. See Coleman et al., *Equality of Educational Opportunity*, 299–302; see generally Boger, "Education's 'Perfect Storm'?" 1413–22 (reviewing the past forty years of such studies).

35. Brief of Amici Curiae, 65 Leading American Businesses.

36. Brief of Lt. Gen. Julius W. Becton Jr. et al., 5.

37. See Orfield and Kurlaender, *Diversity Challenged* (offering research and reports on the educational value of desegregated education); D. Black, "Case" (collecting and analyzing the social scientific research).

38. Dewey, *School and Society*.

39. *Tuttle v. Arlington County School Board*; *Eisenberg*, both of which cited the Supreme Court's decisions in *City of Richmond v. J. A. Croson Co.* and *Adarand Constructors, Inc. v. Pena*.

40. *Grutter v. Bollinger*, 318, 328, 330, 334.

41. Kahlenberg, *All Together Now*, 147–50 (describing "the American attachment to the neighborhood school").

42. See generally Willie and Alves, *Controlled Choice*.

43. *Comfort ex rel. Neumyer v. Lynn School Committee*, 270–71.

44. *McFarland v. Jefferson County Public Schools*, 837.

45. *Comfort*; see also *Parents Involved in Community Schools v. Seattle School District No. 1*.

46. Ibid., 38, 67–70 ("a wealth of data suggests that middle class children are not in fact, hurt by the presence of disadvantaged classmates, even as disadvantaged classmates benefit from such an environment, so long as the schools remain predominantly middle class and so long as some ability grouping is employed"; best teachers are drawn to schools whose students come from the highest socioeconomic levels).

47. *Milliken v. Bradley*, 813–14 (Marshall, J., dissenting).

Bibliography

Abbott v. Burke, 575 A.2d 359 (N.J. 1990).

Adams v. Richardson, 356 F. Supp. 92 (D.D.C. 1973).

Adarand Constructors, Inc. v. Peña, 515 U.S. 200 (1995).

Alexander v. Holmes, 396 U.S. 19 (1969).

Alexander v. Sandoval, 532 U.S. 275 (2001).

Ambach v. Norwick, 441 U.S. 68 (1979).

"America 2004: The 2004 Democratic National Platform: Strong at Home, Respected in the World." 10 July 2004. ‹http://www.democrats.org›. 1 August 2004.

American Educational Research Association. "AERA Position Statement Concerning High-Stakes Testing in Pre-K–12 Education." Washington, D.C.: AERA, 2000. ‹http://www.aera.net.about/policy/stakes.htm›. 11 March 2002.

American Educational Research Association, American Psychological Association, and National Council on Measurement in Education. *Standards for Educational and Psychological Testing.* Washington, D.C.: AERA, 1999.

American Federation of Teachers. *Making Standards Matter 2001: A Fifty-State Report on Efforts to Implement a Standards System.* Washington, D.C.: AFT, 2001.

Anderson v. Banks, 540 F. Supp. 472 (S.D. Ga. 1981).

Anderson, James D. *The Education of Blacks in the South, 1860–1935.* Chapel Hill: University of North Carolina Press, 1988.

Anderson, Judith, Debra Hollinger, and Joseph Conaty. "Re-Examining the Relationship between School Poverty and Student Achievement." *ERS Spectrum* 11 (Spring 1993): 21–31.

Anyon, Jean. *Ghetto Schooling: A Political Economy of Urban Educational Reform.* New York: Teachers College Record, 1997.

Armor, David J. Testimony before the House of Representatives Committee on the Judiciary, Subcommittee on the Constitution, 16 April 1996.

———. Expert report to the court in the case of *Capacchione et al. v. Charlotte-Mecklenburg Schools*, 1998.

———. *Forced Justice: School Desegregation and the Law.* New York: Oxford University Press, 1995.

Armor, David J., Christine Rossell, and Herbert J. Walberg. "The Outlook for School Desegregation." In *Desegregation in the Twenty-first Century*, edited by Christine Rossell, David Armor, and Herbert Walberg, 321–34. Westport, Conn.: Praeger, 2003.

Asher, Steven E. "Note: Interdistrict Remedies for Segregated Schools." *Columbia Law Review* 79 (October 1979): 1168–74.

Ashmore, Harry S. *The Negro and the Schools.* Chapel Hill: University of North Carolina Press, 1954.

Assignment by Choice. "About ABC." ‹http://groups.msn.com/Assignmentbychoice/aboutabc.msnw›.

———. "Home." ‹http://groups.msn.com/Assignmentbychoice/home.msnw›. 16 October 2003.

Baker, Eva, and Robert Linn. "Alignment: Policy Goals, Policy Strategies, and Policy Outcomes." *CRESST Line*, Winter 2000, 1–3.

———. "Validity Issues for Accountability Systems." In *Redesigning Accountability Systems for Education*, edited by Susan H. Fuhrman and Richard F. Elmore, 47–72. New York: Teachers College Press, 2004.

Ballou, Dale, and Michael Podgursky. "Rural Teachers and Schools." In *Rural Education and Training in the New Economy: The Myth of Rural Skills*, edited by Robert M. Gibbs, Paul L. Swaim, and Ruy Teixeira, 3–21. Ames: Iowa State University Press, 1998.

Banks, Karen. *The Effect of School Poverty Concentration in WCPSS*. Research Watch Series, Report 01.21. Raleigh: Department of Evaluation and Research, Wake County Public School System, 2001.

Bankston, Carl, III, and Stephen J. Caldas. "Majority African American Schools and Social Injustice: The Influence of De Facto Segregation on Academic Achievement." *Social Forces* 75 (December 1996): 535–55.

Bass, Jack. *Unlikely Heroes: The Dramatic Story of the Southern Judges of the Fifth Circuit Who Translated the Supreme Court's Brown Decision into a Revolution for Equality*. New York: Simon and Schuster, 1981.

Beard, Charles A., and Mary R. Beard. *New Basic History of the United States*. Garden City, N.Y.: Doubleday, 1968.

Beatty, Alexandra, Ulric Neisser, William T. Trent, and Jay P. Heubert, eds. *Understanding Dropouts: Statistics, Strategies, and High-Stakes Testing*. Washington, D.C.: National Academies Press, 2001.

Belk v. Charlotte-Mecklenburg Board of Education, 269 F.3d 305, 316–17 (4th Cir. 2002) (en banc), *cert. denied*, 535 U.S. 986 (2002).

Belk et al. v. Charlotte-Mecklenburg Board of Education, 465 U.S. 122 (2002).

Bell, Derrick. "*Brown v. Board of Education* and the Interest-Convergence Dilemma." *Harvard Law Review* 93 (January 1980): 518–34.

———. *Faces at the Bottom of the Well: The Permanence of Racism*. New York: Basic Books, 1992.

———. *Race, Racism, and American Law*. 4th ed. Gaithersburg, Md.: Aspen Law and Business, 2000.

———. *Silent Covenants: Brown v. Board of Education and the Unfulfilled Hopes for Racial Reform*. New York: Oxford University Press, 2004.

Belluck, Pam. "Reason Is Sought for Lag by Blacks in School Effort." *New York Times*, 4 July 1999, sec. 1, p. 1.

Berry v. School District, 195 F. Supp. 2d 971 (W.D. Mich. 2002).

Bester v. Tuscaloosa Board of Education, 722 F.2d 1514 (11th Cir. 1984).

Bethel School District no. 403 v. Fraser, 478 U.S. 675 (1986).

Biegel, Stuart. *The Report of the Consent Decree Monitoring Team*. Report 20. San Francisco: San Francisco Unified School District, 2002–3. ‹http://www.gseis.ucla.edu/courses/edlaw/sfrept20.htm›. 10 November 2003.

Billingsley, Bonnie. “Teacher Retention and Attrition in Special and General Education: A Critical Review of the Literature.” *Journal of Special Education* 27 (Summer 1993): 137–74.

Bishop, John H., and Ferran Mane. “The Impact of Minimum Competency Exam Graduation Requirements on College Attendance and Early Labor Market Success of Disadvantaged Students.” In *Raising Standards or Raising Barriers? Inequality and High-Stakes Testing in Public Education*, edited by Gary Orfield and Mindy L. Kornhaber, 51–84. New York: Century Foundation, 2001.

Black, Derek. “The Case for the New Compelling Government Interest: Improving Educational Outcomes.” *North Carolina Law Review* 80 (March 2002): 923–74.

Black, Earl, and Merle Black. *The Rise of Southern Republicans*. Cambridge: Belknap Press of Harvard University Press, 2002.

Blank, Rolf K., Andrew Porter, and John Smithson. *New Tools for Analyzing Teaching, Curriculum, and Standards in Mathematics and Science: Results from the Survey of Enacted Curriculum Project Final Report*. Washington, D.C.: Council of Chief State School Officers, 2001.

Board of Education v. Ambach, 436 N.Y.S.2d 564 (N.Y. 1981).

Board of Education of Oklahoma City Public Schools v. Dowell, 498 U.S. 237 (1991).

Board of Education v. Pico, 457 U.S. 853 (1982).

Boddie v. Connecticut, 401 U.S. 371 (1971).

Boethel, Martha. *Diversity: School, Family, and Community Connections*. Austin, Tex.: National Center for Family and Community Connections with Schools, 2003. ‹http://www.sedl.org/connections›. 6 December 2003.

Boger, John Charles. “Education’s ‘Perfect Storm’? Racial Resegregation, High Stakes Testing, and School Resource Inequities: The Case of North Carolina.” *North Carolina Law Review* 81 (May 2003): 1375–1462.

———. “Willful Colorblindness: The New Racial Piety and the Resegregation of Public Schools.” *North Carolina Law Review* 78 (September 2000): 1719–96.

Boger, John Charles, and Elizabeth Jean Bower. “The Future of Educational Diversity: Old Decrees, New Challenges.” *Popular Government* 66 (Winter 2001): 2–16.

Boger, John Charles, and Judith Welch Wegner, eds. *Race, Poverty, and American Cities*. Chapel Hill: University of North Carolina Press, 1996.

Borman, Kathryn. “A Half Century after *Brown v. Board of Education*: The Impact of Florida Education Policies on Student Outcomes and Equity.” *American Educational Research Journal*. Forthcoming.

Boser, Ulrich. “Pressure without Support. Summary: Standards-Related Policy Tables.” *Quality Counts 2001: A Better Balance. Education Week*, Special Report, January 2001. ‹http://counts.edweek.org/sreports/qc01/articles/qc01story.cfm?slug=17policy.h20›. 28 October 2003.

Braddock, Jomills Henry, II. “The Perpetuation of Segregation across Levels of Education: A Behavioral Assessment of the Contact-Hypothesis.” *Sociology of Education* 53 (July 1980): 178–86.

Braddock, Jomills Henry, II, and James M. McPartland. *More Evidence on Social-Psychological Processes That Perpetuate Minority Segregation: The Relationship of School Desegregation and Employment Segregation*. Report 338. Baltimore, Md.: Center for Social Organization of Schools, Johns Hopkins University, 1983.

———. "Social-Psychological Processes That Perpetuate Racial Segregation: The Relationship between School and Employment Desegregation." *Journal of Black Studies* 19 (March 1989): 267–89.

Braddock, Jomills Henry II, and Tamela Eitle. "The Effects of School Desegregation." In *Handbook of Multicultural Education*, edited by James Banks, 828–46. Menlo Park, Calif.: Jossey-Bass, 2003.

Branch, Taylor. *Parting the Waters: America in the King Years, 1954–1963*. New York: Simon and Schuster, 1988.

———. *Pillar of Fire: America in the King Years, 1963–65*. New York: Simon and Schuster, 1998.

Breed, Alan. "One-Race Schools Gain New Champions: Advocates Look Back, Say Desegregation Proved to Be a Failure." *Charlotte Observer*, 2 January 2002, 5B.

Brewer v. West Irondequoit Central School District, 212 F.3d 738 (2d Cir. 2000).

Brief of Amici Curiae 65 Leading American Businesses in Support of Respondents, *Grutter v. Bollinger* (2003).

Brief of Amici Curiae Amherst, Barnard, Bates, Bowdoin, Bryn Mawr, Carleton, Colby, Connecticut, Davidson, Franklin and Marshall, Hamilton, Hampshire, Haverford, Macalester, Middlebury, Mount Holyoke, Oberlin, Pomona, Sarah Lawrence, Smith, Swarthmore, Trinity, Vassar, Wellesley, and Williams Colleges, and Colgate, Wesleyan, and Tufts Universities in Support of Respondents, *Grutter v. Bollinger* (2003).

Brief of Amici Curiae Columbia University, Cornell University, Georgetown University, Rice University, and Vanderbilt University in Support of Respondents, *Grutter v. Bollinger* (2003).

Brief of Amici Curiae Harvard University, Brown University, the University of Chicago, Dartmouth College, Duke University, the University of Pennsylvania, Princeton University, and Yale University in Support of Respondents, *Grutter v. Bollinger* (2003) (no. 02–241).

Brief of Amicus Curiae General Motors Corporation in Support of Respondents, *Grutter v. Bollinger* (2003).

Brief of Amicus Curiae the School of Law of the University of North Carolina Supporting Respondents, *Grutter v. Bollinger* (2003).

Brief of John Conyers Jr., Member of Congress, etc. et al., *Grutter v. Bollinger* (2003) (nos. 02–241 & 02–516).

Brief of Lt. Gen. Julius W. Becton Jr. et al., *Grutter v. Bollinger* (2003).

Brookhart v. Illinois State Board of Education, 697 F.2d 179 (7th Cir. 1983).

Brown v. Board of Education (I), 347 U.S. 483 (1954).

Brown v. Board of Education (II), 349 U.S. 294 (1955).

Brown, Kevin. "Implications of the Equal Protection Clause for the Mandatory Integration of Public School Students." *Connecticut Law Review* 29 (Spring 1997): 999–1042.

Brown, Marilyn. "Beyond Black and White." *Tampa Tribune*, 10 February 2000, A1.

Brown, Shelly. "High School Racial Composition: Balancing Excellence and Equity." Paper presented at the annual meeting of the American Sociological Association, Chicago, August 1999.

Bryk, Anthony, and Mary E. Driscoll. *The High School as Community: Contextual Influ-*

ences and Consequences for Students and Teachers. Madison, Wis.: National Center on Effective Secondary Schools, 1988.

Bryk, Anthony S., and Valerie E. Lee. "Is Politics the Problem and Markets the Answer? An Essay Review of *Politics, Markets, and America's Schools.*" *Economics of Education Review* 11 (December 1992): 439–51.

Bush Administration Statement on University of Michigan Affirmative Action. Office of the Press Secretary, 15 January 2003. ‹http://www.whitehouse.gov/news/releases/2003/01/20030115-7.html›. 3 June 2003.

Caldas, Stephen J., and Carl Bankston III. "Effect of School Population Socioeconomic Status on Individual Academic Achievement." *Journal of Educational Research* 90 (May–June 1997): 269–77.

———. "The Inequality of Separation: Racial Composition of Schools and Academic Achievement." *Educational Administration Quarterly* 34 (October 1998): 533–57.

California Department of Education. *Class of 2004: Estimated Overall Cumulative Passing Rates for the California High School Exit Examination (CAHSEE), March 2001 through May 2002.* Sacramento: California Department of Education, 2002.

Campaign for Fiscal Equity, Inc. v. the State of New York, 100 N.Y.2d 893 (2003).

Capacchione et al. v. Charlotte-Mecklenburg Schools, 57 F. Supp. 2d 228 (1999).

Carson, Clayborne. *In Struggle: SNCC and the Black Awakening of the 1960s.* Cambridge: Harvard University Press, 1981.

Carter, R. L. "The Unending Struggle for Equal Educational Opportunity." In *Brown v. Board of Education: The Challenges for Today's Schools*, edited by Ellen Condliffe Lagemann and Lamar P. Miller, 19–26. New York: Teachers College Press, 1996.

Carter, Thomas P., and Roberto D. Segura. *Mexican Americans in School: A Decade of Change.* New York: College Entrance Examination Board, 1979.

"Catalogue of Federal Domestic Assistance, Desegregation of Public Education." ‹http://12.46.245.173/cfda/cfda.html›. December 2003.

Cecelski, David. *Along Freedom Road: Hyde County, North Carolina, and the Fate of Black Schools in the South.* Chapel Hill: University of North Carolina Press, 1994.

Cenzipur, Debbie. "New Standards Hit Minorities Hard." *Charlotte Observer*, 17 December 2001, 1A.

Chambers, Mike. "Judge in KY Lifts Order to Desegregate Schools." *Charlotte Observer*, 21 June 2000, 4A.

Chang, Mitchell. "Racial Diversity in Higher Education: Does a Racially Mixed Student Population Affect Student Outcomes?" Ph.D. diss., University of California, Los Angeles, 1996.

Chapman v. California Department of Education, No C. 01–01780 CRB, Preliminary Injunction (N.D. Cal. February 21, 2002).

Charles, Camille Zubrinsky. "The Dynamics of Racial Residential Segregation." *Annual Review of Sociology* 29 (2003): 167–207.

Charlotte-Mecklenburg Schools. *2003–2004 Lottery Results Compared to 2002–03 Twentieth Day Enrollment.* Charlotte: Charlotte-Mecklenburg Schools, 2003.

———. "Board Resolution 2001." ‹www.cms.k12.nc.us/studentassignment/boardresolution2001.asp›. 3 April 2003.

———. "Board Resolution 2002–2003." ‹www.cms.k12.nc.us/studentassignment/boardresolution02–03.asp›. 31 July 2003.

———. *Class Counts.* Charlotte: Charlotte-Mecklenburg Schools, 1996–2002.

———. *Monthly Reports.* Charlotte: Charlotte-Mecklenburg Schools, 1970–2003.

———. *Pupil Assignment Plan Study.* Submitted by the Administrative Staff to the Board of Education 6 March, revised 27 September 1973. Charlotte: Charlotte-Mecklenburg Schools, 1973.

Chicago Metropolis 2020. "One Region, One Future." ‹http://www.chicagometropolis2020.org›. 6 December 2003.

Chipman, D. E. "Spanish Texas." In *The Handbook of Texas Online.* Austin: Texas State Historical Association, University of Texas at Austin, 2001. ‹http://www.tsha.utexas.edu/handbook/online/articles/view/SS/nps1.html›. 28 May 2002.

Chubb, John E., and Terry M. Moe. *Politics, Markets, and America's Schools.* Washington, D.C.: Brookings Institution, 1990.

Citizens' Commission on Civil Rights. *Closing the Deal: A Preliminary Report on State Compliance with Final Assessment and Accountability Requirements under the Improving America's Schools Act of 1994.* Washington, D.C.: Citizens' Commission, 2001. ‹http://www.cccr.org/ClosingTheDeal.pdf›. 20 August 2004.

City of Richmond v. J. A. Croson Co., 488 U.S. 469 (1989).

Civil Rights Project, Harvard University. "2000 Segregation Levels for U.S." *Schools More Separate: Consequences of a Decade of Resegregation.* 17 July 2001. Washington, D.C., Press Briefing, National Press Club, 3 April 2001.

———. "The Impact of Racial and Ethnic Diversity on Educational Outcomes: Lynn, MA School District." February 2002. ‹http://www.civilrightsproject.harvard.edu/research/diversity/LynnReport.pdf›. 6 February 2004.

———. *Overview of Constitutional Requirements in Race-Conscious Affirmative Action Policies in Education.* Cambridge: Civil Rights Project at Harvard University, 2003.

Clotfelter, Charles T. *After Brown: The Rise and Retreat of School Desegregation.* Princeton: Princeton University Press, 2004.

———. "Private Schools, Segregation, and the Southern States." Paper presented at the conference on "The Resegregation of Southern Schools?: A Crucial Moment in the History (and the Future) of Public Schooling in America," University of North Carolina at Chapel Hill, August 2002.

———. *Public School Segregation in Metropolitan Areas.* Cambridge, Mass.: National Bureau of Economic Research, 1998.

Clotfelter, Charles T., Helen F. Ladd, and Jacob L. Vigdor. "Racial Segregation in Modern-Day Public Schools." Unpublished paper. 2003.

———. "Symposium: Segregation and Resegregation in North Carolina's Public School Classrooms." *North Carolina Law Review.* 81 (May 2003): 1463–1512.

Cohen, Jacob. *Statistical Power Analysis for the Behavioral Sciences.* 2d ed. Hillsdale, N.J.: Erlbaum, 1998.

Cohen, Michael. *Review of State Assessment Systems for Title I: Memorandum to Chief State School Officers from the Assistant Secretary for Elementary and Secondary Education, U.S. Department of Education.* Washington, D.C.: U.S. Department of Education, 2001.

Coleman, James Samuel, Ernest Q. Campbell, Carol J. Hobson, James McPartland, Alexander M. Mood, Frederic D. Weinfeld, and Robert L. York. *Equality of Educational Opportunity.* Washington, D.C.: U.S. Department of Health, Education, and Welfare, Office of Education, National Center for Educational Statistics, 1966.

College Board. "2003 College Bound Seniors: A Profile of SAT Program Test Takers." ‹http://www.collegeboard.com/about/news_info/cbsenior/yr2003/html/2003reports.html›. 5 April 2003.

Comfort ex rel. Neumyer v. Lynn School Committee, 263 F. Supp. 2d 209 (D.Mass. 2003), *affirmed in part, reversed in part,* 2004 U.S. App. LEXIS 21791 (1st Cir. 2004), *opinion withdrawn and rehearing en banc granted,* 2004 U.S. App. LEXIS 24662 (2004).

Cook, Thomas. *School Desegregation and Black Achievement.* Washington, D.C.: U.S. Department of Education, 1984.

Coons, John E., William H. Clune III, and Stephen D. Sugarman. *Private Wealth and Public Education.* Cambridge: Belknap Press of Harvard University Press, 1970.

Cooper v. Aaron, 358 U.S. 1 (1958).

Council of Chief State School Officers. *Helping Students to Be First in the World: Recommendations for Federal Action on Legislation, 107th Congress.* Washington, D.C.: Council of Chief State School Officers, 2001.

Crain, Robert. "School Integration and Occupational Achievement of Negroes." *American Journal of Sociology* 75 (January 1970): 593–606.

Cruz, J., Jr. "Political Influence and Educational Change: A Selected Case Study." Ph.D. diss., University of Wisconsin, 1973.

Cruzan v. Director, Missouri Department of Health, 497 U.S. 261 (1990).

Cumming v. Board of Education, 175 U.S. 528 (1899).

Cutler, David M., Edward L. Glaeser, and Jacob L. Vigdor. "The Rise and Decline of the American Ghetto." *Journal of Political Economy* 107 (June 1999): 455–506.

Dailey, Don, Kathy Zantal-Wiener, and Virginia Roach. *Reforming High School Learning: The Effect of the Standards Movement on Secondary Students with Disabilities.* Alexandria, Va.: Center for Policy Research on the Impact of General and Special Education Reform, 2000.

Darden, Edwin C., Arthur L. Coleman, and Scott R. Palmer. *From Desegregation to Diversity: A School District's Self-Assessment Guide on Race, Student Assignment, and the Law.* Alexandria, Va.: National School Boards Association, 2002.

Darling-Hammond, Linda. "Unequal Opportunity: Race and Education." *Brookings Review* 16 (Spring 1998): 28–32.

Davis v. School District, 95 F. Supp. 2d 688 (E.D. Mich. 2000).

Dawkins, Marvin P., and Jomills Henry Braddock II. "The Continuing Significance of Desegregation: School Racial Composition and African American Inclusion in American Society." *Journal of Negro Education* 63 (Summer 1994): 394–405.

De León, A. "Mexican Texas." In *The Handbook of Texas Online.* Austin: Texas State Historical Association, University of Texas at Austin, 2001. ‹http://www.tsha.utexas.edu/handbook/online/articles/view/MM/npm1.html›. 13 June 2002.

Debra P. v. Turlington, 474 F. Supp. 244 (M.D. Fla. 1979); *affirmed in part and reversed in part,* 644 F.2d 397 (5th Cir. 1981); *remanded,* 564 F. Supp. 177 (M.D. Fla. 1983); *affirmed,* 730 F.2d 1405 (11th Cir. 1984).

Denton, Nancy. "The Persistence of Segregation: Links between Residential Segregation and School Segregation." *Minnesota Law Review* 80 (April 1996): 795–824.

Devins, Neal. "Judicial Matters." *California Law Review* 80 (July 1992): 1027–70.

Dewey, John. *Democracy and Education: An Introduction to the Philosophy of Education.* New York: Macmillan, 1916.

———. *The School and Society.* Chicago: University of Chicago Press, 1900.

Doherty, Kathryn M. "Accountability." *Education Week on the Web,* 16 July 2004. ‹http://www.edweek.org/context/topics/issuespage.cfm?id=49›. 16 July 2004.

Donahue, P. L., R. J. Finnegan, A. D. Lutkus, N. L. Allen, and J. R. Campbell. *The Nation's Report Card: Fourth-Grade Reading, 2000.* NCES 2001-499. Washington: U.S. Department of Education, Office of Educational Research and Improvement, 2001.

Donato, R., M. Menchaca, and R. R. Valencia. "Segregation, Desegregation, and Integration of Chicano Students: Problems and Prospects." In *Chicano School Failure and Success,* edited by R. R. Valencia, 27–63. London: Falmer, 1991.

Du Bois, W. E. B. *Black Reconstruction: An Essay toward a History of the Part Which Black Folk Played in America, 1860–1880.* New York: Russel and Russel, 1935.

Dulaney, Chuck, and Glenda Burch. *2000–2001 End-of-Grade Multiple-Choice Test Results.* Measuring Up Series, Report 01.37. Raleigh: Department of Evaluation and Research, Wake County Public School System, 2001.

Dulaney, Chuck, and Roger Regan. *2001–2002 End-of-Grade Multiple-Choice Test Results.* Measuring Up Series, Report 02.31. Raleigh: Department of Evaluation and Research, Wake County Public School System, 2002.

———. *End-of-Grade Multiple-Choice Test Results: 2002–03.* Measuring Up Series, Report 03.17. Raleigh: Department of Evaluation and Research, Wake County Public School System, 2003.

Eaton, Susan. *The Other Boston Busing Story.* New Haven: Yale University Press, 2001.

Edgewood Independent School District v. Kirby, 777 S.W.2d 391 (Tex. 1989).

Educate! Charlotte, N.C.: Swann Fellowship, 2003. ‹http://www.educateclt.org/default.asp›. 2 August 2004.

Education Trust. "Education Watch Online: Data to Drive Education Change." ‹http://66.43.154.40:8001/projects/edtrust/index.html›. 3 March 2004.

———. *The Other Gap: Poor Students Receive Fewer Dollars.* Education Trust Data Bulletin. Washington, D.C.: Education Trust, 2001.

Ehrenberg, Richard G., Daniel D. Goldhaber, and Domminic J. Brewer. "Do Teachers' Race, Gender, and Ethnicity Matter? Evidence From the National Educational Longitudinal Study of 1988." *Industrial and Labor Relations Review* 48 (April 1995): 547–61.

Eisenberg v. Montgomery County Public Schools, 197 F.3d 123 (4th Cir. 1999), *cert. denied,* 529 U.S. 1019 (2000).

Eitle, Tamela McNulty. "Special Education or Racial Segregation: Understanding Variation in the Representation of Black Students in Educable Mentally Handicapped Programs." *Sociological Quarterly* 43 (Fall 2002): 575–605.

Elmore, Richard F. *Building a New Structure for School Leadership.* Washington, D.C.: Albert Shanker Institute, 2000.

———. "The Problem of Stakes in Performance-Based Accountability Systems." In *Rede-*

signing Accountability Systems for Education, edited by Susan H. Fuhrman and Richard F. Elmore, 274–96. New York: Teachers College Press, 2004.

———. "Testing Trap." *Harvard Magazine*, September–October 2002, ‹http://www.harvard-magazine.com/on-line/0902140.html›. 11 December 2002.

———. "Unwarranted Intrusion." *Education Next*, ‹http://www.educationnext.org/20021/30.html›. 11 December 2002.

Elmore, Richard F., and Susan H. Fuhrman. "Opportunity-to-Learn Standards and the State Role in Education." *Teachers College Record* 96 (Spring 1995): 432–57.

Elmore, Richard F., and Milbrey Wallin McLaughlin. *Steady Work: Policy, Practice, and the Reform of American Education*. Santa Monica, Calif.: RAND, 1988.

Elmore, Richard F., and Robert Rothman. *Testing, Teaching, and Learning: A Guide for States and School Districts*. Washington, D.C.: National Academy Press, 1999.

Entwistle, Doris, Karl Alexander, and Lee Olsen. *Children, Schools, and Inequality*. Boulder, Colo.: Westview, 1999.

Equal Open Enrollment Association v. Board of Education of Akron City School District, 937 F. Supp. 700 (N.D. Ohio 1996).

Erik V. v. Causby, 977 F. Supp. 384 (E.D.N.C. 1997).

Evans v. Buchanan, 416 F. Supp. 328 (D. Del. 1976).

Fair Housing Act of 1968, P.L. 90–284, Title VIII, 82 Stat. 81 (codified as amended at 42 U.S.C. secs. 3601–19, 3631 [2000]).

Fairclough, Adam. *Better Day Coming: Blacks and Equality, 1890–2000*. New York: Viking, 2001.

Farley, Reynolds. *Recent Trends in School Segregation and Enrollment by Race: An Analysis of New Data from the Office of Civil Rights. Final Report*. Ann Arbor: Center for Population Studies at the University of Michigan, 1981.

———. "Residential Segregation and Its Implications for School Integration." *Law and Contemporary Problems: The Courts, Social Science, and School Desegregation* 39 (Winter 1975): 164–93.

Farley, Reynolds, and Walter R. Allen. *The Color Line and the Quality of Life in America*. New York: Sage, 1987.

Feldman, Paul. "N.J. Plans More Rigorous Competency Testing; New Graduation Standards to Be Determined." *Education Week on the Web*, 12 January 1983, ‹www.edweek.org/ew›. 8 September 2001.

Ferguson, Ronald F. "Paying for Public Education: New Evidence on How and Why Money Matters." *Harvard Journal on Legislation* 28 (Summer 1991): 465–98.

Finn, Jeremy, and Charles M. Achilles. "Tennessee's Class Size Study: Findings, Implications, Misconceptions." *Educational Evaluation and Policy Analysis* 21 (Summer 1999): 97–109.

Flake, Floyd. "Drowning Kids in Failure." *New York Post*, 20 March 1999, 1A.

Fleming, Tristan. "Note: Education on Equal Terms: Why Bilingual Education Must Be Mandated in Public High Schools for Hispanic LEP High School Students." *Georgetown Immigration Law Journal* 17 (Winter 2003): 325–46.

Flinspach, Susan Leigh, Karen Banks, and Ritu Khanna. "Socioeconomic Integration Policy as a Tool for Diversifying Schools: Promise and Practice in Two Large School

Systems." Paper presented at the Color Lines Conference, Civil Rights Project, Harvard University, Cambridge, Mass., August–September 2003.

Florida Department of Education. *School Diploma, Certificate, and GED Report.* Tallahassee: Florida Department of Education, 2003.

Foley v. Connelie, 435 U.S. 291 (1978).

Foner, Eric. *Reconstruction: America's Unfinished Revolution, 1863–1877.* 1st ed. New York: Harper and Row, 1988.

Ford, Richard Thompson. "The Boundaries of Race and Political Geography in Legal Analysis." In *Critical Race Theory: The Key Writings That Formed the Movement*, edited by Kimberlé Crenshaw, Neil Gotanda, Gary Peller, and Kendall Thomas, 449–64. New York: New Press, 1995.

Fowler, Frances C. "The Great School Choice Debate." *Clearing House* 76 (September–October 2002): 4–7.

Frankenberg, Erica, and Chungmei Lee. *Charter Schools and Race: A Lost Opportunity for Integrated Education.* Cambridge: Civil Rights Project at Harvard University, 2003. ‹http://www.civilrightsproject.harvard.edu/research/deseg/CharterSchools.php›. 31 October 2003.

———. *Race in American Public Schools: Rapidly Resegregating School Districts.* Cambridge: Civil Rights Project at Harvard University, 2002.

Frankenberg, Erica, Chungmei Lee, and Gary Orfield. *A Multiracial Society with Segregated Schools: Are We Losing the Dream?* Cambridge: Civil Rights Project at Harvard University, 2003. ‹http://www.civilrightsproject.harvard.edu/research/reseg03/reseg03_full.php›. 8 July 2003.

Franklin, John Hope. *From Slavery to Freedom.* 4th ed. New York: Knopf, 1974.

Freedle, Roy O. "Correcting the SAT's Ethnic and Social-Class Bias: A Method for Reestimating SAT Scores." *Harvard Educational Review* (Spring 2003): 1–43.

Freeman v. Pitts, 503 U.S. 467 (1992).

Fuhrman, Susan H. "Conclusion." In *From the Capitol to the Classroom: Standards-Based Reform in the States*, edited by Susan H. Fuhrman, 263–78. Chicago: University of Chicago Press and the National Society for the Study of Education, 2001.

Fuhrman, Susan H., M. Goertz, and M. Duffy. "Slow Down, You Move Too Fast: The Politics of Changing High Stakes Accountability Policies for Students." In *Redesigning Accountability Systems for Education*, edited by Susan H. Fuhrman and Richard F. Elmore, 245–73. New York: Teachers College Press, 2004.

Fuller, Howard. "The Continuing Struggle of African Americans for the Power to Make Real Educational Choices." Paper presented at the second annual Symposium on Educational Options for African Americans, Center for Educational Reform, Milwaukee, March 2000. ‹http://edreform.com/school_choice/fuller_choice.htm›. 25 March 2000.

Gaillard, Frye. *The Dream Long Deferred.* Chapel Hill: University of North Carolina Press, 1988.

Gallup Opinion Index. February 1976.

Galster, George C., and W. Mark Keeney. "Race, Residence, Discrimination, and Economic Opportunity: Modeling the Nexus of Urban Racial Phenomena." *Urban Affairs Quarterly* 24 (September 1988): 87–117.

Gamoran, Adam. "American Schooling and Educational Inequality: A Forecast for the Twenty-first Century." *Sociology of Education* 74 (Extra Issue 2001): 135–53.

———. "Student Achievement in Public Magnet, Public Comprehensive, and Private City High Schools." *Educational Evaluation and Policy Analysis* 18 (Spring 1996): 1–18.

Gayler, Keith, Naomi Chudowsky, Nancy Kober, and Madlene Hamilton. *State High School Exit Exams Put to the Test.* Washington, D.C.: Center on Education Policy, 2003. ‹www.cep-dc-org›. 23 October 2003.

Gehring, John. "States Open Fiscal Year on Shaky Ground." *Education Week,* 6 August 2003, 24, 29.

George, Francis Cardinal, O.M.I. "Dwell in My Love: A Pastoral Letter on Racism." 2001. ‹http://www.archdiocese-chgo.org/cardinal/dwellinmylove/dwellinmylove.shtm›. 30 September 2003.

G.I. Forum v. Texas Education Agency, 87 F. Supp. 2d 667 (W.D. Tex. 2000).

Glaeser, Edward, and Jacob L. Vigdor. *Racial Segregation in the 2000 Census: Promising News.* Washington, D.C.: Brookings Institution, 2001.

Godwin, R. Kenneth, Frank R. Kemerer, and Valerie Martinez. "Comparing Public Choice and Private Voucher Programs in San Antonio." In *Learning from School Choice,* edited by Paul E. Peterson and Bryan Hassel, 275–306. Washington, D.C.: Brookings Institution Press, 1998.

Goertz, Margaret E., and Mark C. Duffy. *Assessment and Accountability across the Fifty States.* CPRE Policy Briefs 33. Philadelphia: Consortium for Policy Research in Education, 2001.

Goldhaber, Dan D., and Dominic J. Brewer. "Why Don't Schools and Teachers Seem to Matter? Assessing the Impact of Unobservables on Educational Productivity." *Journal of Human Resources* 32 (Summer 1997): 505–23.

Goldschmidt, Pete, and Jia Wang. "When Can Schools Affect Dropout Behavior? A Longitudinal Multilevel Analysis." *American Educational Research Journal* 36 (Winter 1999): 715–38.

Gordon, Milton M. *Assimilation in American Life.* New York: Oxford University Press, 1964.

Graglia, Lino. "Public Schools in Black and White." *Justice Talking* (National Public Radio), 13 April 2001. Transcript and CD available from National Public Radio.

Grass Roots Innovative Policy Program (GRIPP). *Briefing Paper on Emerging Issues and Best Practices.* Oakland, Calif.: Applied Research Center, 2000. ‹http://www.arc.org/gripp/publicEducation/grippPublicEducPg03.html›. 2 August 2004.

Gratz v. Bollinger, 539 U.S. 306 (2003).

Green v. County School Board of New Kent County, 391 U.S. 430 (1968).

Grieco, Elizabeth M., and Rachel C. Cassidy. "Overview of Race and Hispanic Origin." U.S. Census Bureau, Census 2000 Brief 3, table 1, March 2001, ‹http://www.census.gov/prod/2001pubs/c2kbr01–1.pdf›. 5 August 2002.

Griffin v. County School Board, 377 U.S. 218 (1964).

Grissmer, David W., Ann Flanagan, and S. Williamson. "Why Did the Black-White Score Gap Narrow in the 1970s and 1980s?" In *The Black-White Test Score Gap,* edited by Christopher Jencks and Meredith Phillips, 182–226. Washington, D.C.: Brookings Institution, 1998.

Grissmer, David W., Sheila Nataraj Kirby, Mark Berends, and Stephanie Williamson. *Student Achievement and the Changing American Family.* Washington, D.C.: RAND, 1994.

Griswold v. Connecticut, 381 U.S. 479 (1965).

Grutter v. Bollinger, 539 U.S. 306 (2003).

Gurin, Patricia. "The Compelling Need for Diversity in Higher Education." Expert reports prepared for *Gratz, et al. v. Bollinger, et al.*, no. 97–75231 (E.D. Mich.) and *Grutter, et al. v. Bollinger, et al.*, no. 97–75928 (E.D. Mich.), January 1999. http://www.umich.edu/~urel/admissions/research/.

Gurin, Patricia, Eric L. Dey, Sylvia Hurtado, and Gerald Gurin. "Diversity and Higher Education: Theory and Impact on Educational Outcomes." *Harvard Educational Review* 72 (Fall 2002): 330–66.

Gutmann, Amy. *Democratic Education.* Princeton: Princeton University Press, 1987.

Habermas, Jurgen. *Moral Consciousness and Communicative Action.* Translated by Christian Lenhardt and Shierry Weber Nicholsen. Cambridge: MIT Press, 1995.

Hallinan, Maureen T. "Affirmative Action in the Classroom: Diversity Effects on Student Outcomes: Social Science Evidence." *Ohio State Law Journal* 59, no. 3 (1998): 733–54.

Hallinan, Maureen T., and Richard A. Williams. "Interracial Friendship Choices in Secondary Schools." *American Sociological Review* 54 (February 1989): 67–78.

———. "The Stability of Students' Interracial Friendships." *American Sociological Review* 52 (October 1987): 653–64.

Hampton v. Jefferson County Board of Education, 102 F. Supp. 2d 358 (W.D. Ky. 2000).

Hanushek, Erin A., John F. Kain, and Steven G. Rivkin. "New Evidence about Brown v. Board of Education: The Complex Effects of School Racial Composition on Achievement." 2004. ‹http://edpro.stanford.edu/eah/papers/jpe.resubmission.feb04.PDF›. 27 July 2004.

———. *Why Public Schools Lose Teachers.* Working Paper 8599. Cambridge, Mass.: National Bureau of Economic Research, 2001.

Hardy, Lawrence. "A New Federal Role." *American School Board Journal* 189 (September 2002): 20–24.

Harlan, Louis R. *Booker T. Washington: The Wizard of Tuskegee, 1901–1915.* New York: Oxford University Press, 1983.

Harrington-Lueker, Donna. "States Raise the Bar: Now Local School Districts Are Accountable for Results." *American School Board Journal* 185 (June 1998): 17–21.

Hauser, Robert M. "Should We End Social Promotion? Truth and Consequences." In *Raising Standards or Raising Barriers? Inequality and High-Stakes Testing in Public Education*, edited by Gary Orfield and Mindy L. Kornhaber, 151–78. New York: Century Fund, 2001.

Hawley, Willis. "Diversity and Educational Quality." Unpublished manuscript, School of Education, University of Maryland, College Park, 2002.

———, ed. *Strategies for Effective Desegregation: Lessons from Research.* Lexington, Mass.: Lexington Books, 1983.

Haycock, Kati, Craig Jerald, and Sandra Huang. *Closing the Gap: Done in a Decade, Thinking K-16.* Washington, D.C.: Education Trust, 2001.

Hazelwood School District v. Kuhlmeier, 484 U.S. 260 (1988).

Helms, Anne D. "Blacks Less Likely to Get Choice of Schools." *Charlotte Observer*, 20 March 2002, 1A.

———. "High-Poverty Schools Undermine Students: Observer Analysis Reveals Detriment Even to Top Students." *Charlotte Observer*, 14 September 2003, 1A.

———. "Parents' Choice May Clinch Schools' Fate." *Charlotte Observer*, 5 January 2003, 4A.

Hendrie, Caroline. "Panel Says Choice's Benefits Worth Risks." *Education Week*, 19 November 2003, 1, 15.

Heubert, Jay P. "Disability, Race, and High-Stakes Testing of Students." In *Racial Inequality in Special Education*, edited by Daniel J. Losen and Gary Orfield, 137–66. Cambridge: Harvard Education Publishing Group, 2002.

———. "High-Stakes Testing and Civil Rights: Standards of Appropriate Test Use and a Strategy for Enforcing Them." In *Raising Standards or Raising Barriers? Inequality and High-Stakes Testing in Public Education*, edited by Gary Orfield and Mindy L. Kornhaber, 179–94. New York: Century Foundation, 2001.

Heubert, Jay P., and Robert M. Hauser, eds. *High Stakes: Testing for Tracking, Promotion, and Graduation*. Washington, D.C.: National Academy Press, 1999.

Hills v. Gautreaux, 425 U.S. 284 (1976).

Hochschild, Jennifer. *The New American Dilemma: Liberal Democracy and School Desegregation*. New Haven: Yale University Press, 1984.

Hochschild, Jennifer, and Nathan Scovronik. *The American Dream and the Public Schools*. New York: Oxford University Press, 2003.

Hodel v. Indiana, 452 U.S. 314 (1981).

Hoffman, Kathryn, and Charmaine Llagas. *Status and Trends in the Education of Blacks*. NCES 2003-034. Project Officer: Thomas D. Snyder. Washington, D.C.: National Center for Education Statistics, U.S. Department of Education, 2003.

Hoke County Board of Education v. State of North Carolina, 358 N.C. 605, 599 S.E. 2d 365 (2004).

Holme, Jennifer Jellison. "Buying Homes, Buying Schools: School Choice and the Social Construction of School Quality." *Harvard Educational Review* 72 (Summer 2002): 177–205.

Hopwood v. Texas, 78 F.3d 932 (5th Cir. 1996).

Hudgins, Kerry I. "A Comparison of Market-Inspired and Equity-Based Reforms in Three North Carolina School Districts." Master's thesis, University of North Carolina at Charlotte, 2003.

Hui, T. Keung. "Magnet Schools Work, Maybe Too Well." *Raleigh News and Observer*, 23 March 2003, 5A.

Hui, T. Keung, and Lorenzo Perez. "Education: Reassignments Frustrate Parents: Wake Schools Reaching Out for Diversity." *Raleigh News and Observer*, 15 December 2000, 1A.

Hunter ex rel. Brandt v. Regents of the University of California, 190 F.3d 1061 (9th Cir. 1999), *cert. denied*, 531 U.S. 877 (2000).

Iceland, John, Daniel Weinberg, and Erika Steinmetz. *Racial and Ethnic Residential Segregation in the United States, 1980–2000*. U.S. Census Bureau Series CENSR-3. Washington, D.C.: U.S. Government Printing Office, 2002.

Improving America's Schools Act. 20 U.S.C. secs. 6301 et seq. 1994.

Individuals with Disabilities Education Act. 20 U.S.C. secs. 1401 et seq. 1997.

Irons, Peter. *Jim Crow's Children: The Broken Promise of the Brown Decision.* New York: Viking, 2002.

Jackman, Mary R., and Marie Crane. "'Some of My Best Friends Are Black . . .': Interracial Friendship and Whites' Racial Attitudes." *Public Opinion Quarterly* 50 (Winter 1986): 459–86.

Jackson v. Pasadena City School District, 382 P.2d 878 (Cal. 1963).

Jacob, Brian A. "Getting Tough? The Impact of High School Graduation Exams." *Educational Evaluation and Policy Analysis* 23 (Summer 2001): 99–121.

James, David R. "City Limits on Racial Equality: The Effects of City-Suburb Boundaries on Public-School Desegregation, 1968–1976." *American Sociological Review* 54 (December 1989): 963–85.

Jargowsky, Paul A. "Ghetto Poverty among Blacks in the 1980s." *Journal of Policy Analysis and Management* 13 (1994): 288–310.

———. *Stunning Progress, Hidden Problems: The Dramatic Decline of Concentrated Poverty in the 1990s.* Living Cities Census Series. Washington, D.C.: Brookings Institution, 2003.

Jencks, Christopher. *Inequality: A Reassessment of the Effect of Family Schooling in America.* New York: Harper and Row, 1972.

Jencks, Christopher, and Susan E. Mayer. "The Social Consequences of Growing Up in a Poor Neighborhood." In *Inner-City Poverty in the United States*, edited by Laurence E. Lynn Jr. and Michael G. H. McGeary, 111–86. Washington, D.C.: National Academy Press, 1990.

Jencks, Christopher, and Meredith Phillips, eds. *The Black-White Test Score Gap.* Washington, D.C.: Brookings Institution Press, 1998.

Johnson v. Board of Regents of the University of Georgia, 263 F.3d 1234 (11th Cir. 2001).

Johnson, Ruth. *Using Data to Close the Achievement Gap: How to Measure Equity in Our Schools.* Thousand Oaks, Calif.: Corwin, 2002.

Johnson, Tammy, Libero Della Piana, and Phyllida Burlingame. "Vouchers: A Trap, Not a Choice." 2000. ‹http://www.arc.org/erase/vouchers/exec_summ.html›. 6 November 2003.

Johnston, Robert, and Debra Viadero. "Unmet Promise: Raising Minority Achievement." *Education Week*, 15 March 2000, 1, 18–19.

Joint Statement of Constitutional Law Scholars. *Reaffirming Diversity: A Legal Analysis of the University of Michigan Affirmative Action Cases.* Cambridge: Civil Rights Project at Harvard University, 2003. ‹http://www.civilrightsproject.harvard.edu/policy/legal_docs/Diversity_%20Reaffirmed.pdf›. 6 June 2004.

Jones, Clifford V., ed. *A History of Major Developments That Implemented the Merger of the Wake County and Raleigh City Public School Districts, 1976–1980.* Vol. 1 of *A History of Merger: Wake County Public School System.* Raleigh, N.C.: Wake County Public School System, 1980.

Jones, Rebecca. "Defining Diversity." *American School Board Journal* 189 (October 2002): 18–23.

Kadrmas v. Dickinson Public Schools, 487 U.S. 450 (1988).

Kahlenberg, Richard D. *All Together Now: Creating Middle-Class Schools through Public School Choice*. Washington, D.C.: Brookings Institution, 2001.

———. "Socioeconomic School Integration." *Poverty and Race* (September–October 2001), ‹http://www.prrac.org/full_text.php?text_id=43&item_id=628&newsletter_id=58&header=Search%20Results›. 22 March 2004.

———. "An Unambiguous Legacy." *Education Week*, 21 February 2001, 28–48.

Kanter, R. M. *Men and Women of the Corporation*. New York: Basic Books, 1977.

Karatinos, T. E. "*Price v. Austin Independent School District*: Desegregation's Unitary Tar Baby." *Education Law Reporter* 77 (1993): 107–19.

Keller, Bess. "More New York Special Education Students Passing State Tests." *Education Week*, 12 April 2000, 33.

Kelly, Sean P. "The Black-White Gap in Mathematics Course Taking." Paper presented at the meetings of the American Sociological Association, Atlanta, August 2003.

Kennedy, Mary M., Richard K. Jung, and Martin E. Orland. *Poverty, Achievement, and the Distribution of Compensatory Education Services: An Interim Report from the National Assessment of Chapter 1*. Washington, D.C.: Office of Educational Research and Improvement, U.S. Department of Education, 1986.

Keyes v. School District no. 1, Denver, Colorado, 413 U.S. 189 (1973).

Killen, Melanie, and Charles Stangor. "Children's Social Reasoning about Inclusion and Exclusion in Gender and Race Peer Group Contexts." *Child Development* 72 (January–February 2001): 174–86.

Kim, Jimmy. "The Initial Response to the Accountability Requirements in the No Child Left Behind Act: A Case Study of Virginia and Georgia." Paper presented at the meetings of the American Educational Research Association, Chicago, April 2003.

Kim, Jimmy, and Gail L. Sunderman. "Findings from the First Phase of School Choice Implementation in Three Districts: Buffalo, New York; Richmond, Virginia; De Kalb County, Georgia." Paper presented at the meetings of the American Educational Research Association, Chicago, April 2003.

King, Martin Luther, Jr. "The Ethical Demands for Integration." In *A Testament of Hope: The Essential Writings of Martin Luther King, Jr.*, edited by James Melvin Washington. San Francisco: Harper and Row, 1986.

Klarman, Michael J. "*Brown*, Racial Change, and the Civil Rights Movement." *Virginia Law Review* 80 (February 1994): 7–150.

Klein, Stephen P., Laura S. Hamilton, Daniel F. McCaffrey, and Brian M. Stecher. *What Do Test Scores in Texas Tell Us?* Santa Monica, Calif.: RAND, 2000.

Kluger, Richard. *Simple Justice: The History of Brown v. Board of Education and Black America's Struggle for Equality*. New York: Knopf, 2004.

Koretz, Daniel, and Laura Hamilton. *The Performance of Students with Disabilities on New York's Revised Regents Examination in English*. Los Angeles: National Center for Research on Evaluation, Standards, and Student Testing, University of California, 2001.

Kornhaber, Mindy L. "Seeking Strengths: Equitable Identification for Gifted Education and the Theory of Multiple Intelligences." Ph.D. diss., Harvard University, 1997.

Kornhaber, Mindy L., and Gary Orfield. "High-Stakes Testing Policies: Examining Their Assumptions and Consequences." In *Raising Standards or Raising Barriers? Inequality and High-Stakes Testing in Public Education*, edited by Gary Orfield and Mindy L. Kornhaber, 1–19. New York: Century Foundation, 2001.

Kozol, Jonathan. *Savage Inequalities: Children in America's Schools.* New York: Crown, 1991.

Krebs, Albin. "George Aiken, Longtime Senator and G.O.P. Maverick, Dies at 92." *New York Times*, 20 November 1984, B10.

Kreft, Ita, and Jan de Leeuw. *Introducing Multilevel Modeling.* Thousand Oaks, Calif.: Sage, 1998.

Krei, Melinda Scott. "Teacher Transfer Policy and the Implications for Equity in Urban School Districts." ERIC Document Reproduction Service 443 932. Paper presented at the annual meeting of the American Educational Research Association, New Orleans, April 2000.

Krueger, Alan B. "Experimental Estimates of Education Production Functions." *Quarterly Journal of Economics* 114 (May 1999): 497–532.

Kulik, Chen-lin C., and James A. Kulik. "Effects of Ability Grouping on Secondary School Students: A Meta-Analysis of Evaluation Findings." *American Educational Research Journal* 19 (Fall 1982): 415–28.

———. "Effects of Ability Grouping on Student Achievement." *Equity and Excellence* 23 (Spring 1987): 22–30.

Kurlaender, Michal. "The Impact of School Racial Composition on Students' Attitudes towards Living and Working in Multiracial Settings." Unpublished qualifying paper, Harvard University Graduate School of Education, 2002.

Kurlaender, Michal, and John T. Yun. "Is Diversity a Compelling Educational Interest? Evidence from Louisville." In *Diversity Challenged*, edited by Gary Orfield, 111–41. Cambridge: Harvard Education Publishing Group, 2001.

———. "School Racial Composition and Student Outcomes in a Multiracial Society." Paper presented at the annual meeting of the American Educational Research Association, Chicago, April 2003.

Ladd, Helen F. "Briefing for the U.S. Civil Rights Commission." Paper presented at a hearing of the U.S. Commission on Civil Rights, Charlotte, North Carolina, 6 February 2003.

———. "School-Based Accountability Systems: The Promise and the Pitfalls." *National Tax Journal* 54 (June 2001): 385–400.

———, ed. *Holding Schools Accountable: Performance-Based Reform in Education.* Washington, D.C.: Brookings Institution Press, 1996.

Lankford, H., Susanna Loeb, and James Wyckoff. "Teacher Sorting and the Plight of Urban Schools: A Descriptive Analysis." *Education Evaluation and Policy Analysis* 24 (Spring 2002): 37–62.

Laosa, Luis M. "Intercultural Transitions in Human Development and Education." *Journal of Applied Developmental Psychology* 20 (July–September 1999): 355–406.

———. "School Segregation of Children Who Migrate to the United States from Puerto Rico." *Education Policy Analysis Archives* 9 (January 2001), ‹http://epaa.asu.edu/epaa/v9n1.html›. 5 August 2002.

———. "Social Policies toward Children of Diverse Ethnic, Racial, and Language Groups in the United States." In *Child Development Research and Social Policy*, edited by H. W. Stevenson and A. E. Siegel, 1–109. Chicago: University of Chicago Press, 1984.

Lareau, Annette. *Home Advantage: Social Class and Parental Intervention in Elementary Education*. Philadelphia: Falmer, 1989.

Lau v. Nichols, 414 U.S. 563 (1974).

Lee v. Butler County Board of Education, 183 F. Supp. 2d 1359 (M.D. Ala. 2002).

Lee v. Opelika City Board of Education, no. 70-T-853-E, 2002 U.S. Dist. LEXIS 2513, (M.D. Ala. 2002).

Lee, Jaekyung. "Racial and Ethnic Achievement Gap Trends: Reversing the Progress toward Equity?" *Educational Researcher* 31 (January–February 2002): 3–12.

Lee, Valerie E., and David T. Burkam. *Inequality at the Starting Gate: Social Background Differences in Achievement as Children Begin School*. Washington, D.C.: Economic Policy Institute, 2002.

Lee, Valerie E., and Julia B. Smith. "High School Size: Which Works Best and for Whom?" *Educational Evaluation and Policy Analysis* 19 (Fall 1997): 205–27.

Lee, Valerie E., Julia B. Smith, and Robert G. Croninger. "How High School Organization Influences the Equitable Distribution of Learning in Mathematics and Science." *Sociology of Education* 70 (April 1997): 128–50.

Lemann, Nicholas. *The Big Test: The Secret History of the American Meritocracy*. New York: Farrar, Straus, and Giroux, 1999.

Lewis Mumford Center for Comparative Urban and Regional Research. *Ethnic Diversity Grows, Neighborhood Integration Lags Behind*. Albany: Lewis Mumford Center for Comparative Urban and Regional Research, State University of New York, Albany, 2001.

Lewis, Anthony. *Portrait of a Decade*. New York: Bantam, 1965.

Liebman, James. "Implementing *Brown* in the Nineties: Reconstruction, Liberal Recollection, and Litigatively Enforced Legislative Reform." *Virginia Law Review* 76 (April 1990): 349–436.

Lillard, Dean, and Phillip DeCicca. "Higher Standards, More Dropouts? Evidence within and across Time." *Economics of Education Review* 20 (October 2001): 459–73.

Lincoln, Abraham. "Address at Gettysburg, Pennsylvania." In *Speeches, Letters, and Miscellaneous Writings*, edited by Don E. Fehrenbacher, 536. New York: Library of America, 1989.

Linn, Robert L. "Assessments and Accountability." *Educational Researcher* 29 (March 2000): 4–16.

———. *The Design and Evaluation of Educational Assessment and Accountability Systems*. Los Angeles: National Center for Research on Evaluation, Standards, and Student Testing, University of California, 2001.

———. *Reporting School Quality in Standards-Based Accountability Systems*. CRESST Policy Brief 3. Los Angeles: National Center for Research on Evaluation, Standards, and Student Testing, University of California, 2001.

Lippman, Laura, Shelley Burns, and Edith McArthur. *Urban Schools: The Challenge of Location and Poverty*. NCES 96-184. U.S. Department of Education, Office of Educational Research and Improvement. Washington, D.C.: National Center for Education Statistics, 1996.

Lipsitz, George. *The Possessive Investment in Whiteness: How White People Profit from Identity Politics.* Philadelphia: Temple University Press, 1998.

Llagas, Charmaine. *Status and Trends in the Education of Hispanics.* NCES 2003-008. Project Officer: Thomas D. Snyder. Washington, D.C.: National Center for Education Statistics, U.S. Department of Education, 2003.

Logan, John R., Jacob Stowell, and Deirdre Oakley. *Choosing Segregation: Racial Imbalance in American Public Schools, 1990–2000.* Albany: Lewis Mumford Center for Comparative Urban and Regional Research, State University of New York, Albany, 2002.

Lord, Dennis. Expert report to the court in the case of *Capacchione et al. v. Charlotte-Mecklenburg Schools.* 1999.

Losen, Daniel J. "Silent Segregation in Our Nation's Schools." *Harvard Civil Liberties Civil Rights Law Review* 34 (Summer 1999): 517–46.

Loury, Glenn C. *The Anatomy of Racal Inequality.* Cambridge: Harvard University Press, 2002.

Loveless, Tom. *The Tracking Wars: State Reform Meets School Policy.* Washington, D.C.: Brookings Institution Press, 1999.

Lucas, Samuel R. *Tracking Inequality: Stratification and Mobility in American High Schools.* New York: Teachers College Press, 1999.

Lucas, Samuel R., and Mark Berends. "Sociodemographic Diversity, Correlated Achievement, and *De Facto* Tracking." *Sociology of Education* 75 (October 2002): 328–48.

Marable, Manning. *The Great Wells of Democracy: The Meaning of Race in American Life.* New York: Basic Civitas, 2002.

Margo, Robert A. *Race and Schooling in the South, 1880–1950: An Economic History.* Chicago: University of Chicago Press, 1990.

Massachusetts Department of Education. *Progress Report on Students Attaining the Competency Determination Statewide and by District: Classes of 2003 and 2004.* Boston: Department of Education, 2003.

———. *Progress Report on the Class of 2002: Percentages of Students Who Have Earned a Competency Determination, Statewide and by District.* Boston: Department of Education, 2002.

———. *Spring 2001 MCAS tests: State Results by Race/Ethnicity and Student Status.* Boston: Department of Education, 2001.

Massey, Douglas S., and Nancy A. Denton. *American Apartheid: Segregation and the Making of the Underclass.* Cambridge: Harvard University Press, 1993.

———. "The Dimensions of Residential Segregation." *Social Forces* 67 (December 1988): 281–315.

Mathews, Jay. "The Bias Question." *Atlantic Monthly*, November 2003, 130.

Mazzoni, Tim L. "State Policy-Making and School Reform: Influences and Influentials." In *The Study of Educational Politics: The 1994 Commemorative Yearbook of the Politics of Education Association (1969–1994)*, edited by Jay D. Scribner and Donald H. Layton, 53–73. Washington, D.C.: Falmer, 1995.

McCleskey v. Kemp, 481 U.S. 279 (1987).

McConahay, J. "Reducing Racial Prejudice in Desegregated Schools." In *Effective School Desegregation: Equity, Quality, and Feasibility*, edited by Willis Hawley, 35–53. Beverly Hills, Calif.: Sage, 1981.

McDuffy v. Secretary of Education, 615 N.E.2d 516 (Mass. 1993).

McFarland v. Jefferson County Public Schools, 330 F. Supp. 834 (W.D. Ky. 2004).

McLaughlin, Margaret J. *Reform for Every Learner: Teachers' Views on Standards and Students with Disabilities*. Alexandria, Va.: Center for Policy Research on the Impact of General and Special Education Reform, 2000.

McNeil, Linda, and Angela Valenzuela. "The Harmful Impact of the TAAS System of Testing in Texas: Beneath the Accountability Rhetoric." In *Raising Standards or Raising Barriers? Inequality and High-Stakes Testing in Public Education*, edited by Gary Orfield and Mindy L. Kornhaber, 127–50. New York: Century Foundation, 2001.

McPartland, James, and Jomills Henry Braddock II. "Going to College and Getting a Good Job: The Impact of Desegregation." In *Effective School Desegregation: Equity, Quality, and Feasibility*, edited by Willis Hawley, 141–54. Beverly Hills, Calif.: Sage, 1981.

Metropolitan School District v. Buckley, 449 U.S. 838 (1980).

Metz, Mary H. *Classrooms and Corridors: The Crisis of Authority in Desegregated Secondary Schools*. Berkeley: University of California Press, 1978.

Meyer, Jeanie Keeny, and Daniel U. Levine. "Concentrated Poverty and Reading Achievement in Five Big Cities." Paper presented at the meetings of the American Educational Research Association, New York, April 1977.

Mickelson, Roslyn Arlin. "The Academic Consequences of Desegregation and Segregation: Evidence from the Charlotte-Mecklenburg Schools." *North Carolina Law Review* 81 (May 2003): 1513–62.

———. "Achieving Equality of Educational Opportunity in the Wake of Judicial Retreat from Race Sensitive Remedies: Lessons from North Carolina." *American University Law Review* 52 (March 2003): 1477–1507.

———. Expert report to the court in the case of *Capacchione et al. v. Charlotte-Mecklenburg Schools*, 1998.

———. "How Middle School Segregation Contributes to the Race Gap in Academic Achievement." Paper presented at the meeting of the American Sociological Association, Anaheim, Calif., August 2001.

———. "Subverting *Swann*: First- and Second-Generation Segregation in the Charlotte-Mecklenburg Schools." *American Educational Research Journal* 38 (Summer 2001): 215–52.

———. "Why Does Jane Read and Write So Well?: The Anomaly of Women's Achievement." *Sociology of Education* 62 (January 1989): 47–63.

Mickelson, Roslyn Arlin, and Carol A. Ray. "Fear of Falling from Grace: The Middle Class, Downward Mobility, and School Desegregation." *Research in Sociology of Education and Socialization* 10 (1994): 207–38.

Mickelson, Roslyn Arlin, and Stephen S. Smith. "Race, Tracking, and Achievement among African Americans in a Desegregated School System: Evidence from CMS." Paper presented at the Stanford University Conference on Race, Stanford, Calif., November 1999.

Milliken v. Bradley, 418 U.S. 717 (1974).

Milliken v. Bradley II, 433 U.S. 267 (1977).

Mills v. Freeman, 942 F. Supp. 1449 (N.D. Ga. 1996).

Missouri v. Jenkins, 495 U.S. 33 (1990).

Missouri v. Jenkins, 515 U.S. 70 (1995).

Morris, Vivian, and Curtis Morris. *The Price They Paid: Desegregation in an African American Community.* New York: Teachers College Press, 2002.

Morrison, Toni. *Playing in the Dark: Whiteness and the Literary Imagination.* Cambridge: Harvard University Press, 1992.

Mosteller, Frederick. "The Tennessee Study of Class Size in the Early School Grades." *Future of Children* 5 (Summer–Fall 1995): 113–27.

Mosteller, Frederick, and Daniel P. Moynihan. "A Pathbreaking Report." In *On Equality of Educational Opportunity: Papers Deriving from the Harvard University Faculty Seminar on the Coleman Report*, edited by Frederick Mosteller and Daniel P. Moynihan, 3–66. New York: Vintage, 1972.

Multicultural Market Statistics, Target Market News. "The Buying Power of Black America." ‹http://www.diversityhotwire.com/business/diversity_statistics.html›. 1 August 2004.

Murnane, Richard, and Frank Levy. "Will Standards-Based Reforms Improve the Education of Children of Color?" *National Tax Journal* 54 (June 2001): 401–15.

Myers, David E. *The Relationship between School Poverty Concentration and Students' Reading and Math Achievement and Learning.* Rev. ed. Washington, D.C.: Decision Resources, 1986.

Myrdal, Gunnar. *An American Dilemma: The Negro Problem and Modern Democracy.* Vol. 1. New York: Harper and Brothers, 1944.

NAACP v. Duval County Schools, 273 F.3d 960 (11th Cir. 2001).

"NAEP Achievement." *Education Week*, 8 August 2001, 24.

National Association of Latino Elected Officials. "Georgia Hispanic Chamber of Commerce, Statistics." 2002. ‹http://www.ghcc.org/Statistics.html›. 24 July 2002.

National Center for Education Statistics. *Common Core of Data (CCD) Public Elementary and Secondary School Universe Data.* Washington, D.C.: U.S. Department of Education, Office of Educational Research and Improvement, 2002.

———. *The Condition of Education, 1997.* Washington, D.C.: U.S. Department of Education, 1997.

———. *The Condition of Education, 2001.* Washington, D.C.: U.S. Department of Education, 2001.

———. *The Condition of Education, 2003.* Washington, D.C.: U.S. Department of Education, 2003.

———. *Digest of Education Statistics.* Washington, D.C.: U.S. Department of Education, 2003.

———. *The Nation's Report Card.* Washington, D.C.: U.S. Department of Education, 2000.

National Commission on Teaching and America's Future. *What Matters Most: Teaching for America's Future.* New York: National Commission on Teaching and America's Future, 1996.

National Opinion Research Center. "General Social Survey." ‹http://www.icpsr.umich.edu:8080/GSS/homepage.htm›. 12 June 2004.

Natriello, Gary, Edward L. McDill, and Aaron M. Pallas. *Schooling Disadvantaged Children: Racing against Catastrophe.* New York: Teachers College Press,1990.

Natriello, Gary, and Aaron Pallas. "The Development and Impact of High-Stakes Testing." In *Raising Standards or Raising Barriers? Inequality and High-Stakes Testing in Public Education*, edited by Gary Orfield and Mindy L. Kornhaber, 19–38. New York: Century Foundation, 2001.

New York Department of Education, Office of Vocational and Educational Services for Students with Disabilities. *2000 Pocket Book of Goals and Results for Individuals with Disabilities.* Albany, N.Y.: Department of Education, 2000.

———. *2002 Pocket Book of Goals and Results for Individuals with Disabilities.* Albany, N.Y.: Department of Education, 2001.

No Child Left Behind Act of 2001, P.L. 107-110, 8 January 2002.

North Carolina Department of Public Instruction. "History of Public Education in North Carolina." ‹http://www.ncpublicschools.org/students/edhistory.html›. 14 August 2003.

———. "N.C. Course of Study Graduation Requirements." ‹www.iss.k12.nc.us/curriculum/cos_requirements.pdf›. 12 September 2003.

———. "Reports of Supplemental Disaggregated State, School System (LEA) and School Performance Data for 2002–2003." ‹http://disag.ncpublicschools.org/›. 10 November 2003.

Oakes, Jeannie. *Keeping Track: How Schools Structure Inequality.* New Haven: Yale University Press, 1985.

———. *Multiplying Inequalities: The Effects of Race, Social Class, and Tracking on Opportunities to Learn Mathematics and Science.* Santa Monica, Calif.: RAND, 1990.

Oakes, Jeannie, and Gretchen Guiton. "Matchmaking: The Dynamics of High School Tracking Decisions." *American Educational Research Journal* 32 (Spring 1995): 3–33.

Oakes, Jeannie, Karen Muir, and Rebecca Joseph. "Course Taking and Achievement in Math and Science: Inequalities that Endure and Change." In *Handbook of Multicultural Education*, edited by James Banks, 69–90. Menlo Park, Calif.: Jossey-Bass, 2003.

Oliver, Melvin L., and Thomas M. Shapiro. *Black Wealth/White Wealth: A New Perspective on Racial Inequality.* New York: Routledge, 1995.

Olson, Daniel V. A. "Dimensions of Cultural Tension among the American Public." In *Cultural Wars in American Politics*, edited by Rhys H. Williams, 237–58. New York: Aldine de Gruyter, 1997.

Olson, Lynn. "All States Get Federal Nod on Key Plans." *Education Week*, 18 June 2003, 1–21.

———. "Final Rules Give States Direction, Little Flexibility." *Education Week*, 4 December 2002, 1–27.

Orfield, Gary. *Congressional Power: Congress and Social Change.* New York: Harcourt Brace Jovanovich, 1975.

———. "Conservative Activists and the Rush toward Resegregation." In *Law and School Reform*, edited by Jay P. Heubert, 39–87. New Haven: Yale University Press, 1999.

———. *Dropouts in America: Confronting the Graduation Rate Crisis.* Cambridge: Harvard Education Press, 2004.

———. "Metropolitan School Desegregation." In *In Pursuit of a Dream Deferred*, edited by john a. powell, Gavin Kearney, and Vina Kay, 121–58. New York: Peter Lang, 2001.

———. "Metropolitan School Desegregation: Impacts on Metropolitan Society." *Minnesota Law Review* 80 (April 1996): 825–74.

———. *Must We Bus?* Washington, D.C.: Brookings Institution, 1978.

———. "Public Opinion and School Desegregation." *Teachers College Record* 96 (Summer 1995): 654–70.

———. *Public School Desegregation in the United States, 1968–1980.* Washington, D.C.: Joint Center for Political Studies, 1983.

———. *The Reconstruction of Southern Education: The Schools and the 1964 Civil Rights Act.* New York: John Wiley, 1969.

———. "Response to Richard D. Kahlenberg: Symposium: Socioeconomic School Integration." *Poverty and Race* (September–October 2001), ‹http://www.prrac.org/full_text.php?text_id=711&item_id=7761&newsletter_id=58&header=Symposium:%20Socioeconomic%20School%20Integration›. 22 March 2004.

———. *Schools More Separate: Consequences of a Decade of Resegregation.* Cambridge: Civil Rights Project at Harvard University, 2001. ‹http://www.law.harvard.edu/civil-rights/publications/resegregation01/schoolsseparate.pdf›. 10 September 2002.

———. *Toward a Strategy for Urban Integration: Lessons in School and Housing Policy from Twelve Cities: A Report to the Ford Foundation.* New York: Ford Foundation, 1981.

Orfield, Gary, and Carole Ashkinaze. *The Closing Door: Conservative Policy and Black Opportunity.* Chicago: University of Chicago Press, 1991.

Orfield, Gary, and Susan E. Eaton. *Dismantling Desegregation: The Quiet Reversal of Brown v. Board of Education.* New York: New Press, 1996.

Orfield, Gary, Rosemary George, and Amy Orfield. "Racial Change in U.S. School Enrollments, 1968–84." Paper presented at the National Conference on School Desegregation, Chicago, 1986.

Orfield, Gary, and Michal Kurlaender, eds. *Diversity Challenged: Evidence on the Impact of Affirmative Action.* Cambridge: Harvard Educational Publishing Group, 2001.

Orfield, Gary, and Chungmei Lee. *Brown at 50: King's Dream or Plessy's Nightmare?* Cambridge: Civil Rights Project at Harvard University, 2004. ‹http://www.civilrightsproject.harvard.edu/research/reseg04/resegregation04.php›. 12 December 2004.

Orfield, Gary, and Frank Monfort. *Racial Change and Desegregation in Large School Districts: Trends through the 1986–87 School Year.* Alexandria, Va.: National School Boards Association, 1988.

Orfield, Gary, and David Thronson. "Dismantling Desegregation: Uncertain Gains, Unexpected Costs." *Emory Law Journal* 42 (Summer 1993): 759–90.

Orfield, Gary, and John T. Yun. *Resegregation in American Schools.* Cambridge: Civil Rights Project at Harvard University, 1999. ‹http://www.law.harvard.edu/civilrights/publications/resegregation99.html›. 27 May 2002.

Orfield, Myron. *Metropolitics: A Regional Agenda for Community and Stability.* Washington, D.C.: Brookings Institution Press; Cambridge, Mass.: Lincoln Institute of Land Policy, 1997.

Organization for Economic Co-Operation and Development (OECD). *Knowledge and Skills for Life: First Results from the OECD Programme for International Student Assessment (PISA) 2000.* Paris: OECD, 2001.

Orland, Martin E. "Demographics of Disadvantage: Intensity of Childhood Poverty and

Its Relationship to Educational Achievement." In *Access to Knowledge: An Agenda for Our Nation's Schools*, edited by John I. Goodlad and Pamela Keating, 43–58. New York: College Board Publications, 1990.

Panetta, Leon, and Peter Gall. *Bring Us Together: The Nixon Team and the Civil Rights Retreat.* Philadelphia: Lippincott, 1971.

Parents Involved in Community Schools v. Seattle School District no. 1, 137 F. Supp. 2d 1224 (W.D. Wash., 2001); 377 F. 3d 949 (9th Cir. 2004).

Patterson, James T. *Brown v. Board of Education: A Civil Rights Milestone and Its Troubled Legacy.* New York: Oxford University Press, 2001.

Pauley v. Kelly, 255 S.E.2d 859 (W. Va. 1979).

Payne, Charles M. *I've Got the Light of Freedom: The Organizing Tradition and the Mississippi Freedom Struggle.* Berkeley: University of California Press, 1995.

Pearce, Diana. *Breaking Down the Barriers: New Evidence on the Impact of Metropolitan School Desegregation on Housing Patterns.* Washington, D.C.: National Institute of Education, 1980.

Peltason, J. W. *Fifty-eight Lonely Men.* New York: Harcourt, Brace, and World, 1961.

Penta, Mary Q. "Comparing Student Performance at Program Magnet, Year-Round Magnet, and Non-Magnet Elementary Schools." Report 01.27. Raleigh: Department of Evaluation and Research, Wake County Public School System, 2001.

People Who Care v. Rockford Board of Education, 153 F.3d 834 (7th Cir. 1998).

People Who Care v. Rockford Board of Education, 246 F.3d 1073 (7th Cir. 2001).

Peterson, Paul E. *School Choice: A Report Card.* In *Learning from School Choice*, edited by Paul E. Peterson and Bryan Hassel, 3–32. Washington, D.C.: Brookings Institution Press, 1998.

Petrovich, Janice, and Amy Stuart Wells, eds. *Bringing Equity Back: Research for a New Era of Educational Policy.* New York: Teachers College Press, 2005.

Plank, Stephen. *Finding One's Place: Teaching Styles and Peer Relations in Diverse Classrooms.* New York: Teachers College Press, 2000.

Plessy v. Ferguson, 163 U.S. 537 (1896).

Plyler v. Doe, 457 U.S. 202 (1982).

Podgursky, Michael, Ryan Monroe, and Donald Watson. "The Academic Quality of Public School Teachers: An Analysis of Entry and Exit Behavior." *Economics of Education Review* 23 (October 2004): 507–18.

Poe, William. Interview with Roslyn Arlin Mickelson, Charlotte, N.C., 22 December 1998.

Porter, Andrew C., and John L. Smithson. "Alignment of State Testing Programs, NAEP, and Reports of Teacher Practice in Grades 4 and 8." Paper presented at the annual meeting of the American Educational Research Association, New Orleans, April 2000.

———. "Are Content Standards Being Implemented in the Classroom? A Methodology and Some Tentative Answers." In *From the Capitol to the Classroom: Standards-Based Reform in the States*, edited by Susan H. Fuhrman, 60–80. Chicago: University of Chicago Press, National Society for the Study of Education, 2001.

powell, john a. "Is Racial Integration Essential to Achieving Quality Education for Low-Income Minority Students, in the Short Term? In the Long Term?" *Poverty and Race* 5 (May–June 1998), ‹http://www.prrac.org/full_text.php?text_id=400&item_id=3884&newsletter_id=38&header=Search%20Results›. 22 March 2004.

———. "Living and Learning: Linking Housing and Education." *Minnesota Law Review* 80 (April 1996): 749–94.

———. "The Tensions between Integration and School Reform." *Hastings Constitutional Law Quarterly* 28 (Spring 2001): 655–97.

powell, john a., Gavin Kearney, and Vina Kay, eds. *In Pursuit of a Dream Deferred: Linking Housing and Education Policy.* New York: P. Lang, 2001.

President's Advisory Commission on Educational Excellence for Hispanic Americans. "From Risk to Opportunity: Fulfilling the Educational Needs of Hispanic Americans in the Twenty-first Century." ‹http://www.yesican.gov/paceea/finalreport.pdf›. 7 June 2002.

Price v. Austin Independent School District, 729 F. Supp. 533 (W.D. Tex. 1990).

Price v. Austin Independent School District, 945 F.2d 1307 (5th Cir. 1991).

Princeton Survey Research Associates. *Public Perspective.* Storrs, Conn.: Roper Organization, 1996.

Rabe-Hesketh, Sophia, and Brian S. Everitt. *A Handbook of Statistical Analyses Using Stata.* Boca Raton, Fla.: Chapman and Hall/CRC, 1999.

Raffel, Jeffrey A. "History of School Desegregation." In *School Desegregation in the Twenty-first Century*, edited by Christine H. Rossell, David J. Armor, and Herbert J. Walberg, 17–39. Westport, Conn.: Praeger, 2002.

Raudenbush, Stephen W., and Anthony S. Bryk. *Hierarchical Linear Models: Applications and Data Analysis Methods.* 2d ed. Thousand Oaks, Calif.: Sage, 2002.

Raudenbush, Stephen W., Randall P. Fotiu, and Yuk Fai Cheong. "Inequality of Access to Educational Resources: A National Report Card for Eighth-Grade Math." *Educational Evaluation and Policy Analysis* 20 (Winter 1998): 253–67.

Reardon, Sean F. "Eighth-Grade Minimum Competency Testing and Early High School Dropout Patterns." Paper presented at the annual meeting of the American Educational Research Association, New York, April 1996.

Reardon, Sean F., and Glenn Firebaugh. "Measures of Multigroup Segregation." *Sociological Methodology* 32 (2002): 33–67.

Reardon, Sean F., and John T. Yun. "Integrating Neighborhoods, Segregating Schools: The Retreat from School Desegregation in the South, 1990–2000." *North Carolina Law Review* 81 (May 2003): 1563–96.

———. "Suburban Racial Change and Suburban School Segregation, 1987–1995." *Sociology of Education* 74 (April 2001): 79–101.

Reardon, Sean F., John T. Yun, and Tamela McNulty Eitle. "The Changing Structure of School Segregation: Measurement and Evidence of Multiracial Metropolitan-Area School Segregation, 1989–1995." *Demography* 37 (August 2000): 351–64.

Reardon, Sean F., John T. Yun, and Michal Kurlaender. "The Limits of Income Desegregation Policies for Achieving Racial Desegregation." Paper presented at the annual Sociology of Education Conference, Monterey, Calif., February 2004.

Reddick, D. C., and R. A. Wooster. "Texas." *Encyclopaedia Britannica.* 2002. ‹http://www.search.eb.com/eb/article?eu=121330›. 29 May 2002.

Regents of University of California v. Bakke, 438 U.S. 265 (1978).

Rene v. Reed, 751 N.E.2d 736 (Ind. App. 2001).

Rickles, Jordan, and Paul M. Ong. "The Integrating (and Segregating) Effect of Charter,

Magnet, and Traditional Elementary Schools: The Case of Five California Metropolitan Areas." Paper presented at the Color Lines Conference, Civil Rights Project, Harvard University, Cambridge, Mass., August–September 2003.

Riley, Richard W. "Reflections on Goals 2000." *Teachers College Record* 96 (Spring 1995): 380–88.

Rivkin, Steven G., Eric A. Hanushek, and John F. Kain. *Teachers, Schools, and Academic Achievement.* Paper 6691. Cambridge, Mass.: National Bureau of Economic Research, 1998.

Robelen, E. "States Sluggish on Execution of 1994 ESEA." *Education Week,* 28 November 2001, 1, 26–27.

Roe v. Wade, 410 U.S. 113 (1973).

Rose v. Council for Better Education, 790 S.W. 2d 186 (Ky. 1989).

Rosenbaum, James E., Nancy Fishman, Alison Brett, and Patricia Meade. "Can the Kerner Commission's Housing Strategy Improve Employment, Education, and Social Integration for Low-Income Blacks?" *North Carolina Law Review* 71 (June 1993): 1519–56.

Rosenberg, Gerald N. *The Hollow Hope: Can Courts Bring about Social Change?* Chicago: University of Chicago, 1991.

Rossell, Christine. *The Carrot or the Stick for School Desegregation Policy: Magnet Schools or Forced Busing.* Philadelphia: Temple University Press, 1990.

———. "The Desegregation Efficiency of Magnet Schools." *Urban Affairs Review* 38 (May 2003): 697–725.

———. "Desegregation Plans, Racial Isolation, White Flight, and Community Response." In *The Consequences of School Desegregation,* edited by Christine Rossell and Willis Hawley, 13–57. Philadelphia: Temple University Press, 1983.

Rumberger, Russell W., and Gregory J. Palardy. "Does Segregation (Still) Matter? The Impact of Student Composition on Academic Achievement in High School." *Teachers College Record.* Forthcoming.

———. "Technical Appendix: The Impact of Segregation on Academic Achievement in Southern High Schools." ‹http://education.ucsb.edu/rumberger/›. 18 June 2004.

Rumberger, Russell W., and J. Douglas Willms. "The Impact of Racial and Ethnic Segregation on the Achievement Gap in California High Schools." *Educational Evaluation and Policy Analysis* 14 (Winter 1992): 377–96.

Rusk, David. *Inside Game, Outside Game: Winning Strategies for Saving Urban America.* Washington, D.C.: Brookings Institution Press, 1999.

Ryan, James E. "The Influence of Race in School Finance Reform." *Michigan Law Review* 98 (June 1999): 432–81.

Ryan, James E., and Michael Heise. "The Political Economy of School Choice." *Yale Law Journal* 111 (June 2002): 2043–2136.

Sagar, H. Andrew, and Janet Schofield. *Classroom Interaction Patterns among Black and White Boys and Girls.* Washington, D.C.: National Institute of Education, 1980.

———. "Interracial Interaction in a New 'Magnet' Desegregated School." 1976. Paper presented at the annual convention of the American Psychological Association, Washington, D.C., September 1976.

———. *Peer Interaction Patterns in an Integrated Middle School.* Washington, D.C.: National Institute of Education, 1977.

San Antonio Independent School District v. Rodriguez, 411 U.S. 1 (1973).

Saporito, Salvatore, and Annette Lareau. "School Selection as a Process: The Multiple Dimensions of Race in Framing Educational Choice." *Social Problems* 46 (August 1999): 418–39.

Scafidi, Benjamin, David L. Sjoquist, and Todd R. Stinebrickner. *The Impact of Wages and School Characteristics on Teacher Mobility and Retention.* Atlanta: Andrew Young School of Policy Studies, Georgia State University, 2002.

Schellenberg, Stephen J. "Concentration of Poverty and the Ongoing Need for Title I." In *Hard Work for Good Schools: Facts Not Fads in Title I Reform*, edited by Gary Orfield and Elizabeth H. DeBray, 132–48. Cambridge: Civil Rights Project, Harvard University, 1999.

Schofield, Janet W. "Promoting Positive Intergroup Relations in School Settings." In *Toward a Common Destiny*, edited by W. D. Hawley and A. W. Jackson, 257–89. San Francisco: Jossey-Bass, 1995.

———. "Review of Research on School Desegregation's Impact on Elementary and Secondary Students." In *Handbook of Research on Multicultural Education*, edited by James A. Banks, 597–616. New York: Macmillan, 1995.

———. "Uncharted Territory: Speculations on Some Positive Effects of Desegregation on White Students." *Urban Review* 13 (Winter 1981): 227–41.

Schofield, Janet W., and H. Andrew Sagar. *Desegregation, School Practices, and Student Race Relations.* Pittsburgh: Learning Research and Development Center, University of Pittsburgh, 1985.

Schrag, P. "Too Good to Be True." *American Prospect* 4 (January 2000): 46–49.

Sedlak, Michael W., Christopher W. Wheeler, Diana C. Pullin, and Philip A. Cusick. *Selling Students Short: Classroom Bargains and Academic Reform in the American High School.* New York: Teachers College Press, 1986.

Serrano v. Priest, 557 P.2d 929 (Cal. 1977).

Shalala, Donna E., and Mary Frase Williams. "Political Perspectives on Efforts to Reform School Finance." *Policy Studies Journal* 4 (Summer 1976).

Shapiro v. Thompson, 394 U.S. 618 (1969).

Sheet Metal Workers v. EEOC, 478 U.S. 421 (1986).

Sheff v. O'Neill, 238 Conn. 1, 678 A.2d 1267 (1996).

Shoemaker, Don, ed. *With All Deliberate Speed.* New York: Harper, l957.

Shujaa, Mwalimu J. *Beyond Desegregation: The Politics of Quality in African American Schooling.* Thousand Oaks, Calif.: Corwin, 1996.

Simmons, Tim. "A Crisis Out of Hiding: Color of Their Skin Guides Destiny of Black Schoolchildren." *Raleigh News and Observer*, 21 November 1999, A1.

Skinner v. Oklahoma, 316 U.S. 535 (1942).

Slate, Ashley Lizabeth. "The Inertia of Moderation: North Carolina's Response to *Brown* and the Desegregation of Raleigh Public Schools." Honors essay, Department of History, University of North Carolina at Chapel Hill, 1999.

Smedley, T. A. "Developments in the Cases of School Desegregation." *Vanderbilt Law Review* 26 (April 1973): 405–12.

Smiley v. California Dept. of Education, U.S. App. LEXIS 26516 (9th Cir. Dec. 19, 2002).

Smith, G. A. "As Few Become Many while Many Become Few: The Ever-Evolving

Cultural Dynamics within and Beyond Skewed Groups and 'Tokenism.'" Ph.D. diss., Harvard University, 2003.

Smith, Stephen S. *Boom for Whom? Education, Desegregation, and Development in Charlotte.* Albany, N.Y.: SUNY Press, 2004.

———. Expert report to the court in the case of *Capacchione et al. v. Charlotte-Mecklenburg Schools,* 1998.

Smylie, Mark A. "Reducing Racial Isolation in Large School Districts: The Comparative Effectiveness of Mandatory and Voluntary Desegregation Strategies." *Urban Education* 17 (January 1983): 477–502.

Snyder, Thomas D., and Charlene M. Hoffman. *Digest of Education Statistics, 2000.* Washington, D.C.: Department of Education, 2001.

———. *Digest of Education Statistics, 2002.* Washington, D.C.: Department of Education, 2003.

Sontag, Deborah. "Power of the Fourth." *New York Times Magazine,* 9 March 2003, 40.

Southern Regional Education Board. *ACT and SAT Scores in the South: The Challenge to Lead.* Atlanta: SREB, 2003.

Stanley v. Illinois, 405 U.S. 645 (1972).

Steele, Roberta L. "Note: All Things Not Being Equal: The Case for Race Separate Schools." *Case Western Reserve Law Review* 43 (Winter 1993): 591–624.

Stowe, David W. "Uncolored People: The Rise of Whiteness Studies." *Lingua Franca,* September–October 1996, 68–77.

Sunderman, Gail L. "Implementing a Major Educational Reform: No Child Left Behind and Federal-State Relationships—First Impressions." Paper presented at the meetings of the American Educational Research Association, Chicago, April 2003.

Swann v. Charlotte-Mecklenburg Board of Education, 402 U.S. 1 (1971).

System Development Corporation. *The Third Year of Emergency School Act (ESAA) Implementation: Report to the U.S. Office of Education.* Santa Monica, Calif.: System Development Corporation, 1977.

Taylor, William. "Standards, Tests, and Civil Rights." *Education Week,* 15 November 2000, 40–56.

———. "Title I as an Instrument for Achieving Desegregation and Equal Educational Opportunity." *North Carolina Law Review* 81 (May 2003): 1751–69.

Tennessee Small School System v. McWherter, 851 S.W.2d 139 (Tenn. 1993).

Texas Education Agency. "Academic Excellence Indicator System, 2000–01 State Profile Report, Student Information." ‹http://www.tea.state.tx.us/perfreport/aeis/2001/state.html›. 29 April 2002.

———. "Public Education Information Management System (PEIMS) Data Standards, 2000–2001." ‹http://www.tea.state.tx.us/peims/standards/0001/index.html›. 9 August 2002.

———. "Student Assessment Program." 2002. ‹http://www.tea.state.tx.us/student.assessment›. 9 August 2002.

Texas State Data Center. *New Population Projections for Texas Show a State Growing Extensively, Diversifying Rapidly and Aging Substantially in the Coming Decades.* College Station: Texas State Data Center, Texas A & M University, 2001. ‹http://txsdc.tamu.edu/tpepp/presskit›. 26 May 2002.

Thevenot, Brian. "Students Who Fail LEAP Can Be Held Back: Court Rules in Favor of High-Stakes Testing." *New Orleans Times-Picayune*, 18 September 2001, 1.

Three Cities That Are Making Desegregation Work. Washington, D.C.: National Education Association, 1984.

Thurlow, Martha. "Biting the Bullet: Including Special Needs Students in Accountability Systems." In *Redesigning Accountability Systems for Education*, edited by Susan H. Fuhrman and Richard F. Elmore, 115–40. New York: Teachers College Press, 2004.

Thurlow, Martha, J. Ruth Nelson, Ellen Teelucksingh, and James E. Ysseldyke. *Where's Waldo? A Third Search for Students with Disabilities in State Accountability Reports.* Minneapolis: National Center on Educational Outcomes, 2000.

Title VI, Civil Rights Act of 1964, 42 U.S.C. sec. 2000(d).

Tribe, Laurence H. *American Constitutional Law.* 2d ed. Mineola, N.Y.: Foundation Press, 1988.

Troxel v. Granville, 530 U.S. 57 (2000).

Tuttle v. Arlington County School Board, 195 F.3d 698 (4th Cir. 1999) (per curiam), *cert. dismissed*, 529 U.S. 1050 (2000).

Twenge, Jean M., and Roy F. Baumeister. "Social Exclusion Increases Aggression and Self-defeating Behavior while Reducing Intelligent Thought and Prosocial Behavior." In *The Social Psychology of Inclusion and Exclusion*, edited by Dominici Abrams, Jose Marques, and Michael Hogg, 27–46. New York: Psychology Press, 2004.

U.S. Bureau of the Census. "2000 Census of Population and Housing. Demographic Profile: Technical Documentation, 2002." Rev. ed. ‹http://www.census.gov/prod/cen2000/doc/ProfileTD.pdf›. 21 August 2002.

———. "2000 Census of Population and Housing. Profiles of General Demographic Characteristics: Texas, 2000." ‹http://www2.census.gov/census_2000/datasets/demographic_profile/Texas/2kh48.pdf›. 19 June 2002.

———. "Census 2000 Redistricting Data (P.L. 94-171) Summary File, Tables PL1 and PL2." 2002. ‹http://www.census.gov/Press-Release/www/2001/tables/tx_tab_4.xls›, ‹http://www.census.gov/census2000/states/tx.html›, ‹http://www.census.gov/Press-Release/www/2001/cb01cn110.html›, and ‹http://www.census.gov/Press-Release/www/2001/tables/tx_tab_3.xls›. 19 June 2002.

———. "Census 2000 Supplementary Survey Summary Tables, 2002." ‹http://factfinder.census.gov/servlet/DTTable?_ts=48017544791›. 21 August 2002.

———. "Census 2000. Table DP-2. Profile of Selected Social Characteristics: 2000. Geographic Area: Texas. (Data based on a sample.)" 2002. ‹http://censtats.census.gov/data/TX/04048.pdf›. 21 August 2002.

———. *Current Population Reports: Money Income in the United States, 2000.* CPS Report P60-213. Washington, D.C.: U.S. Government Printing Office, 2001.

———. "Historical Income Tables." 2000. ‹http://www.census.gov/hhes/income/histinc/incperdet.html›.

———. "Income in 1999 by Selected Household, Family, and Individual Characteristics: 2000." Census 2000 Summary File 3 (SF 3): QT-P33.

———. *Migration by Race and Hispanic Origin: 1995 to 2000.* CENSR-13. Washington, D.C.: U.S. Government Printing Office, 2003.

———. *Money Income in the United States: 2000.* September 2001. ‹http://www.census.gov/prod/2001pubs/p60-213.pdf›. 19 December 2004.

———. "Percent of Population by Race and Hispanic or Latino Origin, for the United States, Regions, Divisions, and States: 2000. Table 2. (Table Based on Census 2000 Redistricting Data [P.L. 94-171] Summary File for States)." 2001–2. ‹http://www.census.gov/population/cen2000/phc-t6/tab02.xls›. 24 May 2002.

———. "Population by Race and Hispanic or Latino Origin, for the United States, Regions, Divisions, and States: 2000. Table 1. (Table Based on Census 2000 Redistricting Data [P.L. 94-171] Summary File for States)." 2001–2. ‹http://www.census.gov/population/cen2000/phc-t6/tab01.xls›. 24 May 2002.

———. *Statistical Abstract of the United States 2000.* ‹http://www.census.gov/prod/www/statistical-abstract-us.html›. 19 December 2004.

———. "United States Census 2000: State and County QuickFacts, Wake County, North Carolina, People QuickFacts." ‹http://quickfacts.census.gov/qfd/states/37/37183.html›. 16 August 2003.

U.S. Commission on Civil Rights. *Ethnic Isolation of Mexican Americans in the Public Schools of the Southwest.* Mexican American Education Study Report 1. Washington, D.C.: U.S. Government Printing Office, 1971.

———. *The Excluded Student: Educational Practices Affecting Mexican Americans in the Southwest.* Mexican American Education Study Report 3. Washington, D.C.: U.S. Government Printing Office, 1972.

U.S. Constitution, amendment XV, sec. 1.

U.S. Department of Education. "Closing the Achievement Gap in America's Public Schools." 2002. ‹http://www.ed.gov/nclb/overview/welcome/closing/index.html›. 5 August 2002.

U.S. Department of Education, Office for Civil Rights. Letter from Safiyyah Muhammad, Team Leader—Team I, District of Columbia Office, to William R. McNeal, Superintendent, Wake County Public School System, 29 August 2003 (on file with the Wake County Public School System).

———. *The Use of Tests When Making High-Stakes Decisions for Students: A Resource Guide for Educators and Policymakers.* Washington, D.C.: U.S. Department of Education Publications Office, 2000.

U.S. Department of Education, Planning and Evaluation Service. *High Standards for All Students: A Report from the National Assessment of Title I on Progress and Challenges since the 1994 Reauthorization.* Washington, D.C.: U.S. Department of Education, 2001.

Unger, Roberto Mangabeira. *False Necessity: Anti-Necessitarian Social Theory in the Service of Radical Democracy.* New York: Cambridge University Press, 1987.

United Nations General Assembly. *The Convention against Discrimination in Education.* 429 U.N.T.S. 93, art. 1(1)(1962), art. 4.

———. *Convention on the Rights of the Child.* G.A. res. 44/25, Annex, 44 U.N. GAOR Supp. (no. 49) at 167, U.N. Doc. A/44/49 (1989) art. 28, entered into force 2 September 1990 (187 states parties).

———. *Declaration on the Elimination of All Forms of Racial Discrimination.* Resolution 1904 (XVIII). 20 November 1963, art. 3.

———. *International Convention on the Elimination of All Forms of Racial Discrimina-*

tion, G.A. res. 2106 (XX), Annex, 20 U.N. GAOR Supp. (no. 14) at 47, U.N. Doc. A/6014 (1966), 660 U.N.T.S. 195, entered into force 4 January 1969, for the United States 20 November 1994.

———. *International Covenant on Civil and Political Rights.* Adopted and opened for signature 16 December 1966, 999 U.N.T.S. 171, art. 2, sec. 1.

———. *International Covenant on Economic, Social, and Cultural Rights.* G.A. res. 2200A (XXI), 21 U.N. GAOR Supp. (no. 16), U.N. Doc. A/6316 (1966), 999 U.N.T.S. 302, arts. 3, 13, sec. 1.

———. *Universal Declaration of Human Rights.* G.A. Resolution 217A (III). Document A/810, arts. 1, 26, sec. 1 (10 December 1948).

United States v. Board of School Commissioners, 456 F. Supp. 183, (S.D. Ind. 1978) *aff'd in part and vacated in part*, 637 F.2d 1101 (7th Cir. 1980), *cert denied sub nom.*

United States v. Missouri, 363 F. Supp. 739 (E.D. Mo. 1973).

United States v. Paradise, 480 U.S. 149 (1987).

Vickerstaff, John M. "Getting off the Bus: Why Many Black Parents Oppose Busing." *Journal of Law and Education* 27 (January 1998): 155–64.

Viteritti, Joseph. *Choosing Equality: School Choice, the Constitution, and Civil Society.* Washington, D.C.: Brookings Institution Press, 1999.

Wake County Public School System (WCPSS). "From 1976 to 2001: Superintendent McNeal Was Here in the Beginning." In *History of the Wake County Public School System.* 2001. ‹http://www.wcpss.net/history/mcneal/index.html›. 7 July 2003.

———. "Goal 2003." ‹http://www.wcpss.net/goal2003/index.html›. 13 October 2003.

———. "Schools Cheer Student Success with Celebration 2003 Events." *News*, 22 August 2003, ‹http://www.wcpss.net/news/celebration_2003_schools/index.html›. 13 October 2003.

———. "Senior Director of Magnet Program Recounts a History Filled with Choice." In *History of the Wake County Public School System.* 2001. ‹http://www.wcpss.net/history/massengill/index.html›. 7 July 2003.

———. "Superintendent McNeal Calls for Celebration of Student Success." *News*, 25 June 2003, ‹http://www.wcpss.net/news/goal2003/index.html›. 13 October 2003.

———. "Superintendent's Budget Message 2003–04." ‹http://www.wcpss.net/budget/2003–04-official-budget/message.html›. 10 November 2003.

———. "WCPSS Overview." ‹http://www.wcpss.net/overview.html›. 9 July 2003.

———. "Year Round Education in the Wake County Public School System." In *History of the Wake County Public School System*, ‹http://www.wcpss.net/history/year_round/index.html›. 15 July 2003.

Wake County Public School System, Community Services. *Resource Guide.* Raleigh: Wake County Public School System, 1999.

Wake County Public School System, Department of Evaluation and Research. *Gaps in Academic Achievement: WCPSS Status 2000–01.* Report 01.24. Raleigh: Wake County Public School System, 2001.

———. *Gaps in Academic Achievement: WCPSS Status 2001–02.* Report 02.23. Raleigh: Wake County Public School System, 2002.

———. *The Impact of Poverty upon Schools.* Research Watch Series, Report 99.20. Raleigh: Wake County Public School System, 1999.

Ware, Leland, and Melva Ware. "*Plessy's Legacy: Desegregating the Eurocentric Curriculum.*" *Georgia State University Law Review* 12 (June 1996): 1151–86.

Ware, Melva L. "School Desegregation in the New Millennium: The Racial Balance Standard Is an Inadequate Approach to Achieving Equality in Education." *Saint Louis University Public Law Review* 18 (1999): 465–83.

Washington v. Davis, 426 U.S. 229 (1976).

Washington, Booker T. *Up from Slavery.* 1901; New York: Heritage, 1970.

Weiher, Gregory R., and Kent L. Tedin. "Does Choice Lead to Racially Distinctive Schools? Charter Schools and Household Preferences." *Journal of Policy Analysis and Management* 21 (Winter 2002): 79–92.

Weinschrott, David, and Sally Kilgore. "Evidence from the Indianapolis Voucher Program." In *Learning from School Choice*, edited by Paul E. Peterson and Bryan Hassel, 307–34. Washington, D.C.: Brookings Institution Press, 1998.

Wells, Amy S. "Reexamining Social Science Research on School Desegregation: Long- versus Short-Term Effects." *Teachers College Record* 96 (Summer 1995): 691–706.

Wells, Amy S., and Robert L. Crain. "Perpetuation Theory and the Long-Term Effects of School Desegregation." *Review of Educational Research* 64 (Winter 1994): 531–55.

Welner, Kevin G. "Ability Tracking: What Role for the Courts?" *Education Law Reporter* 163 (2002): 565–71.

———. *Legal Rights, Local Wrongs: When Community Control Collides with Educational Equity.* Albany, N.Y.: SUNY Press, 2001.

Welner, Kevin G., and Jeannie Oakes. "(Li)Ability Grouping: The New Susceptibility of School Tracking Systems to Legal Challenges." *Harvard Educational Review* 66 (Fall 1996): 451–70.

Wessman v. Gittens, 160 F.3d 790 (1st Cir. 1998).

West, Cornel. *Keeping Faith: Philosophy and Race in America.* New York: Routledge, 1993.

Wheelock, Anne. *Crossing the Tracks: How Untracking Can Save America's Schools.* New York: New Press, 1992.

Wilhoit, Francis M. *The Politics of Massive Resistance.* New York: George Braziller, 1972.

Wilkinson, J. Harvie, III. *From Brown to Bakke: The Supreme Court and School Integration, 1954–1978.* New York: Oxford University Press, 1979.

Willie, Charles V., and Michael Alves. *Controlled Choice: A New Approach to Desegregated Education and School Improvement.* Providence, R.I.: Education Alliance Press and New England Desegregation Assistance Center of Brown University, 1996.

Willms, J. Douglas. "Social Class Segregation and Its Relationship to Pupils' Examination Results in Scotland." *American Sociological Review* 51 (April 1986): 224–41.

Wills, Garry. *Lincoln at Gettysburg: The Words That Remade America.* New York: Simon and Schuster, 1992.

Wilson, William Julius. *The Declining Significance of Race: Blacks and Changing American Institutions.* Chicago: University of Chicago Press, 1978.

Wise, Lauress L., Carolyn DeMeyer Harris, Lisa E. Koger, Emily Dickinson Bacci, J. Patrick Ford, D. E. Sipes, Shaobang Sun, Milton E. Koger, and Richard C. Deatz. *Independent Evaluation of the California High School Exit Examination (CAHSEE): AB 1609 Study Report.* Vol. 1. Sacramento: California Department of Education, 2003.

Wise, Lauress L., D. E. Sipes, Carolyn DeMeyer Harris, Carol E. George, J. Patrick Ford, and Shaobang Sun. *Independent Evaluation of the California High School Exit Examination (CAHSEE): Analysis of the 2001 Administration.* Sacramento: California Department of Education, 2002.

Woodward, C. Vann. *The Strange Career of Jim Crow.* 3d ed. New York: Oxford University Press, 1974.

Wright, R. E. "Spanish Missions." In *The Handbook of Texas Online.* Austin: Texas State Historical Association, University of Texas at Austin, 2001. ‹http://www.tsha.utexas.edu/handbook/online/articles/view/SS/its2.html›. 28 May 2002.

Wygant v. Jackson Board of Education, 478 U.S. 1014 (1986).

Youngstown Sheet and Tube Co. v. Sawyer, 343 U.S. 579 (1952).

Ysseldyke, James E., Martha Thurlow, Karen L. Langenfeld, J. Ruth Nelson, Ellen Teelucksingh, and Allison Seyfarth. *Educational Results for Students with Disabilities: What Do the Data Tell Us?* Minneapolis: National Center on Educational Outcomes, 1998.

Zabetakis, Amy S. "Note: Proposition 227: Death for Bilingual Education?" *Georgetown Immigration Law Journal* 13 (Fall 1998): 105–28.

Zehr, Mary Ann. "Once 'Sacred,' School Aid Falls Prey to Budget Cuts, NCSL Report Finds." *Education Week*, 7 May 2003.

Zelman v. Simmons-Harris, 536 U.S. 639 (2002).

Ziegenbalg, Dawn. "Civil Rights Inquiry into Schools Ending: No Major Redistricting Changes Expected." *Winston-Salem Journal*, 7 January 2000, A1.

Contributors

Karen E. Banks is assistant superintendent for evaluation and research in the Wake County Public School System. She also holds adjunct appointments at the University of North Carolina at Chapel Hill and North Carolina State University. She holds a B.S. from Texas A & M University and a Ph.D. in educational psychology from the University of Texas at Austin. Her research interests focus on equity issues in student achievement, and she has held offices in several state and national organizations focusing on educational research and accountability.

John Charles Boger is a professor of law at the University of North Carolina School of Law and the deputy director of the UNC Center for Civil Rights. A former assistant counsel with the NAACP Legal Defense and Educational Fund, Inc., Boger has represented parties and amici in various school resource/finance cases in Connecticut and North Carolina. He holds an A.B. from Duke University, an M.Div. from Yale University, and a J.D. from the University of North Carolina.

Erwin Chemerinsky is the Alston and Bird Professor of Law at Duke Law School. Until recently, he was the Sydney M. Irmas Professor of Public Interest Law, Legal Ethics, and Political Science at the University of Southern California Law School. He holds a B.S. from Northwestern University and a J.D. from Harvard University. Chemerinsky is one of the nation's most respected constitutional scholars and is a frequent author on constitutional topics, including a leading treatise, *Constitutional Law: Principles and Policies.*

Charles T. Clotfelter is the Z. Smith Reynolds Professor of Public Policy Studies and a professor of economics and law at Duke University. He also serves as the director of Duke's Center for the Study of Philanthropy and Voluntarism and as a research associate with the National Bureau of Economic Research. He holds an A.B. from Duke University and a Ph.D. in economics from Harvard University. Clotfelter is the author of *After Brown: The Rise and Retreat of School Desegregation*, two books on higher education, and many articles on issues of educational policy.

Susan Leigh Flinspach is a researcher in the psychology department at the University of California, Santa Cruz. She holds a Ph.D. in education from the University of Chicago and a B.A., an M.A., and a Ph.D. in anthropology from the University of Iowa. Her recent publications deal with educational policy and district leadership of reform.

Erica Frankenberg is a doctoral student in education policy at the Harvard Graduate School of Education. She is a research assistant at The Civil Rights Project, where she has coauthored a series of reports on public school segregation trends, including *A Multiracial Society with Segregated Schools: Are We Losing the Dream?* with Chungmei Lee and Gary Orfield. She holds an A.B. from Dartmouth College and an Ed.M. from Harvard University.

Catherine E. Freeman is a research associate at the U.S. Department of Education. She holds a B.S. from Vanderbilt University, an M.Ed. from the University of Texas at Austin, and a Ph.D. from Vanderbilt. She concentrates on educational policy issues and resource allocation consequences. She is currently working on the update to *Trends in Educational Equity of Girls and Women* in addition to developing a new financial resource allocation publication for the department.

Jay P. Heubert is a professor of education and law at Teachers College, Columbia University, and an adjunct professor of law at Columbia Law School. He received his B.A. from Swarthmore College, his M.A.T. from Duke University, and his Ed.D. and J.D. cum laude from Harvard University, where he taught from 1985 to 1998. He has also served as chief counsel to the Pennsylvania Department of Education and a trial attorney in the Civil Rights Division of the U.S. Department of Justice. His recent publications concern the effects of graduation and promotion testing on achievement and persistence of students of color, English-language learners, and students with disabilities.

Jennifer Jellison Holme is a research associate on the University of California, Los Angeles–Teachers College, Columbia University, Understanding Race and Education Study. She received her Ed.M. from the Harvard Graduate School of Education and her B.A. and a Ph.D. in educational policy studies from UCLA. Holme recently published "Buying Homes, Buying Schools: School Choice and the Social Construction of School Quality" in the *Harvard Educational Review.*

Michal Kurlaender is an assistant professor at the University of California, Davis. She received her Ed.D. from the Harvard Graduate School of Education and her B.A. from the University of California, Santa Cruz. She has worked as a researcher at The Civil Rights Project since 1997. Her work focuses on educational stratification and inequality. She is currently working on a national study on the impact of school racial composition on educational outcomes. She is the author of several articles and is a contributing editor to *Diversity Challenged: Evidence on the Impact of Affirmative Action*, edited by Gary Orfield.

Helen F. Ladd is a professor of public policy studies and economics at Duke University and associate director of Duke's Sanford Institute of Public Policy. She holds a B.A. from Wellesley College and a Ph.D. in economics from Harvard University. Much of her current research focuses on education policy. From 1996 to 1999 she cochaired the National Academy of Sciences Committee on Education Finance, which generated the book *Making Money Matter: Financing America's Schools.* She is the editor of *Holding Schools Accountable: Performance-Based Reform in Education* and the coauthor, with Edward B. Fiske, of *When Schools Compete: A Cautionary Tale.*

Luis M. Laosa obtained his Ph.D. from the University of Texas at Austin. He was the chief school psychologist of a large school district in Texas and taught at the University of California, Los Angeles. He retired as principal research scientist from the Educational Testing Service in Princeton, New Jersey. He is the author of many studies. His continuing research interests include schools and families as environments for learning and for human development.

Jacinta S. Ma is a civil rights attorney who lives in the Washington, D.C., area. She has worked at The Civil Rights Project at Harvard University, the Massachusetts Attorney General's Office, and the U.S. Department of Education. Ma received her B.A. from the University of California, Berkeley, and her J.D. from New York University.

Roslyn Arlin Mickelson is a professor of sociology at the University of North Carolina at Charlotte. She holds a B.A. in anthropology, an M.A. in education, an M.A. in sociology, and a Ph.D. in sociology of education, all from the University of California, Los Angeles. Her research focuses on the political economy of schooling and school reform, particularly the equity effects of market-oriented educational reforms on low-income and ethnic minority students and the effects of segregation, including racially identifiable tracking, on academic outcomes. She is the author of *Children on the Streets of the Americas: Globalization, Homelessness, and Education in the United States, Brazil, and Cuba.*

Gary Orfield is a professor of education and social policy at the Harvard Graduate School of Education and the Kennedy School of Government. He is codirector of The Civil Rights Project at Harvard University and has for more than thirty years been a leading expert on desegregation in public education. He holds a B.A. from the University of Minnesota and an M.A. and Ph.D. in political science from the University of Chicago. He has coedited many books and studies, including *Dismantling Desegregation: The Quiet Reversal of Brown v. Board of Education.*

Gregory J. Palardy is an assistant professor of educational psychology at the University of Georgia. After graduating from the University of Michigan, Ann Arbor, he taught high school science for eight years. He holds master's degrees in both statistics and research methodology and a Ph.D. in education from the University of California, Santa Barbara. His research focuses on applications of research methodology, models for evaluating school and teacher effectiveness, and how family, teacher, and school characteristics impact student achievement and other educational outcomes.

john a. powell is executive director of the Kirwan Institute for the Study of Race and Ethnicity and a professor at the Moritz School of Law at Ohio State University. The founder, in 1993, of the Institute on Race and Poverty at the University of Minnesota Law School, powell is also a former national legal director of the American Civil Liberties Union. He holds a B.A. from Stanford University and a J.D. from the University of California, Berkeley. Previous publications include *In Pursuit of a Dream Deferred: Linking Housing and Education Policy.*

Sean F. Reardon is an associate professor of education and sociology at Stanford University. He received his B.A. from the University of Notre Dame and his doctorate from the Harvard Graduate School of Education. His research interests include the causes and consequences of school and residential segregation, the causes of racial and socioeconomic educational inequality, and the effects of community and neighborhood context on adolescent development and behavior.

Russell W. Rumberger is a professor of education at the University of California, Santa Barbara. He holds a Ph.D. in education, an M.A. in economics from Stanford University, and a B.S. from Carnegie-Mellon University. His recent research focuses on school dropouts, student mobility, school segregation, and the educational underachievement of minority students. Recent publications include *Student Mobility and the Increased Risk of High School Dropout* and *The Distribution of Dropout and Turnover Rates among Urban and Suburban High Schools.*

Benjamin Scafidi is an assistant professor in the Andrew Young School of Policy Studies, Georgia State University. He is currently on loan to the state of Georgia, where he serves as the education policy adviser to Governor Sonny Perdue. Scafidi earned his B.A. from the University of Notre Dame and his Ph.D. in economics from the University of Virginia in 1997. His recent refereed publications include articles on the Georgia Lottery, the causes of neighborhood racial segregation, the price of college, and K–12 accountability.

David L. Sjoquist is a professor of economics in the Andrew Young School of Policy Studies, Georgia State University, and holder of the Dan E. Sweat Distinguished Scholar Chair in Educational and Community Policy. He holds a B.A. from the University of St. Thomas and an M.A. and a Ph.D. in economics from the University of Minnesota. His research interests span topics in public finance, urban economics, and educational policy. He recently published *State and Local Government Finances at the Beginning of the Twenty-first Century.*

Jacob L. Vigdor is an assistant professor of public policy studies and economics at the Terry Sanford Institute of Public Policy at Duke University. He received a B.S. in policy analysis from Cornell University in 1994 and a Ph.D. in economics from Harvard University in 1999. He has written extensively on the topics of education and housing policy, with a particular interest in segregation in both schools and neighborhoods.

Amy Stuart Wells is a professor of sociology and education at Teachers College, Columbia University. She holds a B.A. from Southern Methodist University, an M.S. from Boston University, and a Ph.D. from Teachers College. Her research and writing have focused broadly on issues of race and education and more specifically on educational policies and how they shape and constrain opportunities for students of color. She is currently the principal investigator of a four-year study of adults who attended racially mixed high schools. She is the author and editor of numerous books and articles, including *Where Charter School Policy Fails: The Problems of Accountability and Equity.*

John T. Yun is assistant professor of education at the University of California, Santa Barbara. He holds a Sc.B. from Brown University and an Ed.D. in education policy research from the Harvard Graduate School of Education. His research includes issues of equity in education—specifically, patterns of school segregation, the impact of funding on educational outcomes, and the effects of high-stakes testing on instructional practice and student progress.

Index

H. Eugene and Lillian Youngs Lehman Series

Lamar Cecil, *Wilhelm II: Prince and Emperor, 1859–1900* (1989).

Carolyn Merchant, *Ecological Revolutions: Nature, Gender, and Science in New England* (1989).

Gladys Engel Lang and Kurt Lang, *Etched in Memory: The Building and Survival of Artistic Reputation* (1990).

Howard Jones, *Union in Peril: The Crisis over British Intervention in the Civil War* (1992).

Robert L. Dorman, *Revolt of the Provinces: The Regionalist Movement in America* (1993).

Peter N. Stearns, *Meaning Over Memory: Recasting the Teaching of Culture and History* (1993).

Thomas Wolfe, *The Good Child's River*, edited with an introduction by Suzanne Stutman (1994).

Warren A. Nord, *Religion and American Education: Rethinking a National Dilemma* (1995).

David E. Whisnant, *Rascally Signs in Sacred Places: The Politics of Culture in Nicaragua* (1995).

Lamar Cecil, *Wilhelm II: Emperor and Exile, 1900–1941* (1996).

Jonathan Hartlyn, *The Struggle for Democratic Politics in the Dominican Republic* (1998).

Louis A. Pérez Jr., *On Becoming Cuban: Identity, Nationality, and Culture* (1999).

Yaakov Ariel, *Evangelizing the Chosen People: Missions to the Jews in America, 1880–2000* (2000).

Philip F. Gura, *C. F. Martin and His Guitars, 1796–1873* (2003).

Louis A. Pérez Jr., *To Die in Cuba: Suicide and Society* (2005).

Peter Filene, *The Joy of Teaching: A Practical Guide for New College Instructors* (2005).

John Charles Boger and Gary Orfield, eds., *School Resegregation: Must the South Turn Back?* (2005).